RUINS OF THE FREE STATE HOTEL LAWRENCE.
From the Daguerreotype taken for Mrs Robinson.

KANSAS;

ITS

INTERIOR AND EXTERIOR LIFE.

INCLUDING

A FULL VIEW OF ITS SETTLEMENT, POLITICAL HISTORY,
SOCIAL LIFE, CLIMATE, SOIL, PRODUCTIONS,
SCENERY, ETC.

BY

SARA T. L. ROBINSON.

THIRD EDITION.

BOSTON:
CROSBY, NICHOLS AND COMPANY.
CINCINNATI: GEORGE S. BLANCHARD.
LONDON: SAMPSON LOW, SON & CO.
1856.

Stereotyped by
HOBART & ROBBINS,
NEW ENGLAND TYPE AND STEREOTYPE FOUNDERY,
BOSTON.

PREFACE.

THIS work, now offered to the public, has been written amid all the inconveniences of tent life. Its pages were penned during a three months' residence of the authoress in the United States Camp, at Lecompton, with her husband, one of the state prisoners.

If a bitterness against the "powers that be" betrays itself, let the continual clanking of sabres, and the deafening sound of heavy artillery in the daily drills of the soldiery, aids in crushing freemen in Kansas, — the outrages hourly committed upon peaceable and unarmed men, — the daily news of some friend made prisoner, or butchered with a malignity more than human, — the devastation of burning homes, by the connivance of the Governor, under the eye of the troops, and no power given them to save an oppressed people, — be placed in the balance against a severe judgment.

If the simple recital serves to strengthen in any the love of liberty, or to arouse in others a hatred to tyranny, then will its mission have been accomplished.

"God give us Men ! A time like this demands
Strong minds, great hearts, true faith, and ready hands ;
Men whom the lust of office does not kill ;
Men whom the spoils of office cannot buy ;

Men who possess opinion and a will ;
  Men who have honor, — men who will not lie ;
Men who can stand before a demagogue,
  And damn his treacherous flatteries without winking !
Tall men, sun-crowned, who livė above the fog
  In public duty, and in private thinking ;
For while the rabble, with their thumb-worn creeds,
Their large professions, and their little deeds, —
Mingle in selfish strife, lo ! Freedom weeps,
Wrong rules the land, and waiting Justice sleeps ! "

CONTENTS.

CHAPTER I.

INTRODUCTION.

CHAPTER II.

THE FIRST ELECTION AND FIRST INVASION.

CHAPTER III.

EASTERN EMIGRATION — BORDER MEN.

CHAPTER IV.

LAWRENCE.

CHAPTER V.

KANSAS HOMES.

CHAPTER VI.

ILLS OF PIONEER LIFE.

CHAPTER VII.

KANSAS LAWS — GOV. SHANNON.

CHAPTER VIII.

GENERAL DISCOMFORTS — MURDER OF DOW.

CHAPTER IX.

WAKARUSA WAR — PREPARATIONS.

CHAPTER X.

WAKARUSA WAR — INCIDENTS.

CHAPTER XI.

DEATH OF BARBER — THE TREATY.

CHAPTER XVI.

THE ATTACK UPON LAWRENCE.

CHAPTER XVII.

THE "REIGN OF TERROR" IN KANSAS.

CHAPTER XVIII.

ARREST OF G. JENKINS AND G. W. BROWN — ARREST OF GOVERNOR ROBINSON.

CHAPTER XIX.

EXCITEMENT IN MISSOURI — OUTRAGES IN THE TERRITORY.

CHAPTER XX.

TWO WEEKS IN JUNE ON THE MISSOURI BORDER.

CHAPTER XXI.

THE U. S. CAMP — DISPERSION OF LEGISLATURE.

CHAPTER XXII.

"LAW-AND-ORDER" MEN — FREE-STATE MEN AROUSED.

CHAPTER XXIII.

NEW INVASION — RELEASE OF STATE PRISONERS.

CHAPTER XXIV.

AN APPEAL TO THE AMERICAN PEOPLE.

KANSAS.

CHAPTER I.

INTRODUCTION.

Far away amid childhood's sunny vales, pleasant memories bring back to me a quiet New England village not far from the noble Connecticut's sparkling waters. Situated upon an elevation, commanding an extensive view of the surrounding country in all directions, the Mt. Holyoke range upon the north-west, and Wilbraham mountains on the south, and being finely diversified with hill and dale, as an inland town its beauty of location can scarcely be equalled. The taste of its inhabitants was visible in the broad, finely shaded streets, and the long, wide common, where the whispering breezes toyed and laughed among the trees. Upon the eastern side of this beautiful green were the churches and town-hall, the lower rooms of which, for many years, had been used for school rooms; and here, especially, memories of bygone days cluster, — memories of teachers and school friends long since passed away, others still living, few of whom I shall ever meet again. But most vividly of all comes before me the bright-colored map, in green, red and yellow, upon which I daily learned my lessons, as to our whereabouts, and that of mankind generally, upon the face of the old earth. Very many were my speculations as to the appearance of one part of the country, laid down upon the map as the Great American Desert. There was mystery to me in its semi-circular lines in fine letters, "Great American Desert, inhabited only by savages and wild beasts," and much childish curiosity was excited thereby. Years came and went; and with them came the increase of wealth and power to the American people, and the progress of the age. As California became a portion of her dominions, gold was found in the bed of her rivers, and in the bosom of her soil. Thousands flocked thither from the whole country. The young and ardent from the Atlantic States, unused to toil and hardships, but eager in their search for gold, left all the comforts of home, and entered the lists. Men from the West, not quite so daintily raised, pressed onwards in the race, and together they sought this far-famed Eldorado. Some realized their anticipations, but many a loved and cherished one "fell and perished, weary with the march of life." Thousands reached the goal of their hopes, by a long passage around the Horn, some by a slow, vexatious crossing of the Isthmus; but thousands more took that route which promised most of health to the traveller, — the one opened from Missouri overland to the Pacific shore, by the courageous, the enterprising, the adventurous Colonel Fremont. This, the finding of which through the mountains by unequalled energy, and endurance, and trials, and sufferings, which would have unnerved ordinary men, became now the general thoroughfare to Oregon and California. This newly opened highway led directly through the Indian Territory, known to my childhood as the "Great American Desert;" and many a one, looking upon its unrivalled and ever varying scenes of beauty, as his route for days lay over its beautiful rolling prairies, decked with the loveliest flowers in every shade of coloring, or camped under the noble trees by the bank of some swiftly flowing stream, felt strong desires for a home, where he could sit under his own vine and fig-tree, in a land like this. Many then resolved to find therein such home, when it should be thrown open to settlement. The face of this country is beautiful beyond all comparison. The prairies, though broad and expansive, stretching away miles in many places, seem never lonely or wearisome, being gently undulating, or more abruptly rolling; and, at the ascent of each new roll of land, the traveller finds himself in the midst of new loveliness. There are also high bluffs, usually at some little distance from the rivers, running through the entire length of the country, while ravines run from them to the rivers. These are, at some points, quite deep and difficult to cross, and, to a traveller unacquainted with the country, somewhat vexatious, especially where the prairie grass is as high as a person's head while seated in a carriage. There is little trouble, however, if travellers keep back from the water-courses, and near the high lands. These ravines are in many instances pictures of beauty, with tall, graceful trees, cotton-wood, black walnut, hickory, oak, elm and linwood, standing near, while springs of pure cold water gush from the rock. The bluffs are a formation unknown in form and appearance, in any other portion of the West. At a little distance, a person could scarcely realize that art had not added her finishing touches to a work, which nature had made singularly beautiful. Many of the bluffs appear like the cultivated grounds about fine old residences within the Eastern States, terrace rising above terrace, with great regularity; while others look like forts in the distance. In the eastern part of the territory, most of the timber is upon the rivers and creeks, though there are in some places most delightful spots; high hills crowned with a heavy growth of trees, and deep vales where rippling waters gush amid a dense shade of flowering shrubbery; all reminding me of dear New England homes, where art and taste had labored long. Higher than the bluffs are natural mounds, which also have about them the look of art. They rise to such a height as to be seen at a great distance, and add peculiar beauty to the whole appearance of the country. From the summit of these the prospect is almost unlimited in extent, and unrivalled in beauty. The prairie for miles, with its gently undulating rolls, lies before the eye. Rivers, glistening in the sunlight, flow on between banks crowned with tall trees;—beyond these, other high points arise. Trees are scattered here and there like old orchards, and cattle in large numbers are grazing upon the hillside, and in the valleys, giving to all the look of cultivation and home life. It is, indeed, difficult to realize that for thousands of years this country has been a waste, uncultivated and solitary, and that months only have elapsed since the white settler has sought here a home.

SOIL.

The soil for richness can be surpassed in no country. It is of a black color, with a sub-soil of clay and limestone basis. Vegetation is most luxuriant. The soil and climate are most admirably adapted to the raising of grains of every known variety. The growth of melons, cantelopes, tomatoes, squashes,—in fact, vegetables of all kinds,—is wonderful. Western Missouri bears most excellent fruit of all kinds, apples of the best varieties, peaches, plums, grapes, etc. The soil and climate in Kansas being similar, a very few years will see the perfection of the same fruits throughout the country.

Wild fruits are abundant. Pawpaws, a fruit resembling somewhat a banana, are very sweet and luscious, in the estimation of some, while others think them quite unpalatable. The mandrake, or custard-apple, is a pleasant fruit, ripe in August, of the size and appearance of an egg-plum, medicinal also in its nature. The wild plum, cherry and mulberry, grow in many places. The plum is very good of itself, and, as a tree to graft upon, valuable. Gooseberries, blackberries, strawberries and raspberries, grow spontaneously. With a very little pains, the settlers in Kansas can soon surround themselves with all the fruits which require several years in New England to cultivate to any degree of perfection. Meat here, especially beef, is much nicer than beef fattened elsewhere. It is owing, probably, to the rapidity with which it fattens in this country. Beef of a year old in many instances is unequalled. Venison, prairie chickens, wild turkeys, rabbits, and squirrels, furnish dainties for the most fastidious epicure.

CLIMATE.

The climate is exceedingly lovely. With a clear, dry atmosphere, and gentle, health-giving breezes, it cannot be otherwise. The peculiar clearness of the atmosphere cannot be imagined by a non-resident. For miles here a person can clearly distinguish objects, which, at the same distance in any other part of this country, he could not see at all. The summers are long, and winters short.

The winters are usually very mild and open, with little snow, — none falling in the night, save what the morrow's sun will quickly cause to disappear. So mild are they, that the cattle of the Indians, as those of the settlers in Western Missouri, feed the entire year in the prairies and river-bottoms. The Indians say that, once in about seven years, Kansas sees a cold and severe winter, with snows of a foot in depth. Two weeks of cold weather is called a severe winter. Then the spring-like weather comes in February; the earth begins to grow warm, and her fertile bosom ready to receive the care of the husbandman.

The winds of March and April are the most disagreeable out-door arrangements in Kansas. It were quite useless for a person of little gravity, or strength, to attempt much progress in locomotion, when from out the halls of Æolus the winds have rushed untrammelled, and unrestrained. The breezes of summer, however, are most delightful. With the sun the wind rises, and makes such a difference in the actual effect of the temperature upon one's senses, as to lead to doubts as to the correctness of thermometers in this country. The mornings and evenings are always cool and pleasant, and one experiences nothing here of those summer nights, so common even in New England, where, between weariness occasioned by intense heat, and mosquitoes, no refreshing sleep will come. Very seldom are the nights, in Kansas, that blankets are not found an essential comfort. The rains are frequent, and copious. So far as my own experience goes, we have no more of a wet or dry season than in Massachusetts. Seldom a week passes in the summer without rain, often coming in most gentle showers in the night, unaccompanied by thunder and lightning; while, early in the spring especially, there is such display of electricity as one seldom sees. The whole heavens will be one perfect sea of flame, and thunder deafening in the continual roar, while the waters fall so abundantly, that they run in all directions, after the earth has filled its pores, like a miniature deluge. There is a sublimity, an awe-inspiring influence, in such displays of grandeur and power, as make the creature feel his nothingness, and that the Creator is indeed all, — the great All-Father, All-wise, All-good, All-powerful. Days, like September days in New England, linger here until the old year has given place to the new; and the last of December has the genial breath, the pleasant sun, and glad look of early autumn. But the changes of weather come suddenly. One may be dreaming all the morning, influenced by the pleasant temperature around him, of the fair Italian land; and, ere the sun finds its setting, may fancy himself nearing the pole. Yet in all these changes no one takes cold. There is something so invigorating in the atmosphere, so bracing, and the lungs have such play and action in it, that vigor is increased where health was before enjoyed; and in many a case, where the pulse was faint and low, and the invalid looked out upon life with little purpose and few aims, feeling that its limits were nearly reached, the roses of health have again bloomed, and the life-blood coursed joyously. For consumptives there can be no better country than this. In many instances, most material has been the change, and permanent the cure.

This country, covering an extent of surface larger than the thirteen Atlantic States, was, by an act of Congress approved March 6, 1820, forever sealed to freedom. This prohibition to slavery is most definitely expressed in these words:

"Sec. 8. Be it further enacted, That in all that territory *ceded* by France to the United States, under the name of Louisiana, which lies north 36° 30′ of north latitude, not included within the limits of the state contemplated by this act, slavery and involuntary servitude, otherwise than as the punishment of crimes, shall be, and is hereby, forever prohibited."

This country, than which the sun shines upon no fairer, with its mountains, prairies and valleys, lying midway between the north and south, east and west, in the very heart of the United States, was never to be cursed with the blackest of all villanies, the bitterest of all evils — human slavery. The clanking of chains was never to create a discord in that harmony, where the wild bird sent forth its gushing lay for freedom, where the whispering breezes through the leafy wood caught up the music, echoing it amid the quivering leaves, and where all nature sang a continual song for freedom. But what has been the sequel? How has this act, entered into as a solemn compact before God and man, been regarded? The slave oligarchists looked with covetous eyes upon this fair region. They had gained, heretofore, whatever they had desired by craft, bribery, or threats; and the North, imbecile in many of its legislators, had acquiesced. They had gained new territory, for slavery extension, by the compromise of 1850, when New England's greatest senator sounded his own death-knell, and, in the passage of the Fugitive Slave Bill, had rendered the entire country slave-hunting ground. Had they not good reason, then, to hope by legislation to get Kansas too?

On the 14th of December, 1853, Mr. Dodge, of Iowa, asked leave to introduce a bill to organize the Territory of Nebraska, which was finally referred to the Committee on Territories. This was a simple territorial bill, in no way undertaking to touch the compromise of 1820, the prohibition of slavery in the territory. This bill was opposed by Atchison, Vice-President of the United States, as well as by other southern men. On the 4th of January, 1854, Mr. Douglas, of Illinois, as chairman of the Committee on Territories, reported this bill back to the Senate, with various amendments, accompanied by a special report.

The whole country was moved at the prospect of such an outrage as this bill proposed — the annulling of a sacred compact, the breaking of a plighted faith. How, through all that long season of discussion upon the bill, more than three months, every freedom-loving heart was moved to hope this great wrong might not be committed! How every honest feeling was stirred at the eloquent words of Chase, Giddings, Sumner, Seward, Hale, and all our noble men in Congress, who battled mightily against this evil! We can never forget what indignation fired the veins of all lovers of God and men, as the wires brought news of the indignity offered to New England's three thousand protesting clergymen, and what shame mantled the cheek of many to remember that the Benedict Arnold of the age should have been born of any *woman* in a beautiful, thriving town nestled amid the Green Mountains. Well will the North remember how the womanly element mingled its influence to stay this current of evil; how the protests, with many thousands of names, poured in through all the avenues of communication to the capital. Woman's heart was touched; all the deep sympathies of her nature were stirred; and, while hourly she prayed that no new field of suffering and woe should be opened for her down-trodden and oppressed sister, she acted too, and, through the melting snows of early spring, each woman in many towns was called upon for her signature, by one of her own sex. Could she see this great country — only a little less in extent than Italy, France, and Spain, together — thrown open to the foul inroads of slavery, so that no woman with black blood in her veins could be a welcome inmate of her father's house, feel safe in the protection of a husband's love, or, in caressing the children God gave her, call them her own, and make no effort in their behalf? No. It was not thus, thank God! Men felt, and women felt. Notwithstanding all that was done, and all that was felt, the bill, odious in the sight of God and hateful to man, was passed. Mr. Sumner made his final protest, for himself and the New England clergy, against slavery in Kansas and Nebraska, upon the night of the final passage of the Nebraska and Kansas Bill, May 25, 1854. After a most stormy and contentious debate, on Sunday morning the bill was passed. The slave power was again triumphant. A consolidated despotism was striving to crush out every aspiration for truth, for goodness, for freedom, from every free-born soul. Southern men argued that by this new compromise the agitation in our country would cease, and peace be restored. How has it been? Civil feud, strife, and continual agitation, have been the result in all communities. The "crime against Kansas" consummated in Congress, the infraction of solemn obligations, has been acted over in frauds upon the ballot-box in Kansas, and has been the occasion of robberies, murders, civil war, in her fair borders.

When, at that dark midnight hour, the bill was passed, the final blow was struck, seemingly the knell for the burial of Liberty was sounded. But there was light also in the hour, in the deed. There could no more be sown in common ground the seeds of harmony and good-will. The hosts of freedom must marshal their forces, and draw their lines against the lines of slavery, and each man fight courageously on the accepted issue. It was the death of all compromises too.

From this period, the passage of the bill, and the throwing open of the territory to settlement upon the principles of "squatter sovereignty," let us note carefully the whole course of those men, who so strenuously urged its passage, and see to what extreme measures, bringing untold sufferings upon the innocent people of Kansas, they have resorted, to bring about their first design — that of making Kansas a slave state. As early as the spring of 1854, Stringfellow, and other men of like calibre in Western Missouri, founded secret societies, called Blue Lodges, Friends' Societies, etc. Their members were sworn, upon peril of their lives, to make Kansas a slave state. There were published accounts of meetings held in several towns in Western Missouri, with most fiery resolutions, denouncing northern men, offering large rewards for the heads of some, and explicitly avowing their purpose of settling the territory with pro-slavery men, and keeping all others out. In May, at a meeting held in Westport, one of the principal speakers continually interlarded his harangue from the court-house steps with "Ball to the muzzle, knife to the hilt!" "Damn the abolitionists!" "We'll put them all in the Missouri river." Two gentlemen from Massachusetts, who travelled in Western Missouri in June and July, 1854, saw Mr. Stringfellow on their way up the river. He was continually reiterating, with horrid oaths, that "Kansas would and should be a slave state," and "no abolitionist should be allowed to live in the territory;" that "if he had the power, he would hang every abolitionist in the country, and every man north of Mason and Dixon's line was an abolitionist;" that "every means should be used to drive free-state men from the territory."

CHAPTER II.

THE FIRST ELECTION — FIRST INVASION.

While these things were being done in Missouri, the press of the North was publishing accounts of the new country opened to settlement, and directing the attention of emigrants, seeking a western home, to this Eden of America. It was evident that a large emigration would naturally flow into Kansas from the North and East; and, to enable the emigrant to reach his destination easily and cheaply, an association was formed, which completed its organization in July. The purpose of this association, as declared by themselves, was to "assist emigrants to settle in the West." Their objects were to induce emigrants to move westward in such large bodies, that arrangements might be made with boat lines and railroads for tickets at reduced rates; to erect saw-mills and boarding-houses, and establish schools in different localities, that the people might gather around them, and not be obliged to wait years for the blessings and privileges of social life, as most early settlers in the West have done. Transplanted into the wilderness, they hoped to bring to them the civilization and the comforts of their old homes.

Mr. Eli Thayer, of Worcester, Mass., was one of the first movers in the scheme. To some suggestions of his the association owed its birth. He, with A. A. Lawrence of Boston, Mass., and J. M. F. Williams, of Cambridge, Mass., acted as trustees of the Stock Company formed July 24, 1854. They are all gentlemen of sterling integrity and noble purpose, and with untiring energy have devoted their labors and money to the cause of freedom. Dr. T. H. Webb has from the first acted as secretary of this association, and by day and night has given himself to the work of aid for Kansas. His courage has never faltered, or his efforts been diminished, in the hour of prosperity, or when dark hordes of invaders hovered in our borders; and, with unabated zeal, he still looks forward to the day of our deliverance from the bonds of the oppressor.

On the 21st of February, an act was passed to incorporate the New England Emigrant Aid Company. The purposes of the act were distinctly stated to be "directing emigration westward, and aiding and providing accommodation for the emigrants after arriving at their place of destination."

The first of August, 1854, a party of about thirty settlers, chiefly from New England, arrived in the territory, and settled at Lawrence. Mr. C. H. Branscomb, of Boston, on a tour in the territory a few weeks earlier in the summer, had selected this spot as one of peculiar loveliness for a town site. A part of them pitched their tents upon the high hill south-west of the town site, and named it Mount Oread, after the Mount Oread School in Worcester, of which Mr. Thayer was founder and proprietor.

When the party arrived, one man only occupied the town site with his family. His improvements were purchased, and he abandoned his claim for the town. This party was met with insult and abuse on the Missouri river, and on their way into the territory. After they arrived in Lawrence, bands of these Missourians gathered along the river bottoms, and wherever they put a stake they made a pretended claim. They invaded the meetings of the actual settlers in the neighborhood, and attempted to control them. Attempts were also made to frighten and drive them from the territory by fomenting disputes about claims, and other quarrels. Sept. 28, 1854, a squatter meeting was held at Homsby & Ferril's store, on the California road, about two miles from Lawrence, at which the free-state men had a majority.

The squatters at length decided by vote that no person, resident of another state, should be allowed to vote at these meetings, etc., and for a while they made their own regulations.

About the first of September, the second New England party arrived and settled at Lawrence. As soon as it was known that a

New England settlement was to be made at Lawrence, every means was resorted to, to break it up.

About the first of October, a man from the Western States, who said Stephen A. Douglas was a better man than Jesus Christ, made his appearance with his friends, and used every effort to break up the New England settlement. The people however proceeded with their improvements, erecting a saw-mill, boarding-houses, and stores.

On the sixth of October, a demand was made that a certain tent, standing within five rods of the house occupied by the original claimant, should be removed from its present location, and no more improvements should be made in that part of the town. Several pro-slavery men, mostly from Missouri, assembled in the vicinity of the tent, and kindly notified Dr. Robinson "that if he did not remove the tent in thirty minutes, they should." The following laconic reply was returned to them: "If you molest our property you do it at your peril." The citizens of the settlement came together to witness the removal, and with praiseworthy patience waited for the half hour to expire. The time at length passed by, and no movement was made toward removing the tent. Another half hour was waning fast, and the thirty New Englanders were quietly waiting for the tent's removal. At last one of the citizens asked another if it "would be best to hit the first man who attempted to remove it, or fire over his head?" The decisive reply was, "I would be ashamed, for the rest of my life, to fire at a man and not hit him."

There was a spy among them, and, as soon as he heard this conversation, so brief, yet pointed, he went over to the enemy's camp. The intelligence he imparted, of whatever nature it might be, had the effect to scatter the Missourians at once. They left with oaths, and threats that "in one week they would return with twenty thousand men from Missouri, and then the tent should be removed."

The week came and went, and about the same number of Missourians as before appeared, but not to remove the tent. For some reason, the people of Missouri, although urgently called upon, did not respond, and the belligerent parties concluded to postpone any warlike action.

The people of Missouri call all eastern and northern men cowards, and are evidently disappointed at the calm determination of the people of Lawrence to protect themselves from mob violence. They do not understand how a people can be brave, yet quiet. With them, loud swelling words are received as evidence of valor; and they could not therefore comprehend the quiet, yet firm preparations for deadly conflict made by the few settlers in Lawrence.

The buildings erected in Lawrence were of most primitive style, of pole and thatch. Most of the people for some weeks boarded in common, and, in such a dwelling, sleeping upon the ground on buffalo robes and blankets.

Oct. 1*st.* — Rev. S. Y. Lune preached the first sermon in Lawrence, in the "Pioneer House." A few rough boards were brought for seats, and, with singing by several good voices among the pioneers, the usual church services were performed. The first Bible Class in Lawrence was formed that day. The people then, as many succeeding Sabbaths, were gathered together by the ringing of a large dinner-bell.

6*th.* — At a meeting of the association, it was decided that the town be named Lawrence, after Amos A. Lawrence, of Boston, who was doing much for the settlement. It had been called previously Wakarusa and New Boston, while the Missourians gave it the name of Yankee town.

9*th.* — Gov. Reeder and other officers appointed by the President arrived in the territory. On the nineteenth of the month they came to Lawrence, and were received with a general greeting by the people. A dinner was provided for them, and with speeches and sentiments some pleasant hours were passed.

The first child born in Lawrence was named Lawrence Carter, the city association presenting him with a lot. He was born October 26.

The first election of the territory was for delegate to Congress, and was held on the twenty-ninth November, 1854. The conspiracy against the rights of the settlers was gaining ground in Missouri, and, before the day of election, armed hordes poured over her borders. In the second district, one of the citizens, who was a candidate for delegate to Congress, was told, by one of the Missourians,

2

he would be abused and probably killed if he challenged a vote. He was at length compelled to seek the protection of the judges. After the election these men mounted into their wagons, crying out, "All aboard for Westport and Kansas City!"

Similar frauds were practised in the other districts. In the eighth district, five hundred and eighty-four illegal votes were cast, and only twenty legal. It was a remote district, with a sparse population. At Leavenworth, then a little village, several hundred men came over from Platte, Clay and Ray counties, camped around the town, and controlled the polls. Many of them were men of influence in Missouri. Gen. Whitfield was, by these illegal votes, elected delegate to Congress.

In January and February, 1855, Gov. Reeder caused the census to be taken. The whole number of inhabitants was found to be eight thousand five hundred and one.

The same day that the census returns were brought in complete, Gov. Reeder issued his proclamation for an election to be held March 30th, 1855, for the Legislative Assembly.

The winter in Kansas was very mild and pleasant. There was not a day that the people could not follow their out-door employments, and but little snow fell. With occasional lectures before the Athenæum just formed, and a general prevalence of kindly feeling, the pioneers passed a pleasant winter amid the uncouth arrangements of the new home.

Before the time of the election in March, the border papers were again rife with their threats of outrage. The following, from the *Leavenworth Herald*, will suffice to show the character of the leaders of the pro-slavery party, and their intentions regarding the manner in which Kansas was to be made a slave state. The plan of operation was laid down in an address to a crowd at St. Joseph, Missouri, by Stringfellow. "I tell you to mark every scoundrel among you that is the least tainted with free-soilism, or abolitionism, and exterminate him. Neither give nor take quarter from the d—d rascals. I propose to mark them in this house, and on the present occasion, so you may crush them out. To those having qualms of conscience, as to violating laws, state or national, the time has come when such impositions must be disregarded, as your lives and property are in danger, and I advise you one and all to enter every election district in Kansas, in defiance of Reeder and his vile myrmidons, and vote at the point of the bowie-knife and revolver. Neither give nor take quarter, as our cause demands it. It is enough that the slave-holding interest wills it, from which there is no appeal. What right has Gov. Reeder to rule Missourians in Kansas? His proclamation and prescribed oath must be disregarded; it is your interest to do so. Mind that slavery is established where it is not prohibited."

Laws, state and national, are to be disregarded; every one tainted with any sentiment of freedom to be murdered; every election district to be invaded, and votes cast in a neighboring territory at the point of bowie-knife and revolver. This same Stringfellow is one of the leaders of the "law and order" party.

A few days before the thirtieth of March crowds of men might be seen wending their way to some general rendezvous in the various counties of Ray, Howard, Carroll, Boone, Lafayette, Saline, Randolph and Cass, in Missouri. They were rough, brutal looking men, of most nondescript appearance. They had, however, one mark upon them, a white or blue ribbon, to distinguish them from the settlers. This was wholly unnecessary, no one ever mistaking one of these men for an intelligent, educated settler in the territory. Those Missourians who did not feel the interest to come over to vote, paid their money, or contributed provisions and wagons for the new raid. The expenses of the vandal horde were paid, and they were *en route* again to overrun the fair country, with drunkenness, and fraud, and murder, if the cause demanded it. Their watchword was, "Neither give nor take quarter."

The people of Missouri had been excited by the inflammatory rumors, put in circulation among them by their leaders, regarding the design and character of eastern emigration. Aided by the oaths of their secret societies, they had acted upon their base passions and prejudices to such a degree that they were fully equal to any deeds of violence.

Provisions were sent ahead of the parties, and those intended for the invaders at Lawrence were stored in the house of W. Lykins. The polls were also opened at the same place. Some of the party came in on the evening previous to the election, and on the morning of the thirtieth of March about one thousand men, under the command of Col. Samuel Young, of Boone county, and Claiborne F. Jackson, came into Lawrence. They came in about one hundred and ten wagons, and upon horseback, with music, and banners flying. They were armed with guns, pistols, rifles and bowie-knives. They brought two cannon loaded with musket balls.

The evening preceding the election, these men were gathered at the tent of one of their leaders, Capt. Jackson, and in speeches made to them by Col. Young, and others, it was declared, "that more voters were here than would be needed to carry the election," and that there was a scarcity at Tecumseh, Bloomington, Hickory Point, and other places, eight, ten, and twelve miles distant. Volunteers came forward, and the next morning left Lawrence for those places.

When this band of men were coming to Lawrence, they met Mr. N. B. Blanton, formerly of Missouri, who had been appointed one of the judges of election by Gov. Reeder. Upon his saying that he should feel bound, in executing the duties of his office, to demand the oath as to residence in the territory, they attempted, by bribes first, and then with threats of hanging, to induce him to receive their votes without the oath. Mr. Blanton not appearing on the election day, a new judge, by name Robert A. Cummins, who claimed that a man had a right to vote if he had been in the territory but an hour, was appointed in his place. The Missourians came to the polls from the second ravine west of the town, where they were encamped in tents, in parties of one hundred at a time.

Before the voting commenced, however, they said, that "if the judges appointed by the governor did not allow them to vote, they would appoint judges who would." They did so in the case of Mr. Abbott, one of the judges, who had become indignant, all law being outraged, and resigned. Mr. Benjamin was elected in his place. Soon after the voting commenced, some question of legality was raised in regard to the vote of a Mr. Page. Col. Young interfered, saying he would decide the matter. Mr. Page withdrew his vote, and Col. Young offered his, saying he was a resident of the territory, but refusing to take the oath. His vote was registered. When asked by Mr. Abbott " if he intended to make Kansas his future home," he replied, that " it was none of his business ; " that, " if he was a resident there, he should ask no more." Col. Young then mounted on to the window-sill, telling the crowd " he had voted, and they could do the same." He told the judges " it was no use swearing them, as they would all swear as he had done." The other judges deciding to receive such votes, Mr. Abbott resigned.

The crowd was often so great around the log cabin, that many of the voters, having voted, were hoisted on to the roof of the building, thus making room for others. Afterwards, especially when the citizens began to vote, a passage-way was made through the crowd. Between a double file of armed men, while they were continually asking for the prominent men in Lawrence, their questions always coupled with threats of shooting, or hanging, our citizens passed to the polls. Several citizens of Lawrence were driven from the ground during the day, with threats of fatal violence. One man escaped by a perilous leap off the high bank of the river, several shots whizzing past him.

As a special favor to the old men, who were weary with travelling, and wanted to get back to their tents to rest, they were allowed to vote first. Many of the Missourians left for home as soon as they had voted, while others remained until morning. They entered freely the houses of the citizens, without ceremony or invitation, in some instances taking their meals with them. So loud were the threats of the Missourians against the town, that a guard was kept around it the following night. There was, however, no disturbance.

The whole number of names on the poll lists was one thousand and thirty-four, of which eight hundred and two were non-residents and illegal voters.

BLOOMINGTON.

Early on the morning of the day of election, five or six hundred Missourians, armed with rifles, guns, pistols and bowie-knives, with flags flying, went to Bloomington, in wagons, and upon horseback. Samuel J. Jones, of Westport, Claiborne F. Jackson, with his volunteers from the camp at Lawrence, and a Mr. Steely, of Independence, were the leaders of this motley gang. The day here was one continual scene of outrage and violence. Scarcely were the polls open, before Jones marched up to the window, at the head of the crowd, and demanded that they be allowed to vote without being sworn as to their residence. Little bands of fifteen or twenty men were formed by Jackson. He gave to them the guns from the wagons, which some of them loaded. Jackson had previously declared, amid repeated cheers, that "they came there to vote;" "if they had been there only five minutes they had a right to vote;" "that they would not go home without voting." Like the party at Lawrence they tied white ribbons in their buttonholes. Upon the refusal of the judges to resign, the mob broke in the windows, glass, and sash, and, presenting pistols and guns, threatened to shoot them. A voice from the outside cried, "Do not shoot them; there are pro-slavery men in the house!" A pry was then put under the corner of the log cabin, letting it rise and fall; but the same fear of injury to pro-slavery men proved the security of the others. The two judges still remaining firm in their refusal to allow them to vote, Jones led on a party with bowie-knives drawn, and pistols cocked. With watch in hand, he declared to the judges, "he would give them five minutes in which to resign, or die." The five minutes passed by. Jones said he "would give another minute, but no more." The pro-slavery judge snatched up the ballot-boxes, and, crying out "Hurrah for Missouri!" ran into the crowd. The other judges, persuaded by their friends, who thought them in imminent peril from the rough and reckless men, brandishing their deadly weapons at every moment, while curses and oaths were a part of every sentence, passed out, one of them putting the poll-books in his pocket. Jones, seeing the movement, snatched from him some papers, which were of immaterial value; but, not finding his mistake, he also ran out crying, "Hurrah for Missouri!" They took Judge Wakefield, one of the citizens, a prisoner, and made him stand upon a wagon and make them a speech. After tying a white ribbon in his button-[illegible] go.

A Mr. Mace was abused by them in a most ruffianly manner. He having replied in the affirmative whether he would take the oath, he was dragged away from the polls by the brutal crowd, with instant death staring him in the face, the incessant yells of the mob being, "Cut his throat!" "Tear his heart out!" "Kill the d—d nigger thief!" After getting him away from the house, they stood around him with bowie-knives drawn and pistols cocked; one man putting to his heart a drawn knife, another holding a cocked pistol by his ear, and another yet striking at him with a club.

A great many threats were made "to kill the judges, if they did not receive their votes;" "no man should vote who would submit to be sworn;" "no man should vote who was not all right on the goose;" and "they would vote by foul if not by fair means."

Cries of "Shoot him!" resounded during the day, and, in such a Pandemonium as would shame even Pluto's dark domains, three hundred and eleven illegal votes were polled.

Will not Americans blush that such indignities have been offered her citizens, and no remedy been afforded by those in power?

In the other districts the polls were taken possession of by bands of these marauders, and similar scenes of violence were enacted. They not only came in numbers sufficient to carry the election over the votes of the actual settlers, but by their outrageous conduct compelled them, in most instances, to keep away from the polls. Not satisfied with once voting, many of them, by changing hats and coats, repeatedly voted in the same precinct, or, after voting at one, went to another. At Marysville, a settlement in the northern part of the territory, twenty-five or thirty men polled one hundred and fifty votes.

Many of the men elected to the Legislature were, and still are, residents of Missouri. The judges of election appointed by Gov. Reeder were obliged, by threats of death, to leave the polls, and others were appointed from among the Missourians. One of the judges of election, for refusing to sign the returns, in spite of many threats, was fired upon on his way home, but fortunately was uninjured. These bands of whiskey-drinking, degraded, foul-mouthed marauders came under the leadership of Sam'l J. Jones, of Westport, Col. Sam'l Young, and C. F. Jackson, Col. Sam'l H. Woodson, of Independence, Mo., Gen. D. R. Atchison, of Platte City, and Gen. B. F. Stringfellow, of Weston.

Col. Woodson was the leader of the rabble of Tecumseh, while B. F. Stringfellow was very active in his efforts to promote the pro-slavery interests in one of the northern precincts. Atchison, the urgent advocate of squatter sovereignty, the former Vice-President of the United States, after controlling one of the primary elections in the fourteenth district, was the acknowledged leader of a gang at the Nemaha. In opposition to the wishes of the actual residents (pro-slavery), he caused a set of candidates to be nominated. His words at the time were, "There are ten hundred men coming over from Platte county, and if that is n't enough we will send five thousand more. We 've come to vote, and will vote, or kill every G—d d—d abolitionist in the territory." In these northern precincts, besides being armed to the teeth with guns, bowie-knives, and revolvers, the ruffians wore hemp in their button-holes, as a pledge to carry out the designs of their secret societies, and singularly significant of the fiendish nature of the institution, while their password was "All right on the hemp."

Major Mordecai Oliver, member of Congress from Missouri,—who, it will be remembered, stated on the floor of the House last spring (during the debates preceding the appointment of a committee to look into the wrongs of the people of Kansas, and was appointed one of the number at his own request), that he knew of no one who came from Missouri to vote in the territory,—was himself present at the election, and, while it is not known with certainty that he voted, he did make a speech, excusing the Missourians for voting. Four hundred and seventeen votes were polled at this precinct, of which no more than eighty can be legal. It is not to be supposed that even wilful blindness could have concealed these facts from his sight. Another instance of the elasticity which one's conscience may attain may be cited here. While the investigating committee were holding their session at Westport, and bands of armed men from the border towns were continually in the streets, making both day and night hideous with their vile curses, and by their oaths calling down the swift vengeance of Heaven, Mr. Oliver to the committee discountenanced such unlawful measures in the attempt to make Kansas a slave state, but was said to have been heard repeatedly urging on the ruffians to deeds of horror, in words of their own choosing, such as "Wipe out the d—d abolitionists!" "Drive them from the territory!" At this precinct, where Major O. made his speech, the voters took the oath as to residence in the territory. The grounds of their residence were the following: One man had cut some poles, and, laying them in the form of a square, it constituted his claim. Another based his right to a claim in having cut a few sticks of wood. Col. Burns recommended all to vote, and not to go home without voting. The pro-slavery residents in this precinct, as in some others, became so outraged at the course pursued by the lawless invaders, that they gladly came over to the ranks of the free-state party, and have since then been among the firmest in the cause of freedom.

In reference to the protests to the election, Major Richardson, who was a resident of Missouri, and whose family still resides there, but who was the pro-slavery candidate for council, with threats, told Dr. Cutter, the free-state candidate, that if he offered a protest, he and his office should be thrown into the Missouri river.

One of the judges in the third district, having at last been driven from his post, where he was determined to do his duty, made affidavit in a protest of the illegality of the election. An indictment for perjury was found against him by the grand jury fifteen months ago, and is still pending. Mr. R. has not been informed what is the nature of the evidence against him, or who is his accuser.

Mr. W. Phillips, a lawyer of Leavenworth, made affidavit also to a truthful protest concerning the election. A meeting was soon called, in which the right of free speech upon the peculiar institution is denied, as being subversive of the quiet of the community, and stigmatized peaceable citizens of free-state sentiments as fanatics, incendiaries and traitors. The following resolve was passed:

"*Resolved*, That the institution of slavery is known and recognized in this territory; that we repel the doctrine that it is a moral and political evil, and we hurl back with scorn upon its slanderous authors the charge of inhumanity; and we warn all persons not to come to our peaceful firesides to slander us, and sow the seeds of discord between the master and the servant; for, as much as we deprecate the necessity to which we may be driven, we cannot be responsible for the consequences."

A committee of vigilance of thirty men was then appointed. These steps were taken preparatory to acts of violence which would follow, that the pro-slavery party might be bound together in their deeds of blood, and, as one man, carry out their nefarious designs. Soon after this meeting, the vigilance committee waited upon Mr. Phillips, notifying him to leave. Upon his refusal to do so, he was seized by them, taken across the river to Weston, Missouri, several miles from Leavenworth. There, after being tarred and feathered, and one side of his head shaved, he was marched about the streets, and finally sold at auction to a negro.

Just one week after the other meeting proposing these acts of lawless indignity upon any and all who should differ from them in sentiment, another meeting was called. R. R. Rees, a member elect of the council, presided at this meeting of the 25th of May, 1855. This same Rees, on the 30th of March, had declared that whoever should say that laying out a town, staking a lot, or even driving down stakes on another man's claim, did not entitle him to a vote, was either a knave or a fool. Judge Payne, a member elect of the House, offered the following resolutions, which were unanimously adopted:

"*Resolved*, That we heartily indorse the action of the committee of citizens that shaved, tarred and feathered, rode on a rail, and had sold by a negro, William Phillips, the moral perjurer.

"*Resolved*, That we return our thanks to the committee for faithfully performing the trust enjoined upon them by the pro-slavery party.

"*Resolved*, That the committee be now discharged.

"*Resolved*, That we severely condemn those pro-slavery men

who, from mercenary motives, are calling upon the pro-slavery party to submit without further action.

"*Resolved*, That, in order to secure peace and harmony to the community, we now solemnly declare that the pro-slavery party will stand firmly by and carry out the resolutions reported by the committee appointed for that purpose on the memorable 30th."

"This meeting was eloquently addressed by Judge Lecompte." Thus, Judge Lecompte, and the men elected by force and fraud, not "inhabitants of" the district for which they were elected, as the organic act requires (this act declaring that "the true intent and meaning of this act is to leave the people there perfectly free to form and regulate their domestic institutions in their own way, subject to the constitution of the United States"), are the leaders and instigators to a series of lawless acts, whose end we cannot even foresee, against the peaceable and order-loving citizens of the territory, exposing them to imminent peril from drunken mobs, and death by fiendish violence, if this judge and these law-makers so desire. In such hands, and at the mercy of such men, are our lives and safety.

No other country than this witnesses so terrible a despotism.

CHAPTER III.

EASTERN EMIGRATION — BORDER MEN.

The first Kansas party of the season left Boston, March 13, 1855, under the charge of Dr. C. Robinson. There were nearly two hundred in the party, men, women and children. We reached Kansas city March 24. The name of Kansas city sounded pleasantly to us, wayfarers, twelve days *en route* from Boston; and, having trunks and carpet-sacks all locked, we were ready to leave the boat in anticipation of our arrival. When the cables were thrown out upon shore, and the planks lowered, we passed off the boat and entered the long parlor at the hotel, only a few steps distant. The mystery was, where could a place be found to stow away so many. Such place, however, was made for all, and sleep without the boat's continual rocking was very sweet.

25th. — Another boat came in with another party of Kansas passengers. I awakened to find the hotel directly on the levee, the street very narrow, the river in front of the house, and Clay county opposite, with forest skirting the shore. Wyandotte, settled by a tribe of Indians of the same name, was also in sight, and in the distance the buildings looked finely, among the trees. My husband made an arrangement to accompany a portion of our fellow-travellers into the country, to look for a pleasant location for a new settlement.

26th. — The party looking for a location left this morning for a trip south, and will return to Topeka and Lawrence. Many of our party are busy getting teams for their trip into the country, buying provisions, and the general outfit for a few weeks; and many left for their new homes in the territory at the "top of the morning." We hear a great deal said here of the preparations the Missourians are making to go over into Kansas to vote on the 30th. We heard the same while on the river; crowds are coming from Lexington, also from one hundred miles below that point. Mr. P., who was to carry us to the Baptist Mission, said he should be ready to start for the mission by ten o'clock. We sat with bonnets and shawls on over an hour; then he concluded we had better stay to dinner. About four o'clock, he said, again, we would leave Kansas city; but, as he was continually interrupted with company, we were not fairly in the wagon until another full hour had passed.

We then had a good view of all there is to Kansas city. It is a most singular location for a town, being a gathering together of hills, high and steep. Houses of very limited dimensions are perched upon all the highest points. They have usually a small porch over the door, or light piazza. There is another peculiarity prevailing here, as elsewhere in Missouri; the chimneys are all built upon the outside of the houses. We passed several of our party with ox-teams. In one of the great lumber-wagons was a young lady from Massachusetts, who in this way was attempting to make the journey of more than a hundred miles into the territory.

It was near evening when we reached Westport. It has a look of recent growth — some good brick buildings and a large hotel. A good deal of the Indian, also Sante Fe, trade comes in here. We were late at Dr. Barker's, having made a call at a house off of the road for some time; and I was completely chilled through on arriving there, so much so as to be unable to walk without assistance. The mission is situated about a quarter of a mile from the great California road, four miles from Westport, and about two from Rev. Thomas Johnson's Methodist Mission. After the road turns from the California road, it descends slightly, and, for an eighth of a mile, is skirted with timber upon either side. The night was not dark, being starlight; and there was novelty in the whole scene presented before us, as we reached the terminus of the road. A large yard was enclosed by a high fence, with stairs by way of entrance. Some four or five steps were on the outside of the fence, a platform, perhaps two feet in width, above it, and as many steps on the inside. The occasion of such an uncouth arrangement I cannot divine, although it prevails all through the country. The houses of log, making five or six rooms, stretch along parallel with the fence, and at some distance from it. The ground is still descending. The first effect upon one used to high lands is most singular. There is a feeling of oppression at the thought of dog-day heats, and insecurity in spring floods. Several dogs gave us greeting as we alighted from the carriage and stumbled over the stairway. We were glad to be at the end of our evening's ride — to feel safe after its insecurity. We had been off on a wild, untravelled road, to see a person who had sent for Mr. P. to come and see him, without telling him the reason of such message. He had urgently, however, pressed his coming. It was dark ere we reached his house, and, to show us a nearer way back, he took us down through fields and by-paths. He walked behind us, and I could not resist the inclination to turn my head occasionally to see what our guide might be doing. A foe in the front would have been more agreeable than in the rear, though the event proved there was no occasion for fear.

We found Dr. Barker's family most hospitable and pleasant, and appreciated thankfully the prospect of a quiet resting-place for a few weeks after this long, wearisome journey. How cheerfully the fire beamed a welcome, and how genial its heat after such a chilly ride! The great logs were rolled into the huge fireplace, and burned and crackled until every corner of the room was light as day. Supper being over, we were soon in dream-land; friends we had left were around us; the "loved and lost" were near.

27th. — The sun shining in at our windows disturbed our slumbers early, just before the little Indian girl came in to start a fire. One glance at the room was sufficient to show that our host and hostess were not born in this western land. Books, pamphlets, pictures, vases, &c., were on all the tables, walls, and everywhere. Sixteen years ago they came to the West; and Dr. Barker has worked indefatigably for the best good of the Shawnees. As minister, teacher, and physician, he has labored for their physical as well as spiritual good, through summer's heat and winter's cold, by day and night, with unceasing effort. Through the evil reports and influence against him of Rev. Mr. Johnson, his school has been discontinued. A colored woman, whom he assisted to gain her freedom, and two little Indian girls, are still in his family. Since this emigration to the territory commenced, their house has been a pleasant home for many on their way thither; some remaining with them six or eight weeks. Their kindness will be gratefully remembered by many.

29th. — The Missourians, for some days, have been passing into the territory. They talk loudly of "fighting, and driving out the free-state men." They go armed and provisioned. There is nothing truer, however, than that "stillest waters run deepest;" and the most courageous men usually have no occasion to boast of their courage.

30th. — It is the election day in the territory. We shall hope to hear something by to-morrow from Kansas. There are several families stopping here, mostly from Indiana, with some pleasant ladies among them. Their peculiarities of speech cause us to smile occasionally, while I dare say our Yankeeisms are as strange to them. This "feeling powerful bad" and "mighty weak" sounds oddly to us; so also when they say, "a right smart chance of calicoes." There is a little English woman boarding here. She is young and girlish. She was born in India, of English parents, and, upon their death, she came to this country. She is very artless and childlike in her manner, and, I fear, will see some hardships in frontier life.

31st. — It is a warm, sunny day. The spring flowers bloom in every sheltered nook. A lemon-colored flower, like adder's tongue in New England, bends its graceful stalk before the gentlest breeze. We have been out over to the high grounds overlooking the main road into the territory for miles; and it is full of people of most desperate look. They come on horseback, in wagons, in carts; in fact, every sort of vehicle seems to have been put in requisition to convey these men into the territory. Now and then a carriage of more pretensions appeared, and was probably occupied by some of the leaders of the gang. The horses, as well as the men, looked wearied out with their journey.

Will these frauds be allowed? or are they a part of the system connived at by a corrupt administration to force slavery into

Kansas against the desire of the actual settlers? Mr. P. arrived from Lawrence this afternoon with a lady, who is going to visit some acquaintances in Independence, Mo. They have passed many of the desperadoes, on their way, armed with all kinds of death-dealing instruments. They carried with them provisions and whiskey, and baked bread by the roadside.

April 2d. — Mrs. C. left to-day for Independence. Mr. S. and family, from New Hampshire, arrived. Their youngest little one sickened on the way, and they are now carrying it with them to Lawrence for burial. There is a good deal of sickness upon the river, especially among children.

3d. — People are continually coming and going. Gentlemen leave their families here, while they look up a situation in the territory. They go into the nearest towns to buy grain and feed for their horses, which are now very scarce and high.

Towards evening, four gentlemen came in from Lawrence. The doctor, with others, soon came; and the number continually increased, until there were fourteen in from Lawrence. A very pleasant family, who were our fellow-travellers a part of the way, have just arrived; Mrs. Nichols also, the Brattleboro' editress and earnest worker for the rights of women, with a young lady, soon to be her daughter-in-law. The son, and chief attraction to this young lady, was already in the territory. Had we just arrived in the West, we should have wondered where all could find resting-places for the night; but we had been here long enough to know the expansiveness of western homes.

4th. — The morning was bright and pleasant. More than fifty slept under the roof last night. I gave up my room to some of the new comers, and slept on comfortables and buffalo-robes on the floor in the attic; and, with the exception of an occasional tug at my pillow, or nibble at my finger, from some stray mouse, I never slept better.

There is a rumor that it is the intention of those Missourians elected to the Legislature, by the votes of the overwhelming forces who went into the territory on the last week and voted on the 13th, to assassinate Gov. Reeder unless he grants certificates of election. They have so declared; and these high-minded gentlemen say also that "he can have fifteen minutes to decide whether he will give them the certificates, or be shot." Gov. Reeder has only allowed four days' time in which the protests against these frauds can be sent in. We fear in many districts the time will be too short to allow them to be canvassed. Besides, the persons who desire to do it are in danger of losing their lives in the attempt, a large number of the Missourians declaring openly their intention to "remain in the territory until the four days are past, and that they will kill any one who endeavors to get signers to a protest." This threat will intimidate many.

Word came from the Shawnee Mission that armed bands, upon horseback and in carriages, were assembling there. The gentlemen who came from Lawrence had mostly gone over. As my husband sat quietly writing, an express came, desiring his attendance also. There have been so many threats upon the part of the Missourians, that, had we any faith in their courage, we should have believed our friends in imminent peril to-day. As it was, we bade them God-speed with light hearts, expecting to see them again at sundown. At noon a messenger returned, and reported all quiet at the mission. Although the Missourians number considerably more than the actual settlers gathered there, they seemed to think their forces insufficient to justify an attack either upon Gov. Reeder or them. Gov. Reeder, having been loudly threatened with assassination unless he granted the certificates of election, examined the papers with pistols cocked near him.

The members elect were holding caucuses during the day. One of the gentlemen from the territory was invited by an acquaintance to attend one of them; and he assured me, as he looked in upon them at his first entrance, their stolid faces, their disordered, rough dress, and their various attitudes, impressed him with anything rather than their wisdom. Some were lying on the benches, others sitting on the backs of the same; and he could hardly believe such a body of men desired to be considered grave legislators. From the appearance of one, at least, to whom a paper was given, who, after scanning it closely, gave it to him with a request that he should read it aloud, he judged he could not read his own mother tongue.

5th.—In every district where the election was contested, and papers sent in showing the fraud, Gov. Reeder refused to grant certificates. As we feared, however, the time allowed was so short, the protests could not reach the mission from a majority of the districts.

6th.—A day of quiet has passed, after the leaving of so many people. We went to Westport this morning. The country was most pleasant. The air was dry and balmy as a day in June. The birds were carolling among the bursting buds and new-springing leaves; the butterflies, flitting here and there, rejoiced in their young life. A part of the way lay through the woods, where a driver needs some skill to pass safely among the stumps. We met a party of the Indians dressed in their native costume, in blankets and moccasins, with much paint upon them, feathers and a large quantity of beads. As I looked back, after we passed them, and saw one of them with most repulsive face also scanning us sharply, with one hand apparently grasping a pistol or gun, I felt an involuntary shiver. I saw, however, at the next moment, it was only a childish fear, and that mutual curiosity actuated us.

The Kaw Indians are the most uncultivated of all, while the Shawnees have made good advances in civilization. They have houses, cultivate their lands, and wear the dress of Americans.

8th.—Attended the little white church upon the rolling prairie to-day. Standing as it does upon quite an elevation, overlooking a great extent of woodland and prairie, being built with spire pointing heavenward, it reminds me of dear New England, and her pleasant villages scattered through all her valleys and upon all her hill-sides. Being early, I noticed the Indian worshippers. Many of the men seated themselves in little groups upon the grass, and entertained each other in their odd-sounding dialect. The women came upon horseback, and, after tying their horses to the fence near by, came into the church, and maintained most strict decorum throughout the entire service. With the exception of the handkerchief upon their heads, in place of bonnet, their style of dress differed in no way from our own. They admire rich materials, and gay colors, and the most of those I saw at church were clad in chameleon silks The service, although we could understand only an occasional word, was very impressive. The speakers, especially the interpreters, had rich mellow voices. Their quick and varied intonations, their rapid mode of enunciation, their graceful and most expressive gestures, singularly enchain the attention of the hearers, and impress upon them the substance of the discourse. The interpreter was a fine-looking man, large, well-formed, and with intelligence speaking in every feature.

9th. — Doctor returned with E. from Kansas city. She will go with him to Lawrence, and he will return for us in a few days. We have some apples sent us from Kansas city. How fresh and nice they taste in these warm spring days! I have been down to the creek, half a mile from the house, for water. The well here is nearly dry, and most of the water used in this large family is brought from the creek. With assistance I succeeded in bringing up a six-quart pail half full of water. A young married lady here, from Indiana, whose whole appearance gives evidence of unabated health, her lively ways bespeaking a rich fund of good nature, who said indeed "she never knew what it was to be tired," laughed merrily at us, that we have accomplished so great a feat. I enjoyed the laugh as much as she, and am quite sure that it borders a good deal upon the ridiculous to go half a mile for water, and get only three quarts. But one's strength is not equal always to their will, and carrying water is entirely novel business for me.

11th. — Doctor left with E. this morning. Soon after they left we were attracted by the sound of carriage wheels, and looked out of the window to see what new comers had arrived. There was a hack stopping at the gate, and two ladies alighted. In descending the steps at the entrance one of them tripped her foot and fell. From the hearty welcome which the ladies received, we knew they must be friends, and we were soon introduced to them as the sister and daughter of Dr. Barker. The daughter has not seen this western home since her remembrance, her parents having taken her on to New England when she was a mere child, and this is her first return, now that she is "budding into womanhood." How strangely all things — this log house and perfect solitude everywhere, fresh as she is from the sympathies, the gayeties, the never-ceasing prattle of young school-girls — must look to her! But most singular of all to be a stranger in one's father's house, where the countenances of the youngest of the flock are unfamiliar. Mrs. B. is a person, the very first impression of whom will be that of her superiority, both mentally and morally, over most others; and we feel that if the mother in this Indian country must commit her child to another's care, she acted wisely in giving it to her charge. Mrs. B. is seeking the boon of health in this change of residence.

13*th.* — One day here is like every other, save in an occasional change of faces around us, as the new comers arrive to take the places of others just leaving. We wrote, read, and walked out into the woods, or took a longer walk upon the prairie. The woods near here were full of gooseberries and grape vines. Bitter-sweet and running roses wound their tendrils upon the branches, and climbed high among the trees. The red berries of the bitter-sweet were still hanging on the vines. We have tried to call upon an Indian family to-day. We followed the trail through the woods, succeeded in getting over a high fence which enclosed a large cultivated field in which the house stands, but found no one at home.

14*th.*—We have been expecting the doctor to-day to take us to Lawrence. After such a journey as this, westward, one will be content with bare comforts, and humble abodes, where there is quiet, and one feels it is really home. There is truly "no place like home." At evening some gentlemen, in from Lawrence, reported our house cut down, and the workmen ordered to stop building, by Dr. Wood, a man notorious for the disturbances he has occasioned in Lawrence.

15*th.* — Doctor arrived at the mission in the early evening, and corroborates the statement of the others. During his temporary absence from Lawrence, on the 13th, Dr. Wood and other choice spirits, armed with revolvers, went up to the house, and, after commanding the workmen to leave, commenced to cut off the timbers with an axe. The workmen, save the gentleman who had the work in charge, ceased their labor, saying they would do so until the doctor's return. These pro-slavery men were determined he should have no house there, although, for a long time, he had held the claim by another building; but, in his absence from the territory, one of these men attempted to "jump the claim." The next morning, the doctor went to the house, and the workmen returned to their labor. While at the house, he met Dr. Wood, who had gone out of Lawrence, swearing that "one of them had got to die that morning." He was, however, very quiet and peaceable. Doctor told him, "he should protect the house, but he could attempt to take it down any time he pleased."

16th. — We went to Kansas city this morning, and made such purchases as we feared we might not be able to make at Lawrence. We met some very pleasant people, who were going to find a home in the territory, and returned to the mission at evening.

17th. — We leave for Lawrence this morning. I have just been into the woods, after some rose and gooseberry bushes, not knowing whether I can get them near Lawrence. The horse is lame, having stood where the wind blew on him during the night. At about nine o'clock our buggy was packed, and we also packed into it, and a carriage never held more or greater variety. There was one valise, three carpet-bags, baskets of crockery, umbrellas, cloaks, bundles, stone pitcher, and a small basket of crackers and gingernuts. And in the midst of all this "plunder," as the western people say, three of us were seated, two ladies in front, and the doctor behind. But after being thus packed, with geometrical precision, that no square inch of space should be lost, we attempted to start. The horse proved in such condition that we proposed walking, and giving him a ride. However, after a mile or two of snail-like progress, my husband walking, and raising the horse's spirit by the cheerful tones of his voice, we began again to cherish hopes of reaching Lawrence, which we had been brought to the point of relinquishing altogether.

We passed the Quaker Mission a little distant from the road, and the peach-trees all about it gave it a cheerful look. Our road lies over the high and rolling prairie, and never was fairer picture hung out between earth and heaven to feast the eyes of nature's lovers. The sky was cloudless and blue as ocean. The air was fragrant with the perfume of apple, plum and grape blossoms, which grew in clumps by the wayside, wherever we passed through small groves. Emerging from these, some new phase of scenery would cause new expressions of delight. Sometimes we would seem to be on the very height of the land, prairies stretching in all directions, noble forests marking the line of the rivers and creeks, while the mounds far away in the distance formed a complete amphitheatre.

At another time we would be passing rapidly into what seemed to be the cultivated grounds of some private mansion, over a smooth lawn, where the tall oaks and walnuts were grouped in admirable arrangement, and with such artistic beauty, in many places, that it was difficult to realize that art had done nothing here, but nature all. At one or two places we passed ledges, where, upon the highest points, the stones were laid up in walls as regularly as if laid by stone-masons. There were deep ravines also, to be crossed, which test the strength of one's nerves somewhat. These are skirted with graceful trees, while the water in their pebbly beds is limpid and clear. Just beyond one of these, with the green branches interwoven above us to shut out the sunbeams, we rested, and dined as best we might on crackers and apples, which an acquaintance gave us, who was baiting his horse at the same spot, while ours nibbled his grass with a most satisfied look at the base of a tree. A large emigrant wagon was broken down near us, and their exertions to right matters for the rest of the journey, as well as their gypsy-like appearance in camp, added not a little to the interest of the half hour. The friend we had overtaken would be our co-traveller the rest of the way. Our afternoon's ride was similar to that of the morning, with the exception of more company.

The stage, filled with young men, settlers just arrived, overtook us in the afternoon, and was sometimes ahead of us, and sometimes in the rear, and the loud tones of the cheerful horn, frequently blown, awakened the musical echoes from prairie and dell. The prairie seemed higher, and for many miles at some points our vision was uninterrupted. A few isolated Indian huts were passed occasionally, and a grave of an Indian warrior, with the skull of his horse and dog still lying upon it. These were to accompany him in the hunting grounds of the Great Spirit. We reached the Wakarusa as the golden sunlight was fading, fast fading, for we have no twilight here, no mountains behind which the sun sinks, still shedding its lingering beams upon earth and sky. We made our descent into the river's bed rapidly, for the bank is steep, and from a clear, gushing spring in the shadow of the trees overhanging the bank, quenched our thirst. A heavily-loaded wagon having reached the top of the opposite bank, and the horses proving refractory, has slid backwards into the river. It was no pleasant sight to us. However, we reached the top safely; and there were still six miles between us and our destination, our new home in fair Kansas. We drove on as swiftly as stumps in every direction in the wood would allow; the trees, which stood most nearly in the road, being cut down, leaving a foot or more of the base, which required a good deal of expertness to avoid. After I had come so near running over a tree, that the gallant steed bearing us had reason to discover which was the harder of the two, his head or the tree, the doctor took the ribbons, and guided us onward through the gathering shadows. We saw the lights from the dwellings in Franklin, as we passed. Another hour, and we were home; yes, home, after a journey of near two thousand miles, and five weeks among strangers, sometimes pinched with cold, and sometimes suffocated with heat, crowded into dusty cars, and jostled at every turn; tired, sick children, and worn out, impatient mothers everywhere. Give us fresh, pure air, cold water plenty, a shelter from the sun and rain, and we will call it home, and soon gather around us home comforts and home joys enough to verify the truth, that the purest joys left of Eden are found under the home roof.

CHAPTER IV.

LAWRENCE.

Last evening we saw a light, which my husband said must be from our house, while we were three or four miles distance. On arriving, we found our trunks, furniture and bedding, had been carried to it. Although the first work done upon the house was upon the Friday before, after taking supper down street, we preferred going to it to stopping elsewhere. One room was clapboarded within a foot of the chamber-floor, loose boards were laid over the joists above to keep out the rains or falling dews. The windows were also similarly protected upon each side, while at the front the glass was set. There were mattresses laid upon the floor and upon the lounge, while upon the table a candle was burning, supported by a candlestick of entirely new invention, being a little block, perhaps three or four inches square, with four nails driven in to support the candle. A broom had also been provided, and a brimming pail of cold water. Blessings on him who was thus thoughtful of our comfort! By nailing a buffalo-robe at the doorway, and arranging some articles of bedding upon chairs, out of one room we made two for the night. Sleep was never sweeter or more refreshing than last night, after a long drive, with the thermometer standing at one hundred degrees.

Was awakened early this morning by a noise around the house, and, looking through a crack in the temporary partition, saw a cow very demurely examining the premises, having stationed herself in the quarter which will soon be dignified with the name of dining-room. My anxiety was considerably relieved, as my thought on awaking was, that we were visited by the same house-destroyers as a few days previous.

When we came to look out upon Lawrence and the surrounding country, as we had nearly run through the vocabulary finding words to express our rapture at the ever-changing beauty of every part of our route, and as this view from our window, and from the hill beyond us, was the master-piece, silence expressed most truly our feelings, stirred as they were by a divine hand. The house fronts the east, and is situated upon an elevation commanding a prospect unequalled for extent, or variety of loveliness, for miles in all directions. Half a mile to the north sits Lawrence, a little hamlet upon the prairie, whose fame has even now crossed the continent, awakening hopes and fears, in the hearts of many, for friends who for six months have battled with pioneer life. Malignity and hatred have been aroused in the souls of others, who see in this little gathering of dwellings of wood, thatch, and mud hovels, the promise of a new state, glorious in its future.

The town reaches to the river, whose further shore is skirted with a line of beautiful timber, while beyond all rises the Delaware lands, which in the distance have all the appearance of cultivated fields and orchards, and form a back-ground to the picture of singular loveliness. To the eastward the prairie stretches away eight or ten miles, and we can scarcely help believing that the ocean lies beyond the low range of hills meeting the horizon. The line of travel from the east, or from Kansas city, passes into the territory by this way. Blue Mound rises in the south-east, and, with the shadows resting over it, looks green and velvety. A line of timber between us and Blue Mound marks the course of the Wakarusa, while beyond the eye rests upon a country diversified in surface, sloping hills, finely rolling prairies, and timbered creeks. A half mile to the south of us, Mount Oread, upon which our house stands, becomes yet more elevated, and over the top of it passes the great California road. West of us also is a high hill, a half mile in the distance, with a beautiful valley lying between, while to the north-west there is the most delightful mingling together of hill, valley, prairie, woodland and river. As far as the eye rests, we see the humble dwellings of the pioneer, with other improvements.

4

19th.—A dark, dull day; almost raining. We sit with cloaks and bonnet on to keep warm, and sew a little. Have some calls. We walk to the door occasionally,—which will, when hung, open into the other room,—forgetting it will not open at one's bidding now. It is cramped up to stay in one room always, though, as I hoped before leaving Massachusetts, we "have out-of-doors a plenty." Doctor brings from town our dinner, to save our going down. It consists of slices of cold ham, cookies and doughnuts. We laugh at him because he brought no bread, which is worth more than all.

20th.—A slight rain to-day. The flowers are springing all over the hill-side; purple and straw-color being the prevailing colors. A little lilac-colored flower, of fern-leaf variety, fragile and beautiful, grows under every step, and yellow flowers, resembling lupine, are everywhere. The hammering, the continual pounding of a dozen workmen is confusing, and we walk out upon the brow of the hill for quiet and rest. How lovely nature has made this Kansas valley, and yet it seems as if, from a full lap of treasured gems, she had poured out the fairest here! More ham and cake to-day,—no bread. Our merriment over it will aid digestion, even though it be cake and ham.

21st.—The floor in the dining-room is laid. The windows are in. The door between the rooms is taken away, and the stove is set, with the pipe out of the window, after the true pioneer fashion. The stove, however, will put one's ingenuity to work in using, it being second-hand. Having been used six months in a boarding-house, not the most carefully, the furniture is minus; and what there is, is of unknown use to me. There is one large iron boiler, which would cover the whole front of the stove, one broken gridiron, one large dripping-pan, two tin boilers holding six or eight quarts, one of which, near the top, has a nose—the other, close to the bottom, has a spout. The furniture, which is the minus quantity, are iron kettles, tea-kettle, spider, shovel and tongs. However, we get supper, stew apples,—brought from Massachusetts,—and have biscuits without butter. It is a real Graham supper, with cold water. Provisions are scarce.

22d.—The old Westminster catechism allows works of necessity and mercy to be done on the Sabbath day, and we baked some pies; but had breakfast of simple griddle cakes with syrup, made of sugar and water. Even the shade of Sylvester Graham might have looked on approvingly. We are in danger of no intermittents from clogged liver at present. So far, so good. We read and write all day. Just at evening walked on the hill above, near the first camping-ground. A gentleman and lady from Massachusetts came in. They live not very far from us. The lady, with a large family of boarders, seventeen in all, in one little room, seemed disheartened. They had had some sickness, too. They feel the change from comforts to privations.

The slit-work for the stairway is set, and we are anticipating the time when we can get into the second story. How our friends in the East would pity us, did they know just how we live; but I dare say there is not one in a hundred of them who enjoys the half we do. We are deprived of no comforts, that is, of anything essential to our happiness; for, coming to the real root of the matter, every one will find that the externals have but little to do with a person's real enjoyment. We have the pure, fresh air, in abundance; we have fine, even spirits, and we feel that to live, to breathe in such a country, is a joy, especially on a day like this.

" Under the hill where the sun shines dimmer,
Shrunk from the eager beam,
The work goes on with a fitful glimmer,
And music for a dream.

" Over the groves and moistened meadows
The steady gray hawks wing,
And down below in the shifting shadows
The merry small birds sing."

A gentleman from Philadelphia, of most polished manners and brilliant address, is here to-night.

24*th.* — Doctor returned last night, after we had retired to rest. The town was full, and his friend returned with him. Doctor made a bed, that is, laid down a buffalo robe on the floor, and, putting another at the door, formed a sleeping apartment of the kitchen and dining-room, *pro tem.* He was missing before we awakened in the morning.

We can get no butter, no syrup, no milk, no potatoes. There is an abundance of nothing save cheese, beef, ham, and sugar. We made doughnuts, and after a consultation fried them in a two-quart tin upon the top of the stove. The smoke of the fire seems to have some strange attraction into the room, and E. and I take turns going out upon the staging to turn the pipe, with like success each time, not being able to move it at all. However, as the smoke poured out more and more with every extra whiff of the wind, and promised to add a seasoning to our cooking which we had not intended, we went each time to test our strength, hoping the emergency had brought an addition. Some strangers called, and, in a room sixteen feet by twelve, containing lounge, table, eight trunks, two dry goods' boxes, and chest, besides chairs, there was no extra room.

25th. — Doctor accompanied three other gentlemen upon a tour of discovery into the country two or three hundred miles. They will be gone ten days. They dined with us before leaving. They are used to the simplicity of Kansas fare at present, else I would have been embarrassed in setting it before them. An old gentleman will do errands and take care of everything in doctor's absence. We hear the wolves howling at night, and the bells on the cattle that have an attachment for this hill keep me awake.

26th. — A most delightful day. It seemed wicked not to gather new life and cull enjoyment from the bright skies and blooming prairies. Soon had the horse put into harness, and was bounding over them. We wanted to call upon a friend, who was of our party, from Massachusetts. We could see her house plainly from ours, but took the wrong road when nearly there.

We came upon an abrupt ravine, and the young lady with me said she must get out. I tried to persuade her to remain — that I would take her safely over; but my persuasions were useless, and she alighted. "Old Gray" and I went through it alone, all right. We soon, however, came upon a second ravine, where even he declined going. He said, as plainly as words could, that he would n't go; but in a twinkling he started off a little to the right, and came upon another and more travelled road, where there was a bridge, rudely constructed, but safe. A few minutes more passed, and we met our friend at her little log cabin door. Everything looked comfortable, she was glad to see us, and we enjoyed our call much. We took a different route home, and found so many beautiful flowers, each one seeming more lovely than the last, that we hardly could be satisfied unless we gathered them all.

27th. — In the afternoon, horse and buggy were again put into requisition for a two miles' drive in search of the friend we met at the mission. She had lived nearly all her life in Boston, and was wholly unaccustomed to hardships, and unused to many things in domestic economy with which country people are familiar, although they may never have lent their own hands to the work. By instinct, almost, we found the cabin on the edge of a bluff, looking as if some high wind might take it over; but the door opened upon a finely rolling prairie, dotted all over with flowers, which, in variety of color, vied with the rainbow.

The cabin was of wood, and small, yet with bed nicely dressed in snowy linen, little table with white cover, upon which were placed a Chinese work-box and vase of flowers, easy-chairs, of home manufacture, just ready for the stuffed covers; a stranger would at once perceive that the presiding genius of all, fragile and slight, dressed in gingham of the smallest plaid, with linen collar, had come from far New England; and, whether the home be humble or lofty, elegance and taste would bring out their treasures to make it pleasant. Her husband, a New Yorker by birth, by profession a lawyer, a poet, and musician, allured by the health-giving clearness of Kansas atmosphere, had sought and found that inestimable treasure. He came in while we were there; had driven home a cow just purchased. It was decided, against my earnest protest, that she should be milked, and that I should carry the milk home with me. It was but four o'clock in the afternoon — an unusual time for milking, I was sure; but they thought one time would do as well as another, and persisted in it, and I carried home the first milking, which proved much to my chagrin when I heard of it the last for that day.

28th. — We attended church. How strangely everything appeared! The hall where the meetings are held is in a two-story wooden building. It is simply boarded with cotton-wood, and that to a person in the country, is explanation sufficient of its whole appearance; for the sun here soon curls the boards, every one shrinking from every other, leaving large cracks between. For a desk to support the gilded, morocco-covered Bible, sent to the Plymouth church, a rough box, turned endwise, and standing near one end of the hall, was used. The singers, with seraphine, were seated upon one side of the preacher, while upon the other side, also fronting the desk, were other seats — rough boards, used until the settees are finished. All this seemed rough and uncouth, and at the first moment we felt that two thousand miles lay between us and the pleasant sanctuaries of our fathers, where they tread the aisles on soft carpets, listen to the word read from its resting-place of richest velvet, and to the pealing organ's deep, rich tones. But when we looked upon the pleasant faces around us, so familiar all in look, in manner, in attire, and the services commenced with the singing of hymns learned long ago, and we heard, in the persuasive, winning tones of the preacher, the same heavenly truths which will render one's life here as holy as elsewhere, let us so will it, we felt that New England was in our midst. We realized more fully the truth, which has been pervading our thoughts for many days, that "a man's life consisteth not in the abundance of the things which he possesseth." Happiness does not consist in the furnishings of the upholsterer. It may be as pure and unalloyed in "gypsy tent as in palace hall." Most of us have come to this far-away land, with a mission in our hearts, a mission to the dark-browed race, and hoping here to stay the surging tide of slavery, to place that barrier which utters, in unmistakable language, "Thus far shalt thou go, and no further." This unlocks our hearts to each other, and at once we recognize a friend actuated by like sympathies and hopes.

At the Sabbath school many children were gathered, who entered with zest into the exercises, while there were learners older in years, young men, buoyant in the active life opening before them, and some with whom gray hairs were honorable.

CHAPTER V.

KANSAS HOMES.

Mrs. T., a young lady from Boston, is dead. Just one year from the day of her marriage she was attired for the grave. In this early spring, when nature is so beautiful in young leaves and opening buds, and full of promise, the hopes of the young husband are blasted. Earth and sky wear a pall. Slowly the mourners wind through the prairie, and over the high hill beyond us, to the lowly cemetery. We all feel that death is indeed here. It has, with unerring aim, stricken down the young and beautiful. Tenderly we would offer sympathy, realizing well that "every heart knoweth its own bitterness" in hours of bereavement, and shrinks from many words, though kindly spoken.

Death to us here, away from one's early friends, one's old home, has more than its usual significance, and the tidings of one laid low in our little settlement awakens a thoughtfulness and a tenderness for the bereaved and heart-stricken, which in the old homes we felt not, save for a dear friend. We make their sorrow, their utter loneliness, our own. So different is it from the olden towns, where life is crowded, and if, in the bustle and jostling of each other, one now and then falls, the crowd presses on, and the gap closes. Here, there is a sad feeling for many and many a day, and we realize that changes as sudden may await us all.

We have showers to-day, quick, pouring showers, and in the intervals the sunlight seems intense with its life-giving powers. How nature is robing herself in the richest of green! For hours I have looked out upon her changing forms, with many crowding thoughts of home, of friends scattered all through New England dells and mountains — of friends passed onward into the spirit life, whose presence is at all times near me, but with peculiar vividness to-day; of the duties of life, especially of those resting upon us in this age, when the spirit of liberty, of manliness even, is giving way before the increasing thirst for gold, which is the god of this country. I have watched the new and varied phase of those noble trees across the river. How the leaves grow! How the rain-drops glitter like gems, as the sun, with clouds passed by, shines out brilliantly again; and as the bow of promise spanned all, this thought, like it, was born of the sunshine and the shower.

We are passing through hours of imminent danger to the liberties of the country. "The old landmarks have been removed," and "men have framed mischief by law." Yet, serenely above all these commotions, this treachery, this fraud of man, holding the seals of justice, sits God upon his throne. And out of all, in his own good time, he will again bring the reign of righteous men, and the laws of our country shall have for their basis love and truth. Give us courage to act when the hour calls for action, and faith to wait when endurance is our cross. We in Kansas can see with clear vision the workings of this hydra-headed monster, whose seat is at Washington, and whose power emanates therefrom, and whose unholy name is Human Slavery.

May 2d. — "Old Gray" is lent to a friend to-day; so we lose our intended ride. Mr. S. brings us a basket of eggs from the Delaware country. We are beginning to get more articles which seemed essential in house-keeping at home, but which are difficult to get here, as many people are ready to take them the moment they are brought in. Many of the new comers neglect to provide themselves with the staples of life at Kansas city; so, as soon as flour and groceries are brought in here, they take them back into the country, leaving us a continual dearth. Somehow, by the happy genius of invention, of which long ago necessity was acknowledged the mother, we have always had enough of the good things of this life, and have most faithfully followed the last clause of the injunction which the rich man in Scripture lays to his soul, "eat, drink, and *be merry.*"

Mr. W., the old gentleman who acts for us in the capacity of prime minister of all work about the house, in the occasional absence — I might more truthfully say occasional presence at home — of my husband, croaks a good deal, that we "will have a famine in the autumn — that starvation will drive us far from the country, because, forsooth, to-day there is no flour in town. It seems to me quite probable, while flour is plenty in Missouri at three and a half dollars per sack, and sells here at six and a half, that the Missourians will bring it over; not so much out of friendly regard for us, "poor Massachusetts paupers," as of interested feeling for their pockets. In that at least I have implicit trust. E. goes on an exploring expedition for yeast, and is successful in getting some which looks neither "lively" nor clean. Indeed, it looks as though some very strong chemical action must be brought to bear upon it, in order to raise good bread.

3d. — Towards night was glad to welcome to our house a young lady, also a fellow-traveller upon the river. The family with whom she travelled are exceedingly fine people. They are intending to settle at Manhattan, upon the Big Blue, seventy-five or one hundred miles from here. The country there is called by many more beautiful than this, yet they who go there must possess courage beyond mine to live so far from any steam line of communication with the states.

Like most Kansas emigrants, this young lady and her friends have tasted the hardships of pioneer life. On leaving Kansas city three days since, and getting out of town a short distance, their horses became entirely unmanageable. Notwithstanding the depth of the mud, owing to the recent heavy showers, the ladies were set out into it, and for quite a distance carried the children in their arms. The effort being ineffectual towards further progress that night, they camped by the road-side and slept amid the dampness and falling rain.

They have also been visited with sickness. While Mr. D., after great prostration, has recovered, the little one, the "pet lamb" of the flock, has "gone home," without tasting earth's trials, or breasting its stormy floods.

4th. — I sent E. to my nearest neighbor's this morning for milk; without success, however. Among all these cows which are grazing over all the hills, reminding one continually of the sweet pictures of pastoral life, where the cattle feed upon a thousand hills, and the dwellers of the land make their homes in tents, it seems strange that milk is so difficult to procure. E. finds more acquaintances at Mr. S.'s, and they too are "passing under the rod." The wing of the dark angel is hovering near to bear away the little child, whose pallor now rivals the linen which the wan cheek presses.

We go out to ride over these glorious old prairies, where till now the moccasined foot of the Indian has alone pressed the soil. We called for a friend, and rode several miles. How I have longed for my eastern friends to be with me in such pleasure-drives as these, that I might hear their bursts of enthusiasm at sight of this world where nature has been prodigal, or their exclamations of fear as we approach some deep ravine lying between us and the fairy land beyond! Flowers of every shade of color, and every variety of form, would entice us beyond the bounds, and my assurance of safe passage over would calm their fears. Tame to them as to me would seem the every-day dull routine of conventional life, its old beaten track of set forms and ceremonies, from which if one deviates, criticism, the stern censor of society, labels him as odd, eccentric, simple, or independent. Freedom is a blessed thing, and thrice blessed is freedom of will, freedom of intellect, freedom of action.

The little wan child is dead. The measles have been fatal here beyond all experience. The bereaved sister will stay with us to-night.

5th.—I rose early this morning. As I reached the dining-room, with my foot on the last stair, a movement at the door, a rustling attracts my attention. The buffalo robe is pulled away, and a familiar face fills the small gap. After little ceremony I run to tell E. that her father has come—just from Massachusetts and home. How the questions crowd upon him, and how strangely it seems to us that, in the two months of our absence from Fitchburg, something of greater moment has not happened! While we have been passing through new scenes, continually meeting people from all parts of the Union, with their peculiarities awakening an interest in us, and giving zest tc their conversation, each day varied with some new incident, we are looking for something new and strange from home.

Some ladies from Massachusetts soon call. One of them came with the second New England company, and has been through the heats of the day. They brought a bouquet, which for beauty would compare favorably with any green-house collection. As they pranced their horses gayly from the door, and over the table land between us and the brow of the hill north, nothing could have looked finer.

The evening shadows fall, another week is at an end, and seated around the table we are writing to home friends, when there is a new rattling at the rickety door-step, and, almost before we can turn to see, doctor comes in under the buffalo robe. He has been just ten days from home. The pleasant light shining from the windows gave him, in advance of us, a glad welcome. They had been two hundred miles back in the country, and there as here a most delightful region invites settlement.

6th. — Exclamations of delight from E.'s room called me early from mine. Words poorly convey an idea of the exceeding beauty of the scene. A mist was slowly ascending from the river. The sun, in a chariot of fire, was mounting upwards from a bed of golden clouds, and his beams encircled earth, air and sky, in a halo of glory; the mists still rising became a silver sheen, through which the foliage on the further bank looked yet more green and brilliant. It was a beautiful harbinger of the Sabbath morning, which to man brings peace and quiet here, and offers glory in the unending ages. The quiet of the day is most grateful. Before time for service, Mr. P. came in from "Fisk's," nine miles from here, in the Shawnee Reserve. We attended church and Sabbath school. In the evening sang Whittier's gem of a Kansas song. Some beautiful bouquets were passed in at the door. They were fairy gifts, the giver remaining unseen.

7th. — The grass is getting so high, and we are so far from the road, Mr. W. spends a long forenoon in beating down the grass, and making a wide path. We ride out again to see our Boston friend. She had been trying to churn, with the cream in a large tin pail, and a large square place cut in the cover for the dasher. She churned, and her husband churned, until they were both weary, and of the opinion that country life has its cares as well as pleasures. A new thought came to the gentleman — he had seen some one pour in cold water to facilitate the butter-making, as it began to look like coming. No sooner thought, than acted upon; but the butter, alas! remained cream in *statu quo*. The day before, a large rattlesnake, attracted by the genial warmth near the stove, had, without waiting for invitation, or being assured of a welcome, crawled in through a huge crack, and stretched out his three feet of length. With a scream or two on the part of the lady, and some dexterous and telling blows by a stronger arm, his snakeship was rendered harmless, though a most ugly object. I noticed a bottle of medicine on the little white-covered table, and over it pinned upon the wall a recipe for rattlesnake bites, and a *sure cure*.

Upon our leaving, my friend was determined to share with me the unfortunate cream. So, with one six-quart pail of cream, and another of milk, and a pretty bunch of flowers, we started for home. It was no easy matter to carry such full measures without spilling; but, by very careful driving down the hills, the friend with me carrying one pail while we steadied the other in the bottom of the wagon, we reached Lawrence in safety.

8th. — I wanted to boil eggs at noon, but, as many times before, when proposing to cook something new, a dilemma arose. This time it came in the lack of a kettle to be used. Doctor's experience in roughing it in California was again useful, and upon his suggestion the eggs came out of the copper boiler properly cooked. A gentleman in at dinner spoke of some beautiful straw-colored flowers he had seen on the hill above us. E. and I started off, after dinner, with shovel in hand, to get some for transplanting. We went half a mile, and found a number of very beautiful bunches, but, after persevering efforts, were obliged to leave them, their firmly-set roots still clinging to the soil. We took up a few rose-bushes to set about the house.

Among the stones down the side of the ledge, a little blue flower, with lily-like leaf, looked out temptingly; and carefully, being most fearful of a fall, I clambered down, and was paid for all my trouble, all my labor in working upon roots I could not remove, in the realization of the fact that one of our garden favorites, the graceful spiderwort, grows wild here.

The house is full of company this evening, and, with the open partitions, there is no quiet anywhere. Dr. C., a practising physician here, who came from Georgia recently, and his brother-in-law, just arrived, are the last who call. They are very gentlemanly men, of northern birth, education and intelligence, with southern ease of manner. Very many of this class of people are looking to Kansas for a home — a home free from the curse, the blighting mildew of slavery, with genial climate, and the intercourse of enlightened, refined people surrounded by the institutions of free labor.

9th. — Our stove smoked terribly. We moved it from the west to the south window before noon, and, as the wind changed before night, returned it to its old place. Mr. G. dug up for us some of the straw-colored flowers, which must be a variety of evening primrose.

10th. — Doctor went to Topeka. We moved the dressing bureau up stairs, which until now has served us for a cupboard. We cut prairie hay, and put down carpet in front room. A young lady, who came to the territory in the autumn, called. She has enjoyed life here very much. Our new book-case was brought up at evening. It is of black walnut, of Kansas manufacture, and very pretty. E. and I spent the whole evening arranging books.

11th. — We hung pictures and engravings on the unfinished walls, and the parlor really begins to have a pleasant look. Doctor came home. He says we have something new every time he goes away, and he proposed to stay altogether, that we may get all things in order. The truth is, when he is at home, the house is at all hours full of company, and we are busily employed in looking after their physical wants. There is seldom a meal that we have only our own family of five, and, more often than otherwise, the strangers number more than we.

12th.—A most curious fish was sent in from Topeka to-day. It has a long, projecting, sword-shaped upper jaw, and no lower jaw, — the mouth being an opening in the under side of the upper one. After being stuffed, it will be sent to Boston. A lady from Maine, who has been located on the hill west of us for a week or two, calls to say they have concluded to leave Kansas. Her husband is much pleased with the country, but the mills do not supply all the lumber people want just now, and he thinks he can't wait. A good deal of lumber has been sawed, but as we remember that the claims for ten miles around Lawrence are all taken, and that they depend upon the mill here for lumber, we can easily see that there must be a scarcity, and that each person must be content with little for the time being.

13*th.* — I attended a Sabbath school to-day, four miles out on the California road. There were quite a number of children present, with some older persons. Some little English girls were very bright and interesting. The family at whose house the school was held are from Ohio. They are such good people that one feels it in their presence, and sincerity and unselfishness are manifested in their actions. They have long been earnest workers in the cause of humanity — have "fed the hungry, clothed the naked," and given the "cup of cold water" to the fainting soul. I attempted to hear a class of girls, whose ages varied from fourteen to eighteen, recite. They were all from the West, and mostly from Missouri. Some of them were bright, quick girls, but with one or two I puzzled my brain to know how to ask questions simply enough to be understood. They had no ideas of their own existence or of God.

14*th.* — The thunder rolls in deafening peals, reverberating across the hills, and the lightnings are one continual flash. There is not a moment that the forked, angry lightnings do not dart chain-like in every and all directions, making the whole country as light as noon-day. Objects miles distant are as clearly seen as by the sun's light. The rains come down a pouring, tumultuous flood, and the winds blow wildly, threatening to overturn everything before them. The house being so unfinished, the saddle-boards not yet on the roof, the staging still standing around it, with crockery covering tables in the dining-room, and no back door, my presence was needed in several places at the same moment. While attempting to move my bed so the rains would not float it off, there was a rattling of glass below stairs. As I reached the lower room, Mr. W. emerged from the other one, and asked, "Are you afraid the house will blow over?"

Upon my replying, "O, no, I am not afraid of anything," he seemed satisfied, and as quickly disappeared.

Concluding, from this present phase of the matter, I need expect no aid from my "prime minister," I went out and took down as much of the staging as I could — those pieces which were partly loose and striking the house. The shower lasted for hours. Although I have been among the Green Mountains when most severe showers raged there, and the reverberating roar was incessant, I never experienced anything equal in sublimity and grandeur to this.

15*th.* — The night brought another shower — if possible, more severe than that of last night. All the evening the lightning flashed in every direction; but at midnight the thunders sounded, and the great drops fell. The grand artillery of heaven could hardly be distinguished from the noise of the furious blasts of wind and fast-flowing streams, which seem to scorn all old-fashioned showers. The shower came from the west, and there was nothing to break its force as it beat upon the house in full fury. There was a crash below. Hastily as possible I descended the stairway against the driving wind and pelting rain, which came full upon me the moment I stepped on to the staircase, almost taking away my breath. The door had been hung the day before; but the slight button which fastened it together was like a flaxen string before the gale, and the door with great force had been driven back against the wall. It was impossible to remove so much crockery and glass ware, which, on account of the unfinished cupboard, was still standing round, to any secure place; and it was but the work of a moment with me to "haul" a trunk of the largest size, filled with carpets, against the door after closing it. The next moment found trunk and me in the middle of the floor, and door again wide open. Another effort must be made; and, quicker than thought, or any calculations as to strength, the trunk was replaced, and a large black-walnut dining-table brought up against it.

At this juncture of affairs, the old gentleman made his appearance; and, after some casual remarks upon the weather, by way of suggestion, I spoke of adjusting the pipe, as it looked likely to fall. He looked at it rather suspiciously, though keeping at a safe distance from it, should some extra breath tottle it over, and, without comment, made good his retreat. I was amused, and pitied his fears; then took down the pipe that it might occasion me no more thought. The storm lasted several hours, as on the previous night. It was quite impossible to shade one's eyes from the continual glare, and sleep came not until the morning shadows were breaking.

16*th.* — One expected this morning to see some devastation — some remnant or vestige of the last night's work — but earth never put on a more smiling face. There was no evidence of the lightning's dread power, although often in the night there was an unmistakable sound of its striking near. Instead of the valleys being full of water, and the earth a perfect sea, its thirsty pores had drank in all, and naught remained to tell of it save the grass bending under its heavy weight of glistening rain-drops.

For ten long months the drouth had been unprecedented. Many times a little cloud had arisen, awakening hopes of rain; but the cloud had passed by. In any other country than this, vegetation would have been entirely killed, root and branch dried up; but, before the rains came, even the gentle showers, the grass was clothing the naked earth in a mantle of greenness, and flowers, fairy-like in their gracefulness, were blooming in every sheltered nook. Now the "windows of heaven were opened," as in old time. The rains came, and the winds blew. Earth was gladdened in her vegetable life, and in her hidden springs. From many a dry spot, heretofore, the clear gushing waters came.

17*th.* — A most glorious morning. How gayly all nature looks! The woods over in the Delaware country are clothed in every shade of green, from the most delicate to the deepest sea-green, while beautiful browns and blue are intermingled. Until now I have never longed for the artist's skill in conveying to canvas these living pictures of beauty by the master's hand — more beautiful than that of any earthly limner, inasmuch as the heavenly is above the earthly. Never until now have I revelled in such manifold and different shades of coloring, or felt so deeply my own insignificance beneath creative power. We admire, we worship, we adore, when His presence speaks in the loveliness of this Eden. We feel it in the voice of his thunders — in their unwritten magnificence and grandeur.

Take a walk down to the town, and call upon one of our fellow-travellers. We find her in a little cabin of mud walls, cotton-wood roof, and with cloth covering the inside. It is tent-shaped, and very small. There is an earthy smell and a stifled feeling as I enter the low door; and, as I at a glance see the want of comfort pervading all, I scarcely can find courage to ask how she likes Kansas. A bed, standing crosswise, fills up one entire end of the cabin, leaving only about eight feet square of space for the family, consisting of father, mother, and four little girls under six years. Two rough benches, about two feet in length, and two rude tables, make up the furniture. The cooking is done out of doors, after camp fashion. The children have been very ill, and the little one now tosses restlessly in its fevered dreams.

I talk cheerfully of the homes we hope to have when a few months are passed — of the comforts, the institutions, which we will gather around us; but my heart is sad for the little, frail, heart-broken looking woman and her four little ones, and involuntarily my mind questions whether like cares shall make their young girlhood wear the look of age. I can bear no longer the oppression, the feeling that the walls will come together, crushing me like a mere shadow between them; and, with a promise to come again, breathe most thankfully the unconfined fresh air.

The mail is in, and, in the office of a friend near by the post-office, we wait for its distribution. Letters from home are a pleasant reward. I met Mr. C., of Philadelphia, who says doctor has returned home with a carriage-load of company. There surely is no end to the company. The house now is full in every corner. I give up my room again, and make two extra beds on the floor. I am not yet rested from my journey, and the constant excitement since. Now there is an ungoverned, noisy child, — a continual presence, — and no quiet place in the house where I can find a safe retreat. Several more strangers were in in the evening. A gentleman, just arrived from Massachusetts, is very ill, and sends up for doctor's attendance upon him. Doctor brought from Missouri a jar of butter — the first we have had — and some potatoes.

19*th.* — A large carriage-load went down to the Wakarusa to visit the proposed site of a new town. I enjoyed the quiet occasioned by their absence beyond measure, and realized more fully than ever the truth of the injunction:

> "Be to thyself a palace,
> Else the world will be thy jail."

They returned late in the evening, much pleased with the country and scenery. Their adventures, in crossing the Wakarusa at high water, occasioned more merriment in the retrospect than in the moment when the water was coming into the carriage-body over the top. They were delayed an hour by the straying off of one of their party, which came near preventing their return that night, as the water was rising very fast.

20*th.* — All went to church save E. and I, and the three-year-old boy, who intended to rule every one around him. A little decision proved very salutary with him, and we had a quiet morning. As we were nearly through supper a whistle sounded. Each one of us looked at every other in blank astonishment, until some one said, "It is the cars." The thought of a boat occurred to me, and was quickly spoken. The table was vacated in a trice. Some were looking out of the windows and doors, while others ran to the chamber windows. A steamboat was really in sight, and a pretty object she was as she floated gracefully towards the landing, now behind this building, and now that, with the tall old forest for a background. A friend brings in some wild strawberries. How they bring back days long ago, when we knew where the sweetest grew, and, with merry school-friends, travelled far for them through the dim woods down into the meadow!

21*st.* — A bright May morning, clear and sunny, reminding one of the beautiful poem of Willis:

"The spring is here — the delicate-footed May —
  With its slight fingers full of leaves and flowers,
And with it comes a thirst to be away,
  Wasting in wood-paths its voluptuous hours;
A feeling that is like a sense of wings,
Restless to soar above its perishing things."

The heat in the afternoon was equal to July weather at home, and the new jar of butter is fast approaching the fluid state. It has to be removed from one place to another, sometimes in the house, and sometimes on the shady side out of the house, to find the coolest place. We propose various ways for keeping it hard, such as digging a place in the ground large enough for the jar; but, at the suggestion of one of the Boston gentlemen, who was interested in the matter, we decided upon the refrigerator as by far the greatest convenience.

To-morrow is the day set for the election of representatives in the contested districts. We hear the Missourians are coming to take possession of the polls, as before. A party of horsemen rode in this afternoon over College Hill, west of us, and at first we thought the report of Missourians coming might be true. The gay blankets, bare heads, and shining ornaments, soon showed them to be a party of Kaw Indians. Mr. Simpson was assaulted to-day by a bitter pro-slavery man.

22*d.* — Election day, and all was quiet. Only eleven pro-slavery votes polled in this district. A very pleasant lady from New York is spending the day. A young gentleman, one of our Kansas party, called. He has a claim on the Wakarusa, with which he is much pleased. Some families of his acquaintance, also of our party, are equally pleased. More gentlemen to tea. We boil ham for doctor, who will leave with three gentlemen on a pleasure trip, or exploring tour, into the country.

23*d.* — Doctor left with his party on their prospecting journey this morning. It is quite an undertaking to get started on such an expedition, as they are obliged to take a good stock of provisions and cooking utensils, so that if their route takes them far from any settlers they will not be reduced to starvation. For such trips usually, we pack a ham, dried meat, hard bread, sugar, a bottle of syrup, cheese, a small box with knives, forks and spoons, and little papers of pepper and salt. Tin cup for drinking, with canteens, are also indispensable. Blankets and comfortables for camping ought not to be forgotten; also provisions for the horses.

Our cupboard was completed to-day, and we have cleared all the tables of crockery. Our house gives promise now of being in reality a house at no distant day.

24th. — The timbers are drawn for the kitchen. We are to have another room sixteen feet by twelve, and with doors opening directly opposite each other. It will be delightful and cool. A large chest, which we have used for a cupboard since the removal of the bureau, is moved up the stairway, and finds a place just fitting it near the head. We find behind it a missing pie, whose sudden disappearance had been a mystery, and awakened some fears of the too neighborly inclinations of prairie wolves, or the nightly visitation of some hungry traveller; our open doors and unfastened windows furnishing no safeguard against any who choose to enter.

The roads for many days have been full of wagons — white-covered, emigrant wagons. We cannot look out of the windows without seeing a number, either upon the road through the prairie east of us, which comes in from Kansas city, where most emigrants leave the boats and buy wagons and provisions for the journey, or, going on the hill west, on their way to Topeka, or other settlements above.

The prairie, too, is alive with people, coming and going. Some are upon horseback, and others in carriages of eastern manufacture; while the busy teams, carrying stone for the hotel and other large buildings, give to the whole town an appearance of unprecedented thrift which renders the name of Yankee Town, bestowed upon it by the border friends, richly merited. At night we see the camp-fires all about us, on the prairies and in the ravines. The appearance of the men, preparing their evening meal, is singularly grotesque and gypsy-like.

26th. — Some young ladies called at the house early this morning. They were just in the territory from Ohio, and came up from town to admire the prospect from Mount Oread. We have similar calls almost daily, while frequently for hours there are persons sitting upon the brow of the hill beyond us. A few days since a rather young-looking man called. He was a clergyman, and had buried his wife not long before. He had come to Kansas with his children, the eldest of whom, a little girl of not more than ten summers, was his housekeeper. I have never heard of them since.

We spend the day with a friend, two miles in the country, who sends a carriage for us. The hills on our way look like one vast garden. Elegant bunches of foxglove stand by the wayside, lifting most proudly their tall spikes of purple, lilac and white flowers, from a beautiful base of dark lustrous green leaves; straw color, orange, and every variety of shade of pinks, from white to deepest red, add their blended beauty. Our road, after leaving the great California road, than which there was never a finer one, is uneven, and we pass several abrupt ravines. We see the house, or, more properly, the flume, a long time before reaching it, and are constantly expecting to be at the door; but we have to learn, what every one else does in these prairies, that eyes unaccustomed cannot judge correctly of distances.

We found the lady much excited, and glad of our arrival, as she had had some very unwelcome visitors in the absence of her husband. Being also half a mile from the nearest neighbor, rendered it yet more unpleasant. A large party of Kaw Indians had passed the house, while three of the stragglers made a call They examined daguerreotypes and jewelry lying on the book-case and by signs manifested their desire for them. The lady remained firm in her refusal, and they relinquished the idea of appropriating them. They soon made signs for something to eat, and, after being most abundantly supplied with meat and bread, one of them, the most repulsive of all, made a circle on the floor, and signs of cutting it, then pointing to his mouth to represent his desire that a pie should be set before them. To comply with such request being considered unnecessary, it was refused; whereupon the young Indian pulled away a cloth, at one end of the room, concealing some shelves, and, with boisterous exclamations of delight, brought out some pies. Seating themselves around them, they were also soon devoured. When we arrived the visitors had scarcely left.

The house, which, when finished, will contain two rooms on the lower floor, with an equal number upon the upper, is now only boarded upon one end, and partially upon the sides, enclosing one room, while the partition, which will be between the rooms when the whole outside is finished, but is now the only protection on the north, is partly of wood and partly of cloth; the roof, also, is shingled over the south part. The cooking utensils and stove are out of doors.

In such houses as these, exposed to all the vicissitudes of climate and weather, and all the discomforts of such a life, there is many a person fresh from all the elegancies, the refinements clustering about a home in our eastern cities. The most I have met bear these hardships cheerfully, and hopefully looking to the hour when Kansas shall come into the glorious sisterhood of states, herself untrammeled by the dark rule of slavery. These privations seem naught in the anticipation of such an hour. This spot is a most delightful location for a house. The bluffs, in a semicircular form, partially enclose a lovely prairie of quarter of a mile in width between them. The house stands near the centre, between the northern and southern ridge, while the bluff rises on the west very near the house. A lovely prairie stretches away nearly two miles eastward, with wood-skirted ravines, and Lawrence rising on an eminence beyond. Means alone are needed to make the grounds as beautiful as any one could desire; and our friends who have chosen the spot for a Kansas home are revelling in golden anticipations for the future.

We ride home as the sun is setting behind massive clouds in orange and violet, in fantastic shapes, resembling Chinese pagodas and temples. The mutterings of the thunder, when we are a little distance from home, warn us of the near approach of another shower, and by dint of much persuasion our friends remain with us during the night.

27*th.*—A pleasant morning. The face of the earth looks bright after such a drenching. We laugh at my night adventure.

I gave up my own room to my friends, and, hastily taking some buffalo robes from the wood-pile, made a bed of them, and of comforters upon the floor in E.'s room. Having been a little time asleep was awakened by a quick stinging pain in my hand, and the consequent thought of a rattlesnake. The dampness about the windows had ruined the matches which lay near, and I could strike no light from any of them. To aid me, however, it still occasionally lightened faintly, and I felt secure in walking over as much of the floor as would be revealed in the light; and slowly, every inch of the staircase being thus scrutinized that I might not step on any snake, if snake it was, I reached the dining-room and struck a light. Then I carefully shook every article composing my bed, hunted behind trunks and in every corner, and found nothing, though the pain in my hand continued the same. Just as I was preparing to blow out my light again, one of the girls, looking over the foot of the bedstead, says, "What are you doing?" and was much amused at my reply, "I am hunting rattlesnakes!"

The pain in my hand was probably the effect of imagination, as we had been speaking of rattlesnakes the day before—of several houses where they had been found coiled up among the logs, and of one which very unceremoniously had crawled in between two persons occupying a bed in a tent.

We went to the Sabbath school in the country with Mr. S. Near the close of the exercises the young man, H., who made the brutal attack upon Mr. S., a few days before, came in with four or five young men. If their faces were any index to their character, they were fitting companions for him. They seated themselves quietly, and offered no violence. If they came with such intentions, the circumstances, or it is not impossible that the good in them for the time outweighed the evil, brutal nature, and prevented their execution.

Towards evening we heard that Mr. Nute, the clergyman sent out by the Unitarian Association, would preach upon Capitol Hill, and we saw the people already gathering. The scene was impressive. The preacher stood while the audience sat upon rough seats and stones upon the summit of the hill. Earth had never spread out a fairer picture than this lying before us. At one glance the eye rested upon river, forest, mountain and prairie, miles and miles distant as well as near, and the last rays of the setting sun shed a halo of glory over all. The novel circumstances under which we met were touched upon; our leaving the old homes among the eastern hills to find a new one in the "waiting West," and the hope which actuates one and all of seeing the same institutions flourish here, which make life desirable there. The protecting care and guidance of the same kind Parent are still over and around us. He provides for us this beautiful temple, "not made with hands," in which to worship him; and if from our work here he calls us home, he offers heaven with its "eternal mansions."

Mr. N. was for some years the pastor of a dearly loved friend of mine, of whom she often spoke, and in this way he seems to me like an old friend. We are glad he has come among us with his genial sympathies, his heart warmth, his earnest ways, his outspoken words for truth, and his abiding love for freedom and the right. We need such manliness among us, in this new, unsettled state of things; such men, with unwearying confidence in God, and the humanity of men; with whom the love for a distressed brother is more than one's faith in creeds, and whose faith is strong that in doing good to one's fellow we show our love to God. That men are born of the times is an old adage. That men, needed for the times, may arise ready for the work in Kansas, ministers as well as laymen, men of nerve, of principle, "wise as serpents, and harmless as doves," is our continual hope. Most propitious, as well as most disastrous, in its influences upon this territory, will be the effect of the institutions now planted here.

30*th.* — More rain has fallen to-day, though the clouds cleared away at noon. There has been no day yet, since we came, that the sun has not shone. The Sabbath school children from three schools are to have a celebration on the morrow.

Death has again come into our little settlement, and taken one of its most loved, most useful members. Since my coming, the prattling infant, like the dying away of the summer wind, has faded and fallen. The bride of a year, with her young hopes still fresh, still gayly looking into the future — earth's future — has passed beyond the unseen veil, and the prairie grass waves over her. Ties of children, the unutterable love of a mother who would leave them orphans indeed, could not bribe the death-angel, and she too has entered the shadowy land. But now, the strong man, with the harness of duty on, has fallen at his post. Yesterday he was well as usual, and to-day he is not. It comes so suddenly upon us, we cannot realize that Dr. Clark is dead.

Hard as it ever is to realize that death is more than a brief parting, that our friends will not return, until time and their long absence force the sad truth upon us, doubly so is it in this case, where but yesterday his patients shared his care. How sadly will this intelligence fall upon the ear of his brother, now absent on a tour in the territory! With the stricken friends of his Massachusetts home we can almost feel the shrinking heart, the overpowering oppression, the utter desolation of earth, as the missive bears to them the mournful intelligence. Earth has its thorny ways, and hedged about with sorrows. Among the saddest of them is for friends we loved so well to die in a far-off home, and we be not there.

No one more than Dr. C. had the esteem, the love of the people, and their grief is heartfelt and sincere.

There has been much sickness on the Wakarusa, and for many days the doctor had taken no rest. Last evening, at tea-time, he said he felt better than usual. He was soon after taken with the disease, which, owing to the exhausted state of his system, quickly ended in death. The procession is now winding over the hill to the place of graves.

CHAPTER VI.

ILLS OF PIONEER LIFE.

June 1st.—The weather is as cold as that of an October morning in New England. The stove having been removed into the kitchen, as soon as the roof was on, we ate our breakfasts in a cold dining-room, with large shawls and cloaks drawn around us. The wind was rising, and, as we attempted to accomplish necessary work by the stove, we found it almost impossible to keep any heat in it. We attempted to nail up buffalo-robes to break the wind, but they came down as fast as we could put them up. Some gentlemen, on the hill beyond us, new comers, looking upon the beauty of the country, seeing our efforts, came to our assistance; but their labors in curbing the wind were as futile as ours, and we only had the exercise and sport of seeing our plans fail. We were kept awake a long time, last night, by the barking of the wolves. They make a shrill, quick bark, and, when a number are together, the sound is deafening. They are harmless, however, always running from man. The most trouble they give us is in eating off the ropes with which we picquet out the horses at night. They eat them so smoothly as to look like being cut with a knife, and what we have occasionally thought must be charged upon emigrants camping in the valley, in want of a rope, we find is wholly owing to the sharp teeth of the cayotes. Doctor returned yesterday from his tour west. Dr. P. heard of the death of his brother-in-law a few miles from here.

2d.—The first communion Sabbath since I have been here. As the table is spread, and the few members gather around, the promise of the Saviour, "where two or three are gathered together in my name, there will I be in the midst of them," seems peculiarly significant and impressive. He knoweth those who seek to follow him, and with his strength will aid their weakness. We hide the promise in our hearts, with new lessons of humility, and go out from the "upper chambers," striving to learn aright the meek, suffering patience of Jesus, which will fit us to be his co-workers here. The gem of patience is among the greatest of the Christian virtues, and blessed is he who wears the jewel in his heart.

3d. — Doctor has gone to a funeral some miles away. If he does not go himself, on all such occasions, his carriage does. The person now dead clung to her jewels. She wore bracelets, rings, etc., until her last breath. Life to her must have consisted in externals; and a weary home Kansas must have been, with its cotton-wood, "shake" cabins, bare floors, and general discomfort.

There has been a good deal of cholera a few miles from here, mostly among Missourians. They lived in most abject filth, and drank of the stagnant water in the bed of the Wakarusa, when the water was at the lowest, from ten months' drouth. One instance of sickness seems almost incredible among civilized people, but there is no doubt of its correctness. The father and mother were ill — very ill. The cabin was very small, untidy, and would of itself almost breed disease. Dr. C. proposed that the children, who were adults, should occupy a tent near by, for their own safety, and yet attend upon the sick. The next morning, what a sight met the kind physician's eyes, as he entered the cabin! One of the parents was lying on the bed, dead; the other was still living, though with little breath left. A little water was standing by the bed; and no one had been in but once since the time of the doctor's leaving the day before. Thus forsaken of their children, they died. Such heartlessness, such barbarity, we can scarcely believe would exist among any people.

6th. — With a friend, who has been several days with me, I visited one of the early pioneers. She lived three months in a cloth tent, and now resides in a log house, which she renders pleasant, by her tact hiding every rudeness. She talked gayly of their tent life, and we learned much of the roughness of pioneer life at the outset.

We staid so long, that E. was fearful we were lost on the prairie, and was just about setting lights in the windows for our guidance, as we reached home. Getting lost on the prairie in the darkness is an easy matter; and it has happened here, several times, that persons have wandered around nearly all night, trying to find the town, when at no time they were more than half a mile from it.

7th. — Mr. H. was very ill with an attack of pleurisy. Doctor being absent, I felt anxious, yet did the best I could. A mustard plaster and some simples removed the difficulty of breathing, and he slept quietly. He said he never was as sick before, but I was thinking he imagined himself sicker than he was. Just before night, and as I was wondering where E. could be, she came in, pale and almost breathless, with just enough left of life to say, "O, that rattlesnake!" I laughed at her at first; but being convinced that seeing a snake of some kind was a reality to her, and not quite liking the idea of their making a home in our neighborhood, we started out with shovel and hatchet for a battle. The spot where she saw him was very easily found, as the pail she had in her hand, while coming up the path from the spring, she set down when she came upon him. She had heard a buzzing noise, like that made by a large grasshopper, for some minutes; but her attention was attracted by a small bird flying backward and forward across the path, and no great height above it, and did not, therefore, perceive the snake until she was within a foot of him. Hastily setting down the pail, as he lay there coiled ready to spring, she took another path to the house. We looked along both paths, above and below, and far out on the hill-side, but found nothing. His fright was undoubtedly equal to E.'s, not being particularly partial to the cold bath she gave him in setting down her pail so hastily.

9th. — Leave home early to spend the day with a sick friend; find her quite ill, lying on a straw pallet on the floor. One small window and door, at the other end of the room, afforded all the air there was; and about everything there was a general look of discomfort. Many a person in health has bravely battled with the ills and privations of Kansas life; but when the pulse throbs with fevered heat, and disease is making a wreck of one's self and every energy, the mind turns sadly backward to the pleasant home, and yearns for the kind friends there with an irresistible longing. With baking for the family in the sun's glaring rays, and taking care of the invalid, I was weary, and thankful for our own home-roof, which has more of comfort.

10th. — Was awakened by a little tree-toad on my pillow this morning. He must have climbed up the low roof of the ell part, and in at the window. I found a mouse in the tub, and a swallow came into the kitchen flapping his wings wildly, and seeming much frightened, as we were at breakfast. I am wondering if all the "four-footed beasts and creeping things" have appointed a place of rendezvous upon our premises; and suggest, laughingly, that "the rattlesnakes will come next." Scarcely had we finished breakfast, before the cry from near the wood-pile was, "Here 's a snake!" It measured about eighteen inches in length, was ugly-looking, and had four rattles.

The people are talking much of what shall be done in view of the oppression forced upon us. Men armed with guns, revolvers, and bowie-knives, from another state, have carried the elections, driving the actual settlers from the polls with threats of certain death. A memorial, stating these facts, has been sent on to Congress; but no relief comes — no promise of any. This Legislature soon proposes to hold its session, and enact laws for the people of this territory. They, many of them residents of Missouri, and all of them elected by Missouri votes, ignorant and brutal men, having gained their election at the point of the bowie-knife, intend to enact laws to govern an enlightened and intelligent people. The question is, shall the laws, whatever they may be, be boldly repudiated as no laws for us, the makers being not of us; or shall the matter be delayed until the so-called Legislature meets? A few days will decide the course to be pursued by our people; and whatever is done will be done thoughtfully, and with a view to the greatest and most permanent good of the country.

12th. — It rained gently all the morning. In the afternoon the clouds cleared away, and we took a pleasant tramp over the hills. We met a party of Indians. Scarcely a day passes that motley groups of Delawares are not in our streets. Instead of going to Missouri for their groceries and clothing, as formerly, they come to Lawrence. They are very friendly, and look upon the rapid growth of the little town near them with as much apparent surprise as we would upon actual creations like the brain-pictures in fairy tales.

Large stone buildings, which would be an ornament to any place, are fast being erected, while buildings of humble pretensions, of wood and stone, are springing up with a rapidity almost equalling the wonderful genius of Aladdin. We can count already fifty dwellings erected since we came; and the little city of less than a year's existence will, in intelligence, refinement, and moral worth, compare most favorably with many New England towns of six times its number of inhabitants.

Many people were in, in the evening. The wind was blowing, and I heard a rustling near me. I looked, but saw nothing. An hour later, as I relinquished my seat, and went to make arrangements for extra beds, a gentleman very positively said, "I hear a rattlesnake." Near where I had been sitting, the yellow-spotted reptile had crawled in between the last floor-board and the siding, and already his head had reached the window-casing. We had serious objections to his further progress towards the chambers, or to his greater length of days. After a moment's more envenomed rattling, all was still. Like the other, he had four rattles, and was undoubtedly looking for his lost mate. One of the gentlemen, Judge Conway, to whom the front room had been appropriated as a sleeping apartment, the mattresses being removed each morning, felt nervous about such companions for bed-fellows, and, to be prepared against the possible contingency of another similar visit, turned his boot-tops into one another upon retiring.

15*th.* — We heard at midnight the rapid approach of a horseman, and soon the loud halloa, with a western brogue, sounded at the door. A friend was very ill with cholera, and "the doctor must go immediately over." He hunted up his horse on the hill-side, and went, first sending to another physician down street to be there as quickly as possible, as he had no medicine. Friends in the East knew nothing of the evils which lie around the path of the new settler when sickness comes. Surrounded by the aids which science has brought to bear against disease, and by all the blessings of a thickly settled community, they cannot realize how death stares one in the face often in these isolated spots, when the case is urgent, and help far away.

In this instance the husband had left home, early in the evening, to attend a meeting in Lawrence, some two miles distant, leaving with his wife, who was but just recovering from illness, a young friend. Over-exertion during the day had somewhat prostrated her, and now cramps and the most urgent symptoms of cholera came upon her with fearful severity. What could be done? They were a full half-mile from any neighbor. It was night, and there was no one to send for help. Every remedy which the house afforded was tried, with poor success, the patient losing courage with her loss of strength. At ten o'clock her husband returned, and, seeing at a glance the need of instant relief, started for a neighbor, who went for a physician.

17*th*. — The doctor brought up a nice side-saddle from town, and, upon my asking whose it was, he replied, "It is a present for Mrs. R." To my question, "From whom?" he said, "From him who gets her the most of her things."

"Old Gray" was soon saddled, and I was on his back to find my way over the prairies to spend another day with sickness. Towards evening, as the horse was saddled, and I was ready to return home, we noticed some threatening clouds, and a shower just upon us. As it promised to be but slight, and of short duration, I concluded to remain until it had passed, in preference to a drenching, and two miles' ride in it. The shower once commenced, there seemed no end to it; and, when an hour had passed away, the wind was still blowing in unabated fury, the rain falling in "rivers of waters," while there was one incessant peal and crash of thunders, and the whole heavens a perfect blaze of dazzling light. I abandoned all hope of seeing home that night; and the question now was, how could we avoid being wet by the rain, which came boisterously in from the north? For a while I sat and read, in the corner most removed from the exposed side; but the wind suddenly shifted, and by agility alone I escaped the deluge pouring in from the east. No place was now secure but the little corner where the straw pallet lay, with the sick lady, weak and nervous, tossing restlessly, and wishing the heavy shower would cease. To avoid cold and sickness, wrapping myself in blankets, I lay down upon the bed, which we supposed the rain would not reach. In all previous showers this had been the dry corner; but the rains were searching. Soon, buffalo robe upon the bed, and umbrella spread over our heads, so arranged that the water should run off on to the floor, was our only protection. Yet we slept at last, wearied out by the furious raging of the elements, and hearing, as the last thing, the pattering rain-drops upon the umbrella.

18*th.* — The morning sun never shone more brightly than now. We found everything in the house damp, but had taken no cold. The cholera patient was doing well. The gentleman of the house assured me he slept well, but it was a mystery to me where he found a dry nook. Had a fine ride home in the early morning light, which gives to every object a double value. "Old Gray" nibbled at the "compass plant," which always points northward in these prairies, occasionally cropping its bright yellow flowers with a satisfied air as he trotted along. The rattlesnake weed was also blooming in profusion. Nature is ever mindful of the needs of her children, and provides an antidote against the bane of rattlesnakes, and a sure guide over the wide prairie in the compass plant. When I reached home, found the doctor gone to attend upon a broken limb. A man, in rafting logs down the river, had met with this misfortune. The doctor has many calls professionally, and, though he assures them all that he is not now a practising physician, he looks in upon many to advise them.

19*th.* — It was just eleven and a half by the clock when a carriage-load drove up from Kansas city. We completed our work at four, P. M. We had more company over night. We had arranged a cot bed to sleep on for the night in the dining-room, and I was just planning my morrow's work before I slept, when the window came in with a frightful crash. With a quick spring, we avoided the effects of broken glass, which fell on the bed and all over the floor. The window was not permanently cased, and the heavy wind of the Monday night previous had loosened the nails.

21st. — A gentleman, just up from Kansas city, brought me some letters which I had long expected, and which have been lying there for weeks. He brought intelligence also of Stringfellow's attack upon Gov. Reeder for the maintenance of an honest opinion. Preparations are being made by our people to celebrate the coming Fourth of July. At this time, when Freedom is but a name; when three millions of human beings, created in the divine image, are sold as chattels in a country boasting of liberty; when the two hundred thousand slaveholders are using every endeavor to enslave the twenty-five millions of our countrymen, and we in Kansas already feel the iron heel of the oppressor, making us truly white slaves, — we will celebrate it by a new Declaration of our Independence, and in the God of our fathers trust that he will lead us safely through this Red Sea of evil, until we plant our feet securely on freedom's bulwarks, having passed from this worse than Egyptian bondage.

July 4th. — The morning of the Fourth came in cloudy, yet pleasant. Word had been sent to the people on the Wakarusa, and many were expected. Invitations also were sent to the Delaware and Shawnee Indians to mingle in our festivities. From the elevated position of our house we saw the people gathering from all quarters. Several teams, of oxen as well as horses, the roughness of the vehicles being hidden under garlands of green leaves and flowers, came in from the Wakarusa. A beautiful flag was presented by a Massachusetts lady to the military companies of Lawrence, in an appropriate speech, in behalf of the ladies of Lawrence. After its acceptance, the procession formed upon Massachusetts-street, and was escorted by the military to a fine grove about a mile from town. Here, in one of Nature's grand old forests, seats had been provided, and a platform raised for the orators and other speakers, for the singers and musical instruments. The number present was variously estimated from fifteen hundred to two thousand. It was a motley gathering. There were many people with eastern dress and manner, and settlers from Missouri, and other far western states, no less distinctly marked by theirs. The Delawares and Shawnees added no little to the interest of the occasion. After the reading of the Declaration of Independence, whose embodied truths seemed to have gained new vitality, new force, since we last listened to it, came the oration. It was, for the most part, a gathering together of the opinions of southern men upon the vexed question of slavery. There were confessions as to the relative value of free and slave labor by some of their best educated men. There was a most perfect condemnation of the whole system from their own mouths. Then the question of our own position, in regard to the encroachments of a neighboring state, was touched upon, with the firm determination to assert our rights, and maintain them.* There were speeches, songs, and sentiments. We received friendly words of welcome from the chiefs of the Delawares and Shawnees.

* The following is the conclusion of Dr. R.'s oration:

"Fellow-citizens, in conclusion, it is for us to choose for ourselves, and for those who shall come after us, what institutions shall bless or curse our beautiful Kansas. Shall we have freedom for all the people, and consequent prosperity, or slavery for a part, with the blight and mildew inseparable from it? Choose ye this day which you will serve, — Slavery or Freedom, — and then be true to your choice. If slavery is best for Kansas, then choose it; but, if liberty, then choose that.

"Let every man stand in his place, and acquit himself like a man who knows his rights, and, knowing, dares maintain them. Let us repudiate all laws enacted by foreign legislative bodies, or dictated by Judge Lynch, over the way. Tyrants are tyrants, and tyranny is tyranny, whether under the garb of law, or in opposition to it. So thought, and so acted, our ancestors; and so let us think and act. We are not alone in this contest. The entire nation is agitated upon the question of our rights; the spirit of '76 is breathing upon some; the hand-writing upon the wall is being discerned by others; while the remainder the gods are evidently preparing for destruction. Every pulsation in Kansas vibrates to the remotest artery of the body politic; and I seem to hear the millions of freemen, and the millions of bondmen, in our own land, the millions of the oppressed in other lands, the patriots and philanthropists of all countries, the spirits of the revolutionary heroes, and the voice of God, all saying to the people of Kansas, 'Do your duty!'"

They were glad to see us coming, not with the hatchet and sounds of war, but bringing with us the sweet fruits of peace and civilization. A long day was quickly passed — the first Fourth of July in Kansas celebrated by its white settlers. In the evening a party of about one hundred was gathered, to strengthen yet more the bonds of social feeling, in our largest hall, which serves the purpose of church, school-room, and hall for all political and social meetings. We had refreshments of cakes and ice-creams, and our house *full*, as usual, at night.

5th. — A little child is dead. The family took the small-pox while on the Missouri river, some two months since, and this child has never recovered from the effects of the disease. We carried a friend to her home on the prairie, and called for the minister to attend the funeral, leaving doctor asleep and alone. We heard at evening that Dr. Wood (who had previously attempted to cut down our house, and was afterwards appointed Probate Judge by the Shawnee Legislature — who was continually with the enemy at the time of the fall invasion, and in the crowd which attacked and killed Barber, and, since removing to Lecompton, procured the indictments for treason) was very angry about the oration on the fourth; also young Andrews, a South Carolinian, and liquor-seller. They both threatened that they would take the doctor's life; but a person in this country soon gets accustomed to such assertions. They mean nothing when uttered by these men, and only prove their utter cowardice. They reported that the doctor was afraid to go down town, while in the simplicity of his heart he had been taking a most quiet nap upon the lounge, with windows and doors open, and alone in the house, not awaking, from the time I left for a two miles' drive, until my return.

7th. — With a carriage-load of ladies I drove on to Dr. B.'s, four miles away. The last part of the way was rough and hilly, reminding one more of Massachusetts hills than anything I had seen since coming to Kansas. For a mile we made a gradual ascent up hills, which look so wondrously New England like, that we forgot we were strangers there. From the house we took a tramp of half a mile down to the lake, and were well repaid for all our labor and fatigue of descending and climbing hills by the beautiful views continually meeting our eyes at every turn in the winding path. There were high, conical-shaped hills, bearing on their tops forest trees, with dense, thick foliage; at the next moment a little shady nook, with silvery rivulet murmuring over its pebbly bed, would peep upon one's sight. A high ledge, with a cool spring gushing from its side, and flowers overhanging it, came next.

Our guide took longer steps than we, and seemed more used to travelling in the woods, for I had scarcely time to see all I wanted to, get over places dry-shod, and climb up the steep hills, before he would be far out of sight. However, if I kept the last straggling one of our party in view, I felt safe. When we all finally came together again, as they at last waited for me, our guide was coming from the lake with his hands full of most beautiful flowers. They were larger than a white pond-lily, and much more beautiful, with the same sweetness. The Indians call the flora "Yonkopen," and they live, at some seasons, upon the seeds of the plant, of which there some eight or ten, of a nut-like appearance, in each seed-vessel. The Kaw Indian women often wade into the water for them as food. Dr. B. informed us there were enough in this little lake for the subsistence of six or seven families for weeks.

Last night some of the gentlemen whose love for slavery was outraged by the out-spoken words for freedom, uttered on the fourth, with guns and pistols, and many muttered threats of revenge, started from town to give us a call. Their discretion was probably greater than their valor, and it might be that the effort of climbing this hill would at least give time for the cooling of their rage.

8th. — Sunday we had company, but they all attended church. How I wish we could have one old-fashioned, New England Sunday, with the ringing of church bells to call us to service, and quiet at home! We are full of company at all times, not excepting even Sabbath day. We now have meetings every Sabbath at five o'clock, at the house, or, as the notice was given, "under the shadow of Dr. R.'s house." The ladies sit in the front room, the gentlemen outside on benches and in carriages, while the preacher stands in the doorway.

"Old Gray" was an attentive listener to-night. Just after the beginning of the service he came around the north side of the house, and took his station close by the speakers, where he remained until the last prayer was said, when he as quietly walked away.

10th. — Yesterday the doctor, Mr. L., and G., went down to Kansas, stopping at Shawnee Mission and Westport. A gentleman at the former place, a pro-slavery resident of Lawrence, said to G., "Is the doctor going to Westport?"

Upon his replying in the affirmative, the gentleman said, "They are going to hang him there."

With characteristic *naïveté* G. replied, "Is that all?" and his informant, turning on his heel, walked away.

The doctor, after looking in upon the grave legislators who hold their sessions at the Shawnee Mission School, but who ride over and back in omnibuses from their homes in Westport, to his satisfaction, pursued his way to Kansas city. There, friends informed him that Dr. Wood had been there attempting to arouse the bitterness of the pro-slavery men against him; that they might offer him some violence. Having completed his business at that place, he came again by Westport on the following day, stopping, as before, at the mission. He saw Dr. Wood there, who was complaining that the stage for Lawrence had gone, and he had no mode of conveyance home. The doctor said to him, "Here is a seat in my carriage, if you like;" at the same time jocosely adding, "but we may get to fighting."

To which the dignified Dr. Wood offered no reply, though his hand seemed to have a strange affinity to something in his coat pocket. The docter came on to Lawrence without fear or molestation, and wholly alone.

19th. — We rode into the country some miles, to dine. We had vegetables, peas, etc., with pumpkin pies for the second course. They were veritable pumpkins,—such as make a New Englander think of home and Thanksgiving holidays,—ripened this year. On our way home we called at another friend's, and, to shorten distances, went across the prairie where there was no road. We found several deep ravines, difficult to cross, but with no actual danger save at one point. There was a deep ravine, with a natural path, or bridge, over it, which was exceedingly narrow, while the chasm below looked frightful, and the bank before us very steep. The doctor thought he could drive safely over. I calculated the chances of broken limbs, should we go off the ledge, and the frightened horse, with an extra pull and a creaking of the carriage, took us again on to safer ground. A short time after, as we were passing along quite gayly upon a side hill, thinking the perils of the way were over, the carriage suddenly slipped down against the lower wheels; but we arrived home safely and in good time.

20th. — We heard of the illness of some acquaintances over at Wakarusa, and I accompanied the doctor to see them. We had a pleasant drive over, though the crossing at the Wakarusa is steep. The little dry ravines beyond are more trying to springs. Our friends live upon the top of "Lone Tree Mound," a high elevation, the "lone tree" and house for many miles being distinctly visible. It is a difficult matter to reach the summit of the hill, and was accomplished by winding around a circuitous way upon the side hill, with the carriage, while the doctor climbed up upon foot. We at length reached the house, and found our friends glad to see us. So far as they are from neighbors, and so difficult of access when sickness has been upon them, one or both, the times have indeed looked dark, and life's road dreary. They sent for the doctor several days since, but the word had but just reached him.

Hoping to find a better road home, we turned into another, but found it infinitely worse. In the bottom of one ravine "Old Gray" made a false step, and fell, breaking both shafts. Yankee ingenuity was brought into requisition, and after tying on poles with anything in the shape of strings which could be produced for the emergency of the hour, and a good deal of merriment, we were en route again. Before the cutting of the poles, there was a most amusing silence. The horse, having been led up to the top of the hill, was looking meekly for further orders. The doctor was standing near by, with his hands upon his sides, and looking the very image of patience, and poor little me, feeling like laughing, and yet feeling sober in view of remaining all night with the prairie wolves, in such a place as this, sat demurely in the carriage. Finally I said, "Shall I get out of the carriage?" And the image of patience came forward, saying "Yes," and assisted me out. I knew then that in some corner of his brain there was a plan for new shafts, and a sure prospect for our return to Lawrence. Within two miles of Lawrence we called at the place where we got our weekly supply of butter, which is of the best quality. While the lady of the little log cabin was weighing it out, her husband came to the carriage, and, after talking a moment, went in again to play us some tunes. His fondness for music amounts to a passion, and while living in Ohio he often taught music. He has a large dairy here.

About a mile further on our way home, two gentlemen on horseback, coming from the direction of Lawrence, rode hastily up, and, with a good deal of excitement in their manner, informed us that a large body of Missourians were encamped near Hickory Point; that they threatened to drive off the free-state settlers; and, lastly, that a fight was expected. They desired the doctor to use his influence with the people of Lawrence, to have a force sent out immediately to aid their neighbors at Hickory Point. He said to them he "thought it was a ruse," and promised to do nothing until more reliable information should come. One of the gentlemen, who has always been famous here for his words of bravado, and want of bravery in action, said, on parting, "I will send an express every hour."

22*d.* — The military companies are on drill to-day. A friend sent us a basket of mandrakes. They have a pleasant flavor, but are quite medicinal. The gentleman's "express" is not yet heard from.

A gentleman, living nine miles distant, sent to the doctor this morning to come and see him. He found him quite il with fever, in a little cabin, alone, with no one to take care of him. So, placing the bed in the carriage, he brought him home with him.

23*d.* — The patient was not injured by his ride, but his nervousness exceeded all bounds. We had a quantity of delicious apples. Apples were first brought into market here on the fourth of this month. A large pailful of grapes was also sent in. These are smaller, and not as sweet as those which ripen in October. We had rain with furious wind beforehand. Such clouds of dust arose as to hide the town from our sight. Several panes of glass blew out, and, in attempting to put boards at the window, to keep out the pouring rain, we were thoroughly drenched. The little calf in the pen seems frightened too, breaks his rope, leaps the fence, and scuds before the wind like a frightened hare. We have a general hubbub. Mr. C., a lawyer here, was assaulted by Dr. Wood, this afternoon. Dr. Wood invited Mr. C. to his house, saying he wanted to talk with him. On reaching the house, however, he declined to go into it, and took Mr. C. around on the east side of it, and there they sat down. Dr. Wood then asked him if he thought so and so in regard to the settlement of the city property, making his own action in the affair fair and honorable. Mr. C. said he thought not; whereupon Dr. Wood struck Mr. C., with a piece of iron, or a slung shot, upon his head, cutting a deep gash in it. He then ran. Mr. C. soon came into the street, and, as the brave doctor was picking up a stone to throw at the wounded man, several of the citizens gathered around and put an end to it.

24th. — We were scarcely up this morning before word came that Mrs. L. was dead or dying. She was taken ill last evening. Two of the children are also dead. It is thought their deaths were occasioned by eating very freely of mandrakes yesterday — a disease like cholera being the result. Remembering her as I saw her in the little, pent-up cabin, I can but think the change a glorious one, for now there must be room, room for the freed spirit, earth's fetters broken. There are now two motherless little girls. The mother and youngest two are buried in one grave.

"Thou hast all seasons for thine own, O Death!"

28th. — As a relaxation, being wearied with constant company and continued care of so large a family, with want of quiet, the doctor proposed a ride to Fish's. With a full carriage load, we made the proposed visit. Fish's is a sort of stopping-place by the way, nine miles from Lawrence, and between thirty and forty miles from Kansas city. Entertainment for man and beast is found there. The building is of wood, two stories in height. Upon the lower floor are a dining-room, which is also used for general reception-room, and a store of groceries, dry goods, and the et cetera, needful to supply the Indians in this region, while the upper rooms serve for sleeping apartments. The worn traveller, after a ride of thirty-five miles, in the broiling sun, or in the piercing winds, is glad of a rest, even in a building so unhomelike as this.

Mr. Fish, who owns the establishment, is a Shawnee Indian, of education and principle. He is a firm believer in the assertion of the Declaration of Independence, that "all men are born free and equal," and gladly extends the right hand of fellowship to those who come desiring to plant the seeds of truth and freedom in this new country. He would, with us, joyfully welcome the hour, when, grown into a mighty tree, its spreading branches should cover the whole land. Two gentlemen connected with Fish are from Boston. Mr. F., who superintends the culinary department, is from Massachusetts, and our appetites attest to his skill in that line. Some Indian women, who came to the store to trade, sit at the table with us. We talk of their dress and ornaments, not supposing they can understand us, while they gravely listen. When we have ceased commenting, they repeat to Mr. Fish, in Shawnee, what we have said, as he tells us; they seem much amused and laugh heartily. They have the advantage of us, being able to speak English as well as Delaware and Shawnee.

July 31*st.* — We have had rain as often as every alternate day, for the last week, in gentle showers mostly, and often at night, the days being clear and pleasant. A part of our guests left a few days since, and on the next day, on a short half hour's notice, we had six gentlemen and a lady to dine. We have now very nice melons. The melons, cantelopes, tomatoes, etc., are finer than any I have ever seen elsewhere. Four more strangers were in, in the afternoon, and we were not able to finish our day's work until sundown. To-day the doctor and I took a short ride on horseback, to get away from care. We found other company, on our return, just returned from the regions of Fort Riley. The cholera is making terrible havoc there, among the men principally engaged on the government works. They are said to have exposed themselves most wilfully, by drinking of poor water, when at a little distance the best was to be had. Major Ogden, a most estimable man, has fallen a victin to the dread disease, also some families of the officers. This afternoon I have been off upon the prairie alone. Was two miles from home at sun-down, and, before I reached it, could not see the path for the darkness, but trusted to "Old Gray." The sick man is so far recovered as to leave.

CHAPTER VII.

KANSAS LAWS — GOVERNOR SHANNON.

Aug. 10. — "All day the low hung clouds have dropped their garnered fulness down."

People begin to come in from the country, miles distant, to the Convention, which is to be held on the 14th and 15th.

On the 2d of July, the Legislature, elected by Missourians, assembled, as ordered by Gov. Reeder, at Pawnee, more than one hundred miles from the border. Mr. Conway, of the sixth district, resigned his seat in the council, on the ground that, having been elected by illegal votes, this pretended Legislature had no claim to that character. The members of the House chosen at the new election, ordered by Gov. Reeder, were deprived of their seats.

On the 4th, the Legislature passed an act, removing the seat of government to the Shawnee Mission, two or three miles from Westport. Gov. Reeder vetoed it, as inconsistent with the organic act.

On the 16th, the Legislature reässembled at that place, and on the 22d, D. Houston, the only free-state member of the Assembly, resigned his seat, not only on the ground that the Legislature was an illegal body, but that, by its removal from Pawnee, it had nullified itself.

The laws passed by the Shawnee Legislature are of an intolerant, Draconian character, allowing to the people of this territory no rights. They are copied from the Missouri statute book, with the exception of those relating to the qualifications of voters of the Legislative Assembly, and the slave code, which are made especially to crush the people of this territory. They allow them no voice in those matters of government which most concern them.

The following is taken verbatim from the "Laws of the Territory of Kansas," furnished to Congress, on its requisition, by President Pierce, and printed as "Exec. Doc. 234."

"CHAPTER CLI. — SLAVES.

"AN ACT TO PUNISH OFFENCES AGAINST SLAVE-PROPERTY.

§ 1. Persons raising insurrection punishable with death.
2. Aider punishable with death.
3. What constitutes felony.
4. Punishment for decoying away slaves.
5. Punishment for assisting slaves.
6. What deemed grand larceny.
7. What deemed felony.
8. Punishment for concealing slaves.
9. Punishment for rescuing slaves from officer.
10. Penalty on officer who refuses to assist in capturing slaves.
11. Printing of incendiary documents.
12. What deemed a felony.
13. Who are qualified as jurors.

"*Be it enacted by the Governor and Legislative Assembly of the Territory of Kansas, as follows:*

"SECTION 1. That every person, bond or free, who shall be convicted of actually raising a rebellion or insurrection of slaves, free negroes or mulattoes, in this territory, shall suffer death.

"SEC. 2. Every free person who shall aid or assist in any rebellion or insurrection of slaves, free negroes or mulattoes, or shall furnish arms, or do any overt act in furtherance of such rebellion or insurrection, shall suffer death.

"SEC. 3. If any free person shall, by speaking, writing or printing, advise, persuade or induce, any slaves to rebel, conspire against or murder any citizen of this territory, or shall bring into, print, write, publish, or circulate, or cause to be brought into, printed, written, published or circulated, or shall knowingly aid or assist in the bringing into, printing, writing, publishing or circulating, in this territory, any book, paper, magazine, pamphlet or circular, for the purpose of exciting insurrection, rebellion, revolt or conspiracy on the part of the slaves, free negroes or mulattoes, against the citizens of the territory or any part of them, such person shall be guilty of felony, and suffer death.

"SEC. 4. If any person shall entice, decoy or carry away out of this territory any slave belonging to another, with intent to deprive the owner thereof of the services of such slave, or with intent to effect or procure the freedom of such slave, he shall be adjudged guilty of grand larceny, and, on conviction thereof, shall suffer death, or be imprisoned at hard labor for not less than ten years.

"SEC. 5. If any person shall aid or assist in enticing, decoying, or persuading, or carrying away, or sending out of this territory, any slave belonging to another, with intent to procure or effect the freedom of such slave, or with intent to deprive the owner thereof of the services of such slave, he shall be adjudged guilty of grand larceny, and, on conviction thereof, shall suffer death, or be imprisoned at hard labor for not less than ten years.

"SEC. 6. If any person shall entice, decoy or carry away out of any state or other territory of the United States, any slave belonging to another, with intent to procure or effect the freedom of such slave, or to deprive the owner thereof of the services of such slave, and shall bring such slave into this territory, he shall be adjudged guilty of grand larceny, in the same manner as if such slave had been enticed, decoyed or carried away out of this territory, and in such case the larceny may be charged to have been committed in any county of this territory, into or through which such slave shall have been brought by such person, and, on conviction thereof, the person offending shall suffer death, or be imprisoned at hard labor for not less than ten years.

"SEC. 7. If any person shall entice, persuade or induce any slave to escape from the service of his master or owner in this territory, or shall aid or assist any slave in escaping from the service of his master or owner, or shall aid, assist, harbor or conceal, any slave who may have escaped from the service of his master or owner, he shall be deemed guilty of felony, and punished by imprisonment at hard labor for a term of not less than five years.

"SEC. 8. If any person in this territory shall aid or assist, harbor or conceal, any slave who has escaped from the service of his master or owner, in another state or territory, such person shall be punished in like manner as if such slave had escaped from the service of his master or owner in this territory.

"SEC. 9. If any person shall resist any officer while attempting to arrest any slave that may have escaped from the service of his master or owner, or shall rescue such slave when in custody of any officer or other person, or shall entice, persuade, aid or assist, such slave to escape from the custody of any officer or other person who may have such slave in custody, whether such slave have escaped from the service of his master or owner in this territory, or in any other state or territory, the person so offending shall be guilty of felony, and punished by imprisonment at hard labor for a term of not less than two years.

"SEC. 10. If any marshal, sheriff or constable, or the deputy of any such officer, shall, when required by any person, refuse to aid or assist in the capture of any slave that may have escaped from the service of his master or owner, whether such slave shall have escaped from his master or owner in this territory, or any state or other territory, such officer shall be fined in a sum of not less than one hundred nor more than five hundred dollars.

"SEC. 11. If any person print, write, introduce into, publish or circulate, or cause to be brought into, printed, written, published or circulated, or shall knowingly aid or assist in bringing into, printing, publishing or circulating within this territory, any book, paper, pamphlet, magazine, handbill or circular, containing any statements, arguments, opinions, sentiment, doctrine, advice or innuendo, calculated to produce a disorderly, dangerous or rebellious disaffection among the slaves in this territory, or to induce such slaves to escape from the service of their masters, or to resist their authority, he shall be guilty of felony, and be punished by imprisonment and hard labor for a term not less than five years.

"SEC. 12. If any free person, by speaking or by writing, assert or maintain that persons have not the right to hold slaves in this territory, or shall introduce into this territory, print, publish, write, circulate, or cause to be introduced into this territory, written, printed, published or circulated in this territory, any book, paper, magazine, pamphlet or circular, containing any denial of the right of persons to hold slaves in this territory, such person shall be deemed guilty of felony, and punished by imprisonment at hard labor for a term of not less than two years.

"SEC. 13. No person who is conscientiously opposed to holding slaves, or who does not admit the right to hold slaves in this territory, shall sit as a juror on the trial of any prosecution for any violation of any of the sections of this act.

"This act to take effect and be in force from and after the fifteenth day of September, A. D. 1855."

Several meetings have been held, taking this matter into consideration, and much talk had in reference to holding a general convention, with the view of forming a state government, and asking for admission as a state at the next Congress.

12th. — It rained pouringly all last night, and without ceasing to-day. Mr. D.'s house, down on the street, was struck by the lightning last night, and one corner of the roof torn off by the fluid. Mrs. D. was alone, save two little children. These were stunned by the shock so that they returned no answer to the mother's repeated call upon them to speak. The wind came in so furiously through the open dwelling, that she was not able to keep a light long enough to assure herself whether they still lived. Thus the weary night passed away; the storm raged without, and many conflicting fears and anxieties within.

The officials at Washington, with President Pierce as their nominal head, have seen that in Gov. Reeder the whole people of the territory have an impartial friend — have seen, too, that he follows to the letter the law under which he acts as governor. They are no less determined now, than at the time of the repeal of the Missouri compromise, to force slavery upon this fair land, and have, therefore, resolved to remove him upon a false charge of speculating in Kaw lands. He has repudiated the acts of the Legislature because of their holding their session in violation of the organic act. Now a creature will be sent here in the form of a man, but ignoring all manliness, and selling body and soul to do the infamous work of the slave power. No man of integrity and sterling honesty can long hold this office, as he will displease both the people of Missouri and the federal head.

13th. — It was beautifully clear this morning, but rain was soon falling. Friends from Boston arrived in the evening, after a long ride from Kansas city, through the treacherous mud and drenching rain. People for the convention are still gathering from all parts of the territory. They feel themselves a wronged and oppressed people. Thousands of men, from another state, armed with instruments of death, and maltreating our citizens, have thus elected men to make our laws. They are men, for the most part, so ignorant, that in any other country they would not be considered eligible to the most unimportant office. It is stated, upon good authority, that some of them can neither read nor write. Such ignorance is not strange when we consider the fact of the scarcity of schools through the border counties of Missouri — one of the most populous boasting only one within its entire limits. Such destitution is one of slavery's trophies. While the *Richmond Enquirer* comes out in wordy tirades upon common schools, why should Western Missouri do more than feed the brutal passions, leaving the mind uncultivated and rough as the shores of her great river?

These men have enacted laws worthy alone of the dark ages. Those of Draco were humane in the comparison, and Nero's blood-thirstiness is transformed into the milk of human kindness before this new light of the nineteenth century. We have looked to him who has sworn to protect the whole people, the executive of the nation. We might sooner look to the granite hills of his own state with hope of sympathy; for, given over to the minions of slavery, to do their bidding, no thunders save those of a long outraged, indignant people will ever awaken him.

14*th.* — Twelve strangers dined with us to-day. They came from one hundred miles back in the territory, and there, as here, they represent the feeling of the people strong against these unheard-of outrages and frauds. We are struggling for our own freedom against a tyranny more unjust than that which King George exercised over the colonies. Though a war, a conflict like that even of seven years' duration, be the result of it, the end, bringing in the glorious reign of freedom, will be a final triumph.

These gentlemen speak of the good appearance of the crops. Corn near the river called the Big Blue is very high. Some of the stalks measure eighteen feet and some inches.

15th — The "windows of heaven" seem literally to be opened, for the rain still pours down in torrents; but it does not in the least dampen the ardor of our people; and they, considering the facts of their want of protection from the government, and being without any law-making power, resolve to act in view of such a state of things. A large and enthusiastic meeting was held in the evening to take the matter into consideration of forming a government of their own.

18th. — The quiet citizens of Lawrence are continually annoyed by the street broils in our midst. Four brothers, by the name of Hopper, living a few miles out, by insult and indignity have endeavored to get our people to that spot where forbearance would cease to be a virtue; where, acting upon the first law of nature, they would give blow for blow. A man, ignorant to the last degree, whose identity is recognized by all our people under the cognomen of "Sam Salters," and who holds an office of deputy-sheriff under the Shawnee Legislature, has also acted with them. Scarcely a day has passed for weeks that the long-sufferance of the people of Lawrence has not been wantonly trifled with. The apparent object has been to get some one to retaliate, and then word would be given to the border counties of Missouri. On the wings of the wind expresses would be sent. By falsehoods and inflammatory rumors, they would so inflame the passions of the people, until, like an avalanche, they would pour in upon us, and a plea be given for the war of extermination they are continually threatening. The border papers are full of threats against the Yankees. An extract from the *Leavenworth Herald* is a sample of all: "Dr. Robinson is sole agent for the underground railroad leading out of Western Missouri, and for the transportation of fugitive 'niggers.' His office is in Lawrence, K. T. Give him a call."

19th. — Two large carriage loads went from our house to attend a camp-meeting on the Wakarusa. It was holden in the woods on the bank of the river, and while seats were provided for the audience in front of the high broad platform used by the speakers, the tents for the night were at a little distance in the back-ground. The carriages, of every possible description, and of every grade of beauty, from a rockaway to a rough, springless cart with board seats, were fastened around the entrance to the grove, and gave to the whole a most novel appearance. There was a large gathering of people, and the services would be impressive were it not for the continued "Amens," in shrill as well as deep guttural tones, which the zealous worshippers are sounding in one's ears from all quarters.

A large proportion of the western emigrants to Kansas are Methodists, and many of them are very fine people. The presiding elder here is a mild, benevolent-looking man, to whom a stranger would at once feel attracted. He came from Georgia, formerly, and for years has been a resident of Missouri. No one more than he can have seen the evils of slavery, and, by his firm adherence to the principles of liberty, he attests his abhorrence of it. There are several clergymen in the territory, who have been residents of Missouri over twenty years, whose souls are strong in their love of freedom.

21*st.* — The little steam ferry-boat, Lizzie, was here to-day. How we wish some enterprising capitalist would build some boats with a draft of only ten or twelve inches without load, such as are used upon the California waters! Every day we might hear the shrill steam-whistle, telling of active business life, and a means of communication between us and the rest of the world. Then the freights which have to be brought forty-five miles by land, on wagons, could more easily be transported into the territory, and passengers would find the journey much less tedious. Now, if a mill gives way, any part of the machinery breaking, nothing in all Missouri, this side of St. Louis, can be found for repairs; and all these heavy freights have to be brought by land from Kansas city. A boat briskly plying on the river would add much to the growth and prosperity of the territory.

22*d.* — I have little leisure for reading and writing. This afternoon I took Mrs. W. to ride, and she acknowledges she never saw so lovely a country, — thinks it would be pleasant to have a summer home here, with a winter home in Boston. Before we took our drive into the country, she received her first lesson in horseback riding, and caused us many a hearty laugh by her fearfulness, calling "Whoa!" "Whoa!" to the horse, when he was standing as still as anything could, and after at last going a little distance, asking, in most plaintive tones, for some one to come and turn the horse around.

24th. — The report of Mr. Dawson's declining the appointment of governor of Kansas is confirmed; also that Wilson Shannon, of Ohio, has been appointed in his place, and will accept the appointment. Coming, as Mr. Shannon does, from the free state of Ohio, where the principles of truth and freedom are engraven on the hearts of her people, deeply and indelibly, we ought to expect a man in whose heart are large sympathies, whose mind is enlightened. But from all the antecedents of his life, his course in Mexico, his daily life of dissoluteness and debauchery in California, which was a shame and burning disgrace upon his countrymen, we have nothing good to expect. Such a man will naturally be the tool of Missouri and the administration. No other could accept the appointment as the second choice of the President since Governor Reeder's removal. We have only to endure with patience the administration of government under such men, still looking forward to the "good time coming."

30th. — There is a Hungarian doctor here, who pretends he has in open field fought for Hungary by the side of Louis Kossuth. Yet, strange as the fact seems to us, he has openly espoused the side of the oppressor here, and for the Hoppers and Sam Salters become a champion. He rolls up his sleeves and daily walks the streets threatening peaceable citizens with annihilation. At the slightest disturbance or refusal of our people to be overawed by him, he runs for bowie-knife and revolver. Threats of "I'll cut your heart out!" "I'll shoot you!" or "Drive the d—d Yankees from the territory!" are of every-day occurrence.

Sept. 1st. — The new governor arrived at Westport, Missouri, and was received into full fellowship, and with demonstrations of joy. Before setting foot in the territory, or looking upon his real constituents, the *bona fide* settlers of Kansas, full of whiskey and elation of office, he made to them a speech. He told them in it repeatedly of *their* Legislature, the laws *they had enacted*, and assured them, with great fervor of manner, that he should call upon them to aid him in their enforcement. All this the people of Westport, Missouri, received with cheers and hurrahs; and, in loud bursts of enthusiasm, they expressed their joy that the *tool* was sure. Governor Shannon's son quietly asked of a bystander "if board could not be obtained in Lawrence, and hinted, in pretty plain terms, that he should prefer to live where there was less whiskey, and men of less ruffianly look. When the boat reached the landing, at Kansas city, a large number of the Missourians went on to meet the governor, and introduced themselves to him as "Border Ruffians." A carriage was soon sent over from Westport, to convey him thither. So, in the course of his rule in Kansas, we shall see what we shall see.

4th.—Emigration again begins to pour into the territory. During the last two months there has been little in this part of the country. Cholera has raged on the river, and summer heats have been too great for any comfort in travelling; but now the prairies are again dotted with white-covered wagons of the western emigrant. They come bringing everything with them in their wagons, their furniture, provisions, and their families. Their stock, also, is driven with the teams. Their wagons to them are a travelling home; many of them having a stove set, with pipe running through the top. They often travel far into the territory; it matters to them little how far, so that they get a location which pleases them. Then they build a cabin, and, with a fixed habitation, they will become the strength and sinew of the country. Being used to the emergencies and the hardships of pioneer life, Kansas will depend upon them mostly, in this early settlement, for the ground work, the substratum, upon which to build up a glorious new state. While they, for the most part, settle in the country, and will gather into their garners of the golden treasures of the rich and fertile soil, eastern capital will form a nucleus, around which the young, the adventurous, the enterprising, will gather, and new cities, new towns, will spring up with rapid growth, emulating in thrift and intelligence those of the old states.

Another street broil occurred to-day. The Blue Lodge has decided to make an attack upon Lawrence before two months are past some of its members informs a gentleman of our acquaintance. Whiskey-drinkers in this country are quite apt to divulge secrets.

6th. — Some gentlemen from Wisconsin have just arrived with their families, and two men, whom they hired in Missouri; one of them is a Missourian, the other a free black. Scarcely had they arrived in Lawrence before Dr. Wood called upon them, and, after a good deal of needless bluster, demanded that the free papers should be shown him. This the negro did. As the design was to create disturbance, and the free papers putting an end to this being done under any show of legality, his rage found vent in threats that the "negro should be thrown into the river, unless he returned to Missouri." However, there is sufficient love of justice, in Lawrence, to prevent any violence being done to any of its quiet citizens, be they white or black.

The weather is, indeed, most lovely. Shadows lie over the whole landscape, painting the prairie in green, from the lightest to the darkest shade. The music of the hay-cutters, with their large mowing-machines, has for days chimed in with the noise of many hammers, the cheerful voice of the teamsters, and the glad carol of singing-birds.

The appearance of the hay-makers is most novel, as they ride in among the tall grass, higher than their heads in many places, and bearing now a beautiful tasseled blossom of red, with yellow stamens, being seated upon their mowers as comfortably as when riding in a buggy.

7th. — The gentlemen with whom the free negro came have hired a claim about two miles from town, and moved out. No attempts were made, last night, to carry out the threats of the pro-slavery men. To-night, however, we heard of loads of people going out to the claim, and shots fired. The facts are, simply, the Hungarian doctor, wishing to exhibit his prowess, and prove his bravery, as our people have invariably suggested that so much rolling up of sleeves, and baring of the bosom, inviting an attack, was only the result of cowardice, selected this opportunity for a display of valor. Armed with gun and pistols, he took the route for the claim. Evans, the young Missourian, with whom the negro was "raised," and whom he says he will protect, at all hazards, came in town with a team. Two of our citizens, who knew the deadly intent with which Dr. Schareff left town, asked a ride with Evans, as he returned home, and they soon overtook the belligerent pill-pedler, who was puffing along in hot haste, as though empires were wavering in the balance at each moment's delay. As the cart passed, he asked for a ride, and sat in front, taking no notice of those behind. Presently, Evans asked him "where he was going;" to which he replied, "he was going hunting," which seemed a little singular, at this time of night. However, no comments were made. After some little desultory talk, the valiant doctor said, "I believe there is a negro out this way, and I am going there." Evans quickly replied, "It is just where I am going."

Doctor Schareff, supposing his errand must be like his own, commenced, at once, a vile tirade upon the negro, and avowed his intention to kill him. Evans heard him a while; then, with decisive tones, ordered him to give him his pistols, which he did, unhesitatingly, and, trembling with fear, dropped his gun upon the bottom of the cart. Evans then commanded him to go on and state his real sentiments. His plaintive "Excuse me," in broken English, gained him no reprieve. He was obliged, while the tears were coursing down his cheeks, to talk, or be silent, at the bidding of young Evans. At one time he commanded him to say, "I eat my words." His sobbing "Excuse me" availed nothing, and upon the threat of "I 'll shoot you," the same he had so often used to others, he repeated, "I 'll eat my words." They soon arrived at the claim, and Evans, commanding him to be seated by the side of the innocent object of much tirade and excitement, said, quite proudly, "The negro is much the better looking of the two."

8th.—The summer, for shortness, has indeed been without precedent. How we long for the good old days of childhood to come back, when a half-hour seemed a month, and the intervening time, between Sunday and Sunday, an age! Now birth-days and annual festivals scarcely knell their departure ere they return. Would there be such a crowding of duties then? One grows weary of doing; also of leaving duties undone.

The loveliness of the weather, the few months I have been here, has never been surpassed. Although the heat often rises high, a fresh breeze makes it in reality seem much less. I have never passed a summer with so little inconvenience from the heat, and have heard many people from Pennsylvania, as well as more northern states, say the same. Coming from the bleak and hilly north, where four months are all we boast of genial weather, free from frosts and north-east winds,—where we cherish with utmost care our garden flowers, protecting them from summer's heat and winter's cold,—where, of wild flowers, we have many a time returned rich, after a long tramp, with short-stemmed violets, one-sided dandelions, and blear-eyed daisies,—to this country, where charming weather predominates from early spring until the new year comes, displacing the old, we have grown wild in our enthusiasm of this beautiful land. We have revelled in flowers growing under our windows and at our doors, which, with much tending, we have tempted to bloom meagerly in garden-borders and green-houses in New England, such as verbenas,—velvet and sweet-scented,—petunias, fox-gloves, phlox, larkspurs, spider-wort, etc., an endless variety.

In the pillared clouds of morning and evening, when the golden and sapphire mingle, we are reminded of the burnished gates, and the streets inlaid with pearl, of the New Jerusalem.

While watching the changing, flitting shadows, which at one moment make the distant landscape of a deep blue, and then of a brown color, with little green spots like oases in the desert, life's changes have been typified in the shadows and sunny light, and we have grown wiser, treasuring the lesson.

9th.—Near the close of an unusually quiet Sabbath, we were attracted by the hasty, furious riding of a horseman upon the prairie going toward town. He soon returned, and others followed in squads of three and four. We heard the merry laugh, and occasional snapping of a gun. They were going out to the claim where the hunted negro lives. It was the hour for the meeting here; but owing to the excitement, few came. A lady, who came from that neighborhood, gave us the fact. A wagon-load of pro-slavery men about Lawrence, with some Missourians, had gathered at Mr. R.'s to take or kill the negro. Some person on a near claim, seeing the crowd, and suspecting the design, had hastily come to him for help. Those we saw passing out were some of the citizens. When the wagon-load of the mob arrived, the negro was out on the prairie, driving in the cattle. The gentleman of the house told them if they wished to fight him they could do so; but they could not have the negro. They left with threats of vengeance, and aid from Missouri.

14*th.* — Gov. Shannon passed within a mile of Lawrence, to-day, on his way to Lecompton — a little settlement some fourteen miles above here. A few little cabins are erected in a broken country; but its greatness lies in the future, as the Shawnee legislators have designated this site as the seat of government. It is also the place where Samuel J. Jones, postmaster at Westport, Missouri, and sheriff of Douglas County, Kansas Territory, has, in most wanton manner, burned down the houses of some free-state settlers. Gov. Shannon passed by us entirely, living in the largest settlement in the territory. Having received the right hand of fellowship from Missouri, what can we of the territory expect? He evidently does not desire the acquaintance of those whom he was sent to govern; but is himself to be governed by the border towns in Missouri.

15*th.* — Gov. Shannon returned to-night. He stopped a moment at the Cincinnati House, and was waited upon by one of our leading citizens, with the request that he would come out and meet the people. He declined; he must go four miles further to-night, and his suite cannot be detained. The offer was at once made to carry him to Franklin, where his party propose remaining over night, after he should have been introduced to our people, and have exchanged mutual greetings. This, also, he declined; and, as he entered his carriage to drive away, smothered groans struck on his ear, — the natural language of an indignation towards a man so weak, so pusillanimous, — a man sent to govern a people, and refusing to meet that people on the most common terms of civility. We deprecate this expression of feeling, knowing that to bear is better than to retort, and to the office we should try to pay that respect of which the man plainly shows he is not worthy. With the Rev. Thomas Johnson, of the Shawnee Mission School, a slaveholder, he will pursue, on the morrow (Sunday), his way thither.

19th.—A delegate convention was held at Topeka to-day to take into consideration the formation of a state constitution. The convention decided, after full discussion, to call a constitutional convention, to be held on the 22d of October, at Topeka, and organized a provisional government to superintend the election of delegates. The executive committee consisted of Messrs. J. H. Lane, Chairman; J. R. Goodwin, Secretary; G. W. Smith, C. R. Holliday, C. P. Schuyler, M. J. Parrott, and G. W. Brown.

Previous to this convention, the mass convention, held at Lawrence August 15th, had resulted in a call for this of the 19th, at Topeka. Also a delegate convention of the free-state party was held at Big Springs, September 5th, to fix a day for the election of a delegate to Congress, and to nominate a candidate. At this convention, the 9th of October was named for the election, instead of the 2d, the day fixed by the Shawnee Mission Legislature, and Ex-Governor Reeder was nominated for candidate. This convention, by resolution, referred the matter of a state organization to the Topeka convention, which was to represent all parties.

22d.—For the last few days nothing had been thought of but company. The house was full all day, and nearly all night. There are also continued rumors of new invasions, which disturb us but little.

Yesterday Mrs. W. and I went out to Mr. N.'s. He has a most lovely location two miles from town, and himself and wife are well pleased with their Kansas home. Last evening there was a melon party at the hall, at which there was a general gathering of old and young.

About this time the people of Lawrence entered into a self defensive organization. The street broils and outrages were becoming so frequent their lives were in daily peril. As soon as the organization was complete, and their badges gave evidence of a secret society, the outrages ceased.

24th.—Rode down to Fish's, after tea with the doctor, who went upon business. There was quite a gathering there, and one of our western orators was making a speech. He said repeatedly, "I have saw," which is their frequent mode of expression. On our way back, we passed several parties camped by the way-side, sitting or lying in the light of the bright camp-fire, while the sentinel leaned against a tree. We passed others, where they had no fires, but slept in and under the wagon, on the bare ground. The air of this country is so pure that persons do not take cold from lying on the ground. Doctor is tired with his various and constant cares, and sleeps sitting in the bottom of the carriage, while I drive on homewards. It was eleven o'clock, and the moon was shining brightly.

30th.—A gentleman called, and inquired for doctor. On being told that he was absent, he inquired for me. After saying to me, "Doctor is not at home," to which I assent, he said, "We have some news." A long pause followed, in which a thousand fears and anxieties rushed upon me. At last, by dint of questions, the following was the substance of the "news" I was able to gather:

Two regiments of men are on their way to Lawrence—one thousand men in each regiment. They have the gallows erected upon which to hang Gov. Reeder, and the rifle loaded with which to shoot Col. Lane.

I raise doubts as to the probability of such a thing; but he is sure, having been "specially informed by one acquainted with their movements, and who saw them as far on their way as the Shawnee meeting-house."

In compliance with his urgent request, I promise to tell doctor the moment he comes, that "he may go down and advise with him." The moment he is gone we have a hearty laugh, at the expense of the timid man, whose courage consists in brave-sounding words, and would willingly be at some personal risk to witness his fright at a visitation from the Missourians. Some people are so sure that large numbers of Missourians are getting ready to attack Lawrence on Tuesday, that messengers are sent out to count the wagons. They return saying all is quiet.

CHAPTER VIII.

GENERAL DISCOMFORT — MURDER OF DOW.

Oct. 14*th.* — A beautiful day. The air is hazy from the many fires on the prairie, which are burning day and night. They are a grand and sublime sight when spreading over a large tract, the tall grass waving with every breeze, now fiercely blazing, and now with graceful undulating motion, looking indeed like a "sea of flame," when the fiery billows surge and dash fearfully; or when the winds are still, like an unruffled, quiet burning lake. Doctor went to Wakarusa again to visit some sick friends. Word had been sent us of a new road, and we attempted to find it. After leaving the old road and riding some distance across the prairie, where there was no track, and through fields partly fenced, we came to a line of timber, where all our directions failed, and the straight way seemed wholly lost. As we were halting to decide upon our course, a woman came toward us from a little cabin not far off. She directed us to a little foot-path through the timber, and we followed it, turning this way and that to avoid crushing the wheels against the trees, and at every moment bending low to save our heads from striking the huge branches. After a quarter of a mile of such travelling, we were at the crossing. And such a crossing! If the old crossing was poor, this was so in a superlative sense, so very steep and abrupt. We went into the water with a lurch, almost tearing the body of the carriage from the wheels. A man came to the opposite bank, which was some twelve feet high, and not lacking much of being perpendicular, and by motions, and a few words we could hear, made us understand that we must keep down the river a little further, in the attempt to cross. Coming to the other shore, there was a little bank about a foot high, then a level broad enough for the wagon to stand upon, before reaching the perpendicular hill. The horse was frightened, and unwilling to take us out of the water. Doctor jumped out to the shore, and I was gathering strength for a similar leap, when one foot broke through the bottom of the buggy, and I was fairly caught. However, as the doctor was holding both my hands, I did not go into the water. The horse, finding himself without a load, walked out of the river. A consultation was then held with the man on the bank, as to the probability of getting to the summit with the carriage. He said he had never seen any carriages go up, but oxen had been. By leading the horse and pushing the carriage, the height was gained, while I clambered up by a winding path, over huge logs, and whatever came in my way. We returned to L. by still another route.

On the ninth of October the election for territorial delegate to Congress, and delegates to the Constitutional Convention, was held. In Lawrence, five hundred and fifty-seven votes were polled for Gov. Reeder.

21*st*.—The weather is getting frosty, and reminds us that bland airs and summer skies do not always last. Mr. W. arrived from Boston. He has had a long and tedious trip through Missouri by cars, boat and stage, and has had some conversation with the people. In fact, he has seen something of the ruffians.

23*d*.—Mr. W. and Mr. P. return from Topeka nearly frozen. Mr. W. is much pleased with the country, though he sees it under most unfavorable circumstances. Business at home makes his stay here very short. He amuses us with his report of the crowded state of the boarding-houses at Topeka. Some dozen or more sleeping in an unfinished room, in berths like those on boats, while the cold was most severe. The place left for a window was wholly open, thus giving a free circulation to the frosty air.

The Constitutional Convention, held at Topeka, was called together at one o'clock, Oct. 22, by J. A. Wakefield. A quorum not being present, the convention adjourned until Wednesday morning. The convention was called to order. Prayer by Rev. H. S. Burgess. Roll called by J. K. Goodin. Thirty members responded. S. C. Smith, of Lawrence, was elected secretary; J. H. Lane, president. The oath of office was administered to the president and the several members by J. A. Wakefield. Rev. Mr. Burgess chosen chaplain; McIntire, door-keeper; Lyman Farnsworth, sergeant-at-arms; S. F. Tappan, reporter for the Herald of Freedom; John Speer, reporter for the Kansas Tribune; E. C. K. Garrey, reporter for the Kansas Freeman; J. Redpath, reporter for the Missouri Democrat.

Nov. 15th. — Rainy and very chilly. A military supper in the evening. For two or three days men have been out in the woods hunting game; and to-night a large number of our citizens have gathered to partake of the supper, and join in the general festivities of the hour. Notwithstanding the rain, the mud being over shoes in depth, at an early hour the large dining-hall of the hotel was full of people, our neighbors and friends, while many came from miles away. A piano stood at the upper end of the room, — parlor and dining-hall being thrown into one, — and over the arch of the folding doors waved the "star-spangled banner," presented to the military companies on the fourth of July. The tables occupying the length of the hall, in double rows, were loaded with wild game, rabbits, squirrels, prairie-chickens, turkeys, and one porker, — whether native of the country, deponent saith not, — while cakes of every variety, with pastry, grace the table. All this cooking was done by one lady, — one of the earliest settlers, — who has the Yankee adaptedness of character to the circumstances in which she is placed. It was a New England gathering, though some, by their dress, tinsel ornaments, or their peculiarity of speech, showed that their home was further west. Some of the latter were asking continually, "When will the supper be ready? If there is going to be anything to eat, let us have it now." That our people are eminently social, the frequent public gatherings here and at Topeka will bear witness. A person coming in to mingle in the scene would never realize he was in a newly settled country, or in a town scarcely a year old.

18th. —We heard yesterday that Mr. C., who for several weeks has been very ill, but had partially recovered, is taken down again with symptoms of fever and ague. The weather is exceedingly cold, and he is in a little "snake" cabin, where the wind creeps in at every crevice, playing hide-and-seek with the papers pasted on the walls. The house has but one room, beside a little attic, which is used for kitchen, dining-room, bed-room, sick-room, and general receiving-room. Worn out with Mr. C.'s long illness, and that of her little daughter, the lady, who has watched over him with a mother's gentleness, is also ill. I send to Mr. C. to come to our house if he can be brought; and soon a carriage drives up with the shadow, pale and ethereal, which sickness has left of Mr. C., wrapped up in coats to the number of three, with comforters and other articles to keep the cold from striking his attenuated frame. He says, in his own peculiar way, "I thought, Mrs. R., I would never be here again; but it is delightful, and I feel better now."

The sun was shining pleasantly in at the windows, the fire was crackling in the stove, spreading a genial warmth throughout the room, and, seated in the nice large rocker drawn up before it, Mr. C. could look out upon the beautiful country miles east and south, and, in his enthusiastic love of nature, would forget his own ills. It was pleasant to see the effect of physical comfort. Now, with outward cheerfulness, came inner strength and courage. Naturally of very slender constitution, with too much mental power for the physical, with energy and inherent love for freedom and justice, Mr. C. has, in working for the cause here, gone beyond his strength, and pays the penalty in a wasted frame and general prostration. There has been a good deal of sickness in the country this fall, — slow fever and chills. They prevail mostly in the low grounds near the rivers. We hear from some settlements, especially from those south on the Neosho, that sickness has laid its heavy hand on the strongest, and scarcely any have escaped the paralyzing blow. So far as we can learn, exposures, either necessary or unavoidable, have been the cause.

The colony at Hampden has suffered most deplorably. The facts, as given me by one of the residents, are these: There were one hundred members of the colony, men, women and children, when they arrived in the territory. When the town site was laid off, there were over sixty men to receive their apportionment of lots. They came in April, and in order to provide for the winter store, they thought first of all it was necessary to get the seed into the ground, they living meanwhile in tents. All their energies, forgetful of present necessities, seemed to be directed to their future good. Health and valuable lives were sacrificed thereby. There was no saw-mill, and whatever houses they made at last were of logs and "shakes." There were very few springs in the vicinity, consequently they drank of the river water, which is slow and sluggish, and, when the dry season came, was covered with a green substance found upon all stagnant water, although good water could be obtained by digging twenty-five feet, as one or two wells proved.

With sickness of body came heart-sickness, and a yearning for pleasant New England homes; and most of those who lived through such discouragements either went to other settlements or returned.

At Osawattomie, situated near the junction of the Potawattomie and Osage, in a pleasant, though rather low country, fever has burned up the blood of many, leaving wan cheeks and livid lips. Yet, every one is free to acknowledge that no country has a purer atmosphere, or more healthful climate. In cases of sickness in Lawrence, they have, so far as I know, been owing to some gross outrage of the physical laws of our being, some unwarranted over-exertion of energies either mental or physical; a knowledge of such undue effort being confessed to by the individual, with the expectation that sickness would follow.

The climate, or the country, should bear no part of the blame. It is a question whether, in the necessary exposures of our new homes, the never-ceasing labors incident to such a situation, we are as guilty as those who court sickness in the states, by rash violation of the laws which govern us.

The cholera raged for a time upon the Wakarusa, for which drinking of the stagnant water in the river's bed, the result of an unprecedented drouth of ten months, and in many cases a sad want of personal cleanliness, was the prolific cause. About the same time, a gentleman near the same region walked into Lawrence in the heat of the day, with perspiration starting from every pore, and blood at fever heat. He plunged into the river for a cooling bath, remaining some time. A pleasant coolness was induced; but the blood was driven back from the extremities, to course madly about the internal organs. Soon after eating a hearty supper, he retired. The awaking, after a short, restless sleep, came with bitter pains, and life-crushing agonies. Death in a few hours closed the scene. The stricken wife, coming to gladden his home, heard of this sudden blighting of her hopes, as she reached Kansas city. On the Missouri river, too, sickness has ruled the hour; and some who bade their friends good-by in the old, dearly loved home, to seek a new one beneath the sunny skies of Kansas, found a grave on those dreary Missouri shores. They call the sickness such as the water produces; we call it the result of their ungoverned appetites. The tables upon the boats are loaded with every delicacy that man can invent. Meats with rich gravies, the richest of pastries and cakes, jellies, ices, fruit and nuts, tempt the palate. Can any stomach bear a mingling together of all these, and give no sign of ill usage, no cry for a reprieve? Yet many are the instances where such overtasking of life's energies has resulted in a brief sickness, and a burial in the waters. Others have lived to reach the territory in time to die there.

One man went on to one of the boats with a large bunch of radishes in his hand. The captain warned him, it being the cholera season, but he said he "could eat them, or anything else, without danger." But ere the morning sun arose, the death damps were heavy on his brow, and the eye recognized no longer the friends, though strangers, who administered to his fast-failing necessities. Another man, who was ill upon the boat, reached Kansas city, and there drank very freely of ice-water, not heeding the suggestions of others who thought it unsafe. The same afternoon he walked out eight miles, and back into the country. The next day he walked out again. He was taken most violently ill. The next evening, at the sunset hour, the tall trees in the leafy wood were waving over his western grave, and the moaning winds sang his requiem.

The poor, homesick youth, whose vision has been bounded by

the smoke of their mother's kitchen chimney, go East again with direful stories of the dread poison in the Missouri waters, and that there is death in the springs of Kansas. Some persons do not drink the water clear, but add brandy, or drink Rochelle powders; as if the drink which God provided for his creatures was not as health-giving as the substitutes of man, making their wisdom greater than his!

It is a fact that in Kansas city, within the short space of two hours' time, ten young men died, — victims to cholera, the papers stated. They did not state that they were most dissolute and intemperate, ready for the sickle when the reaper came.

Many statements have appeared in eastern papers, from the pens of some fresh from the counting-rooms of their employers, or the school-room, and unfitted either by nature or by habit to battle with life in its stern realities. They came to this country, dazzled by the lure of their own visionary hopes, which, with many people, makes all in the distance look bright and golden, but the intervening space passed over has the same dull hue of the last stand-point. These statements wear the color of disappointment, with a sly vein of revenge upon somebody running through all; a bitterness, and a general tone of falsehood. The little discomforts by the way, of crowded cars and overloaded boats, with perhaps a bed upon the cabin floor, instead of the private chamber with its nice appliances for comfort they have left, cause the bright vision to which distance lent enchantment to grow suddenly dim. They reach Kansas city, and find the levee a perfect crowd of men and horses, Mexican drivers from Santa Fe, with their mules half wild, and always headstrong — each man looking out for himself, as the one thing especially uppermost in his mind, not mindful of the attractions these kid-gloved, gaiter-booted, jewelled gentry display. They look upon the brick walls of stores and warehouses along the levee, upon which the sun glares wildly, and upon the water, where the reflection gleams and glitters, and at length reach the hotel whose rooms are already full of wearied mothers and sick children. Where will our dainty selves find rest? is a question anxiously asked by them, but unanswered. Shall we wonder, then, that they turn a lingering look homeward, unimpressed as they are with the reality, that life's mission is to "battle and be strong?" When they find no softly-cushioned car ready to transport them to the little town of Lawrence, to which distance still lends a charm, and if the stage and hacks are full, the emigrant wagons alone affording a passage, can we wonder at the lengthening of their wayworn faces? The hill difficulty is to be surmounted, and stands between them and the end of their journey, like a towering mountain. Little hearts, carried along, until now, upon the smooth travelled paths which their fathers have marked out, and buoyed above deep waters by encouraging words of doting mammas and flattering friends, and lulled into silken dreams by the general consenting voice of society, that life has in it nothing "real," nothing "earnest," save to float gayly on its summer tides, — where is your courage now? Where is your hope for success in life? Where that energy which will scale mountains amid winter's battling snows? Where, with such automatons as you, would have been the world's great men — her Howards, her Newtons, her Washingtons, or her Napoleons?

Some of these poor apologies of humanity leave directly on the next boat, on a home-bound ticket. As an excuse for the shortness of their stay, they recapitulate the thousand-and-one stories which the Missourians repeat to many emigrants; such as no water, no wood, the ground parched, and cracked open in large seams, the people dying of starvation, etc. etc. Some others, however, a little afraid of the jests which would meet them did they return with the old story, "There are giants in the land," make a prodigious effort, and, upon a springless cart, it may be, reach Lawrence. As they approach the little town, with buildings of wood and stone erected and being erected, with the pioneer buildings thatched (now used as stables) intermingled, how their visions fade, and the glittering palaces of their imaginations fall! The town of six months' existence boasted nothing but bare comforts; but these foolish youths write home how they have to sleep upon the floor, with a buffalo robe only between them and the cottonwood boards, with five or six others in the same room; that the windows to the boarding-house are of cloth instead of glass; that there are large cracks in the wall, through which the wind and dust blow; that there are larger cracks in the floor overhead, and through them the straw falls upon the table below; that butter is scarce; and many other like troubles, which make them say, in vexation of spirit, "I am weary, I am weary, I am sick of this poor life!" Does any one need further evidence that they are men of sense? These temporary arrangements were the growth of the hour. They were not intended as permanent institutions, and more comfortable dwellings have taken their place. The Yankee enterprise and thrift which remained after the thorough sifting of the early spring, in spite of fear of cholera and lack of general comforts, have added things most needed. The absence of those delicate youths who needed sofas to lounge upon, and silver forks for their especial use, is the greatest blessing of all. A new country, especially, wants no drones in the hive; and in a country like this, and in this age, when the battle is for freedom, and the hue and cry of our enemies, "Death to the Yankees!" is ever ringing in our ears, we want men, and not creatures claiming to be possessed of manliness, who have not enough of that spirit to be willing, for freedom's sake, to forego some trivial comforts, and, like the fathers of '76, who bore the severest privations, bide the hour, and with willing hands and strong hearts aid to make this country, in its institutions as in soil and climate, the garden of the world. Where would have been the liberties, which, as a precious heir-loom, have come to us, had our fathers been of such sickly, such squeamish sensibility? We do not deny there have been discomforts; but what new country was ever settled without them? The people of Illinois, in times of low water on the Ohio, in the early settlement of that country, have had nothing to eat but bread made of shorts with stewed pumpkin. In Pennsylvania, with no over supply of mills, fifty miles often being the shortest distance to one in running order in low water, for weeks the early settlers lived on potatoes. Did not our great grandmothers live on bean-porridge, weave all the clothing for the family, and, at the same time, gird their husbands and sons for the battle, out of their love for justice and right? We have fallen on degenerate times. The "lines have fallen to us in pleasant places;"

but the love of liberty has grown weak. A sad wailing comes up over the land — a wailing for the departed spirit of '76.

21st. — Charles Dow, a young free-state man from Ohio, was killed to-day by Coleman, a pro-slavery man, at Hickory Point. Some dispute had arisen about a claim, and Coleman had repeatedly threatened to kill Dow. This morning Dow went to a blacksmith's shop, at some distance from Mr. Branson's, where he boarded. Mr. Branson proposed he should take his gun with him as a means of protection, but he declined doing so. Having finished his business at the shop, he left to return to Mr. Branson's; and when a few rods on his way, hearing the click of a gun, he turned around, and received the whole charge in his breast. The gun was a double-barrelled shot-gun, and loaded with slugs. This happened about one o'clock; and the murdered body was left by the barbarians lying by the side of the road where he fell until sundown. Some of the accessories then sent word to Mr. Branson "that a dead body was lying by the roadside." He had begun to fear some ill had befallen his friend, and, at once recognizing the body, conveyed it to his house. Coleman is his murderer, while Harrison Buckley and Hargous were privy to it. There is no doubt that it was a deliberate act.

Such things are winked at by our governor, no effort being made to bring offenders to justice. Our courts are the very mockery of justice. Cole McCrea, a free-state man, having, in self-defence, killed Malcolm Clark, is confined for months. Judge Lecompte packs the jury in order to get him indicted. A meeting was held at Leavenworth, in May, at which resolutions most intolerant in their character, proposing outrage and violence upon the persons of free-state settlers, were passed. Thirty men, as a committee of vigilance, were also appointed, "to observe and report all such persons as shall, by the expression of abolition sentiments, produce disturbance to the quiet of the citizens, or danger to the domestic relations; and all such persons so offending shall be notified and made to leave the territory." "The meeting was ably and eloquently addressed by Judge Lecompte, Col. J. N. Burns, of Western Missouri, and others" Such is the judge the federal government has sent us — a man of partisan character, who throws his whole influence upon the side of violence and disorder, and is aiming to form the domestic institutions of the territory. Collins, a free-state man, was shot, not long since, by Pat Laughlin, and no notice was taken of it by the government. If Coleman should be arrested, have we not good reason to believe, though the evidence was clear as the sunlight that his hand was stained with the blood of a fellow-creature, that Judge Lecompte would so pack a jury as to clear the culprit? The design of the pro-slavery men is to drive out all who are firm and true to the principles of freedom, and in this design the officials sympathize. Justice weeps at the shameless course of her executors in this territory.

24th. — A friend is over from Blanton. The citizens of that region and Hickory Point are much aroused by the murder of Dow. He was a mild and peaceable young man, much esteemed by those who knew him. He had recently received a letter from his friends, in which they urge him to come home, as they fear his life is in danger. Our friend S. has just answered the letter, and borne to them also the sad tidings of their son's decease by the bloody hand of slavery's minions. Another martyr has fallen on the green plains of Kansas for those rights which Heaven vouchsafes to every human creature with his breath of life. A meeting to take into consideration the bloody deed, and their murderous designs, as the lives of other free-state men are sought after with vile, fiendish threats, is called for next Monday, Nov. 26. The murderer has fled to Missouri.

27th. —Tuesday morning. At about four o'clock, this morning, was awakened by the hurried tramp of horses' feet approaching the house. A loud knock upon the door soon followed, with the instantaneous halloa, so common in this western country, used instead of the more courteous civilities of conventional life, saving the rider the trouble of dismounting. Recognizing the voice, my husband asked, "What 's wanted?"

The voice outside replied, "Jones, with a party of Missourians, had taken from his house a Mr. Branson. He has been rescued by a party of free-state men, and they are now on their way here.

Runners have gone to Missouri, and there will be a battle fought this morning."

The simple question asked was, "Where?"

And the brief reply, "Down here on the plain," was only a little startling.

The horseman drove away, and we heard already the sound of the drum, and the quick words of the captain of the little band of rescuers, as they came upon the brow of the hill beyond us. Scarcely had the fire been built ere the simple word, "Halt!" in a tone of command, was spoken, and a line fronting the house quickly formed. The slight form of the leader stood a little nearer the door; and, when his peculiarly dry manner of speech fell upon the ear in his brief inquiry, "Is Dr. R. in?" his identity was also known. The doctor opened the door, and invited them in.

The fact of the rescue was stated, and Mr. Branson, being in the ranks, was ordered to "step forward, and tell his story," which he did with much feeling, and with the appearance of a person who is heart-broken. I shall never forget the appearance of the men in simple citizen's dress, some armed and some unarmed, standing in unbroken line, just visible in the breaking light of a November morning. This little band, of less than twenty men, had, through the cold and upon the frozen ground, walked ten miles since nine o'clock of the previous evening. Mr. Branson, a large man, of fine proportions, stood a little forward of the line, with his head slightly bent, which an old straw hat hardly protected from the cold, looking as though, in his hurry of departure from home in charge of the ruffianly men, he took whatever came first. As he, in simple, unaffected style, told of this outrage upon humanity, we felt that, as in days when men left their ploughs in the furrows at their country's call, so now have come again "days which try men's souls," and that this may be the beginning of a contest which shall drench the whole country in blood. Now, as then, we need strong hearts to battle for the right — to die, it may be, if the sacrifice is needed.

The drum beat again, and the rescuers and rescued passed down to Lawrence. After telling E. she had better take another nap, in order to be prepared for any emergency which might arise, I again fell asleep, leaving my husband thinking over the matter by the parlor stove, and was awakened again, as the sun was rising, by the screams of cayotes in the distance. The first impression was that the Missourians had come. The facts of the rescue are these : The people of Hickory Point yesterday held the proposed meeting in reference to the murder of Dow, and passed resolutions condemning the wanton outrage, and that Coleman should be brought to justice. He, in the mean time, had gone to Gov. Shannon, at the Shawnee Mission, for protection. He was there taken into custody by Samuel J. Jones, who, it will be remembered, was engaged in the burning of two settlers' houses at Lecompton, on the pretence that the claims were his, while he is a citizen and acting postmaster at Westport, Mo. This pretence of taking Coleman into custody was done without any warrant being issued, or examination had.

On yesterday morning a peace-warrant was made out by Hugh Cameron, of Lawrence, at the instigation of Bradley, a pro-slavery man living at Hickory Point, against Jacob Branson, the friend of the murdered Dow, and was placed in the hands of Jones. In the evening, after Mr. Branson, with his family, had retired, Jones, with a party of mounted men, rode up to his lone cabin upon the prairies, a half-mile from neighbors. He knocked at the door. To the question, "Who is there?" the reply was given, "A friend." "Come in, then," was the response, and the little cabin was full of men — rough, savage, armed men. Jones went to the bedside, and, presenting his pistol to Branson's breast, said, "You are my prisoner."

Mr. Branson asked, "By what authority?"

Oaths, and the threat, "I will blow you through," were the decisive answer. The others, with guns cocked, gathered around, and took him prisoner. Thus, in the night, was an innocent, defenceless man taken from his home and family by a gang of twenty-five whiskey-drinking ruffians, showing no papers of arrest, and answering with oaths and threats of instant death any questions as to the cause of such summary, unlawful proceedings. They proceeded to Buckley's house, and, after stopping a while, by a long and winding way to elude pursuers, they took the route to Blanton's Bridge. They strengthened their valor by taking another "drink." Jones, running in his horse by the side of Mr. Branson, said, "I heard there were one hundred men at your house to-day," and talked a good deal "of the sport they would have had with them," and regretted "being cheated out of it."

This affair, though done in the darkness, was soon brought to light. The people felt that the life of another of their citizens was to be taken by the hands of a lawless mob, at the suggestion of two men who were the accessories to the murder of Dow, and who were connected with this new outrage. Earnestly, as honest men will act when they feel that life is at stake, and that the life of a valued friend, these settlers acted; and the tidings flew on the speed of wings from one claim to another, until a few, a lesser number than the party with Jones, were gathered together. With the intention of rescuing the prisoner from a cruel death, they took a nearer route than that taken by Jones, and reached the house of Mr. Abbott, where they made a stand. The settlers were only ten or twelve in number, partially armed, and on foot, while the party now with Jones, whose numbers had somewhat fallen off, was mounted and armed. Soon after the settlers had reached Mr. A.'s house, and had recovered their breath after their running walk, Jones and his party appeared on a full canter. As soon as they saw the little band of footmen, they endeavored to avoid them by passing the other side of the house. The settlers understood the ruse, and passed quickly around to meet them, forming, as they did so, in a line across the road.

Jones and his party halted, and asked, "What's up?"

The reply was, "That's what we want to know — 'What's up?'"

Some one from the band of settlers asked, "Is Mr. Branson with you?"

He answered for himself, "I am here, and a prisoner."

The word of command given from the little band of footmen was, "Ride out to our side," which he did without hesitation, notwithstanding Jones' threat of "I'll shoot you." A question then was raised by the free-state men as to the ownership of the horse he was riding; and, as he said it was not his, he was ordered to dismount, which order likewise he obeyed. With threats of aid from Missouri, which long ago became stereotyped, Jones and his party wheeled about, leaving the few unarmed footmen the winners of the night. Not a word was lisped of the rare "sport" they would have had if they could have found the one hundred assembled men; and now, when the party was smaller than their own, Jones shook nervously, and offered nothing but wordy violence. Jones and party rode on to Franklin, the little village below Lawrence. The whole matter, the rescue, etc., was talked over there, Jones standing by. It was suggested that a decision be made as to the propriety of sending for aid to Col. Boone, of Westport, Mo., Jones' father-in-law, or to Gov. Shannon. The question seemed to be, which would be most likely to furnish the desired assistance in demolishing the doomed town of Lawrence. Now was the time for the war. The time specified by the Blue Lodges, two months since, had arrived. The harvests in Missouri were in, and the people there could, without injury to their business, attend to the matter; and navigation on the Missouri river had closed for the season. Jones therefore wrote a despatch, and sent it by a messenger, remarking, as he started, "That man is taking my despatch to Missouri, and, by G—d! I will have revenge before I see Missouri." Some complaint was made by a bystander that this despatch was not sent to the governor, whereupon he sent one to him, Hargous being the messenger.

Early on the morning of the 27th, the drum-beat, calling the citizens together, was heard in the little town of Lawrence. The noise of the hammer was still; but in the firm tread and thoughtful countenances of the men, as they walked up the stairway to the hall where the meeting for consultation was to be held, the spirit of '76 was visible, and a determination, if they must fight against oppression as our fathers did, that a new Lexington or Concord on Kansas plains should go down to posterity with the unsullied honor of her defenders.

S. N. Wood, Esq., was appointed chairman of the meeting. He spoke briefly of the murder, of the meeting of the day before in the same neighborhood, of the arrest of Mr. Branson, with whom Mr. Dow had lived, of the rescue of the prisoner without

10

bloodshed, and of the necessity that he and the rest of the community be defended from similar threatened attacks. Mr. Branson then made his statement. He is an elderly man, of most quiet and modest deportment. He was much moved, the emotions of his heart, broken by the death of his friend, almost forbidding utterance. Now the laceration was made yet deeper by this wanton assault upon himself, and there was the thought of the terrible suspense as to his fate, making the hours long and weary for the desolate wife in that lone cabin. All these things tended to crush the spirit of the man, unused to such barbarities; and, with tears at times stealing down his weather-beaten cheeks, he said he had been requested by some friends to leave Lawrence, to seek some other place of safety, so that no semblance even of an excuse could be given to the enemy for an attack upon Lawrence. He said he would go — Lawrence should not be involved in difficulty on his account. If it was the decision of the majority, he would leave. He would rather go to his home, and die there, and be buried by the side of his friend. This statement, full of feeling, touched the hearts of the men, who felt they, too, might soon be battling in the death-struggle for their own hearth-stones, and cries of "No! no!" resounded through the still room.

G. P. Lowrey, Esq., then proposed a committee of ten should be appointed to advise for the common defence. He had not hitherto acted in these matters, but the threatening aspect of affairs now demanded action upon the part of all our citizens. The measure proposed was purely defensive. Mr. Lowrey's remarks met with a warm response in the feelings of all, and his proposition was adopted.

Mr. Conway said they were on the eve of important events, and they must have a care to take every step properly. They ignored and repudiated the Legislature which held its session at the Shawnee Mission. They would never give in their allegiance to such a monstrous iniquity. To the United States authorities, to the organic act, to the courts created under it, and to the judges and marshals appointed by the President, they would yield obedience. They might oppress them, but they would submit and seek redress for grievances at the United States Supreme Court, which would give them a fair hearing. They must move with prudence, and, having resolved upon the true course, maintain it fearlessly.

S. N. Wood did not hesitate to say he was in the rescue of the night before; he knew the importance of the step. He was unable to express his feelings when the clicking of the gunlocks sounded in the darkness, telling that the hour had come for a deadly conflict. He was equally unable to do so when, without firing one shot, these men, who had boasted so much, gave up the prisoner, declining to fight a number less than their own, and with fewer arms. When he spoke of the justice of the peace who figured in this transaction, and received his office from the bogus Legislature, and whose name was Cameron, a general hiss expressed the utter abhorrence of the audience. Others spoke of this man living in our midst, who had professed to be a free-state man, and who was now a willing instrument, in the hands of these vile men, to enforce such measures upon us. It was moved that a committee of three be appointed to wait on Cameron, and demand by what authority he acted. The meeting then adjourned until two o'clock.

CHAPTER IX.

WAKARUSA WAR — PREPARATIONS.

We cannot now tell what an hour may bring forth. This whole affair is probably gotten up to test the power of Gov. Shannon, and his accomplices, in carrying out the laws of the Shawnee Mission School Legislature, which he says "shall be enforced;" in the accomplishment of which he said he would call upon Missouri for aid, even before coming into the territory whose people he was sent to govern. No writs of arrest have been attempted to be served upon our people for breaking any of their infamous laws. Now the time, in the estimation of the worthy law-makers, seems to have arrived, when the laws shall be enforced, or at least an excuse be found for destroying Lawrence, whose prosperity has long been a terrible eyesore to the stockholders in the town of Lecompton.

Will the free-state men yield their rights? Will they obey these laws? As we look each man in the face this morning, we read there manliness and determination, — no crouching to tyrants. And each man remembers that "resistance to tyrants is obedience to God."

We have nothing good to expect from the territorial officers, and Gov. Shannon is sold, body and soul, to the oppressing party. The events of last summer, especially of the last few months, have shown, too clearly to be mistaken, the infamous designs of those in power here. On Saturday, April 30th, McCrea, a lawyer of Leavenworth, shot Malcolm Clark, a pro-slavery politician, in self-defence. He had a long and rigorous imprisonment at the fort, and in the jail. At the court in September they failed to find a bill of indictment against him, as the Grand Jury could not agree. At that time Col. Lane, of Lawrence, went to Leavenworth to offer McCrea his services as counsel, which Judge Lecompte refused, as Col. Lane would not take the oath to support the laws of the Legislature of the Shawnee Mission. A majority of the jury were for acquittal, and the remainder were divided, one thinking the prisoner guilty of murder, and a few of manslaughter. At the adjourned term of the court in November, Judge Lecompte had added seven new members to the Grand Jury, and a bill of indictment for murder in the first degree was found against him. Four of the counsel within the bar, and officers acting at this tribunal, including the clerk of the court, were connected with the lynching of Phillips, also a lawyer at Leavenworth, on the 17th of May. At this adjourned session of the court, a motion was made, by one of the attorneys, to dismiss the clerk, and one of the attorneys who had been thus engaged, affidavits having been filed to prove the facts; but the court did not grant the motion. Thus, while one man is imprisoned for months, a jury packed that a bill may be found against him, and he is tried by those who are guilty of the most abominable crimes, they go unpunished, no effort being made to bring them to justice.

Several of these grand jurors were standing outside of the court-house, one day, while several free-state men were within, and, speaking of them, asked " if it would n't be best to take out a few of those fellows, and string them up. Could n't the laws be so construed as to render it legal? " What justice can any one expect from such executors of the laws? At this time, also, the following call for a convention of the " law and order " party was published in all their papers:

" GRAND MASS CONVENTION AT LEAVENWORTH CITY, NOV. 14TH, '55.

" The law-abiding citizens of Kansas Territory, without distinction of party, will hold a grand mass convention, at Leavenworth, on November 14th. Let there be a grand rally of the law and order citizens of the territory. Friends of the constitution and laws, turn out, appoint delegates from every neighborhood, and come yourselves, and show that there is a grand and glorious party in the territory, who are determined to stand by the constituted authorities of the land. Let come what will, show that you are determined to rally around the bulwarks of the constitution, and maintain the laws. Let every county in the territory be fully represented. By order of

"Andrew J. Isaacs, R. R. Rees,
John A. Halderman, L. F. Hollingsworth,
D. J. Johnson, D. A. N. Grover,
Wm. G. Mathias, } *Com.*"

Some of these men are President Pierce's appointees in the territory. A part of these were connected in the mobbing of Phillips, while others were of the invading horde who trampled upon the constitution, and all the rights it ensures to freemen, at the election of the 30th of March. This talk of rallying around the constitution, and maintaining the laws, sounds well coming from such men! At this meeting Gov. Shannon presided, committing himself wholly to the partisan movement. He declared that the iniquitous laws passed by men from, and chosen by, Missouri, "shall be enforced." He entered into a league with these men that he would do all in his power to oppress the other party. He called the free-state party a "faction," although he knew that the convention at Topeka was elected by votes of at least three fourths of the residents of the territory, and was comprised of men of all political opinions. He yet rushed on recklessly, led by blind leaders, and desiring nothing but that free Kansas shall bear the galling yoke of slavery.

Gen. Calhoun addressed the meeting. Among other choice titbits, he said: "Shall abolitionists rule you? No, never! Give them all they demand, and abolitionism becomes the law of the land. You yield, and you have the most infernal government that ever cursed a land. I would rather be a painted slave over in Missouri, or a serf to the czar of Russia, than have the abolitionists in power. (Tremendous cheers.) Look at the outrages mentioned in their journals, of babies shot through the sides of houses, etc. There is nothing so low or mean but abolition papers are found to tell it. We, the Union-loving and State-rights party, of Kansas, have kept too still, and allowed the nullifiers to proclaim millions of lies. This is a great question for abolitionists to make capital out of. We must not allow it to go on here. We must stop its growth. It tramples upon the laws of the land. Say to your governor, 'Enforce the laws; we will stand by you, and, if necessary, we will spill our life's blood to enforce them!' The governor will be with you. The governor calls for all to help him, except abolitionists. He calls to men of all states; but he don't want abolitionists."

After Gen. Calhoun had pursued this strain of remark a while longer, he took his seat, and Mr. Parrott arose to speak. He, however, gave way to an amendment offered by Gen. Clark to the motion of Dr. Stringfellow, "law and order" men being substituted for "pro-slavery" men, in constituting a delegate to the meeting. Mr. Parrott had an interview with the governor, before the evening session, and stated his desire to speak; to which the governor, with very pro-slaveryish leanings, replied, "He did not think anything he would say would be at all congenial to the feelings of the rest." Twice, after the first attempt to speak, Mr. Parrott addressed the chair; but his honor by no sign acknowledged he heard a sound. The feelings of the "law and order" gentry were expressed in hisses, and groans, and cries of "Put him out!" Mr. Parrott's patience still lasted, and as he again appealed to the chair, the gray head turned, as though on a pivot, upon the shoulders which bore the weight of some sixty years, and the coarse features were hidden from his sight. He continued: "By the order of this convention, I am a delegate (groans and hisses), and I claim the right to be heard (hisses and groans). As the friend and advocate of 'law and order,' I shall congratulate myself and the country if your labors shall result in strengthening that sentiment in the territory. ('Put him out,' and groans.) I was, as you know, a member of the Topeka Convention, and am unalterably attached to that cause (hisses and groans). Governor, your presence reminds me of other days, when, as the standard-bearer of an undivided democracy, you stemmed the tide of political opposition which threatened to subvert our cherished principles, in the state from which we hail. May I not venture to invoke the recollection of that time, to ask of you, and the friends by whom you are now surrounded, a patient hearing of the cause I advocate." At this juncture, Dr. Stringfellow informed Mr. Parrott that the convention did not wish to hear a free-state man. A good deal of confusion ensuing, Mr. Parrott gave way to the bully crowd.

A person after Gov. Shannon's own heart now took the floor, and, among other *peaceful* and *patriotic* sentiments, which brought down the house in cheers long and loud, were the following. Speaking of Kansas laws, he said, "For the safety of our property we must enforce them, for the preservation of our lives against higher law marauding. I endorse the sentiments of Gen. Calhoun's speech, and, had I the tongue to be heard to every limit of this Union, I would proclaim it, so that old men, now standing on the brink of the grave, might hear it; and I would sooner my tongue should cleave to the roof of my mouth, or my right arm be severed from my body, than silently give over our beautiful country to ruthless abolitionism. We must enforce the laws, though we resort to the force of arms; trust to our rifles, and make the blood flow as freely as do the turbid waters of the Missouri, that flows along our banks." Judge Lecompte said he would support "law and order." Dr. Stringfellow, and Johnson, one of the foremost in the gang who lynched Phillips, added their words of counsel. Such were the prime movers in this meeting — the governor, the judge, the surveyor-general, appointed by the national head, yet, first and foremost in a meeting made up of border desperadoes. Stringfellow, the pro-slavery apostle, was acting with them, a prominent officer of the meeting, and, only a few days previous, published an extra, which has the following significant sentence: "Thus it is that the fight so long talked of has begun, and it is to be hoped that it will not be discontinued until Kansas Territory is rid of this 'higher law' and blood-thirsty set of negro thieves and outlaws." This was said in reference to the murder of Collins by Pat Laughlin. Gov. Shannon, in conversation, said, "The laws are not so very bad," — notwithstanding, for even having in one's house the Declaration of Independence, or saying aught against slavery, one is exposed to incarceration within prison walls. After the meeting, Gov. Shannon and Surveyor-General Calhoun were the invited guests of Lyle and Johnson, notorious ruffians, and ringleaders in the mobbing of Phillips. Such being the facts of Gov. Shannon's course here, what can we expect? Jones threatens that he will return to destroy Lawrence; "not one stone shall be left standing." He asserts that "Shannon has promised him ten thousand men, to enforce the laws." It seems a little singular that such a promise should have been made, when not even one arrest has been attempted, to test the temper of our people. Where will the poor governor find ten thousand men to do his bidding?

With all these truths before them, our people cannot but see that preparations for defence are necessary; and in the afternoon the adjourned meeting came together again. The pledge reported by Mr. Lowrey, as chairman of the committee, was carried through the hall, by the secretary of the meeting, and was signed, by those of the audience not belonging to volunteer companies, upon the stock of a Sharpe's rifle, that being used as the most convenient article at hand. The following was the pledge of union and mutual support: "We the citizens of Kansas Territory, finding ourselves in a condition of confusion and defencelessness so great that open outrage and mid-day murder are becoming the rule, and quiet and security the exception; and whereas the law, the only authoritative engine to correct and regulate the excesses and wrongs of society, has never yet been extended to our territory, thus leaving us with no fixed or definite rule of action, or course of redress, we are reduced to the necessity of organizing ourselves together on the basis of first principles, and providing for the common defence and general security; and here we pledge ourselves to the resistance of lawlessness and outrage, at all times, when required by the officers who may from time to time be chosen to superintend the movements of this organization."

It is rumored that the Missourians will make the attack to-morrow night. To complete the farce, Gov. Shannon, in person, it is said, will lead on his red-shirted, butternut-colored-trousered allies from Missouri, to subdue and crush his own people. Has he no sense, or has his brain become so muddled in the bad whiskey in which it floats, as to dull all his perceptions of justice or right?

28th. — Wednesday morning. A beautiful morning dawned

upon us — so lovely one could scarcely realize, that under the quiet soothing influence of such sunny skies, the brutal passions of mer could so rage as to seek the destruction of their fellows. Difficult, indeed, is it to feel that destruction is sworn against our homes, and a price set upon the heads of some dear to us. Yet, our people, having decided upon their course of action, are again at their usual places of business. The warlike aspect of yesterday has given place to the busy, enterprising spirit of the past daily routine which has characterized our people, and made the little city of a year give good promise of its future. Though at a moment's warning they could spring into line, armed for defence, externally everything looks peaceful. Occasionally, a horseman rides rapidly into town, and, after stopping a few moments, goes as rapidly out.

It is rumored that a large force is gathering at Franklin; also another at Lecompton, fourteen miles above here. We do not credit such reports. Whom will they fight, if they come? Will they dare, in this nineteenth century, in this boasted land of freedom, to make a raid upon us, crying, "Extermination, and no quarter!" A wholesome fear of consequences to themselves will prevent this. There will, probably, be a good deal of useless bravado, and they will strive to place us, if possible, in a wrong position before the world. There is a rumor, at evening, that an attack is threatened from Lecompton. The night is dark. E. and I are alone. About nine o'clock some gentlemen call, for a few minutes, who have been looking around on the hill beyond us, but saw no enemy. The hours were rapidly passing; it was nearly eleven o'clock, and no one came from town. E. fell asleep in her chair; I went out upon the hill alone, in the darkness, and listened; I heard nothing. I nearly dropped asleep upon the lounge, and was aroused by a loud knocking at the door, and three young men with Sharpe's rifles, and a cheerful "Good-evening," entered. They came as a guard, to see that no force comes into town from the Lecompton road. We talked a while of the prospect of the war, and were fully agreed as to the general character of the enemy, their failure of courage when they meet a foe equal in number, as Jones and party proved on the night of the 26th. We brought in extra candles and blankets, and went up stairs for a little sleep.

29th. — It is Thanksgiving day in Massachusetts, as in several other states. How anxious for us our friends would be, did they know just what dangers threaten us! But as they now draw around the cheerful fire, which November's chilly breath in New England makes social and pleasant, they will think of us as enjoying milder skies, and dream not of the dire visitation of the ruffianly horde gathering in our borders, and thirsting for our blood. The little home circle, now sadly broken in upon by life's changes, the revered head having passed onward beyond the dark portal, will think of her who in young girlhood made one of the number around the bright hearth-stone, and, having entered upon the responsibilities of life's drama, finds her post of duty in this far-away land. Thanksgiving will be kept by some families here, and the old custom of inviting one's friends to dine will not be forgotten; though the "wars and rumors of wars," with the necessary preparations in case of an attack, prevent its assuming its usual festive character.

The town has grown much in the few last weeks. The large hotel is complete externally, and, with its large, airy-looking windows opening upon a prospect of indescribable loveliness, its black-walnut doors with a mirror-like surface adding beauty, promises comfort in the future to the weary traveller. There are other buildings, nearly as large, almost complete, while others are in process of erection. One has to look all around them to avoid running into piles of sand and lime, against the hod-carriers and busy workmen. The Missourians have not forsaken us yet, or left us to starve, as plenty of their market-wagons are standing at every store. The Yankee's money is as good as anybody's money; and too much of it, while the borderers treat us so ill, has gone into their hands. It is estimated that over a million dollars have been paid them for horses, wagons, provisions, and freights, within the last year.

A friend came in from the border at evening, and brought reliable information of quite a camp at Franklin, four miles from us, and people continually on the way. He says there never has been before such excitement in the border towns. All kinds of teams are pressed into service, and are generally, together with the riders, of most uncouth, nondescript appearance. A box of provis ions, some shot-guns, and a jug, usually complete the outfit; and, coming with ox-teams, as quite a number of them do, there must also be embarked for the journey a supply of patience. The possibility of a retreat has probably never entered the heads of these valiant warriors of the ox-team battalion.

The following extraordinary document, sent by Secretary Woodson to Gen. Easton, of Leavenworth, has just appeared:

"(Private.) Dear General: The governor has called out the militia, and you will hereby organize your division, and proceed forthwith to Lecompton. As the governor has no power, you may call out the Platte Rifle Company. They are always ready to help us. Whatever you do, do not implicate the governor.

"Daniel Woodson."

General Easton was appointed, by the Shawnee Legislature, general of the territorial militia. The following, also, was sent from Westport:

"Westport, *Nov.* 27.

"Hon. E. C. McClarem, *Jefferson City:* Gov. Shannon has ordered out the militia against Lawrence. They are now in open rebellion against the laws. Jones is in danger."

Dec. 1*st.* — Saturday night has come again, bringing the close of another week — a week of anxiety to the leaders here, upon whom the responsibility of our safety rests. Messengers have been sent to the other settlements, at different times, notifying them of the threatened attack, with the desire that they hold themselves in readiness to come to our aid at a moment's notice.

Last night, at midnight, a friendly band of armed men came in from Ottawa Creek, having heard of the invasion. With flag flying, a company of mounted riflemen have come in from Palmyra, also. The Indians, both Shawnees and Delawares, have offered their warriors for our defence. While we would not accept aid from the Indians, knowing that it would furnish a pretext to the government for their extermination, their friendly feelings will go far towards sustaining the courage of any who might falter.

Several gentlemen from Lawrence have been down to the enemy's camp to-day, as they have, in fact, every previous day. They found some of the men in the camp quite communicative. They say that "a good many are on the way;" that they are coming "to help the governor." It is estimated that not more than one hundred and fifty are now in camp at Franklin, and on the Wakarusa, two or three miles below. At the former place, to-day, about fifty of these barbarians were shooting at a mark. Two covered wagons, with flags flying, were standing in the centre of the town. Some horses were fastened near.

As one of these gentlemen from Lawrence went below the Wakarusa, where some half a dozen of humanity's roughest specimens guard the ford, on his return, their anxiety was expressed in the question, "Have you seen many coming?" At one point he overtook a covered wagon, with two men and boxes of provisions and ammunition, with an escort of a dozen horsemen. A large flag, of singular appearance, waved over the wagon. It was a "lone star," of deep crimson, upon a white ground. As one of the emblems of their secret oaths, as members of the Blue Lodge, it was hailed with loud shouts by those already in camp.

Business is nearly given up here. Men gather in groups to talk of the probabilities of flying rumors. Never were there more in circulation. A committee of safety, also the leaders in this emergency, have been appointed. They are taking all possible steps for the defence, learning as much as they can of the movements of the enemy. It is rumored, also, that Gov. Shannon has telegraphed to President Pierce for the military force at Fort Leavenworth. The poor people of the territory would wonder what it 's for, were it not explained by the following despatch from Missouri:

"WESTON, MO., *Nov.* 30.

"The greatest excitement continues to exist in Kansas. The officers have been resisted by the mobocrats, and the interposition of the militia has been called for. A secret letter from Secretary Woodson to Gen. Easton has been written, in which the writer requests Gen. Easton to call for the rifle company, at Platte city, Mo., *so as not to compromise Gov. Shannon.* Four hundred men from Jackson Co. are now en route for Douglas Co., K. T. St. Joseph and Weston are requested to furnish each the same number. The people of Kansas are to be subjugated at all hazards."

Yes! Kansas is to be subjugated at all hazards! and at the bidding of a governor who has never yet visited the people of the territory, but has entered into league and copartnership with the people in the border counties of another state, he being their "tool," while they find blood and treasure for the accomplishment of the designed subjugation. How the memory of such a lofty purpose must gladden his days as he treads softly the down-hill side of life!

2d. — Sunday. Last evening a meeting was held, according to previous arrangement, to discuss the merits of the new constitution. Judge Smith, Col. Lane, and others, addressed the meeting. Quite naturally the times in which we live, and the present circumstances surrounding us, occupied quite largely the attention of the meeting.

Several utterly false and distorted accounts of the officers in and about Lawrence were read from a *Leavenworth Herald* of the evening before, which so aroused the indignation of the meeting that they appointed a committee to collect carefully all the facts and have them published. The paper which was read also contained the information that Shannon had called out Richardson, of Mo., general of the militia. Some incendiary appeals from that as well as Independence papers were read.

A gentleman has just remarked that "it is the one act in Shannon's course which is perfectly consistent; a Missouri leader should have command of Missouri banditti."

Dr. Robinson, having been called upon several times to speak, also having been called from the hall two or three times, at last said, in a plain way, and in brief, that "It was a time, in his opinion, for acting rather than speaking; that Shannon had placed himself in a bad situation. At his bidding all these Missourians had come over to help him enforce the laws; but when they come to Lawrence they will find that nobody has broken any laws; for the people of Lawrence are a law-abiding people. Their real object was to destroy Lawrence; but it was a question whether they would attempt it without some pretext; and before the American people Shannon would be responsible for their conduct. Fearful of some atrocious act upon the part of his drunken rabble, he has been compelled to remove the most of them to the camps on the Wakarusa. They really were in a predicament. They were afraid to attack Lawrence without a pretext, and with reason. He had learned, but would not vouch for its truth, that Shannon had telegraphed to President Pierce for the troops at the forts. It was also reported that Pierce had telegraphed back again that he might have them, and, of course, he would get them. Of course he would disarm the people when an invading force of drunken Missourians was almost at our doors, and we have no protection in the government of the country. (Laughter, and cries of 'Of course.') Men of Lawrence, and free-state men, we must have courage, but with it we must have prudence! These men have come from Missouri to subjugate the free-state men, to crush the free-state movement, — their pretence, that outrages have been committed. They are sustained by all the United States authorities here; and while they do not think it essential that a good cause for fighting be given them, the authorities will wait at least for a plausible excuse before commencing to shed blood. This excuse must not be given them. Each man must be a committee of one to guard the reputation as well as lives of the free-state men. If the Missourians, partly from fear and partly from want of a sufficient pretext, have to go back without striking a blow, it will make them a laughing-stock, and redound fearfully against Shannon. This is the last struggle between freedom and slavery, and we must not flatter ourselves that it will be trivial or short. The free-state men must stand shoulder to shoulder, with an unbroken front, and stand or fall together in defence of their liberties and homes. These may be dark days, but the American people and the world will justify us, and the cause of right will eventually triumph." The enthusiasm with which these remarks were received evinced the deep feeling and determined spirit of the meeting.

A gentleman in from Lecompton, yesterday afternoon, reported a most cowardly affair, in which Gen. Clarke was the actor. He is the Indian agent, a most infamous man; so notorious for his evil deeds before coming here, that it is said his life would not be a moment safe where he previously lived. His infamy renders him, however, a better tool for this corrupt administration, and a proper ally for the other officials here. He has become alarmed for his safety, and a few evenings since sent to some of his pro-slavery friends to come to his house to act as guard. They, answering his request by their presence, were saluted by being fired upon as they reached his house. It happened on this wise. His fears were so great, causing him to hear an enemy in every footstep, or the rustling of a leaf, that, supposing the knock at the door was that of some free-state man, he ran out of the back door, around the corner of the house, shot the man who proved to be the friend he had sent for, and ran back again.

E. and I were sitting alone last evening, when loud shouts in the distance told of some new arrival. We opened the door, and looked out into the darkness. We could see nothing but the friendly lights, in the humble dwellings over the prairie, to the eastward, while they burned more brightly yet in the hall, and in the hotel, whose upper rooms are used for the committee and council rooms. Though a half mile from town, and nearly a quarter of a mile from neighbors, and those strangers, while the lights show that no one will be "caught napping," even at this late hour, we have no fears of danger. We feel sure the shouts were not those of invaders, as *their* yells are most unearthly. Again, in the distance, we heard the cheerful sounds go up to heaven, and reëchoed among the hills. We know, instinctively, that it is the spontaneous burst of welcome to some new relief-company.

The guard comes up ere long. They say to our queries of "What news?" "The 'Bloomington Boys' are in." "We've had a grand meeting." "We are going to protect ourselves." One laughingly says, "Protect ourselves from whom?" And after suggestions from the trio of young men, who have now been on guard four nights in this part of the town, making our house head-quarters, "that Shannon will not fight;" that "the Missourians will run at the first fire," and that "they, having been taught to believe the Yankees are cowards, will find their mistake;" that they are expecting to get land-warrants to pay them for their trouble in coming here, but may get an actual preëmption claim six feet by two instead; we are all of our old opinion that there is really very little actual danger. They may take the trouble to come here, some coming hundreds of miles, with their threats, their whiskey and their old shot-guns, — giving them a right to the name with which our guard has christened them, "The Shot-gun Battalion," — they may come with their music, in the shape of an old violin, and a rough, fierce-looking biped, to whom soap and a razor are unknown, clad in buckskin breeches, and red shirt; but the inspiration of the "Arkansas Traveller," among these half-drunken creatures, will never equal the "moral suasion," or the wholesome fear of a few Sharpe's rifles.

Our house was full last night, and of the capacity of our Kansas homes our eastern friends have no idea. Doctor brought several strangers home with him at a very late hour.

A startling incident occurred last night. One of our picket guards was fired upon. Two of the guard were sitting together, when a party of Missourians approached and fired six shots at them. Our men had strict orders not to fire, unless the emergency was desperate, and so bore the insult with remarkable prudence, and obeyed orders.

Our people are acting strictly upon the defensive, and these provocations are continually offered us to provoke a collision. They are endeavoring to draw them from the position which all the world will justify, that they may have a pretext for the destruction of Lawrence, which is really the whole cause of the invasion.

A clergyman was with us last night. He had come in from a neighboring settlement, and has been a resident of Missouri twenty-seven years. He knows them well therefore; their cruel and desperate characters. With the few who came with him to

Lawrence, he was attending a meeting some miles from home, but hearing that Lawrence was in imminent peril, without going to his home, or being sure that the word he sent his family would reach them, he put spurs to his horse and came to our relief.

Another clergyman from Vermont, with others, came in to breakfast this morning. So the time has come again when men, whose vocation it is to preach the word of truth, and to battle heroically in fierce struggles with error, have girded on another sword than that of the spirit; and if the victory is to be won by sharp fighting, while they "pray and watch" they work, too — the working evincing the spirit of the prayer.

The times seem strange! Ministers of the gospel of peace buckling on the armor which is to insure them physical safety! Two thousand years have passed away since the angel-choirs rejoiced together, ushering in the glad news of a new gospel, and the tidings of good-will and peace reverberating over Judea's hills. When will men learn the lesson? With our defence strong and secure, made fully known to our foes, there will be no bloodshed. So we all feel, and things which seem warlike are in reality peace-bearing measures.

Another event happened last night, which occasioned uneasiness, viz., the appearance of McCrea, an escaped prisoner, in our midst. His presence, were it known to the enemy, would be a new source of difficulty, and at once cause an outbreak. Few of the citizens knew he was here, and he is already on his way to a land of safety.

How the blood boils in our veins, when we think of all the indignities imposed upon us by the slave power, by the infamous, the execrable corruption of the administration! No words can express the depth of infamy to which it has gone, in endeavoring to crush out on this soil, made sacred to freedom by a pledge inviolate, free speech, free action and free men.

McCrea had been for months imprisoned in a close, ill-ventilated place. A bill was found against him for murder, but a change of venue was at last effected. These men, who saw themselves about to be foiled of their prey for which with unabated eagerness for six months they had hunted, had made preparations to take him from the jail and lynch him; when, foreseeing this, McCrea escaped. He came to this place, which has been regarded by all our friends as the Sevastopol of Kansas, expecting to find safety and repose. But we can offer none. The same power which sought his life so desperately, seeks ours with the same malignity. We abide the hour with patience, and feel sure that all the tears, the anxieties, the sleepless nights, and weary days, of the heart-stricken wife, now left in uncertainty as to her husband's fate, are all counted by Him, "who seeth the end from the beginning," and that they who have mingled this cup of bitterness will find their reward.

Everything has been so quiet to-day, having no extra company, save some gentlemen to tea, that we forget we may be on the verge of a civil convulsion; that, ere another Sabbath sun arises, we may be homeless, ay, and friendless, if our enemies perform a tithe of that they threaten.

A friend has sat here all day, quietly writing for the eastern press. He takes great interest in the success of the cause, and has several times been in the camp of the enemy, spying out the land. He has brought back interesting "notes of travel," and passed through some hair-breadth escapes. He has a genial, happy nature, peculiar to the Scotch, and, as he tells his adventures with a slight brogue, and a quick, rapid utterance, enlivened by his sense of the ridiculous, one cannot help feeling that he is surrounded by Gov. Shannon's half-tipsy military, or hears the sounds of music drawn out of a violin by some fierce disciple of Paganini, and sees the gaping crowds of men, armed with bowie-knives and pistols, nodding their admiration.

To-day was set for the attack, and the day has passed. The weather has become much colder, and I fancy there are some in the camps who would be glad if they were home again, by a cheerful fire. The men in the camps are getting impatient, but slowly are they reïnforced in small numbers. They come with an appearance of reluctance, but the offer of a dollar and a half a day and a land warrant is said to be the successful inducement to aid in this infamous invasion, and its author no less infamous.

CHAPTER X.

WAKARUSA WAR—INCIDENTS.

Dec. 3d.—Last evening the governor's proclamation, though issued on the 29th, was received. It is one mass of falsehoods and misstatements, and an incendiary appeal to the bad passions of the border men to come in to assist him in our destruction. Jones goes to him with most malignant untruths of a rescue from his hands of the prisoner, by a band of forty men, etc. (It is now stated that Coleman was with the posse, and armed himself at Franklin with pistols and bowie-knives to act with Jones' posse.) The rescue was ten miles from Lawrence. Two men in the rescue are all who have ever been citizens of Lawrence. Gov. Shannon, without the discretion which a man possessing even a common share of sense would show, issued his bloody proclamation, which deserves no place in the archives of history, against the citizens of Lawrence.

While no effort has been made to make a single arrest, he says they are in a state of rebellion against the laws, and utters fierce cries of "revolution," and "civil war." We would that we had a governor less imbecile and senseless.

On Saturday the immortal Jones came into town. While he sat upon his horse, bolt upright, looking defiant, his eyes wandered restlessly here and there, as if expecting some unseen enemy, and his hands trembled. Some boys, whose fun was brimming over, asked him if he was cold.

His thin lips parted, and an abrupt "No" was uttered.

"Then have you the chills?" asked they in a sympathetic tone.

The same sound, and the same monosyllable, only a little more abrupt and stern, was issued.

He evidently did not like the Yankee sympathy when such weighty matters were resting on his shoulders. But, being asked what he wanted in Lawrence, he replied, "I will let you know when I get ready." Then, putting spurs to his horse, he wheeled around, amid the laugh of the three or four frolicksome youths, and the blue coat of the Missourian was last seen going over the hill on the way to Lecompton. He had made, in his estimation, no doubt, a fearful escape from the stronghold of the rebels.

Yesterday, the rumors of war being still rife, and so many citizens of the near settlements having come in, arrangements were made for the companies to go into barracks. The large dining-hall of the new hotel being fitted up with stoves, several of the companies will occupy it, while others have a "soldier's home" in the hall which has been used for school-room, church, etc. The quartermaster and commissary-general have been appointed. Beef and corn are brought in in large quantities, and preparations are being made for a siege.

The soldiers are drilling out on the prairie, and under the command of Col. Lane, who has seen actual service and hard fighting in Mexico. Their evolutions are well performed. As we look upon them, going through the drill soberly, without noise, and no rabble of boys following, we feel that, before yielding to the unjust exactions of a partisan government, they would meet death.

There is young manhood in the ranks, and some who have not yet counted their score of years; but the mantle of discretion and prudence has fallen upon them. The blood of '76 runs in their veins, and the fires of its unquenched love of liberty sparkle in their eyes.

We are yet in the hollow of His hand who "hates the oppressor," and "the crooked ways before us He will make straight."

A Mr. N., of Vermont, is just in. He called to see doctor a few moments since, and has now returned with him from the council-room, and will make our house his home. He brings news of our pleasant Scotch friend, who left us this morning on another tour of observation, in the enemy's camp. He met him at "Fish's," some two miles below the ford, on the Wakarusa, of which the enemy have taken possession, having escaped from their hands. They recognized him as some one from Lawrence, he having been so frequently in their camp. They disarmed him at first; but, on his threatening them with proceedings, they returned the pistol, and he is now on his way to report to Gov. Shannon the conduct of his militia. As they kept him a good while in camp, he learned much of their method of proceeding. Sentries are posted at all the fords on the Wakarusa, with strict orders to search and disarm every one attempting to pass. An old gentleman from Lawrence is a prisoner in their camp. They keep him bound.

Mr. P. attempted to persuade Mr. N. to go further up the river before attempting to cross, it being utter folly to try to get past them at that point; but, by a most skilful manœuvre, he blinded the enemy in gallant style, and came through bearing important despatches.

He has a very military air about him, and, as he reined in his horse a moment, then dashing in among the rough outposts at the crossing, and, in a stern voice, said, "Why don't you demand the countersign?" they looked astonished, and he passed through. They evidently supposed him to be one of their officers. Coming, as they have, from several different counties, the majority of the men and officers are strangers to each other.

In the camp Mr. N. gave the military salute, and commenced an easy off-hand talk with the men. One of the unshaven apologies for manhood asked, "Did you see many of our boys coming?"

Mr. N. replied, "No, I saw more returning;" as he in fact met fifty, whose faces were set homewards, their patience being wearied out with waiting for the gathering together of their sheriff's posse.

The questioner, with downcast look, then said, "Then we may as well give it up; for the Lawrence boys will take us like mice."

When some of the men very blandly asked if they should take care of his horse, his reply, that "he thought he would look around a little first," satisfied them, and he pursued his journey.

He soon reached the village of Franklin, where fifty or more of these men were loitering, and attending most assiduously upon some half a dozen groceries. It seemed at first a matter of some doubt whether he could pass them; but, with the military salute, and gracefully bowing, he went on unmolested, and reached us in safety.

Another fact of some moment, learned to-day, is that as the invaders pass the Shawnee Mission, they are all enrolled by the governor.

One's indignation would exceed every other feeling were it not for the wonder that any man can be guilty of such consummate folly!

Spies from the enemy's camp are in Lawrence every day. They gain all the information they can, which, I judge from the merriment of the guard, in talking over the visit of a spy, is not always so reliable as it might be.

Dr. Wood has moved his family out of town. So, also, have other pro-slavery men. Dr. Wood is in the camp of the enemy. A young man, who claims to be free-state, has repeatedly warned a lady of his acquaintance — a widow with small children — of the approaching onset, and that no one in the town will be safe from indiscriminate slaughter. He begs of her to remove to a pro-slavery residence, a mile out, and there he will insure her safety.

She sends her children to the proposed place of security to sleep; but, like a true woman, remains at home, to perform those duties which the hour renders imperative.

This youth, who, notwithstanding his protestations of being a free-state man, has had a wondrous fellow-feeling for the pro-slavery party, — opening his house for their storage of provisions at the time of the first invasion, — now complains of illness, and neither comes into town, nor goes down to the enemy's camp. Another man, a Mr. Cox, who has been strong in his expressions of sympathy with the free-state cause, is now a spy among us. He has hoisted upon his store a sign telling who he is, and asking that his property may not be destroyed.

Our fair-weather friends are now obliged to show their true colors, and the certain knowledge of their treachery is worth much to a community situated as we are. Eighty men from Topeka have arrived.

4th. — Early morning calls are all I see of the doctor now, as there is continually something in the council-room to demand attention, and last night they held a council of war to decide upon what further measures shall be taken for our defence.

Forts and entrenchments are to be thrown up, under the direction of Col. Lane. Reports have come in of three hundred men between here and Westport, three hundred at the Wakarusa, some two hundred now crossing the Delaware Reserve towards Lawrence, — the Platte County Rifles being of the number, — making in all a force eight hundred strong for the destruction, the annihilation of Lawrence.

Our guard are now fired upon nightly. Last night a bullet passed through the hat of one of the guard, instead of his head, for which it was doubtless intended.

The chilly breath of the last few days has given place to the warm, balmy airs of September. I watch the guard upon the hills, and stationed at different points in the prairies — foot guard as well as mounted. Some are standing quietly, while the two hours of some others have expired, and they are going through a rapid change of position. There are horsemen, also wagons, passing up over the Lecompton road, to reïnforce the company at Lecompton, and swift riders are going in and out of town, while the flag — the sign of invasion — floats over our house. This flag was run up days ago, and can be seen at a great distance.

In the midst of my reveries arising from all this strange scene, the uncouth face of a Missourian presented itself close by me, only the window between. That we looked at each other, I am sure, and from the looks of his physiognomy, and from a certainty as to the nature of my own feelings, I am equally sure neither of us were pleased. He, however, seemed strongly attracted towards the house, was only content after taking a general survey of three sides of it, and came a little nearer than any rules of propriety would allow. He passed on, at length, and seated himself in the tall grass on the top of the hill for half an hour. He was evidently a spy, not upon us only, but the whole town.

While we were at dinner, two other men, evidently in authority, rode out on the point of the hill, to take a survey of the town. They rode very slowly past the house, examining the whole premises, and looking backwards, until they reached the summit of the hill beyond. It looked like a silent threat, coming at the hour, too, when they supposed we would have company to dine, and the leaders of the defence.

Just before noon one of the "staff" (just appointed) came up, and, upon my opening the door, he said, "Good-morning, Mrs. R.; the doctor sent me after his horse;" and, as he vaulted into his saddle, with a ringing laugh he said, "Excuse me, Mrs. R., I meant the general."

So I suppose that the quiet doctor, who has always been remarked for the meekness of his bearing, is metamorphosed into a general. He was appointed last evening. To the never-failing question, "Is there anything new?" he tells me, "The men are anxious to form companies of riflemen, and go down to Franklin;" that "with one round the Missourians would fly like frightened hares." "The people are getting impatient, and nothing but giving up their position, of acting strictly upon the defensive, keeps them from driving them out of the borders."

Soldiers are on drill all the afternoon. A cavalry company is also formed. There are about four hundred armed men in Lawrence now, and if there is a fight there will be terrible slaughter among the Missourians. This they know, and they are still waiting for reïnforcements. What an unheard of sheriff's posse this will be! The companies have been firing at a mark set on the hill near us, and the rifle-balls went far beyond.

5th. — More than a week has passed since an attack was threatened, and not one blow has been struck yet. I was awakened early this morning — about four o'clock — by a loud knocking at the door. It was quickly opened. Mr. P. and our Scotch friend — whose name has also the same initial letter — have had narrow escapes from the enemy, and an escape less fearful from a grave in the Kansas. They were dripping wet, and so chilled with the water and the keen air, that the stove heat did little good, and they

12

soon tried a warm bed, leaving me to dry their clothes, papers, and money, which were all thoroughly soaked.

After Mr. N., who arrived here on Monday, left "Fish's," the brave Scotchman started for the mission, to bring his grievances before the governor. He was not at the mission, and, hearing he was at Westport, he followed on, went to the hotels, but could find him nowhere. He learned there, however, that Gov. Shannon had received instructions from Washington, authorizing his proceedings, and that many more are going to his aid from Westport; large numbers having already congregated there from the border towns. He heard many of their plans thoroughly discussed, as he sat by, the substance of which seems to be that there shall be a war, that the rescuers shall be delivered up, that all arms shall be given up, the leaders lynched, and the others driven from the country. He heard men high in authority say, that "now was the time; the river was just about to close; no reïnforcements could arrive for the free-state men; there were only some thirty-five hundred of them in the territory, and if they were not cut off now, they never could be; that slavery must and should go into Kansas; that they would have Kansas, though they have to wade to their knees in blood to get it; that they should fight, and let the Union go to the d—l!" Judge Johnson, and a young man who recently came with him, had been arrested, and the threats were not few that they would be lynched in a few days.

Learning that the governor had left Westport, our friend pursued his journey towards Kansas city; and, when about half way there, was again arrested by a band of armed men. They said, to his query, "By what authority am I a prisoner?" "By Gov. Shannon's orders." They seemed a little puzzled at his pertinent remark upon this information, "You forget, gentlemen, that we are in Missouri;" and, in the moment of wavering which followed, our friend hoped that the scales would turn in his favor, and he be allowed to go quietly on his way. But the fiat had gone forth. No one but a known pro-slavery man, or the territorial authorities, who are given over, with all their interests, to the furthering of the nefarious schemes of Atchison and Stringfellow, can travel safely in the territory, or in Missouri. Our friend was conducted to a house a little way from the road, and, as he stood before the fire, hearing their expressions of glee at the capture of some prominent free-state men, and their threats of soon lynching them, also ruminating upon his own chances of escape, he espied upon one of them a sign of membership of an odd-fellow's lodge. He made to him the sign of distress, and, by the rules of the order, he was bound to protect him. This man at once interested himself. He said to the others, the examination of the prisoner must be private, and he must make it. The rest of the ruffians agreed to it, and, in a room by themselves, he took the papers in his hand, which the prisoner gave him, then returned them, and said, "His life has been saved at his own peril."

This examination was made somewhat superficially, and with apologies. The next morning, through the interposition of this brother odd-fellow, the prisoner was released, the odd-fellow taking his hand at parting, and asking his pardon. He said, also, "Don't think hard of me, brother. I have done all I could. You were in danger, and I had two duties to perform. I am a member of another order, and am bound to act, and *dare not refuse.* Nor do I want to. I am a border ruffian, nor am I ashamed of it. We shall have Kansas — we won't be cheated out of it. When they passed the Kansas bill, the pledge to us was that the South should have Kansas, and the North Nebraska; but the d—d emigrant aid societies, and other abolitionists, expect to cheat us out of it. But they can't. We are going to have Kansas, if we wade to the knees in blood to get it."

After reaching Kansas city, our friend, in company with Mr. P., left for Lawrence. As it was impossible to go by Westport, they crossed the river about a mile from Kansas city, and came up the north side, thus being obliged to cross again at Lawrence. As they went into the ferry-boat, two men, whom they had seen hanging about the hotel at Kansas, were sitting on the bank. On seeing them, they arose and hastily took the direction towards Kansas city. The evident plan was to go back to Westport, and there get a crowd to intercept them as they should pass through the Delaware Reserve. By taking the Indian trails, now one, and then another, they reached a friendly mission-house, where an

Indian guide was furnished them. At about ten o'clock they left there for Lawrence, twenty-six miles lying between them and the end of their route. As noiselessly as possible they pursued their way through the woods and darkness. They moved on stealthily as men would whose lives were in hourly peril from the enemy seen and unseen. Our young friend, having already been twice in their hands, could have little to hope for on a third arrest. When within three miles of Lawrence, they came upon a camp-fire which had been recently left, but saw no one. The Indian overheard them talking of forcing their way through the guard, should they come upon one, in preference to being taken into their camp, and refused to go further. Every inducement offered was unavailing. So, without a guide, chilled with the keen night air, weary with the excitement and want of rest, they pressed on.

Before this, however, the question of the ford at Lawrence had been discussed. Mr. P. had "never been over, but he thought he knew where it was." The young traveller "had seen people cross, and perhaps he could find it." And now the ford was reached. The ferryman lived in Lawrence, the other side of the river. The enemy might be lurking behind any of these trees. It would not do to halloo for the boat, and the ford must be attempted on horseback.

Mr. P. said to the very slenderly-built young man, who was mounted on a little Indian pony, "You go in first." He replied to the other, who rode a strong horse, and is himself of aldermanic proportions, "I do not know the ford. I have only seen people cross."

But delays were dangerous, and the young man thought "it would not be right to urge such an old man to encounter the dangers first," and gently urged his little pony in. The channel was very deep, and the waters swift. He was carried into the current, and was being borne rapidly down. He was swept out of the saddle, and held on by the pommel. He struggled long in the water, and for a few moments he thought "the *Tribune* would require another Kansas correspondent." At last, by extraordinary effort, he was again on terra firma, having for several moments only been able to keep his head above water.

Mr. P., in the mean time, went in a little way, but, seeing the desperate condition of his friend, returned to the shore. The young Scotchman said, in his facetious way, "I was so thoroughly chilled and exhausted then, I had as lieve fall into the enemy's hands as die so, and we hallooed for the boat for half an hour."

Word came this morning from Franklin that teams, loaded with freight for our merchants here, had been overhauled at the camp on the Wakarusa. All powder and ammunition were taken from them, while the wagons, loaded wholly with apples, potatoes and flour, were stopped entirely, and not allowed to proceed. So they intend to starve us out, or make us surrender.

The hot blood of some of our men chafes at these indignities, and they can hardly be restrained from an attack upon the camp, leaving not one to tell the tale of the infamous invasion.

A despatch must be sent to Washington, and Mr. P. accepts the mission. He is to go through Iowa, and will leave this afternoon, but thinks he must go to Kansas city first. We attempt to dissuade him, knowing the dangers of the route, which thicken every hour.

Early in the afternoon he left for Kansas city, going through the Reserve, to go thence to Iowa.

Soon after he went, I called upon some new neighbors in the valley west of us. They are western people, and the lady especially has the western peculiarities of speech.

She was sweeping the door-way as I approached the little log cabin; and, never having seen her, I said, "Good-afternoon. Is it Mrs. ——?"

"Yes; come in," was the hearty reply.

There was wealth of good-nature and a whole-souled welcome in the very manner of the greeting. As I stepped in, I told her who I was; but, rather in doubt as to who I might be, she said, "Mrs. or Miss?"

Although I replied Mrs., she looked still doubtful, and said, "Do you live in the house on the hill?"

My reply being in the affirmative, and my identity being distinctly understood, we sat down and talked of the war. In the mean time I noticed with how little room one can make comfort and draw enjoyment. There were two beds, one double and the other single, looking so nicely with their white spreads and clean linen. There were table, stove and book-case, all in the same small room. There were white curtains at the one little window; and the room was really so small, that at meals they were obliged to sit down around the table before the leaves were spread, having everything placed on the middle of it.

They say they would rather live in Iowa, where they came from. They do not like to live where there is so much disturbance, and, when the husband and father is from home, they are continually fearful lest some evil has befallen him.

He soon came in. He is a tall, blue-eyed man, of most prepossessing appearance, a native of Georgia, and has come to add his influence in the early settlement of his country, hoping to plant all the institutions of freedom. He said "he had looked with indescribable interest upon all the means taken for our defence, and though as a minister he could not bear arms, he still has faith in Cromwell's motto, 'Trust in God, and keep your powder dry.'"

As we were talking of the war, Mrs. —— said, with her clear, ringing voice, "What does your old man think of it?"

I answered as well as I could, and am amused at this appellation, purely western, she has given my husband.

The Missourians threaten to kill all our men, and save the women for a more bitter fate; and the black flag, now waving over their camp, is eminently suggestive of their piratical designs, — plunder, blood and rapine.

The evening was cold and dark, and chilly gusts of wind swept around the house, flapping the flag wildly, while the staff strikes against the roof. The wind creeps in too through the half-inch siding, and the stove continually cries "more wood."

All this reminds us of chilly days coming, and of the cold winds, and snows, against which the unplastered houses are a poor defence; and we realize that this invasion, let it end as it may, is not only a source of suffering in the present, but in the future will be the occasion of distress, to this persecuted people.

Now is the time when they ought, and would be, prepaing for winter.

As we looked out into the chilly night, we saw the great fires blazing around the forts, and the men busily plying their shovels. Night and day, taking turns by fifties, with unabated ardor, the work goes on. There will be five strong forts commanding the river and all the entrances to the town.

The men, as they work the hard-frozen earth, think of home, wife and little ones. Some are here, but some are far away, not dreaming of the dire evils which threaten the loved one. They think of their country and their God, and courage and the consciousness of doing well fill the heart, and strength nerves the arm. A tyranny less outrageous than this was overthrown by their fathers, and shall they falter when more precious rights are in peril?

As the faithful time-piece says the night is fast waning towards its mid hour, there is a welcome knock at the door, and, opening it, I find our Scotch friend is standing close to the door, with a long rifle by his side. I had tried to persuade him not to go down town after so much excitement and weariness of the last two days and nights; but his enthusiasm in the cause will not let him rest, — besides, he is one of the general's aids, and has been attending the council of war held this evening. He says, "It is decided to send a messenger to Gov. Shannon, to ask him what is the meaning of this armed body of men quartered near our town; why he allows them to commit robberies upon our people and harass travellers, disarming them and taking them prisoners; requesting him also to order their removal." To my inquiries, Mr. P. said, "There is danger in the undertaking, but L. and B. are going. They are acquainted with the governor, and they know the password." We hope they may get through without detention.

After making beds upon the floor, and putting extra blankets on the lounge for any who may drop in for a nap before morning, replenishing the fire, I leave for my own room. And before sleeping, I wonder if we do indeed live in America, — the so-much-boasted land, — or whether, in her prosperity, her love of power and aggrandizement has proved the grave of all honor, patriotism and love of freedom. The question will arise, also, whether Gov. Shannon's heart has become a stony heart, thus to bring a force against his own people. This has puzzled wiser brains than mine, and so I sleep, restlessly. I dream of a royal palace where there are men sitting. They are steeped in wine. There is revelry and confusion. They talk boldly of the evil deeds with which their lives are filled, and they swear they will fill up the measure of their wickedness. They ask aid of one who seems to be in authority; and with the brimming beaker he pledges them he will go with them heart and soul in their deeds of blood. What to him is his plighted honor to a great people, or what murdered innocence and the cries of heart-stricken widows and orphans, whose homes are made desolate by the strong arm of the oppressor? Naught to him are these; so he retains the seat in the royal palace which he has disgraced, and is the representative of the law he has rendered a sad mockery. But the wine-cup falls, his knees knock together, his glaring eyes are fixed, and on the wall are characters written in living colors, unseen by all save him; but the bony, bloodless hand — death's hand — writes, and the words burn his soul, "Mene, mene, tekel, upharsin."

The dream is over, and with the waking comes a realization that the days of the tyrant will end, as surely as revolution is born of oppression; peace and quiet springing from the broken system of tyranny, as surely as morning cometh from the night, and strength is born of sorrow.

CHAPTER XI.

THE DEATH OF BARBER — THE TREATY.

Dec. 6th. — Thursday. We were awakened again, long before daylight. Some friends have had a long journey from the country above. They were not considered safe here, and had gone far away, but they heard that Lawrence had been attacked, doctor and fifteen others killed; and thinking that the war had fairly opened, they had walked thirty miles in the last few hours, that they might with their friends strike and die for liberty.

The guard are again fired upon, and more of our messengers to different parts of the territory and to the states taken prisoners. Horsemen, in companies of four and six, are continually riding over the hills. They are the leading men in the ranks of the enemy; and we hear their design is to plant their artillery on Mt. Oread, and take this house for barracks. They seem to be looking around with the intention of concluding their plans. We feel perfectly safe so far as the planting of their artillery is concerned. Not one man could stand before the deadly fire of the Sharpe's rifles, from the town or ravine. The Missourians are still slowly gathering in at Lecompton, and the camp near Franklin, and the new one on the Wakarusa, south of us, and only about four miles from town. Our supplies are cut off. People are turned from their homes at midnight, and their corn-cribs and hay-stacks burned.

Some other gentlemen also dined with us. They were unexpected guests, nevertheless welcome. Just before dinner, we saw a large mounted party of the enemy's force going over the hill beyond us. We also saw two men on the west side of the hill, coming cautiously towards the house. It looked to us as though it were impossible for them to escape the observation of the enemy, and we watched them anxiously, almost breathlessly, as they slowly were nearing us. The horsemen, fortunately, instead of going on to the summit, kept a little under the eastern slope, and, thank God! our friends were safe. The reason of their coming over was a simple one. They had been guilty of aiding in the rescue of an innocent man from a gang of desperadoes. A gang of men had been prowling about their house all the morning; not all in one body, but at different points, and in such a manner as to excite suspicions of evil intended against them. Finally, this scouting band of the governor's militia all at once started in the direction of their head-quarters, and our friends immediately came over the hills, seeking a safer place. Our messengers fly back and forth to town, and one of them concludes to go to his home in the states, for a little time. We send to his wife to come and see him, and for the first time I begin to feel that the horrors of war are opening upon us. Men, for doing an act of kindness, are hunted for their lives, and daily and nightly watching alone saves them from falling into the hands of the enemy. I go continually from one part of the house to the other, to see if any spies are about, and once fell into a laughable mistake. Having gone up stairs to have a long look out over hill and prairie, I saw a woman upon the west side of the hill. I ran down and said to the gentlemen, "There is a woman coming to the house. Will you step in the dining-room and see if it is any one you would like to see; if not, you can go up stairs." They looked out, and one of them said, "Why, that's my wife."

I laughed as heartily as they, but did not diminish my watchfulness, because once I was "more scared than hurt."

The men were at work on a part of the forts, while some were complete; entrenchments were being thrown up on each side of Massachusetts-street; the soldiers were drilling through the centre of the broad street; ladies were standing in the doorways looking on; while little boys, having caught the general spirit of a resort to arms, were marching about in martial array, with feathers in their paper cocked-hats and imitation guns.

D. R. Atchison, with twenty-five men, was said to be crossing the reserve, towards the camp on the Wakarusa. The men were anxious to go out, and bring him in a prisoner, but the general was firm. We are acting only on the defensive.

The howitzer has just arrived, and several men are guarding it in one of the lower rooms. Some ladies go in to look at the grape and bomb-shells.

It was rumored that Mr. P. has been taken prisoner by the Missourians, and taken into their camp, on the Wakarusa. The indignation of the people is increasing in intensity, and their forbearance growing less. The twelve-pound brass howitzer was brought in by a manœuvre evincing tact and skill, as well as bravery. The council, having heard of its arrival at Kansas city, decided if possible it must be brought up, and three or four of our citizens, willing to encounter the danger, offered their services for the undertaking. They found the boxes in which it was packed, at the warehouse, consigned to one of our merchants. The proprietor of the warehouse suggested there might be rifles in them, and, to quiet all suspicion, Mr. B., with an axe, raised a board from the largest box, saying, "Let's see what there is."

As they looked in, and saw only wheels, he said, "It's only another of H.'s carriages."

Everything was satisfactory. The board was renailed. The boxes were loaded in the wagons, with mattresses and other furniture on the top, and they left Kansas city, by the ferry route. The wagons getting set as they went up the steep bank on the opposite side of the river, Mr. B. called upon a band of Missourians, standing by, "to give them a lift at the wheels," which they did, and without difficulty they reached Lawrence, where they were received with loud acclamations by the citizens. The little besieged town received with it good cheer, hope and courage.

A lady from Ohio, whose husband has ever been most active in the free-state cause, and for whom the enemy feel no little bitterness, has offered her little "shake" cabin, next the hotel, for the general use. Daily and nightly the ladies meet there, in the one room, with its loose, open floor, through which the wind creeps, to make cartridges; their nimble fingers keeping time with each heart-beat for freedom, so enthusiastic are they in aiding the defence.

At evening, the young Scotchman with his constant companion, the long rifle, came in. He looked sedate, as, seating himself on the lounge, he said, "The war has commenced. They have shot a man, about five miles from here."

"Who?" and "Is he dead?" were the questions which followed in quick succession.

"A Mr. Barber, one of the men who came in to our assistance from Bloomington. He died almost instantly. It is said that Dr. Wood was in the crowd that shot him."

He said besides, "It is almost impossible to restrain the men to-night. Their imprecations of vengeance are loud and deep, and the general has something to do to restrain his own feelings. A guard have gone out to bring in the body."

The plot thickens. Our men are shot down in the broad sunlight by this ruffianly horde. Can the governor say, "My soul is clear of my brother's blood?" The messengers sent to him have returned, and they come with the promise from him that he will be here to-morrow. The governor sent a long letter to General R., and others in command. It was very indefinite, and non-committal, and evinced some tact in the author, to write so much, and yet say so little to any purpose. Upon one point alone was it clear; that is, the enforcement of the laws. In his conversation he was a little more definite. He said he was unable to restrain the men, his militia, though he had repeatedly commanded them to preserve order. He was endeavoring also to shake off the responsibility of this Missouri mob, but the following pass, given to a gentleman who dined with us to-day, will show he has some connection with it:

"Mr. Jones, Sheriff, *or any other in command.* Mr. Winchell is going, on business of his own, to Lawrence; please pass him without detention or molestation. WILSON SHANNON."

Col. Lane has received a small limb of a tree, with a bullet in it, and hemp bound round it, from the enemy's camp, with the compliments of Col. Burns, of Missouri. Dr. Wood was in company with Burns at the time it was sent.

7th. — The murdered man was brought into town last night, and in his usual dress, laid upon a table in the hotel. His look was one of perfect repose, with the pallor of the death sleep. The circumstances of his death show more clearly than anything which has previously transpired, the malignity, the utter heartlessness of the foe with whom we have to deal. This certainly convinces us that no mercy will be shown any who fall into their hands.

Mr. Barber, hearing that the lives of the people of Lawrence were in peril, had come, with others in his neighborhood, to lend his aid in making good our defence. Yesterday he mounted his horse, and, bidding his comrades "Good-by," saying that he "would be back in the morning," wholly unarmed, started for his home. Doubtless, as he sped over the prairies on his way, he thought of the glad surprise his coming would give his wife after this few days' absence, and with whom, on leaving for Lawrence, the bitterness of the parting, her unwillingness for him to go, seemed but a foreshadowing of his sad fate. A little after he had left the main road, with his two friends who accompanied him, two horsemen rode out from a company of twelve on the California road, Dr. Wood being one of them. They told him to go with them. In reply to their several questions he said, he "had been to Lawrence, was unarmed, was going to his home;" and, putting spurs to his horse, rode on; but the deadly bullet of the foul creature, the tool of the administration, entered his back, and, saying "O God! I am a murdered man!" he never spoke again.

The home to which he hasted he never reached, but his spirit is an avenging witness before the Higher Court, where all these deeds of blood are held in remembrance.

General George W. Clarke, the Indian Agent, went on his way to meet Governor Shannon at the Wakarusa head-quarters, and there declared with horrid oaths, "I have sent another of these d—d abolitionists to his winter-quarters."

The feeling that her husband would be murdered had haunted the timid wife, but friends kept this dread knowledge from her until this morning.

Words can never convey the mingling emotions which moved the crowd, or the heart-crushing agony of the young wife. There were no children in the household, and all the affections had twined around this one idol. All of life, all of happiness, were centred in him; and to be bereaved thus, was adding bitterness to the agony. It seemed as though her heart must break, and, in her distress and shrieks, the brave, strong-hearted men mingled tears and muttered imprecations of vengeance upon the murderers, and upon him who had brought these murderers into our midst.

The hour approached for the arrival of the governor, who is coming to treat of peace. Already he was coming over the prairie with his suite. The carriage was a covered double-seated one, in which he occupies the back seat. With horsemen riding front and in the rear, the cavalcade moved on. In front of the hotel, lines of citizen soldiery were drawn out, and they knew there was a prospect of a settlement of these difficulties without further bloodshed. Can these men, whose murdered comrade now lies within these walls, make peace and he be unavenged? Their feelings revolt at such a proposal; but the magnanimity of their leaders, who propose pacification, calms the troubled waters, and they realize that peace is better than war, though the hot blood, crying revenge, still chafes. The carriage passed in through the soldiery to the door, and Gen. Robinson and the governor went through the halls, and up the unfinished stairways to the council-chamber.

As the eyes of the governor fell upon the rigid limbs, and the death-pallor of the young man, who yesterday was so full of life, hope, and strength, he gave a perceptible shrug of his shoulders. The governor's suite also entered, and as they passed the silent dead, Col. Boone, of Westport, said, "I did not expect such a thing as this." What else could they expect from the barbarous men gathered here by their murderous appeals?

They were introduced to the Committee of Safety in the large reception-room. Then the governor and Col. Boone, on the part of the invaders, and Gen. Robinson and Col. Lane, on the part of the citizens, held a private session in the council-chamber. They talked over the whole matter. The governor asked that the arms be delivered up. He was soon satisfied, however, that such conditions of peace would never be complied with, and said at last that such a demand was unreasonable. The papers which are to be signed will be made out to-night, and signed by both parties on the morrow.

The governor sent for troops from the fort this morning at three o'clock. He wants to gain time, and delay signing the papers, as he said that "he could not control the force he has brought against us." "If they knew a treaty had been made, they would at once raise the black flag, and march against the town." So, as he is hoping Col. Sumner will send his troops for the defence of Lawrence, this delay is made. When our citizens sent to him days ago for aid, he refused, because he had no orders from the President; and the question is, will he come now?

About three o'clock the governor and suite, consisting of Col. Boone, of Westport, Col. Kearney, of Independence, and Col. Strickland, also of Missouri, with Col. Lane, dined with us.

The governor is a gray-haired man, tall and well-proportioned. He has coarse features and a hard-looking face, generally. Nature must bear a part of the blame, but the weather and bad whiskey, doubtless, come in for a share. However, mild eyes, and a good height of forehead, show that naturally he is not a cruel man; but his head lacks firmness, as we speak phrenologically, and his course here, as well as elsewhere, is evidence that he is vacillating, weak, ill-suited to be the leader of other men; that he is credulous, and easily made a tool in the hands of base men; that, in brief, he is the exponent of the purposes and actions of the men, or party, with whom he is most thrown in contact.

Crowds of horsemen were passing over and down the hill. Some of them were our mounted guard — others were from the camps of the invaders. The enemy have now nearly surrounded us. The camp on the Wakarusa, just south of Lawrence, cuts off connection with the southern settlements. There are strolling bands of men all through the Delaware Reserve, while quite a body of them are camped in the woods just opposite the town, preventing people passing to and from Leavenworth, and other colonies north. They still have camps at Lecompton, and below Franklin.

Yesterday, two of our ladies went out some ten miles, and brought in two kegs of powder. The guard of the invaders halted them, but apologized by saying, "I thought you were gentlemen."

Some of the enemy entered the house of Judge Wakefield, six miles from Lawrence. They ransacked it; and, going into the chambers, fired through the floor, the ball passing directly by the head of a sick lady, who was lying on a bed in the lower room. They have committed depredations upon the property of the Indians, at which they felt outraged. They are constantly taking prisoners any people from other settlements, coming to our aid, unless in large numbers; and we feel constant anxiety for our messengers who have been out some time.

Coleman, the murderer, fired into our guard; the fire was returned, the ball taking effect in the mule he was riding. It died soon after reaching Franklin. Had the guard known the man, he would have escaped less easily.

Gov. Shannon was in town again to-day. Col. Sumner declined to send any force, because he cannot act without orders from the President. The treaty was made with the people. The governor made a speech to the soldiers, telling them he has been laboring under a mistake; that if there were Missourians here they came of their own accord; that he had called upon none but the people of the territory. They would now disperse. He believed the people of Lawrence were a law-abiding people; indeed, he had learned that he had misunderstood them, and that they were an estimable and orderly people. He was glad to find there was no occasion for an attack upon the town, and no laws had been violated, etc. Cheers were attempted, but the muffled sound was little like the spontaneous, outgushing gladness of a satisfied people. There was yet a suspicion among them that the terms of peace had been too easily entered into; that something of their rights had been conceded by their leaders. The officers in command also made addresses, which more heartily called forth the expression of the people; and, with the governor, Generals Robinson and Lane went down to Franklin to meet the officers in the invading army. The governor had desired them to do so, because many of the leaders in his army were determined upon the guns being delivered up, and he wished some other convincing arguments than his own to be used with them.

The night was exceedingly tempestuous. The wind raged with unequalled fury, and was full of driving snow and sleet. All of the afternoon it had been so strong and furious, that boards, ten or twelve feet long, lying in a pile back of the house, had been blown, end over end, in every direction. But the night had added violence to the storm, and scarcely anything could make headway against, or live long out in it. Our Scotch friend had just come in with ears almost frozen.

We pity the guard who faithfully watch for our safety in such a wild night as this. The password for the night, "Pitch in," given by our gallant Adjutant-General Dietzler, who has command in the temporary absence of General Robinson, was in strange consonance with the wildness of the terrific storm. A double guard was put on, that each man might be oftener relieved from the watch, and to be in better readiness for any attack, which many fear. The anxiety felt for the safe return of the officers from Franklin was intense, so little faith have our people in the honor or the plighted word of the invaders.

At Franklin Generals Robinson and Lane met thirteen captains of the invaders in a little room. The governor made a long statement of the existing state of things. He told them that a misunderstanding had occurred; that the people of Lawrence had violated no law; that they would not resist any properly appointed officer in the execution of the laws; that the guns would not be given up; and concluded by advising them to go home to Missouri.

An escort had been promised to Generals R. and L. back to Lawrence; and when, at about seven o'clock, they left for home, one man only was provided to go with them. After going about one hundred yards, he too bade them "Good-evening," and wheeled his horse, leaving them in the enemy's country, without escort to pass the picket-guard. In this Egyptian darkness, the wind and sleet driving, and effectually blinding their eyes, they trusted to their horses to keep their way homeward, knowing they were in the road only by the sound of their hoofs upon the frozen earth. But safely, though once General Robinson's horse fell under him, without injury to himself or it, they reached Lawrence. Later in the night word came in that a party of the ruffians had taken possession of a house a mile or two from town, driving the family out in the storm. General Dietzler went out to bring them in. The three prisoners were armed with a large number of deadly weapons, and were almost frozen. Their plea for going to the house was that they had lost their way. Suspicion was strong against them, from all the circumstances, that they left Franklin with the design of assassinating Generals Robinson and Lane, but were unable to keep the road, and very truly may have lost their way.

9th. — The governor having ordered his men to disperse, many did so, while many other turbulent spirits, who had been dragged out of Missouri by their cupidity, by much persuasion, and by being told that now was the time, if ever, for the extermination of the Yankees, made loud complaints, and were determined upon a fight. Their anger towards the governor was also expressed loudly at this peaceful termination of the raid. With the terrible discomfort of the last night in camp, many of the men having no tents, with the failure of the whiskey, there arose a general dissatisfaction.

They carried home to Missouri their dead bodies — one killed by the falling of a tree, one shot by the guard accidentally, and one killed in some sort of a quarrel. One of Kansas' best citizens had lost his life, and much property been destroyed, all from a "misunderstanding." The following are the articles of negotiation and adjustment:

"Whereas there is a misunderstanding between the people of Kansas, or a portion of them, and the governor thereof, arising out of the rescue, near Hickory Point, of a citizen under arrest, and some other matters; and whereas a strong apprehension exists that said misunderstanding may lead to civil strife and bloodshed; and whereas it is desired, by both Governor Shannon and the people of Lawrence and vicinity, to avert a calamity so disastrous to the interests of the territory and the Union, and to place all parties in a correct position before the world, —

"Now, therefore, it is agreed by the said Governor Shannon, and the undersigned people of Lawrence, that the matter in dispute be settled as follows, to wit:

"We, the said citizens of said territory, protest that the said rescue was made without our knowledge or consent, but, if any of our citizens were engaged, we pledge ourselves to aid in the execution of any legal process against them; that we have no knowledge of the previous, present, or prospective existence of any organization in the said territory for the resistance of the laws, and that we have not designed, and do not design, to resist the legal service of any criminal process therein, but pledge ourselves to aid in the execution of the laws, when called on by proper authority, in the town or vicinity of Lawrence, and that we will use all our influence in preserving order therein; and we declare that we are now, as we ever have been, ready at any time to aid the governor in securing a posse for the execution of such process: provided, that any person thus arrested in Lawrence or vicinity, while a foreign force shall remain in the territory, shall be duly examined before a United States district judge of said territory in said town, and admitted to bail; and provided, further, that Governor Shannon agrees to use his influence to secure to the citizens of Kansas Territory remuneration for any damages sustained, or unlawful depredations, if any such have been committed by a sheriff's posse in Douglas County; and, further, that Governor Shannon states that he has not called upon persons residents of any other state to aid in the execution of the laws, and such as are here in this territory are here of their own choice; and that he has not any authority or legal power to do so, nor will he exercise any such power, and that he will not call on any citizen of another state who may be here. That we wish it understood that we do not herein express any opinion as to the validity of the enactments of the Territorial Legislature.

"(Signed), "WILSON SHANNON,
"C. ROBINSON,
"J. H. LANE."

The prisoners on both sides were released. Several who had been in the camp of the enemy were in town to-day. In times of war there are no Sabbaths, and we had no service to-day. The governor, with Jones and General Strickler, came in this morning.

A dinner was provided for them at the Cincinnati House; and, in a private room, some who are not averse, either by nature or principle, to a social glass, had provided such entertainment for the governor. Every one coming in, who ever thus degraded his higher nature, "must drink with the governor." At each glass which he drank he said, "Now here 's to the Baptist preacher."

When the dinner was ready, and the blessing about to be implored, the governor broke out in this new strain: "This is the happiest day of my life, by G—d!"

The story of the Baptist preacher is simply this: When Mr. Pomeroy left Lawrence for Kansas city, some men, watching him in Lawrence, immediately notified the camp at Franklin, and a company of men forthwith was sent out to intercept him. Having nearly reached the Baptist Mission, the party came up, and asked where he was going.

He said briefly, "To our mission;" and at once the party gave him the soubriquet of "the Baptist preacher." One of the party, however, quite unfortunately as it regarded his further progress towards "our mission," recognized him. He was taken by them across the river again; and wet and cold, without fire, he slept in their camp on the Wakarusa. Threats ran high against him; and his peril became so imminent, that, when his guard had fallen asleep, Atchison, to whom the ruffians had given the euphonious title of "Old Dave," took him to Blue Jacket's, an Indian house, where some of the officers had their head-quarters.

Atchison has declared to the rough men who follow him, "that they cannot fight now. The position the Lawrence people have taken is such that it would not do to make an attack upon them; it would ruin the democratic cause too. But, boys, we'll fight some time, by G—d!"

Mr. Redpath, a young Englishman, came in from Leavenworth, and in his facetious way, which makes the most common thing replete with interest and life, and turns the dull and serious into fun and gayety, told the story of his departure from Leavenworth, in company with four or five others, to come to Lawrence; how they were intercepted, and at last taken prisoners, and only released this morning.

My husband had not now been home for several days, save to dine on Friday. Towards evening he sent a carriage, and a request that I should come down town. So, quickly donning heavy English shawl and furs, we were soon there. I sat in the carriage while a messenger notified him of my arrival. He returned, bringing the word, "The general says, 'Come up to the council-chamber;'" and, under his escort, I passed through a file of soldiers guarding the door, also through halls similarly guarded, and up the rough staircases, until I reached the further end of the third story, where, upon a slight knock, the door was opened, and, with ceremony, I was ushered into the presence of, and introduced to, Gen. Robinson. This being through with, I noticed several ladies, friends and acquaintances, sitting by; and, when a few more were gathered together, we were informed by the general that "the war is over; the hatchet is buried; that the late enemy have expressed a desire to cultivate a conciliatory and friendly spirit with their neighbors in Lawrence; that it is better to bridge over past differences by the kindly, pleasant offices of good-will and friendship. As a token of our willingness to accept and give any pledges of our good offices in the future, we will to-morrow invite Gov. Shannon, and any of his friends from Missouri who will remain, to a social gathering." The ladies were also informed that to them they would look for the necessary refreshments for the evening.

How New England's high-toned propriety would be shocked at the idea of "getting up" a party on so short notice, and some seven or eight hundred guests expected! What would occupy a month's time there, and any amount of unnecessary words, is done here equally as well in an eighth part of the time, with a greater amount of pleasure coming to all.

Another reason for the meeting of the morrow's evening is that Gov. Shannon might see that the people neither have the look of "paupers" nor "rebels." The ladies found time amid the arrangements to speak to the governor, who sat by, an occasional word; and to one and all he was free to say, "This is the happiest day of my life." He stated also, "that he liked the people of Lawrence so well, he should come to live among them." Had the people undergone a sudden transformation?

A rumor came in during the evening from the invading horde still lingering in the borders, and reached the watchful ear of the governor. "His militia" were so indignant with him for the truce, that they threatened him with lynching, and an immediate attack upon Lawrence. He is fearful, and lacks the boldness of a man who has done his duty. Lynching is rather an unpleasant mode of making one's exit, and especially undignified to a person holding the honorable office of governor. Such a terminus to his career must be avoided. A simple remedy is at hand, and the fluttering heart says "Save me from my friends." Feeling doubtless like the man who "digged a pit for his enemies, but into it he fell," he signed the commission of Generals Robinson and Lane, authorizing them to use the force under them, a properly constituted militia, and make good their defence.

The following is the document in question: —

"To CHARLES ROBINSON AND J. H. LANE. You are hereby authorized and directed to take such measures, and use the enrolled forces under your command in such manner, for the preservation of the peace and the protection of the persons and property of the people of Lawrence and vicinity, as in your judgment shall best secure that end.

"(Signed), WILSON SHANNON.

"*Lawrence, Dec. 9th*, 1855."

10*th.* — The early morning finds us busy in the culinary department. The making of seven loaves of bread and five of cake, with other necessary work, leaves only a few stray moments in which to finish a letter, which is to be a messenger of good tidings to friends far away under the home-roof, whose nights on our account have been sleepless and days filled with suspense. It is already three and a half o'clock, and the ladies were to meet at four o'clock. So pressing into the service, as bearers of burdens, two young men, who called opportunely, I went down, and was soon astonished by the huge baskets of provisions which were provided. Had the Missourians looked in upon the well-filled tables prepared on so brief notice, they would have given up the idea of starving us to terms; and had New England added her presence among the welcome guests, with her well-filled pockets and stocks in trade, she would have realized that, in the large open-heartedness and freedom from conventionalities of her frontier children, there is much of the real, true enjoyment of life.

During the speeches of the early part of the evening many of the ladies stood upon tables ranged around the walls, and their position even there was one of compactness. The incidents of the last few weeks were recalled, and those of the war recited. The bringing in of the cannon through the enemy's country, and of the powder by the ladies, had honorable mention. A "compromise measure" also afforded a good deal of merriment. The first week of the invasion a gentleman heard at Lecompton that it was the governor's plan to demand that the arms of the people of Lawrence should be delivered up. Upon this gentleman's return to Lawrence, he asked Gen. Robinson what answer he would make to such a demand.

His reply was brief: "I would propose a compromise measure; keep the rifles, and give them the contents."

Gov. Shannon did not stay to the "party." When the morning came he found his business required his attention at the mission, and he went on his way. But "Sheriff Jones" was there, and there were some there beside who did not cherish that spirit of forgiveness and conciliation, which makes man magnanimous in the treatment of an enemy; and the general's party at one time came near proving anything but a "peace party." There was a spirit there full of ambition, and a desire for office. And while the murder of young Barber was fresh in the minds of his friends; while the voice of poor, weak human nature would say revenge if the right chord was touched; and while "Sheriff Jones," an officer of the territorial courts, was an invited guest of Gen. Robinson, and political capital could be made; with what wonderful ingeniousness it wrought to keep alive this spirit of revenge in their breasts! The object was evident to all, and the indignation of many was hardly kept within bounds. The event, however, proved but another instance of the evil, which was intended for another, recoiling upon one's own head.

After this unpropitious opening of the evening, we had music and social pleasant converse with many friends we seldom meet.

Dr. C., a young Kentuckian, one of the released prisoners, was here last night. He was in the enemy's camp at Lecompton. After a sickness of several weeks at Topeka, and a week or so of feebleness at our house, he left on Tuesday the 27th for his home at Doniphan. On his way thither he was attacked by the mob, disarmed and brought back some sixty miles. Being brought to the camp the other prisoner, Mr. W., also being with him, they were given in charge to "Sheriff Jones." Weak as Dr. C. was from his recent illness, the fever still lurking in his veins, he was carried this long distance, then placed in a cold and very open room which was used as a liquor store. Beside all the noise and confusion usually attendant upon such resorts, Jones and others came in at night and "played poker at twenty-five cents ante." The room was so filled with men that he was obliged to sit up all night. There was constant talk of hanging, and most bitter threats used. Jones did not hesitate to tell Mr. W., in regard to a certain matter, that he must "tell or swing." Kelly, of the *Squatter Sovereign*, told him he thirsted for blood, and should like to see him hung on the first tree.

Dr. C. was very weak, and had now become delirious from the intense excitement and fatigue. Dr. Stringfellow and one or two other physicians were in attendance all night. One of the guard reasoned with Jones upon his treatment of the prisoners, until he desisted.

Other prisoners were similarly treated. One old man, whose years among civilization would have been a guaranty against insult, was treated with like cruelty. The rope with which they threatened to hang him was repeatedly shown him; but, heedless of their threats, and above the raging of the storm, which gave fair promise of leaving the hangman without any upon whom to exercise his office, his voice was heard, " Send it a little colder, O Lord ! "

And amid the fearful oaths and unceasing threats of evil, there was the same earnest plea: " O Lord, send it a little colder."

12th. — The different companies were drawn out in lines yesterday, and farewell addresses were made them by their officers. The Lawrence companies then escorted those from the other settlements a little way out of town.

The war is over for the present. Yet we cannot hope for any permanent peace until the strong arm of an executive, who will not disgrace his office, be interposed for the protection of the settlers, who in good faith came to make homes, rebuilding the old landmarks so ruthlessly torn down by the corruption of men in power.

So long as the excitable, brutal men along the borders are wrought upon by every incentive which can influence them, by such men as Atchison and Stringfellow, so long are we exposed to murder, rapine and pillage, at their hands. The sheriff in this invasion was prime mover, and upon him rests the chief guilt. At Lecompton, soon after the peace, he declared, " Major Clark and Burns both claim the honor of killing that d—d abolitionist, and I don't know which ought to have it. If Shannon had n't been a d—d old fool, that peace would never have been declared. He would have wiped Lawrence out. He had men and means enough to do it." Nothing could illustrate better the bitterness and treachery of his character, when he accepts the invitation, and makes one of the " peace party " in Lawrence.

At Douglas, Stringfellow informed his motley gang that the " thing is settled; " that " they are sold; " that " Shannon has turned traitor; " " he has disgraced himself and the whole pro-slavery party."

By the misrepresentations of Jones, Gov. Shannon brought this force from a neighboring state, against a peaceable community. He saw his error, and entered into a treaty. Who ever before heard of a governor entering into a treaty with the citizens over whom his own jurisdiction extends, having in view their obedience to the laws ? This treaty states, moreover, that Gov. Shannon "had not called upon persons residents of any other state to aid in the execution of the laws." Yet several gentlemen from Missouri come up with him to Lawrence, and in council treat for peace. When our officers go to Franklin, at his urgent request, it is to meet, at their head-quarters, the captain and officers of his army. Does this look like any variation from the truth? The governor is complained of bitterly by the men who say that on the first evening of his return from Lawrence to the head-quarters on the Wakarusa, he stated distinctly the arms were to be given up. The rabble, with many expressions of dissatisfaction, have sought their homes. The leaders, suffering from the smart of mortification, consider themselves sold, Judas-like, by one who should be the soul of honor, integrity and justice, and whom they trusted as a strong ally in the subjugation of this freedom-loving and down-trodden people. Feeling that their defeat has indeed been ignoble and signal, they, nursing secret discontent, and thirsting for revenge, will plan a new invasion, new schemes of villany. There is no settlement of the difficulty. It is only the present lull of the late storm, gathering, it may be, greater fury. While the border leagues are still in being, and they as strongly determined now, as for a year past, to make Kansas a slave state; while the settlers in Kansas have grown yet more strong in their devotion to the principles of freedom from the infamous measures taken by Gov. Shannon, and the other officials, to forcibly wrest them from them, there is no certainty of peace. Since Gov. Shannon has brought a mob against Lawrence; since he, with Judge Lecompte and other appointees of the President, have fraternally sympathized with Atchison and Stringfellow, the depth, the intensity of the feeling of our people against such a tyrannical rule cannot be estimated.

The seeds of difficulty are sown broadcast, and no one can tell what trivial circumstance shall cause a sudden, terrible outbreak. There is ignorance among this excitable class of men in the border counties, but the ignorance is not the principal cause for fear. Such men as Col. Boone of Westport, who was Gov. Shannon's chief adviser, rule these men; and when Col. Boone came to Lawrence, with his portly bearing and most dignified manners, one could hardly believe he was a "border ruffian." While the words, "he came to see if everything was done right," were repeatedly upon his tongue, his inflammatory appeals for men and money to aid in this invasion, in which there was no shadow of truth, were sent through all the border. He has, beside, never failed to be active in these invasions and frauds upon the ballot-box.

Unless the federal government interposes for the relief of the actual settler, there is yet imminent danger that other martyrs for liberty will fall beneath the assassin's blow; that these broad prairies, whose very air breathes life and freedom, consecrated by God when fresh from his forming hand, sealed by a sacred compact of men, shall again be consecrated by their blood.

CHAPTER XII.

FUNERAL OF BARBER — DEATH OF R. P. BROWN.

Dec. 15*th.* — The day of the election upon the adoption of the state constitution. The vote for the constitution was small, coming as it did on the heels of the invasion. In some of the districts the constitutions were not received. There was no opportunity to canvass the territory; and where appointments had been made for meetings, there was no speaking. At Leavenworth there was a gathering of some of the forces who had been before Lawrence. As the election was proceeding quietly, Charles Dunn, with a party, smashed in the window of the building where the election was being held, jumped in, and drove off the judges of election. One of the clerks of election, in attempting to save the ballot-box, was seized by the throat by Dunn. He was also struck in the face by Dunn, and by another person, until he fell, when the crowd rushed upon him, kicking him in the head and sides. Dunn and party then carried off the ballot-boxes.

16*th.* — It is a clear, bright December day, and the snows, which came in small quantity, are fast melting, and mingling with the clayey soil. So, besides the burden of rubbers, one has to carry no little portion of the native earth. But, as Mr. Barber was to be disinterred from his hasty burial in town, to be buried with martial honors to-day, we made the half-mile walk. First, however, arranging for the sick man at home. Mr. C. had gone beyond his strength, in an attempted journey, and he was again a fixture in the chimney-corner. He threatens, with a mixture of "quinine and sulphuric acid," to drive away the chills;

but whether he may not drive himself away, his fragility continually suggests. However, in these days of reform and progress, it has become fashionable to "die of the doctor rather than the disease."

As we reached the hotel, which had indeed become the place for all assemblies, meetings to discuss the affairs of the country, or pleasure-gatherings, the barracks for soldiers, and now where the services for the dead were to be performed, the wagons and carriages standing around, and the groups of people hurrying in all directions, showed that the feeling of the people was aroused. We passed among the crowd, and, narrowly escaping a fall into one of the ditches made by the throwing up of the entrenchments, ascended the inclined boards at the doorway, which served for steps.

As I entered the long dining-hall, where but a week since was the sound of rejoicing, it seemed as though every place was full. But a friendly heart, though a stranger's, made room on one of the long settees. Long boards had also been brought in for extra seats, and these were full of this sympathizing community.

It was a strange, a motley group. There were hats of satin and velvet, with plumes, and Paris flowers, with dresses of rich material, and costly furs. There were brides of a few months, just arrived in this western home, and city belles come out for a winter's sojourn where the artificial has wholly given place to simplicity and nature. There were some with log-cabin bonnets of black silk, or cotton velvet, and dress of plain coarse stuff, giving to the wearer an odd, strange look. There were others whose apparel is the safer medium between the two, which ever bespeaks the taste and intelligence of the wearer.

There were many who have lived their whole lives in cities, accustomed to their elegancies and refinements, who are now roughing it with the simple dwellers in nature's halls. Yet, over all this immense crowd, who had gathered from many miles around to take part in this mournful service, was spread the hallowed, chastening influence of this great sorrow. There was not one present but would willingly have taken part of the burden, could it have lessened the crushing woe of the lone bereaved one.

Silence pervaded the assembly, and many a heart whose tendrils yet cling unbroken around their loved ones, who seemingly had been in perils more and greater, felt a deep thankfulness that, rudely torn asunder, they did not then lie bleeding, the fond object dying, withering.

There was a sound of people moving, the tread of many feet, a heart-breaking sob, and many turned to look. Had they passed through hours when the death angel had stricken down the loved from their own pathway, they would have realized how like sacrilege is this gazing of the multitude upon the broken, crushed spirit, burying its dead.

Then the sob came from the other end of the hall, and the tall, white-haired, blue-eyed man, who knew her husband, and would perform the service, bent over her, to speak some comforting word. But, like Rachel, she refused to be comforted. A hymn was read, and the audience sang an old, familiar tune; but ever and anon, amid the singing, there came this wailing, this moaning, as though the heart must break through its earthly fetters. Short speeches followed from Generals Lane and Robinson, and then a sad sermon.

When the preacher spoke of death finding the one taken in the performance of his duty, a duty cheerfully performed for his country; that from this service he had been taken to a higher; of him who will be to the widow more than husband or child; of the evanescence of human life, and of that fairer country, beyond the dark waters of death, where the cruel reign of the tyrant is over; we felt that a response went out from the poor lone one's heart, — that she had caught a glimpse of the bright chain reaching from heaven, earthward, — and that she would realize, more fully than in life, the nearness of the loved spirit.

The services were over, and preparations were made to bear the lamented dead to the burial. The military companies, with arms reversed, walked first, the generals, upon horseback, leading the way. There was the company from Lawrence, and the "Barker Guards;" then the body of the dead, and the sad mourners — the widow and brothers; then the neighbors of the quiet, inoffensive man, who felt most keenly his death; then the whole community. All kinds of vehicles, wagons, and carriages, fell into the rear, and in solemn procession made a long line over the prairie. Soon they wound up the lone, steep way, over Mount Oread.

A mile further over the level prairie the procession moved on slowly, "for it was a man they bore." The soldiers formed in lines on either side, with bowed heads and lifted hats. The mourners passed through, and stood around the open grave. The coffin was gently lowered, the falling earth rattled upon its lid — a dread, fearful sound; the bitter wailing of the desolate, childless, earth-stricken widow rose above the sad moaning of the winter wind, and broke in upon the words, "Dust to dust," — "I am the resurrection and the life."

The mourners fell back, giving place to the soldiers, who then stood around the grave, and each division fired their rifles into the last resting-place of their loved and honored comrade.

Such a scene as this the actors in it had never before witnessed, and with similar emotions never will again. In this glorious old country, with its hills so smoothly terraced, its prairies boundless, over which, a twelvemonth since, the Indian alone roamed with the wild deer in the venerable forests, now in concord the white man dwells with his red brother. There is no war between them, no enmity. But another power, more hideous, more grasping, has arisen. These beautiful lands are coveted by the slave power. It threatens boldly, and with all its treachery, all its hateful wiles unmasked, to bring the dark-browed race, whose color is their crime, to suffer here; that with the sweetly-perfumed breath of these green prairies shall come to our ears the wailing of her who is worse than widowed, and the sad cry of children who know no tenderer words of man than those of the bloody task-master and tyrant.

For this the slave power has another victim, and the solemn prairie has witnessed the burial of liberty's third martyr to-day. Stern men, unused to weep, and timid women, have bowed with the stricken, and shared their grief. The blow, falling most heavily on her, leaves them not untouched, and the warning is loud and deep, "Death to your liberties." The love we had always borne to freedom is tenfold increased, while the hatred of oppression is intensified and strengthened. A new consecration of our energies, in this unequal fight for freedom, is made over the new-made grave. And it is no child's play,— no work merely of to-day,— but a life-service. It is easy to boast of putting on the harness, and to be full of courage, when quiet sits by one's own fireside, and when the crowd are pressing eagerly on to victory, with banners waving, and music filling the air; but it is another thing in this frontier land, where for very weariness with watching the soul faints, where there is no gloss of military trappings, where the plumes are tattered, and the little army, weary and struggling, is passing through sorrow and the wilderness.

In the prospect of freedom's bulwarks raised high and strong we can yet exult. It will be accomplished by no magic power, but by faithful service, and patient endurance. Strong arms will hew out the timber, dig broad and deep the trenches, and rear high the walls. It will cost many tears and cares, anxieties and prayers, and the sorrow of many spirits hopeful to-day. It may cost many valued lives; but we will lay each corner-stone of this altar of freedom with the serene, abiding strength of a holy faith; trust all to Him who maketh "the darkness as the noonday," and the end will be glorious.

Sheriff Jones called at the door, before the day was over, for S. and T., two young men of New England origin, and of whom she may well be proud. They went with him to Lecompton for trial, having been engaged in the "rescue" case, and from that court will appeal to the Supreme Court of the United States, hoping thus to test the validity of the territorial laws. We hope this willingness of theirs to be the instruments in testing these laws will not be at too great a cost. Another of the rescuers was sitting in the parlor when Jones called for Smith and Tappan, upon whom he had previously served the warrant; but his eye did not fall upon the man he had so much longed to arrest.

22*d.* — A convention was holden to-day in Lawrence to nominate state officers. It was fully attended. The forenoon was warm and pleasant; but the change in the weather, soon after dinner, was terrible.

The cold every moment increased, and snow commenced falling with the evening shadows. E. wrapped herself in blankets, and took a nap on the lounge. I tried to write a letter, sitting on a cricket, close to the stove, with lamp upon a music-stool; but it required so much time to change positions, to keep some part of me from freezing, that I concluded to lay it by for a warmer day The next suggestion was, as it would be late before they would return from the convention, to try to go to sleep. There was a crispy sound of new-fallen snow, the moment one's foot was on the stairway, and all through the chambers, over trunks, bureaus, beds, and everywhere, was spread this white mantle. The roof was impervious to rain, but the fine snow sifted in everywhere. So, gently shaking the pillows, I lay down, and the fleecy covering was still falling. Twice I went down to replenish the fire, lest when they came they would be almost frozen, and the clock struck three, ere, through the wildness of the night, I heard cheerful voices approaching the house. Some of the gentlemen had frozen their ears, and were free to declare that the night was awful.

We New Englanders consoled ourselves by thinking that in her borders it was even colder than here, while our guests, who had been used to the mild climate of southern Illinois and Kentucky, could hardly believe that this was the " very mild climate " which travellers have termed it, or that "cattle could graze" and "flowers bloom the whole year." Before the gentlemen retired, I made an effort to remove the snow from their bed; but it was continually falling, and the attempt was nearly useless.

23d. — T. and S. have returned from Lecompton. They were committed for trial, but Jones let them out on parole, until the time they are to go to Leavenworth to be imprisoned.

24th. — Still snowing, and the weather terribly severe. The thermometer seventeen degrees below zero, wind is blowing, and the snow drifting into all imaginable shapes. To travel in it seems impossible, and many times to-day I am querying what will become of the party who left here last evening. To face a Missouri mob is nothing to facing these winds which sweep over the prairies.

Four young men — two from New England, one from England, and our Scotch friend — are stopping here. They try to write, but the ink can only be kept in a fluid state by keeping it on the stove, while it freezes in their pens. Were it not for their good spirits, and fun-loving natures, I believe we should all freeze together. As it is, there are many things to provoke a laugh even amid the discomforts, and a little warmth remains. We think such weather as this can only last a day or two; for last year, at Christmas, people sat with doors and windows open.

The cows and mules, wandering about without shelter, not being able to get a nibble for themselves, look at me pleadingly, as much as to say, "Why don't you feed me?" while many of them find their way into our barn and help themselves.

25th. — Cold, bitter, stinging cold; not so windy as yesterday, but the cold more intense. Thermometer ranging between twenty and thirty degrees below zero. The water freezes in the tumblers at breakfast, and everything eatable, or intended to be eaten, is frozen hard. The bread can only be cut as we thaw it by the fire, setting the loaf down and cutting one piece at a time. Potatoes, squashes, pumpkins, citrons, and apples, are as hard as rocks. Several glass pickle-jars, filled with ketchup, are broken open from top to bottom.

26th. — It is no warmer yet. What will the poor settlers do who have no floors in their cabins? — and there are many such. Will their hopeful, cheerful spirit, which has borne them through the dark hours now scarcely passed, sustain them against physical suffering, it may be actual want? The sacking of their granaries and open houses will cause untold ills.

Now, when New England hears of the destitution of her own children, fighting her battles, trusting their all in this dangerous strife, will she put her hands into her well-filled pockets, and send of her fulness for their necessities? Hungary, yes, poor, bleeding Hungary, sought aid and found it here. The nation's heart responded. Greece stretched forth her hands not in vain. Shall the imploring cry of destitute, starving Kansas reach no pitying heart?

Gov. Shannon has been at Lecompton for some time. He did not come to Lawrence, as he proposed, and it is said he is soon going home. The glory won here in his famous war will probably suffice him for the remnant of his life, and he may conclude to retire upon his laurels.

The circuit court should have met last week at Lecompton, but after keeping the prisoners there all of the week, the judge not then appearing, the court was adjourned until the March term. Some of the rescuers have given bail, but T. and S. still refused to do so, as it would be recognizing the Missouri territorial justice. Getting weary of waiting for Judge Lecompte's appearance, the patience of the border ruffians at Lecompton was exhausted. They even went so far as to threaten his removal, and cursed him in no stinted terms. S., with his love of a good joke, said,

"If you want to get him removed, I 'll tell you how you may easily do it."

"How is it?" asked the renowned Sheriff Jones.

"Why, get him to join the free-state party."

Another outrage has been committed at Leavenworth. During Col. Delahay's absence, while attending the convention here, his press was thrown into the river. It looks singular, as he is a national democrat, and a personal friend of Stephen A. Douglas. He has also always been wonderfully conservative, and ever counselled no resistance to the laws. He was, with other leading men at Leavenworth, so fearful of doing anything to offend the border men, that he declined to do anything for the defence of Lawrence. Some of them said, "They have got into a scrape; let them get out the best way they can!" and one of them, a bachelor, said, "We must stay at home and defend our own wives and children." Col. Delahay, however, was a member of the constitutional convention, and it may be for this that the Missouri mob treated his press so rudely.

29th. — Doctor arrived home from Kansas city. He had, in addition to his heavy fur coat, fur gloves, and fur-lined overshoes, a heavy shawl and mittens, and was very cold even then. On his way down he suffered so severely from the cold, that with assistance he went into an Indian hut to warm, and for a half hour lay fainting on the floor. The cold at Kansas city has been even greater than here. It is apparently quiet along the border, yet the press in the frontier towns, as well as those papers of pro-slavery sentiments in the territory, are endeavoring to inflame the populace in such articles as the following, taken from the *Kickapoo Pioneer*, of Dec. 26:

"But the abolitionists, or free-state men, if you please, have become dissatisfied, and are willing to violate the constitution of their country, which explicitly recognizes slavery, and disfranchise themselves as loyal citizens, for the purpose of stealing negroes, and committing other unconstitutional and unlawful depredations. Should such men receive any compassion from an orderly, union-loving people? No! It is this class of men that have congregated at Lawrence, and it is this class of men that Kansas must get rid of. And we know of no better method than for every man who loves his country, and the laws by which he is governed, to meet in Kansas and kill off this God-forsaken class of humanity as soon as they place their feet upon our soil."

While articles like these are circulated through the borders, letters, calling for men and money, are industriously written and published throughout the South. Southern Kansas aid societies are being formed, and it is rumored that Gen. Quitman, of Mississippi, of fillibuster renown, has given twenty-five hundred dollars to this society, and will be here in the spring with several hundred men from that state. Major Buford, of Alabama, has contributed twenty-five thousand dollars for a similar purpose, and upon the opening of navigation proposes to be here with three hundred southerners. Notwithstanding the hue and cry made over northern emigrant aid societies, will there be aught said against these?

Jan. 1st. — A beautiful, sunny morning ushers in the new year, but the air is still keen and cold. For nearly ten days the cold has been without precedent, and we, of New England, who came hoping to find warm and pleasant winters, begin to surmise we are in the wrong latitude, and talk of a new emigration still southward.

A gentleman here to-day, who has lived in Missouri over twenty years, says he has never seen such weather as this. With his large, blue blankets, a place being cut in the centre through which he slips his head, his ears and nearly the whole of the face being protected by a worsted fabric of gray color, one can hardly tell whether he belongs to the Anglo-Saxon or the aboriginal race.

The little boy, whose family has but recently moved into the next house beyond us, has been in, nearly frozen. He carries all the water the family use from our spring, making a distance of nearly half a mile. He is a slight little fellow, and only twelve years old. He has two pails, and dips the water with a half-pint cup. He sits a long time by the dining-room stove, and seems to suffer much from his frost-bitten fingers. There is to be a new-year's party at the hotel, and the lovers of gayety will be there.

6th. — Who ever saw so clear a morning as this? The smoke from the Indian houses over in the Delaware Reserve, and five miles away, could be seen gracefully curling and rising above the trees, as plainly as that from the house nearest us. The smoke rising from so many dwellings, far and near, from the compact settlement of Lawrence, and the sun shining upon the snow, making it look like a broad mantle studded with glittering gems, formed a pleasing, novel sight, well worth a place in memory's gallery.

10th. — What odd-looking sleighs our people ride in, and how they glide over the smooth, level way! Yankee invention, so much despised, brings a mine of comfort to her frontier children. A sleigh is wanted; the enterprising youth goes into the woods, and cuts two poles long enough for runners and shafts. A little part between the shafts and runners, leaving each the required length, is shaved from the upper side, so that they will bend easily. A few little cross-pieces being put in, and two or three cross-boards on the runners, with a box for a seat, the vehicle is complete. This is the most simple contrivance of all. There is another variety of wagon-body on runners, which has the advantage of greater safety over the other, with sufficient lightness. From the first we have learned of some laughable accidents. A day or two since, two young men were riding quite briskly along, when, coming to a drift, the horse stopped suddenly, and one of our friends, quicker than thought, found himself head foremost in a deep bank, little more than boots being visible. He was so completely pinioned by the depth of snow, and by the force with which he was sent from the slight vehicle, that it was only after extra help had arrived that he was extricated. He suffered no injury, and joined in the laugh of the bystanders.

19*th.*—Word came in last night, about eleven o'clock, of an attack at Easton, two messengers having narrowly escaped with the intelligence. S. had gone down, late at night, to see if there was any news, and he brought back the startling intelligence that a fight had occurred at Easton. One pro-slavery man, named Cook, mortally wounded; some free-state men in the hands of the mob, whom they threatened to hang if Cook dies. The council of war was to be held, and doctor went down with S. immediately. Not long after I was awakened again by a loud knocking at the door. I opened the window and asked, "What 's wanted?" The reply was, "The general wishes T. to saddle the horse and send him down by me." After some amusing and fruitless efforts, T. was at last awakened enough to know that war was abroad, and the horse was soon on his way to head-quarters.

Two or three horsemen left immediately for Leavenworth, to apply to Judge Lecompte for a writ of *habeas corpus*, that the prisoners might be released from the gang, while others started for Easton, the scene of the trouble. Our people are feeling much excited, and ready to lend any assistance to their neighbors in peril.

Owing to the disturbances at Leavenworth on the fifteenth of December, and from rumors of another mob gathering just across the river, to prevent this election of the fifteenth of January, the mayor issued a proclamation forbidding an election to be held at Leavenworth. A few of the free-state men then went to Easton, about twelve miles from Leavenworth, where the election had been postponed until the seventeenth. On their way to the polls, some persons were stopped and disarmed by a body of armed men. In the afternoon a company came to Mr. Minard's house, where the election was held, and threatened to destroy the ballot-boxes. Late at night, as Mr. Sparks and his son were leaving for home, they were attacked and taken prisoners by three men. Information of it reached Mr. Minard immediately, by a man who left his house in company with Mr. Sparks. Mr. Brown and a company of others went to the relief of Mr. Sparks, and saved him when in imminent peril. As the rescued returned with the rescuers to the house, they were fired upon. They returned the fire, and an irregular fight, firing from behind buildings, commenced. One or two free-state men were slightly wounded, while a Mr. Cook, of bitter pro-slavery feelings, was wounded mortally.

21st. — Sunday. Our messengers returned to-night, and brought certain knowledge of the murder of R. P. Brown. The blood chilled in our veins as we heard the recital of the horrid outrage, and the beating heart cried, is there no justice — no avenger? After Mr. S. left for Lawrence, Mr. Brown, and seven others from Leavenworth, attempted to return there. They were followed, and taken prisoners by the Kickapoo Rangers, headed by Capt. John W. Martin. Mr. Brown was placed in a room apart from the others of his party. The hours were passing, and the men who had them in their power were becoming yet more brutal by the free use of liquor, and they were bent upon the death of Mr. Brown. Capt. Martin used his influence to prevent such a deed; but, after doing all in his power to save him, he went home. The cruel crowd then took him out of the house, and, with blows and kicks, and knocking him upon the frozen earth, and literally hacking him in pieces with a hatchet, they showed themselves fiendish beyond the unenlightened savage. Then throwing him into a wagon, with wounds undressed, he was borne several miles, through the piercing cold of a January night, to his home. He could only say to his wife, "I am murdered by a set of cowards," and death ended his sufferings.

The slave power has another victim, and the shame, the eternal infamy of his mournful death will forever, like an incubus, rest upon his soul who has the power, yet offers no interference against the hunting down of our citizens, by worse than Florida blood-hounds! Was there ever an administration so utterly vile as this?

Mr. Brown was a tall man, with pleasant dark eyes, olive-brown complexion, and dark abundant hair. He was at Lawrence during the siege; one of the few from Leavenworth who ventured so far from home. He leaves a wife and child to mourn over his sad, heart-rending fate. While Kansas' wrongs are written in the blood of her citizens, the cruel, bloody death of her fourth martyr for freedom will never be effaced from the memories of the dwellers in this far-away land.

23d. — More messengers are in from Easton; men driven from their homes upon peril of their lives, and with continued threats of violence. They come to Lawrence, as to a city of refuge. Mr. Sparks is now in peril from bands of armed Missourians. Some twenty-five men go up from here and Topeka. One man, who came down to notify the people here, escaped from a band of twelve men in hot pursuit,—something after Gen. Putnam's mode, of revolutionary memory, — by leaping over a precipitous bank, while the enemy did not dare follow. While they were looking for a smoother descent, he had time to escape. After Mr. M. had been obliged to leave his home, some of the ruffians went to his house, asking "if they could come in to get warm." Mrs. M. replied, "they could do so by giving her their guns." As they sat by the fire, they told her "they had killed her husband." However, she gave no credence to it.

Major Robinson, of Tecumseh, died to-day. He has been ill most of the time since the invasion of Lawrence, the disease having been contracted from exposure at that time. For some time he was sick at the Cincinnati House; but there is little room there for sick people, and no quiet; and the noble woman, who has sacrificed much for the cause, in the exposures of last winter and this, and the constant absence of her husband, offered her cabin, under the shadow of the hotel, as a place of rest and quiet to the sick stranger. The unconsciousness of disease was upon him much of the time, and when his mind was dull to things about him, far-away scenes were fresh in his memory, and friends he had long loved were ministering by his bedside. He talked much with his mother, when clouds darkened his mental vision. He said to her, "Take off my shoes, mother, for I am tired and weary, and I cannot travel further." So, with this sweet consciousness of loved friends around him, his life's journey closed.

24th. — It was a little milder this morning; and, not having been out since the cold weather came, I proposed to T. to take me to call on a friend, and to the stores. Not knowing my arrangements, the doctor had lent both horse and carriage; and, as I came down stairs, cloak and bonnet on, they were already out of sight. T. said, "We 'll not lose our ride in this way," and suggested taking Mr. P.'s buggy, which was in a sadly dilapidated condition, and a mule of somebody's else, quartered in the barn for a few days. My only question was as to safety, and we were soon rattling over the drifts, now one side inclining far down, threatening to spill us out, and then the other. This incessant rattling put speed into the wild mule, and a John Gilpin ride we had of it for the first quarter of a mile. However, by clinging to the frame-work of the seat, for there was nothing left of it but the frame-work, we passed over the ravine at the foot of the long sloping hill west of the house, in safety, and the mule took an easier gait both for himself and us. We reached the place of our destination. A gentleman opened the door, and asked very blandly, "Is this the state carriage?"

Doctor having had a more recent title than that of general bestowed upon him, I answered, "Yes; and will your wife accept the honor of a ride?"

He looked with a dubious expression at the broken dasher, swinging forward and back at every motion, the bottom half broken out, the shafts tied on with ropes, and the seat cushionless, and destitute of every bit of leather it ever boasted, to say nothing of broken springs, and wheels with tire half off, and said, "Yes, if you will insure her safety."

With blue blankets before and around us, instead of buffalo-robes, we were soon on our way to town, and hurried along at the mule's own pace. We laughed until we were weary at the mule's antic motions, never before having had the honor of a ride after one. T. and Mrs. C., both Boston bred, laughed at the idea of what an impression such an establishment, and such speed, would make down Washington-street some pleasant winter's day. After a short call at our stores, than which there are none better in most New England villages, neatly furnished as some of them are with black walnut shelves and counters, we went home.

Letters from Kansas city and Leavenworth state that some deep-laid scheme for our ruin is being planned. They do not know what it is, yet advise us to prepare for the worst. There is a perfect lull at those places, — no bravado, no threats, — all of which reminds us of the fearful calm always preceding the bursting out of a volcano. Prominent pro-slavery men are seen riding into a town; they hold a few moments' conversation with the leaders of their party there, then disappear. Quickly they are at another settlement; but no word is dropped as to the designs.

A half ton of lead, and nearly as much powder, arrived to-day. Other teams, loaded with the same needful, are on the way. Provisions, too, are fast coming in, and we will soon be able to stand quite a siege. Sixty men, detailed from the various companies, are at work upon the different fortifications. A guard is again to watch hourly for our safety.

The *Kickapoo Pioneer* office issued, on the morning after the murder of Brown, January 18th, the following extra, commencing, "Rally! rally!" After making several misstatements, — among others, that an abolition company from Lawrence had made an attack upon the pro-slavery men,— it goes on: "Forbearance has now ceased to be a virtue; therefore, we call upon every pro-slavery man in the land to rally to the rescue. Kansas must be immediately rescued from the tyrannical dogs. The Kickapoo Rangers are at this moment beating to arms. A large number of pro-slavery men will leave this place for Easton in twenty minutes. The war has again commenced, and the abolitionists have again commenced it. Pro-slavery men, law and order men, strike for your altars! strike for your firesides! strike for your rights! Avenge the blood of your brethren who have been cowardly assailed, but who have bravely fallen in defence of southern institutions. Sound the bugle of war over the length and breadth of the land, and leave not an abolitionist in the territory to relate their treacherous and contaminating deeds. Strike your piercing rifle-balls and your glittering steel to their black and poisonous hearts! Let the war-cry never cease in Kansas again until our territory is wrested of the last vestige of abolitionism."

25th. — Still more snow. The beautiful white covering lies two feet in depth on a level, and four or five in the drifts all over the country. It is the shield, the protection of the good Father for our defence. While the administration, with that corruption which will make it infamous in the annals of our country in all coming time, turns a deaf ear to the agonized cry of widows and orphans; while the President says, "No acts prejudicial to good order have occurred under circumstances to justify the interposition of the federal government," the ear of Him, who will call to account for his stewardship any who make so base a use of power, is open, and he sends, for the present safety, this weather of unequalled severity, and fast-falling snows.

Horses go ploughing through it, with difficulty making any headway. The most people we see moving to-day are with heavy sleds of wood, drawn by three or four yoke of oxen. We burn a cord and a half of wood a week, and, our wood-pile growing less not very gradually, we have watched with a good deal of interest a load which attempted to come up the hill this afternoon. The oxen pulled with all their strength; the driver now coaxed, and then scolded. The oxen would lose their foothold, and plunge headlong into the deep drifts. Sometimes the forward yoke of cattle would turn fairly around, and face the load. All exertions to right them were of no avail until they were unyoked. As the night was coming fast, and the driver two miles from home, the load was thrown off about half way up the hill. The next morning the man came back, and succeeded in getting half of the load to the house. He was until midnight getting home the previous night, as he lost his way and wandered about hours in the darkness.

Wood is one of the principal articles of consumption here this winter. Most of that burned is black walnut. There is also no lack of provisions here. Flour of the best quality can be bought in Missouri for four dollars and a half per hundred. We have always had good flour until this winter. Just after the invasion, a load of flour made of grown wheat was brought in. Apples, of the best quality and flavor, are very plenty. They sold in the autumn for one dollar a bushel. Sweet potatoes were abundant at one dollar twenty-five cents. These, with the apples, came from Missouri, but the nicest of squashes and other vegetables were raised in the territory. Squashes sold for one cent per pound, and pumpkins one dollar and fifty cents per hundred. Butter, made here, is very nice, and until quite recently has been plenty at twenty-five cents. Milk varies from four to ten cents per quart. Beside the meats, beef, etc., venison, prairie chickens, turkeys, rabbits and squirrels, are often in the market; also oysters, in sealed cans. Yet, with all these gratifications for the palate, it is more than probable that, all these long days, some of our people have not tasted of them for want of money to buy them. Many a person gave freely of what he had in the siege of December, and while on guard at Lawrence lost all of his crops at home. As a people we are bankrupt. Remittances from the East are lost, or the same thing to us, retained, with letters, by the officious meddlers in government pay in a neighboring state. Money drafts are months on their way, when twelve or fourteen days is all-sufficient time for the journey. The people in the territory are at no time safe. The cabin of the lone settler on the prairie is momentarily exposed to attack, yet no light comes from Congress — none from its head.

This winter will be ever remembered for its unprecedented severity, and for that wicked use of power by the administration which would make the career of Caligula magnanimous and spotless in the comparison. Those who sit in sealed houses, and by warm hearth-stones, no foes without or fears within, can never realize, as we in Kansas, on the exposed outposts, what a winter this has been to us. Our senses sharpened by the actual necessities of life, and our perceptions quickened by their unsleeping vigilance and constant action, none better than we can realize the terrible infamy which will cling to those who have been the chief abettors in filling up this cup of evil. Wrong-doing has marked their pathway, and shame will be their reward. Yet there is a golden bow of promise over us, the bright rainbow of hope; and, in characters clear as the sunlight and radiant as truth, beneath the arch encircling the snow-clad hills and prairies, and the sad dwellers among them, is written: "The days of the tyrant are numbered. He will hasten on his own downfall."

CHAPTER XIII.

THE WINTER IN THE TERRITORY — STATE LEGISLATURE.

26th. — The men were early at their work this morning upon the little cabins in the forts. Stoves are to be put in them as soon as finished, and then soldiers will board in them as in times of war. The largest fort, which is at the foot of Massachusetts-street, commanding the way to the river, is of circular form, about five feet high, with a broad walk upon the top, perhaps four feet wide. It is about one hundred feet in diameter, and is built of earth and timbers. A sentinel is continually pacing the rounds upon the top.

The general and other officers are at all times busy in the council-room. Scarcely six weeks have passed since Gov. Shannon's famous treaty; he has now gone home, and the plan seems to be to do what is to be done in his absence, while Woodson is acting governor. He, having been instrumental in getting the Platte County Rifle Boys to come to the invasion of Lawrence, will not hesitate to do anything now which a Missouri mob asks of him.

In the evening T. was asleep on the lounge, E. and I were sitting in the bright moonlight, when the loud booming of cannon, the shouts of men, and the barking of dogs, startled us. With the door open we could see no strange thing, but the noise continued. It could not be Missourians, for they would not attack the town so early in the evening, or on such a bright night.

T. awakened, and as we gave him no satisfactory answer to his question of "What 's that?" he rose hastily, saying, "I believe those hounds have come." His pistol-belt was soon fastened on, and, as he left the door, he said, "Good-by, if I don't see you again." He was hastening away, when I said to him, "You must let me know somehow what is doing."

"Yes, I will send you word, if I cannot come myself."

As through the still night-air these words were borne to me, the young, city-bred youth, whose heart beats warmly for freedom — freedom for all, was far down the hill-side. Home friends were continually writing him, "Why don't you leave that God-forsaken country, and come home?" With the earliest settlers he embarked in the holy cause of saving Kansas to freedom, and with those principles deeply implanted in his nature, in the full vigor and strength of early manhood, with hope mounting high, he has buckled on the armor of a righteous self-defence, and with the watchword of victory he is ever ready for active service. I smile often at his enthusiasm of manner as he says, "I used often to go to the theatre at home, life was so dull; but here we have a new scene in the drama every day." I sympathize in the feeling, and have half a mind that all of us, living where we actually realize the truth, "Ye know not what a day may bring forth," would find New England paths dull and tame. Like him, there are many other young men, who, with unchecked aspirations and unblasted hopes, have in the trials of the hour put on the soberness, the prudence of life at its noon. Side by side with furrowed brows, and dark locks silvered o'er by time's fingers, they have prepared for the onset. Our people have grown strong in themselves under difficulties. Young men of education and talent, who sought their home here, have put forth new powers. Stripped of all the artificial accompaniment of old towns, driven by the circumstances of the times to exertions almost superhuman, the happy brightening up of unused faculties, and the quickening of relaxed energies, have followed; whereas, amid the hum-drum paths of the old homes, surrounded by their gloss, gilding, and effeminacy, they would have passed along life's even ways, attaining only middling ranks in their professions.

The women, too, of Kansas have shared in this quickening of the perceptive and reflective faculties — the effect of their surroundings. Some, who would have floated gayly down life's smoother tides, amid the glitter, the false show of society, bound down by an iron rule to King Custom's absurd ways, and would have asked not the great questions of life, of its import, of its destiny, have learned that "life is real, life is earnest." In the simplicity of nature, in a new country, there is a mutual dependence between all, which is not realized at home, and the very needs of humanity demand that one should live, not for self, but out of self, and in realizing the beauty of the poem,

> "We live in deeds, not years,
> In thoughts, not breaths, in feelings,
> Not in figures on a dial. He lives most
> Who thinks most — feels the noblest — acts the best."

With a constant use of faculties and sympathies, the useless ornament of a city drawing-room becomes the strong, the active, earnest woman.

The hours were passing, the noise down street had ceased, and T. returned. He laughed as he said "No Missourians yet. The company have returned from Easton, and the boys were giving them a salute." He said, moreover, that they had speeches, and went through certain military manœuvres, and finished off with a supper prepared for them. They encountered no difficulties by the way; the enemy having heard of their proposed visit, fled to Missouri, leaving a clear field. One of the men, who has been threatened very grievously by them, they found so strongly barricaded in his house, that the enemy could never have taken him. His wife and six sons compose the family. The old lady has all the fire, the spirit of a Spartan mother.

Jan. 27th. — Still another snow. No security from the murderous midnight assassin can be more sure than the heavily drifting snows which cover the whole country. Plans of a guerilla warfare had been laid through the whole border. The murder of Brown and the invasion at Easton were the forerunners of intended attacks upon the whole territory. The leaders of the free-state party being destroyed, they calculated upon an easy victory over the remainder. A letter of Atchison, written just before the murder of Brown, reveals the plan. The following are a few extracts from it.

* * * * "We are in a constant state of excitement here (Platte city). The 'border ruffians' have access to my room day and night. The very air is full of rumors. We wish to keep ourselves right before the world, and we are provoked and aggravated beyond sufferance. Our persons and property are not for a moment safe; and yet we are forbid, by the respect we owe our friends elsewhere, by respect for the cause in which we are engaged, to forbear. This state of things cannot last. You are authorized to publish the whole or a part of what I have written; but if Georgia intends to do anything, or can do anything for us, let it be done speedily!

"Let your young men come forth to Missouri and Kansas. Let them come well armed, with money enough to support them for twelve months, and determined to see this thing out! One hundred true men will be an acquisition. The more the better. I do not see how we are to avoid civil war; come it will. Twelve months will not elapse before war — civil war of the fiercest kind — will be upon us. We are arming and preparing for it. Indeed, we of the border counties are prepared. We must have the support of the South. We are fighting the battles of the South. Our institutions are at stake. You far southern men are now out of the nave of the war, but, if we fail, it will reach your own doors, perhaps your hearths. We want men, armed men. We want money — not for ourselves, but to support our friends who may come from a distance. I have now in this house two gallant young men from Charleston, S. C. They are citizens of Kansas, and will remain so until her destiny is fixed.

"Let your young men come on in squads as fast as they can be raised, well armed. We want none but true men. Yours truly,

"D. R. Atchison.

"P. S. — I would not be astonished if this day laid the groundwork for a guerilla war in Kansas. I have heard of rumors of strife and battle at Leavenworth, seven miles from this place, but the ice is running in the Missouri river, and I have nothing definite. I was a peace-maker in the difficulty lately settled by Gov. Shannon. I counselled the 'ruffians' to forbearance, but I will never again counsel peace. D. R. A."

It is Sunday to-day. We hear no pleasant sound of church-going bell, but, instead, the pounding on the little cabins in the forts. The hotel is again turned into barracks, and through the driving snow we see the sentinel at his post. Rough times our men see. Strong hearts and brave hands have come in to strengthen the town, leaving, in the rude cabins at home, wife and little ones without protector. The officers in the council-room sleep on the floor, or rude settees, when their tired energies must have some respite. Our people have great faith, great hope; nothing but these could keep them so brave, so full of courage, when dangers lurk around.

A gentleman just returned from a town south, some miles, said, "I have been in many cabins where there was no floor, and the snow came in at every crevice, and the cold was intense, yet I have seen a wonderful cheerfulness everywhere." They endure present suffering, and forego present comforts, in hope of an hour when the battlements of freedom shall be high and strong, and out of the rich and fertile earth shall arise pleasant homes, at the bidding of free labor. Their faith is more potent than that of the children of the wilderness, who looked to the brazen serpent for healing.

Some gentlemen were in yesterday from a neighboring settlement which has been threatened by Missourians. Signals are agreed upon, so that, should an attack be made there or here, mutual and speedy assistance might be rendered.

Pistols lie around the room loaded, and rifles are standing in safe places. How strange to our eastern friends would seem this familiarity with fire-arms, and stranger yet the necessity of carrying them to our sleeping apartments, and carefully watching them lest any dampness cause them to corrode!

The last thought of our waking hours is now the possibility that ere the morning's gray light the fiendish yells of the brutal assassins may be heard at our own doors, crying for blood. But we sleep with the same quietude as in dear old New England homes, where safety was the rule, and crime was met by swift-footed justice. Even this sense of insecurity is not without its use, for, with the early waking, comes a deep sense of thankfulness for another night safely passed, our home and friends still spared.

Feb. 10th. — Still cold. How the weather prophets have all spoken falsely! The Indians and traders, who have lived many years in the country, have never seen a winter like this. Many people have frozen their feet, so that for weeks they have been unable to walk. The general hilarity of the young people has not, however, been prevented by it. Sicoxie's dwelling has been open to visitors from Lawrence, and an occasional party, of a winter's evening, has shared the hospitalities of his house.

The Delawares are daily in our streets, and, with their gay dress, half-civilized, retaining always the Indian blanket, add a pleasant variety. Other tribes, less civilized, driven by the cold to winter near a settlement, have pitched their tents on the further bank of the Kansas. They also buy their provisions here, and pack them on ponies in bags. The poor little human, too, is encased in a red flannel bag, and carried on the back of the mothers.

People are now getting out ice for the next summer's heat. Several hundred tons are already cut. Those who work at it look oddly with their dress, half Indian, adopting blankets, leggins, and moccasins, as very conducive to comfort, while gloves, mittens and neck comforters, are the relics of a former civilization. As the party starts off, they might be mistaken for voyagers to the polar regions.

There was a wedding, yesterday, of rather novel character. Early in the autumn a man of some forty-five years of age came to Lawrence. A few more weeks passed, and sickness came to him, then death. He left a widow, over whose head scarcely eighteen summers had flown, to whom he was married just before coming here. Yesterday a second marriage was contracted. How full of change is life, and how in such a case as this the affairs of life jostle each other!

T. came up from town this afternoon saying, "Lawrence is to be attacked on the morrow!" The foundation of this present rumor rests upon the conversation of a pro-slavery resident near Lawrence, and a stranger, which was overheard by one of our citizens. T. brought up quite a quantity of lead, and busied himself a while running bullets.

We are much amused by the eastern newspaper accounts of the Kansas war, especially the part taken in it by the ladies. One would suppose, from reading these, that all the women had given up all the duties of life usually assigned them, and armed with rifles and revolvers, with bravado and threats, were ready at all times to resent injuries by an appeal to the former. Whereas, with the exception of a dozen ladies, more or less, who have busied themselves in making cartridges, most of us have had sufficient employment in the accumulated duties of our own households, in preparing for an unwonted number of guests. Some, far removed in the country, have manifested their sympathies by busily engaging in the baking of bread for the soldiers.

Lawrence and vicinity, numbering some fifteen hundred inhabitants, boasts many fair ladies; more who combine the advantages of personal beauty with intellectual merit, than in any place I ever lived. Our friends east need have no fears that in this "roughing it," not only with the necessary inconveniences, and inelegancies, of a new country, but with the tyrannous acts of a vile administration's tools, that they have lost any of the instinctive gentleness or modesty of woman. Firmness and a purer love of justice have been the gain of many. The acts of one woman here have probably given rise to the false impression which has gone over the country. Sheriff Jones made the arrest of a resident of Lawrence, after a previous unsuccessful attempt, Mrs. B. threatening to shoot the sheriff if he attempted to arrest her husband, and with pistols cocked gave sufficient proof of her sincerity in this determination; enough certainly to satisfy the sheriff, who was effectually cowed, and, amid the laugh of the by-standers, turned away muttering, he "had rather face an army of men than one furious woman." During the war, too, she had evinced her boldness on several occasions.

Statements of this kind have, probably, in the minds of many, given a wrong coloring to the actual character of the womanly element here; when, on coming, they might expect to meet a real Amazon, or Joan of Arc, they would be disappointed to see still uppermost the native refinement, sensibility, and modest dignity of a true woman.

22d. — No attack yet made upon us. In spite of all the talk, and all the marshalling of armed men in the border towns, we awake each morning, with wonder, to say we "still live." We might, however, have lived in greater security, had the mighty genius, who made these words memorable in his last hour, been ever true to the instincts of his great nature; had he in his declining days spoken honest words for freedom, as in his life's morning, or in its noon of splendor. "Lawrence is" not "in ashes," and her citizens still go unhung, notwithstanding the efforts of government officials to the contrary.

The following are the exact copies of letters from Gov. Shannon to the murderer of Barber, Gen. George W. Clarke, Indian Agent, and will show the direction of his efforts:

"Executive Office,
Shawnee Mission, K. T., *Jan.* 4, 1856.

"My dear Sir: Your two last favors are received; and I regret exceedingly to hear of your unpleasant situation. I hope things will grow better. The evidence you speak of must satisfy every one that you did not kill Barber. This difficulty out of the way, I hope you will have nothing to fear. I think that all organizations to take the law into the hands of self-constituted judges or conservatives of the peace will only lead to bad consequences. The other party will do the same by the way of retaliation, and no one will know when he is safe. I am glad to learn that you discourage all such movements.

"I will leave in the morning for Washington city, stopping some days at home on my way. I shall urge on the President the policy of stationing a company of United States troops in Lecompton, or such other place in that region as you may all think best. I shall also urge on him the policy of quietly stationing a company at Topeka about the middle of February next. The free-state government, you know, is to be inaugurated on the 4th of March, and the Legislature at that time will commence its session. The President has the power to station the troops at any place he sees proper, and there will be no necessity of his saying for what purpose he stations a company at Topeka. It will be looked upon by the free-state men as a significant sign, and may induce them to pause in their mad career of folly and treason.

"I would be glad if you would write to your friends in Congress, and get them to back me up in what I may seek to accomplish for the territory. Moreover, I desire to see and talk with the leading men of the South in relation to matters in this territory. I wish to post them upon the real state of things out here, and what the South must do the coming year, or lose all dominion in a few years in the affairs of the republic.

"Write to me frequently at Washington city, to the care of Gen. Whitfield. Post me at least once or twice a week as to all that is going on out here. I shall feel great solicitude as to the state of things in Kansas while I am gone.

"Yours with great respect,

"WILSON SHANNON.

"GEORGE W. CLARK, Esq."

The other brief epistle was filed "Gov. Shannon, Dec. 3, 1855. Advice to join the army with public funds." It is as follows:

"EXECUTIVE OFFICE,
SHAWNEE MISSION, K. T., *Dec.* 3, 1855.

"MY DEAR SIR: I think you had better join the command of Col. Childs or Gen. Richardson with your money. It is unsafe to remain at your house with so large an amount of money.

"Yours, etc.,

"WILSON SHANNON.

"Major CLARK."

The President, with the most abject servility to the slave power, has issued his anathemas against us. So base a document as his special message never before emanated from the White House. Has he read all history aright to suppose such bondage as this will not break its own chain? He talks of "treason." Treason against what? Not the United States surely, as, with earnestness stating our manifold and outrageous wrongs, we ask to be admitted into the sisterhood of states. Himself imbecile as the head of the government, he has bowed himself to the trappings of office. Stupid with the lust of power, and paving his way with the blood, the tears, the woes of Kansas, he has answered the question, "For what will a man sell his own soul?" Southern votes. Traitor to the mother who bore him, to his native state, to his country, and his God, when this great and mighty people shall arise from the blindness of their unparalleled prosperity, and break the bands of evil as tender withes, then shall he, calling upon the mountains even of his own state, find no place deep enough, no covert broad enough, to hide his shame; but in the annals of our country's history will this dark page be written, and he, the chosen guardian of the people's rights, shall wear the crowning infamy. It shall remain as a beacon light, as a warning to all seeking office, like the flaming sword guarding the entrance to Eden, that they sell not their honor, their principles, their very souls even. "So fallen, so lost!" the pitying heart cries.

This evening of the 22d of February witnesses a gathering here in honor of our first President, "whom the nation delights to honor." In strange contrast will his integrity, his uprightness, and his abiding hold upon the people's love, go down to posterity with the hollow-hearted truckling, the treachery, the imbecility, of the present incumbent of the presidential chair. The truth is again clearly maintained that justice sways the world.

Co. A. gave the party to-night, and many were there to partake of their hospitality, notwithstanding the inclemency of the weather. Co. A. are our strong defenders. At a moment's warning they are ready for any perils which endanger us. Much praise is due them for their unwavering courage and steadfast zeal when the rays of hope in other quarters have been few and flickering. They have taken to themselves the name of "Stubs," not particularly euphonious, but suggestive of their stature. A song has also been prepared by some of them, which they sang to-night, giving zest to the other amusements of the evening. It is in ballad style, sung as a solo by one fine voice, while all join in the chorus.

24th. — How genial the air is to-day! The icy bands upon the river have fairly given way, and the fast dissolving snows say loudly that spring is here. The golden haze of last evening, through which the setting sunbeams lingered and floated, spreading a halo of singular loveliness over this unrivalled landscape, gave a promise of warmer days. "The days of the singing-birds have come." With the life-giving days of spring, how could we hope for peace and tranquillity! Yet there is no just ground for such hope. Companies of mounted riflemen have been forming along the border; and a late "Independence Despatch" states that the militia of the border counties in Missouri are to rendezvous at Fort Scott, in this territory, on the 29th of February. Atchison also, a few days since, in his speech at Platte city, called upon his friends to "hold themselves in readiness against the 4th of March," as then there would be a new invasion of the territory." The "six weeks," which Jones pledged upon his honor should be free from invasion, are nearly over. A gentleman of Easton has received a threatening letter from his pro-slavery neighbors, warning him to leave. Everything looks threatening.

March 4th. — The doctor, with many more from Lawrence, left for Topeka yesterday, as the Legislature meets to-day. Lawrence is really deserted. Judge Elmore has, in conversation with the leaders of the free-state party, expressed strong desires that the members should not take the oath of office, as such an act would be considered treasonable, and they would be immediately arrested. Letters written from Washington also say that it is the design of the President to carry this matter thus far. By failing to take the oath of office, the present free-state constitution would be of no account. A gentleman has just been in, who reports a member of the Legislature arrived an hour since from Washington. He says the United States Marshal is on his way to Topeka, to arrest all who take the oath of office. He wishes to be arrested with the others, and will leave for Topeka this evening.

A strange farce this, of arresting freemen for no sin but a desire to maintain their rights as freemen, and for doing what California and Michigan have done before us. No iron rule bound them down like the hateful tyranny crushing Kansas.

Were it not for these continual attempts on the part of government to oppress us, Kansas would be peopled with a rapidity unprecedented in the settlement of any state. Her genial climate and rich soil offers attractions, while the class of people emigrating here afford the inducements of society, as intelligent and refined as any in the states.

Four religious societies have already been formed in Lawrence, and churches will this summer be erected. With the reviving of business this spring, a circulating library has been opened, where its members can find standard works, new books and publications, as soon as issued. There is also a bookstore, where the busy reader can suit his taste. The parish library connected with the Unitarian Church is large and valuable, and, when the room is ready for .ts reception, will form a valuable acquisition. With othei settlements there have been similar organizations, and means for improvement.

Beside Lawrence there are six other settlements, mostly eastern. Osawattomie, at the junction of the Potawattomie and Meradizine, which at that point takes the name of the Osage, is most pleasantly located. It derives its name from a fanciful clipping and mingling together of the words, Potawattomie and Osage. A pleasing variety of prairie and woodland marks the spot. Though the first settlement was made only a year since, with its large mill and enterprising people it bids fair to be a prominent point in the territory.

Hampden is still further south, and, notwithstanding the sickness which came so severely among them last year, its surpassing richness of soil and heavy tember, as well as its central position in the southern part of the territory, will induce many to locate in the region.

Topeka, the third town in size, is situated twenty-five miles above Lawrence, on the Kansas. The principal part of the town is about a fourth of a mile from the river, on the high prairie, which slopes gently to the shore. Webster Peak rises some four miles in the distance south, while the lands of the Potawattomie are but five miles away. The first settlement was made in December of 1854, by some members of the fifth party. When the spring opened emigration poured in there. Constitution Hall, a large hotel, several stores, and dwelling-houses of wood, brick and stone, show clearly their Yankee origin, and that in coming to the West they had not forgotten thrift and enterprise.

Wabousa is forty miles above Topeka, also on the Kansas river, while Mill Creek flows into it at this point. This location, which has many admirers, both for its surroundings of hill and plain, and richness of soil, was selected as a town site in the fall of 1854, by the fourth party, which came from New England. (The New Haven Company have since located there.)

Manhattan, at the junction of the Big Blue and Kansas, is seventy-five miles west of Lawrence, and eighteen from Fort Riley. It was also decided upon as a good location for a town by a portion of the fourth New England party.

Their numbers were strengthened in the spring of 1855 by the company from Providence, and afterwards by a company from Cincinnati, called the Manhattan Company. It has a very fine location upon the high prairie, with a bold prominence of singular beauty near by, upon whose sides dwarf cedars grow. Finely rolling prairies extend back of the town about four miles, where high bluffs surround all like a strong fortress. Being near the fort, and in the midst of a rich farming country, the productiveness of the soil for years must repay in large measure all labor bestowed upon it. A friend, who located not many miles from Manhattan in the spring, and cultivated a few acres, in the fall found himself the possessor of one thousand dollars more than when he came. He sold at the fort whatever he raised, at large prices. As all supplies for the fort at present are brought from Missouri, near one hundred and fifty miles, it must furnish a market for the fruits of the earth, could they be raised near by.

Council city, about forty miles south-west of Lawrence, and a few miles from the Santé Fe road, under the auspices of the New York Settlement Co., is situated upon the head waters of the Osage. A pleasant population are gathered there upon the half-mile claims. A lady of intelligence, residing there a few months, told me she had become very much attached to the people, and on no account would return to her old home, near New York city. Mills are being erected, and when they are in operation, as at the other settlements, nothing but quiet is needed for it and them to increase in population, in intelligence and wealth. Let Peace spread her broad wings over us, and no one can estimate the human tide sweeping westward which will be turned into these channels.

16*th*.—The following are the names of state officers and members of Senate and House, elected under the State Constitution:—

C. Robinson, *Gov.*
W. Y. Roberts, *Lt. Gov.*
S. N. Latta, N. F. Conway, M. Hunt, *Supreme Judges.*
J. A. Wakefield, *Treasurer.*
P. C. Schuyler, *Secretary.*
G. A. Cutter, *Auditor.*
E. M. Thurston, *Rep. of Sp. Ct.*
S. B. Floyd, *Clerk* " "
J. Speer, *State Printer.*

Members of Senate.

—— Adams,
J. M. Cole,
J. Curtis,
J. Daily,
—— Dunn,
L. Fish,
P. Fuller,
J. C. Green,
B. Harding,
G. S. Hillyer,
H. M. Hook,
J. M. Irvin,
D. E. Jones,
S. B. McKenzie,
B. W. Miller,
J. H. Pillsbury,
G. R. Rhaum,
T. G. Thornton,
W. W. Updegraff.

Representatives.

S. N. Hartwell,
J. B. Abbott,
John Hutchinson,
H. F. Saunders,
James Blood,
C. Hornsby,
E. B. Purdam,
J. McGee,
M. C. Dickey,
W. R. Frost,
W. A. Simmerwell,
S. McWhinney,
S. T. Shores,
S. R. Baldwin,
David Rees,
D. W. Cannon,
Isaac Landers,
J. M. Arthur,
Thos. Bowen,
H. B. Standiford,
H. H. Williams,
J. Brown, Jr.,
Isaac B. Higgins,
H. W. Tabor,
Henry Todd,
T. J. Addis,
A. B. Marshal,
J. Hornby,
D. Toothman,
J. D. Adams,
Abraham Barre,
Wm. McClure,
T. W. Platt,
Richard Murphy,
J. B. Wetson,
Rees Furby,
Wm. Hicks,
Wm. B. Wade
B. H. Brock,
B. R. Martin,
A. Jameson,
John Landis,

Wm. Bayliss,	W. T. Burnett,	R. P. Brown,
A. D. Jones,	J. K. Edsaul,	F. A. Minard,
E. R. Zimmerman,	S. Sparks,	G. Goslin,
J. W. Stevens,	L. P. Patty,	A. Fisher,
Wm. Crosby,	S. J. Campbell,	Isaac Cady.

The election for these offices was holden on the 15th January; on the same day M. W. Delahay was chosen representative to Congress.

The Legislature was organized on the 4th, and the state officers took the oath of office. Everything was quiet at Topeka. No attempts were made to arrest any one, although Sheriff Jones and a deputy marshal were there to witness the inaugural ceremonies of the new state government. With the exception of the fears of one of the members, harshly wrought upon by some lovers of mischief, there was nothing exciting. Yesterday, a friend arrived from the East. He came up from Kansas city in company with some of the office-holders under government. They were particularly anxious that the free-state government should not be organized. He also came up just in the wake of Gov. Shannon. He is, according to his report, highly spoken of by all the bar-tenders and others on the way, and had a grand reception at Lexington — which signifies, without any adornings of word or sentiment, "one big drunk."

Rumors came in to-night that a box of Sharpe's rifles, consigned to the territory, have been taken off the boat at Lexington and placed in the warehouse to await Governor Shannon's orders. Rumors fly as fast as autumn leaves, and we scarcely know what to believe. If, however, they have taken them, they will be useless to them as the slides are understood to be in another place, and it will puzzle them quite as much to use a rifle open at both ends as it did the one they threw away in December as useless, because there was no ramrod.

31*st.* — The last of March, and still all quiet. The grass is growing everywhere, and the tiny flower-bells sway gently in every breeze. In many places they spring up without leaves, and in the dusty roads.

Doctor left on the 24th for Washington, at noon, not thinking of going only an hour or two before. The 26th witnessed the laying of the corner-stone of the Unitarian church with impressive exercises. Ministers of different denominations took part in the service. Many people, of various beliefs, were there, as the first church was planted in the wilderness, and a common interest was pervading all classes. Beneath the corner-stone were laid copies of several papers in the territory, a sketch of Lawrence, and other articles of interest.

Gov. Shannon has returned to Lecompton, and Mr. Hoyt, in whose charge were the rifles, has waited on him in reference to their being restored. The poor governor is in a dilemma, neither horn of which he thinks quite safe. Shall he please border ruffians, or restore property to its rightful owners? Fear weighs down the scale on the border ruffian side, and the sage decision is, the guns must remain in Lexington.

The little boy, who had so much water to carry, errands to do, and so many times has come into the house nearly frozen, is dead. He was delirious a few hours and died. Startling as the intelligence was to us, in the dreary shadows of twilight, not having heard of his illness, and only three evenings since he had made us a longer call than usual, there was mingled a sense of relief There was a broken-spiritedness about the boy which was difficult to account for and is not natural to childhood.

Many houses are going up, and, every time we drive down, some new building or fence closes up the old travelled road. Men are digging at the quarries above us, and teams continually going up and down both sides of the house for buildings in town, and for the church half down the hill. We had recently had a house moved quarter of a mile to join our premises. It will be most conducive to our comfort, and that of our frequent lodgers.

Our house is at last completed, amid all the confusion of lathers, plasterers, paperers, and varnishers, with company all of the time, spending the day, the week, or longer. When the noise has been too unendurable, the horses and carriage have been put in requisition, and a ride over the beautiful prairies been enjoyed by our guests.

The house is entirely of black walnut; the finish, doors, window-casings, and mantels, of the same, all nicely polished. The paper of white satin, with a neat flower, in one room, while pretty wood-colors, in rosebuds and leaves, cover other walls, and give the whole a pleasing contrast. The furniture is mostly of the same wood, in pretty styles, while library, seraphine, pictures, which I prize both for their beauty and my long vested rights in them, with many other treasures of my girlhood, make this new home seem indeed like the old one, though so far transplanted. I would exchange its simplicity for no place where art and splendor have sway, while possessor of such living beauty as spreads itself around us.

In my drives of the last few weeks circumstances have brought me in contact with people of various mould, and I have been a learner of life by contrasts. The illness of a lady called me to the low door of her dwelling. It was built against a rock in a side hill, that forming one side. Logs and thatch completed the remaining sides and roof. The inside had the same rough aspect. Rude tables, of home-made manufacture, and three-legged stools, with one rocking-chair, completed the furniture. Several little children, neatly though poorly dressed, clung around the sad-looking mother, upon whose brow care had furrowed deep lines; but whose manner and appearance betokened better days than these in the past. Although ill, she was performing some domestic drudgery. She had friends east who would feel sadly did they know the circumstances which surrounded her here. The trials of the Kansas home had been many, yet she was still hopeful. Assuring her that anything we could do for her comfort should be gladly done, and thinking what a sad, thorny way the life-path is to many, we bade her "good-by."

Another day our fleet horses took our guests and us to see a person whose acquaintance was formed on the river, who was now boarding about six miles from Lawrence. The carriage halted in front of a large cabin, or two cabins rather, the space which is usually left open between them being made into a broad hall. G. said, "This is Judge W.'s." The lady whom we came to see opened the door before we reached it, being glad to see a familiar face. She was very pretty and intelligent, and the mother's heart could be seen in the soul-full eye as she caressed the little boy of a twelvemonth. Their home had been Wisconsin, while her husband was from the aristocratic old state of Virginia, and of a gentlemanly, dignified bearing.

This house is a home for travellers, and its capacious rooms were now full. Young mothers with their little children sat by the fire, and looked weary with their travels. Supper, too, was being prepared for the old judge, who came in from Lawrence, and with cheerful words, always so full of humor, greeted us as he distributed the letters he had brought from there. The beds were partitioned from this common sitting-room by long curtains. Baskets were hanging on poles over our heads, and bags of most capacious size were suspended from the walls, while meat and other articles for cooking found a place in the room. Judge W. is from Iowa, and has been, since his first coming here, one of the standard-bearers in freedom's army.

As we were returning, we met a very youthful lady and her husband, who have had some of the romance of life, and who are testing the sweets of not exactly love in a cottage, but love in a log-cabin, on the wide prairies. The lady was from a wealthy family in Cincinnati. Her friends opposed her in the choice of a husband, and while from home, at boarding-school, the marriage ceremony was performed, the young husband leaving the same day for Kansas. Some months after, when she had made known to her friends that she was already married, she also came.

A gentleman from Wisconsin was here in the early part of the month. He came to examine the country, its inducements to settlers, with reference to the sending out of a large company from Wisconsin. As he wished to meet the people of Lawrence, a reception had been proposed. The last afternoon of his visit had arrived, and the gentlemen in whose hands the arrangements had been left, declared themselves unable to accomplish anything on so short notice. Two of our ladies then took the matter in charge, and the evening found some one hundred persons assembled in a large hall, with refreshments of cake, nuts, fruit, and lemonade, provided.

A few days after, the New Haven company arrived. They

must have a welcome and the right hand of fellowship extended to them by our people. The hall was filled to its utmost capacity, and as our people briefly recounted the history of their stay here, their dangers and perils, they offered to the newly-arrived people the blessings of the civilization which a year and a half has wrought; while they offer, with the shield of an unwasted hope, and the buckler of unwearied energies, to stand by us in hours when evil shall threaten our liberties. Pleasantly thus the hours passed away, and the "Stubs" were loudly called for to close the assembly with their song.

CHAPTER XIV.

COMMITTEE OF INVESTIGATION — "SHERIFF JONES" SHOT.

THE second month of spring was quickly passing away, and quiet reigned — a quiet which seemed almost fearful from the very stillness. Since the threats of arrest in the early part of March, the voice of Missouri had been mostly silent. Save the oaths and imprecations which still fall on the ear, on passing her citizens, and an occasional opening of boxes designed for the territory, at Kansas city, there has been no outrage, and the press is silent as to her plans. Notwithstanding the persevering efforts of Douglas, the champion of the slave power, and the no less zealous exertions of Missouri's representatives, who hesitated not to utter untruths, declaring that no one came from Missouri to vote, — one of them, at least, being present at the election, — a committee has been appointed to investigate the wrongs of which Kansas has complained to Congress. We, as well as our eastern friends, anticipated that quiet would continue while the investigation was entered into; that, from motives of policy alone, the enemy would hide in their lair, and attempt to gain the favor of the committee by a present show of fairness. Emigration was again pouring into the territory; a company of one hundred, from Ohio, had just arrived, while the camp-fires at evening, and the white-covered wagons of the western emigrant, dotting the highways, told of a general desire to make one's self a home in Kansas.

About the 17th of April the commissioners arrived. The hotel, which we had long waited for, was nearly finished, and rooms for their accommodation were put in order by our people, before the proprietor of the hotel could get his furniture up from Kansas city. The commissioners went to Lecompton, and spent two or three days in copying the records of the elections from official books kept there.

On the 19th, Sheriff Jones, who has from the first seemed to be the apple of discord among us, his presence at once making tumult of quiet, again appeared in our midst, and attempted to arrest S. N. Wood, just returned from Ohio, after a winter's sojourn. He said to Wood, "You are my prisoner."

"By what authority?" was the very natural reply.

"As Sheriff of Douglas County."

"I do not recognize such authority," said Wood, adding, however, that he would go with him if he would allow him to go to his house, only a few steps distant, first.

This the sheriff refused, and Wood declared, "Then I'll not go with you at all!" and very coolly walked away.

Jones walked away also, minus a pistol, which had passed from his pocket. The whole affair only lasted two or three minutes.

The next day Jones came in town again to disturb the Sabbath's quiet, and arrest somebody. He was accompanied by four men from Lecompton, and he called upon a number of our citizens standing by to act as a posse, in assisting in the arrest of Wood. These citizens were looking on, simply, and it was an established fact, whenever Jones was seen in the streets of Lawrence, that something rich would happen, and, involuntarily, almost, they gathered around to see.

Jones looked for Wood in his house; but he was not there. Seeing T., another of the Branson rescuers standing by, and who had made the attempt to carry his own case to the Supreme Court, but had never been able to get a hearing at Lecompton, Jones pounced upon him. He took hold of him so fiercely, T. thought it was his intention to knock him down; so, forgetting his non-resistance, he struck Jones, whereupon the bold sheriff, with his comrades, left for Lecompton, muttering, however, "he would bring in the troops, and the arrests should be made. He had now some forty names on his paper, against whom warrants should be served."

The following letter, written by Jones to Marshal Donaldson, shows that the attempt to arrest Wood was made without a shadow even of territorial law:

"LECOMPTON, *April* 20, 1856.

"MAJOR I. B. DONALDSON, — My dear Sir: Samuel N. Wood is now in Lawrence, and I wish you to send me the writ against him. I arrested him on yesterday, and he was rescued from my hands by a mob. The governor has called upon Col. Sumner for a company to assist me in the execution of the laws. I will have writs gotten out against Robinson, and some twenty others.

"In haste, Yr obs.

"S. J. JONES."

The committee of investigation finished their work at Lecompton on Tuesday, the 22d, and returned to Lawrence the afternoon of that day. This first effort of theirs, showing clearly that the work of investigation would be carried on systematically, struck terror into the heart of the wrong-doers. That all their labors hitherto might not be foiled at one blow, they felt that a desperate effort must be made to break up the sittings of the committee, and the plan unfolded itself.

Also, on the afternoon of the 22d, word came into Lawrence that a band of men were encamped in the timber across the river. Two messengers immediately went out from Lawrence to see if there was truth in the statement, and returned, not only to verify it, but the bloody character of the gang. One of our messengers was fired upon, and only escaped falling into their hands by quickly plunging into a ravine until they, in their search, had passed by. They were men from Lecompton and vicinity, and were stationed there to intercept any persons who should attempt to escape from the bogus sheriff.

On Wednesday, 23d, the committee commenced examining witnesses in reference to the invasions. Dr. Stringfellow, Capt. Martin, of the Kickapoo Rangers, and others of like character, were in town. Some twelve came with Gen. Whitfield. In the afternoon of the 23d, the redoubtable sheriff, with authority vested in ten soldiers, under command of Lieut. McIntosh, following, again came into Lawrence. Without the least resistance on the part of any, six men, not implicated in the rescue of Branson, but having arrested no one to place in Mr. Jones' custody, were taken prisoners. They were lodged in a small building on the street, under the guard of the dragoons, and the sheriff occupied the tent of the officers, instead of going to the Cincinnati House, as usual.

In the evening the choir met at our house for a rehearsal. At about nine and a half o'clock T. came in. As the rest were singing, and scarcely noticed his coming in, I said to him, "Why, where did you come from? I thought you were in a safer place than Lawrence for rescuers."

He replied, "I have been out of town to-day; but I thought I would come over the hills to-night, and write a letter."

So, quickly getting him stationery and a light, he went out into another room to write. There was laughing and jesting among the singers, as they left soon after; a doubt arising whether they would all get to their homes safely, they having been on the street the day of the attempted arrest, and, as Jones had forty names, there was little reason to hope theirs were not in the list.

Doctor carried two ladies to their homes, each two miles from ours, and a mile apart. Just after they had gone, two gentlemen came from town. One was a stranger to me, and the other was W. He too had been from town during the day, and had gone home for a night's rest, when he was aroused by the other gentleman. They said "Good-evening," and walked in. W., espying T., who had finished his letter, and was about leaving for a safer residence than ours, said, "Well, T., our best friend is shot."

"Who?" was the question asked simultaneously by several voices; and W.'s reply, in the same solemn manner, "Sheriff Jones," startled us. Not because for him we had any esteem, any respect; but who was there in Lawrence that would take a brother's blood? Unlike the Missourians, who shot down inoffensive people with no more compunctions than they would a wild part-ridge, they feel there is a sacredness in human life, and would not rashly assume the power of the avenger.

The silence which momentarily followed was broken by the question, "Will he die?"

"They say he cannot recover."

The gentleman waited until the doctor returned, and then went back to town. He at once recognized in it a plan to involve our people in difficulty. It was either to be made the occasion of a new invasion, or at least to break up the sittings of the committee.

Jones, while sitting in the tent, the outline of his figure being clearly revealed by the light inside, was shot in the back. He fell to the ground, saying, "I am shot!" Some little time passed away before any physician saw him. At length Dr. Stringfellow was sent for, and the sheriff was removed to the hotel, into one of the rooms so lately fitted up, at the door of which a soldier stood on guard. Some physicians of Lawrence examined him that night and in the morning. The wound was between the right shoulder and spine. Though constantly groaning, Jones was able to turn himself in bed. Notwithstanding Gen. Whitfield's express to Missouri the next morning, with the intelligence that Jones was in a dying condition, he was removed to Franklin in the afternoon of the same day, accompanied by Gen. Whitfield and the friends who came with him, with an escort of dragoons. Gen. Whitfield declared it was not safe to remain in Lawrence; their lives were in peril; and he attempted to persuade the commissioners also to remove, upon the plea that Lawrence was an unsafe place to hold their sessions; that his witnesses could not come into town without risk of losing their lives. He did not hesitate to say, "The commission was at an end; they might as well return to Washington." The brave general stopped a few days at Franklin, then went to Lecompton, and finally returned to take his seat before the committee, positively asserting that "he did not leave Lawrence through fear."

Early in the afternoon of the day Jones was shot, a party of troops, who had been out in the Indian country, passed through town, and, having crossed the river, camped on the other shore. After the shooting, Lieut. McIntosh sent an express for them to return to Lawrence, which they did that night or the next morning.

The morning after the attack, our citizens called a meeting to take steps in regard to it. Speeches were made in reference to the whole matter, and the following resolutions, expressive of the sense of the meeting, were passed:

"*Resolved*, That the attempt made in our town, last evening, upon the life of S. J. Jones, Esq., while claiming to act as the sheriff of the county, was the isolated act of some malicious and evil-disposed individual, unexpected and unlooked for by our community, and unsustained by any portion of them.

"*Resolved*, That, in the opinion of this community, it was a cowardly and atrocious outrage upon Mr. Jones, and an insult and injury to the public sentiment and reputation of our town, and a crime deserving condign punishment.

"*Resolved*, That notwithstanding the unpleasant relation which existed between Mr. Jones and our citizens, if the attack could have been foreseen, or considered at all probable, we would have neglected no means to prevent or defeat it. We deeply sympathize with the wounded man, and will afford him all the aid and comfort in our power.

"*Resolved*, That we deeply regret that the perpetrator of this deed is unknown; and, if known to us, we would unhesitatingly expose and denounce him as the criminal.

"*Resolved*, That it is due to the reputation of our town, and loudly demanded by the deep and universal indignation which pervades our community, that the guilty author should, if possible, be sought out and surrendered to justice.

"*Resolved*, That a committee of five be appointed, whose duty it shall be to investigate the circumstances connected with this deplorable occurrence, and, if possible, to ferret out the guilty agent; and pledge ourselves that, although not responsible as a community for this act of a depraved individual, we will use our best efforts to show to the world that we have no sympathy for crime in any shape, and are prepared to treat the perpetrators with that stern justice which shall not stop to inquire whether they are friends or foes."

No sympathy was manifested for the cowardly act, and a committee was appointed to ferret out the assassin. Before the six prisoners were taken to Lecompton, efforts were made to arrest others of our citizens, in which they failed. Sam Salters acted as deputy sheriff. Some laughable incidents occurred, in consequence of these efforts.

This attempt to arrest our citizens for no crime but looking on, with hands in their pockets, when Jones calls upon them to assist him, — the person he wishes to arrest being missing, — is an outrage which arouses their indignation. They are not willing to be taken from their business, from their homes, to be imprisoned, or to recognize his authority in vexatious suits at law, by giving bail. Neither will they resist the United States government by an open resistance to the army and navy, which President Pierce says shall enforce these laws; a course, however, which the territorial authorities have earnestly and anxiously desired they should take. The only way then left to escape from such arrests was to keep out of sight of the troops; and this for several days was done most effectually.

Two young men, who had been stopping out of town for a day or two, came in one morning, thinking not to leave again, and were just flattering themselves of their present safety from molestation, when they saw the troops, with the notorious deputy, coming towards them. They quickly left all, and struck into the ravine west of the town; and, once in its friendly covert, they took different directions. The one whose course the troops followed, dropped his pistol as he ran, and, stopping to pick it up, he saw the deputy in advance of the troops, upon whom he was calling loudly to run. Mindful of the dignity of the United States uniform, the blue coats marched steadily on, not heeding his cry, and seeing the pistol again in the hand of the pursued, the sheriff seemed to regard the present as an opportune moment to take breath, and waited for them to come up. Whether the sight of the pistol may not have suggested such action, was but little doubtful. Be it as it may, sufficient time was given by the delay for our friend to make good his escape, and in the intricacies of the ravines find a safe retreat.

The same day another of the fugitives was sitting on the side of the hill above us, and did not perceive the troops until they were just upon him. He immediately started for our house, the sheriff calling, "Stop, or I 'll shoot you!" Quickening his pace, he replied, "Shoot then!" and was soon at the house. As he passed through the back room, whose doors were opposite, he said, "I want to leave my rifle here, for I can't run with it."

The troops were in sight; there was only time for me to ask, "Will they take rifles if they see any here?" and for him to reply, "Yes, the sheriff may order them to."

As the dragoons came so far down the hill that the house obstructed their vision of what was passing beyond, he slipped down the side hill north of us, and entered a little house, partly built, at the base. His wife, learning of his whereabouts, carried him his dinner, which he was leisurely enjoying, when the six prisoners, escorted by some eight or ten dragoons, passed by, on their way to Lecompton.

As soon as he left the house, we saw the troops, with Salters at their head, were fast coming, and E. and I stowed away the rifles, — several being in the house, as the guard were again on their watch at night. I called to E., who was noting their progress then, and asked, "Are they really coming?"

'Yes, they have taken the road leading to the house."

"Will I have time to change my dress?" The question was prompted by a desire to appear in proper costume before such dignitaries.

She replied, "No;" but had scarcely pronounced the word, before she said, "They are not coming. Salters has turned his horse down the hill." Running to the window, there they were,— President Pierce's army of subjugation,— going into the prairies. Salters had concluded to postpone his call upon us until some other day.

The next morning, before all of us had eaten breakfast, some who had come in late, and spent the night, thought they could venture down street thus early, and one of them had started down the hill. The others looking out, already saw the troops on the prairie, about a mile distant. A tap on the window, and a look in the direction to which a friendly hand pointed, was sufficient to bring the youth back. Hastily crowding into the pockets of the two cold meat, bread, cake, and apples, for their dinner, should they be where no dinner could be had, they started in an opposite direction from the one they had proposed earlier. By taking a circuitous route, they reached another house, where their welcome was always sure.

Soon a gentleman came up on horseback. The movements of the troops could be seen so far from our house, that it was a good standing-point for observations. He had scarcely seated himself, before the dragoons, their sabres flashing in the sunlight, came prancing out of town, and took the road which led near his house. He rose hastily, saying, "I'll call again some other day. I must go and tell the boys, now."

Mounting his horse, he was soon dashing along at a wild rate. Horse and rider were down through the valley, and over the summit of the hill, a half mile distant, as the dragoons came into sight around the brow of the hill north of us. The hills are in such a position that they did not notice the swift horseman, and as he rode up to his own door, more than a mile away, we knew that the fugitives were safe.

We at all such times left our doors unlocked, so the guard could come in for luncheon, or a short nap, and often in the morning we found as many again had slept beneath the roof as we supposed there would be on retiring.

The family of one of the men so savagely hunted for, removed from town to a little cabin a mile or two out. On coming home one night from a retreat still further in the country, about eleven o'clock, thinking to see his family for a short time, as he approached the house he heard a horseman coming slowly, then a voice from the ravine said something to him, and they held a low conversation. His suspicions were at once aroused. Could they have learned where his family are, and were they looking for him? are the quick suggestions of these circumstances, and, heeding the voice of prudence, he took another route, without going to his house, and came to ours.

The night was dark, and very wet, the rainy season having fairly set in. I had left fire and light burning, and had just gone up stairs. Hearing the door open softly, I went down again, and so perfect was the disguise of this familiar friend, that, without recognizing him, I said, "Good-evening;" and was only sure of his identity, though I took the extended hand, when he said, "You don't know me?" The life of this friend would not have been one moment safe had he fallen into the hands of the foe. They swore vengeance upon him hourly, and it was decided that, as his life was precious, not only to his family and friends, but to the free-state cause, he risked too much by remaining here, and he must leave. He had had several narrow escapes; at one time, driving near a house, and dismounting, while the enemy were in hot pursuit, he taking a footpath into a ravine close by, while a friend near put spurs to his horse, outstripped the enemy, and effectually misled them.

The house of Mr. Speer had been repeatedly searched for him. Sam. Salters went again with some dragoons, a few days since, and entreated them that they would do the despicable work for him. They refused to do so, as it was beyond the province of their duties. So, striking around with a hammer, which he picked up, to show his valor, he at last declared, "he would go in," and, opening the door, was greeted by a dash of hot water in his face.

Mrs. Speer then said, "I have respect for the United States troops. You can search the house, but, as for this puke of a Missourian he shall not come in." The troops enjoyed this unceremonious salutation, given by the Ohio lady to the brave official.

Over at the Wakarusa, something like the following colloquy passed between the troops and Salters. They had approached a house where Salters was hoping to find one of the rescuers. Salters said to them, pointing to different localities, "You stand at those points." The design evidently was to intercept any one who might attempt to pass from the house.

The dragoons replied, "It is not our business to arrest citizens."

With oaths, the sheriff again told them to take the places designated; but their reply, "We are to protect you, and how can we do it, if we are stationed so far away?" mollified his anger somewhat, as he remembered he had not had his life insured.

His courage, too, was exemplified by an attempted arrest of one of the rescuers last winter. He called at the house of one of the men on the Wakarusa, against whom he had a process, and Mrs. A. opened the door. Salters inquired, "Where is Mr. A.?"

She knew the sheriff by sight, and was determined he should not see Mr. A., and said, very calmly, "He is in the house."

"I want to see him."

"What do you want to see him for?"

"I have business with him."

"Well, you can't come in."

Some other like conversation followed, when Salters turned away to report that Mrs. A. had a pistol in her hand, and he had been in danger of being shot. When he knocked, Mrs. A. was putting wood in the stove, and went to the door with a little stick in her hand. Thus are our people continually harassed at the instigation of the administration. For several days the troops were about, attempting to find some one to assist the sheriff in arresting; although, in the manliness of their hearts, they loathed such service, and sympathized in the expression of one of them, on their first arrival at Lawrence, "We have never been ashamed of the United States service until now. We never were in such vile work before." Indignation fires the hearts of many of our people. The feeling is so strong, that continual efforts, on the part of the leading men, are necessary to restrain the men from resistance, and the danger is imminent that some one, pressed beyond the verge of human endurance, may, in an unguarded hour, yield to his impulses, and a hasty but ill-judged resistance bring on us the horrors of civil war.

Called, a few days since, upon a friend, who was living in a house, which was scarcely a shelter from the storms, and whose husband had been trying to make it more comfortable by his own efforts, when he was driven away by these villains, under the cover of law. The lady had been telling me, how, amid discouragements, this house had been erected; how she had been hoping to have it finished, so the rains would not beat in; and, just as the lumber was sawed, her husband, leaving her ill, had to flee out into the country.

She said, that morning she placed the rifle in the window, and told a young girl in the family, if she saw Salters coming, to let her know, and she would shoot him before he reached the house. By the determination of her countenance, I have no doubt she would have carried the resolution into effect. Yet, naturally, she was not a bold woman, but one of a timid, sensitive nature, to whom the change from the refinements and ease of city life to pioneer privations was enough to bear.

While I was there the husband came in, saying, as he sat down his rifle, and wiped the moisture from his brow, "I will not run again."

"But what will you do?" was the simultaneous query of us both.

"I will protect myself," was the bold, defiant reply.

"And resist the troops?"

"Yes, I will fight anybody. If I live under a government that does not protect me, then I will protect myself, Frank Pierce or no Frank Pierce."

This reveals the state of feeling as well as mere words can. It is intense, and every hour deepens it.

No clue has been found to the intended murderer of Jones. All efforts in that direction have proved futile. The safety of all our people demands that perpetrators of such deeds should be brought to justice. Many feared, at first, that the act was committed by some free-state man, who had been goaded on to vengeance by wrongs unparalleled under forms of law, which leave the wrong-doer to go unwhipt of justice, and oppress innocent and peaceable men. The impression prevailing now, in reference to the attempted assassination of Jones, is, that some fellow-gambler sought his life, and, by making the blow upon him in Lawrence, thought to screen himself, and fasten the odium of the dastardly act upon this oppressed people. The suggestion, too, made by some, that, as the killing of a free-state man in the fall proved a failure in causing a war of extermination, now the pro-slavery ranks must furnish a victim, that the crusade may meet with success, has some show of reason.

Reports are fast circulating through Missouri that Jones is dead, with handbills, of flaming character, calling upon them to the rescue, and their papers are full of the most vile fabrications, whole columns devoted to sentiments like the following: "Reeder and Robinson were the aiders and abettors in the deed, and, at the time, were in some gully behind the town, setting on their accomplices." And some of the papers are exceedingly bitter in their denunciations of the commissioners; all of which looks like exciting the people to another invasion.

The only thing which has been learned, in reference to the attack upon Jones, is the following. Early on the evening of the twenty-third, two men riding upon horseback, one very tall, and the other very short, stopped at a house about a mile from Lawrence, and not far from the Lecompton road. Their first question was, "Is Jones in Lawrence?"

The gentleman replied, "I believe he is."

The taller man then said, "I am a pro-slavery man, but Jones shall never leave town alive."

They left immediately, taking the direction towards Lawrence. A little time after, these men, marked by the differences in their stature, fastened their horses in front of a provision store in Lawrence, and walked hastily down the street towards the tents of the soldiers. Soon after, the firing was heard, and they, quickly mounting their horses, drove off furiously. Who they were has never been ascertained, and they were strangers to the few who noticed them.

CHAPTER XV.

REDOUBLED EFFORTS FOR A NEW INVASION.

May, the month of flowers, has come again. Sweet-scented, rose-colored verbenas are blooming side by side with a most delicate straw-colored flower. It grows in heads like the verbena, each separate flower being a little larger, and with serrated edge. The roses and pinks make the air heavy with their perfume. Since the taking of the prisoners to Lecompton, and the ill success of Salters in arresting any more, there have been a few days of quiet.

On the second of May, the ladies of the Literary Charitable Association gave a social entertainment at the hotel. There were the old settlers of Lawrence, who had pitched their tents on Mt. Oread eighteen months before, mingling with the newly-arrived citizens, the commissioners and their suite. The evening passed merrily, and, to add to the pleasure of many, the prisoners at Lecompton arrived. Through the intervention of the soldiers, their guard, word had been sent to Lawrence, that the lives of the prisoners were in danger, and some of our prominent citizens went up in the morning to effect their release by giving bail. The soldiers were convinced, from the continual threats against them, that there were intentions of foul play, and, against the wishes of the ruffians, they accompanied the prisoners half way to Lawrence. The returned men seemed to have the same feeling one would be likely to experience in escaping from a lion's den, and were glad to receive again the kindly sympathies of their friends. Refreshments of cakes, fruits, and ice-cream, were brought in at a late hour, and some lovers of the dance were there.

The outrages of the pro-slavery men are again becoming frequent. Mr. Mace, residing a few miles from Lawrence, the evening after having given in his testimony concerning the ill treatment he received at the hands of the Missourians at the election in the spring, was shot. Hearing his dog bark, he stepped out of his house, and reports of pistols resounded in the air, a ball striking him in the leg. At the same time, he heard one of the assassins say, "There 's another d—d abolition wolf-bait!"

A young man, living on the Wakarusa, has been for many days missing. He had been seen to enter the timber bottoms, on his way to Lawrence. Soon after, a pro-slavery man was also seen taking the same course, and a shot was heard. Mr. B.'s horse was found with saddle on, in the woods. The Stubs, of which young B. was a member, searched for him, but failed to find him.

The second week in May, the First District Court held its session at Lecompton, Judge Lecompte presiding. The congressional committee also held a session at Tecumseh, twenty miles above Lawrence, for the better accommodation of witnesses in that region; and of General Whitfield, who had declined to bring his witnesses to Lawrence, promising, however, to have them at Tecumseh.

The weather being lovely, the doctor proposed that Mrs. S. and I should accompany him to Topeka, five miles beyond Tecumseh. A little later than the committee we left Lawrence, our Scotch friend, who had just returned from the states, accompanying us.

A little way on the road we passed T., who was again going to Lecompton for trial, making the third visit there for the same thing.

We reached Big Springs near noon. A collection of houses and a store were here, upon exceedingly high ground. The site gained its name from a number of springs of excellent water in the deep ravines near the town.

A mile further on was Washington; unlike the Washington with its broad avenue on our eastern slope, where Congress-men, fresh from gambling-hells and deeds of sin which the darkness hides, shoot down their fellows; where our senators, for words of eloquence and truth, born of holy aspirations for freedom, are beaten by southern chivalry. (?) O, how the boast of the South, their chivalry, their gallantry, has in these latter days proved itself only the shadow of a substance, the semblance of a reality!

At this Washington, where its log house, kept by Pennsylvanians, bears the reputation of good meals, and quickly served, we stopped for dinner. The huge stone fire-place, the lounge covered with brocatelle, the damask curtains, the little fancy clock, and flower-vases, gave an air of comfort to the rude arrangements of a pioneer home. A Botany, Mrs. Lincoln's Botany, bringing back our school-days and wild romps for flowers, lay open on the lounge, and told of a student here. To our question of who it might be, seeing only the proprietor and his wife, the mother, with a mother's pride, said her son was studying at home; that he missed much the schools of Pennsylvania, but was hoping that soon good schools would be established here.

The afternoon's ride was over a country of most enchanting loveliness. Timber was more abundant, not only marking the line of the creeks, but crowning the summit of many an elevation. As we rode through the woods, we saw little log cabins, with a clearing around them, and grounds fenced in. The creeks were all high from recent rains, but as we crossed several without difficulty, and when upon the further side of each one, safely over, I asked the doctor if there were any more, I grew almost impatient at the stereotyped answer, "One or two," and Mrs. S. laughed, and said, "Why, what a timid little thing you are!" It was not fear of any personal danger which annoyed me, but the unpleasantness of detention by the breaking of the carriage. The horses were very restive in going down the steep banks, and it would not be the most delightful thing in the world to find one's self taking an unintentional plunge-bath in such muddy waters as the pouring rains of the last week had occasioned.

But we had accomplished the journey to within three or four miles of Tecumseh without hindrance; and, as we approached another creek, which had precipitous banks, we found four heavily-loaded emigrant wagons, each drawn by five or six yoke of oxen, in advance of us. One or two teams had just crossed, and one was then going down the bank, while the last one was waiting, and we drove in ahead to be ready for the next passage. There was a bridge over the water when at its usual height, but this rise had covered the bridge, and everything by which we could tell its actual position.

The heavy wagon of the emigrants struck the bridge a little too far on the right, and the wheels slid off into the water. The danger at this time was that the wagon would be upset into the creek. We could not pass it, and must wait just where we were, half down the winding bank, a high ledge on one side of us, and a miniature precipice on the other, where old dead branches of trees abounded. The driver of the wagon took off all the oxen save one yoke, and he cudgelled them in a manner, which the ancient text, "The righteous man is merciful to his beast," proved him to be entirely lacking in the kindly element, but not one step did the poor cattle stir.

A half hour passed away. The other yokes were put on again. The man stood on the lower side, in the water, and attempted to steady the wheels; but the oxen did not pull. The wagon was a fixture directly on this highway between Lawrence and Topeka. The oxen seemed unused to the yoke, and the teamsters equally new in driving them, and the question of our getting to Topeka began to grow serious. At last the oxen were taken from the front of the wagon, and placed on the other end; also some other cattle were taken from the wagon on the road, making ten yokes in all. The attempt to start the wagon backward was now to be made, and we were directly in the way. Our carriage was driven as far out on the edge of the bank as it could stand, leaving just room enough for the oxen and wagon to pass out by the side of us, if they behaved well, and with a laudable regard for other people's rights, made no encroachments upon ours. Mrs. S. seemed to have a doubt of their doing so, and with the gentlemen left the carriage, and me all alone in it. Mr. P., however, was not far away. Doctor at last took the whip, and tried his skill at driving the patient creatures. Another, with whip in hand, which he brandished with amazing dignity, stood between them and the carriage; still another was holding the tongue of the wagon. After various ineffectual efforts, and much loud hallooing, mingled with doubts and fears on our part, the oxen gave one "long and strong pull together," and the wheels moved. The man standing nearest them fell into the water, but he came up again with a broad grin upon his face, and we could not help making it general. With three pulls, and three several "dips" of the man into the creek, the laugh each time being louder as his good-natured face appeared dripping with the muddy water, not a jot of his cheerfulness abated, the wagon was removed from the way. Our party being quickly reseated in the carriage, by the aid of the drenched man, who offered to stand by the bridge that we might know where it was, we reached the other shore safely, and were on our way again. We asked the doctor, who had had a California trip overland, how this compared with some of their crossing of streams on the plains, and he answered us very energetically, that "it was nothing in comparison to those." On our arrival at Tecumseh, we found the party who had started ahead of us had had trouble in crossing, the water being so high that they had to leave their carriage for a time, getting over themselves at some other point, or climbing among the dead logs.

Tecumseh is a fine location for a town; high from the river, with a heavy growth of wood near by. A court-house of brick, with pillars, is being built, also a large brick store, while the hotel, which is a wooden building, is quite capacious. Stinson, a white man, who married a Shawnee wife, resides here. He is a pro-slavery man, and owns two or three slaves. By the treaty, every member of his family is entitled to two hundred acres of land; hence, he is quite a landholder. Judge Elmore also resides here. It has been currently reported, and never contradicted, that, during the severe cold of last winter, the judge and his wife were obliged to take care of their nineteen slaves — he hauling wood, and cutting it, to keep them warm; that one old man froze to death in his bed, while another was crippled for life.

The district here is largely free-state, notwithstanding some of the owners in the town are pro-slavery. Col. Woodson, of Independence, Missouri, acting counsel for Gen. Whitfield, had business at home which required his immediate attendance, when he learned the commissioners were going to Tecumseh. The singularity and suddenness of the move was explained satisfactorily, when examining the poll books of the 30th of March election, the name of Col. S. H. Woodson, Independence, Missouri, was found registered in full.

We arrived at Topeka towards night-fall, after crossing two more deep ravines, and one strong bridge, a mark of civilization and progress. We drove to a building which had been kept as a hotel by an acquaintance. They had gone out of town, and were living on a claim. Having found the direction, we went out there, stopping on the way, however, at "Commercial Head Quarters," to learn if accommodations for a few days could be had there. The reply was, "We are building, everything is topsy-turvy, but we will see what we can do for you."

We found our Boston friend living some two miles from town, and no road running near. There was a lovely prospect in the distance, but solitude unequalled all around. The house was neither a shelter from the winds nor storms. The floor-boards were loose, moving at every step, with large cracks between, and, through fear of snakes, she slept upon a few boards laid upon the beams near the roof, and scarcely dared step from the door, so great was her fear of them. She was ill with a severe cold, taken by exposures, and seemed a little nervous too, in regard to the continual outrages of the Missourians, but was hoping soon to get back to her house in town.

We returned to "Commercial Head Quarters," and entered through a long, narrow room; cooking-stove and table were standing upon one side, and table with chairs upon the other, while upon the end, leaving only room for the door into an entry, were a large number of shelves, with other shelves also near the door, on the side of the room. They were all empty, and Yankee ingenuity does not suggest for what purpose they were hung. Two or three cages of canaries hung overhead, and they twittered and sung continually. Back of the little entry was the dining-room, with just room enough left for stairway between the two rooms.

The stairs were little, narrow boards laid on insecurely! How dizzy one's head grew at the first steep ascent! Time and use even did not render them wholly safe to me, with nothing to steady one's self by, and there was no security against reaching the bottom by a quicker mode than stairways usually anticipate. On reaching the landing at the top, we found ourselves in a room of the same size as the lower one. This, evidently, was a general sleeping apartment, for there were beds, beds, nothing but beds. They stood along the sides of the room, the foot of the first reaching the head of the second, and leaving only a space a few feet square by the stairway. Stepping about two feet in a straightforward direction, we came to another little entry, from which stairs to the attic ascended. On the left was a door opening into the printing-office, and on the right a curtain, which supplied the place of door, was uplifted, and we were ushered into an apartment. We sat down on a sofa (two were standing close together, and filled one side of the room), and realized that, as Mr. G. said, "they are topsy-turvy," and not that exactly, but that there is a great deal of furniture in one room. The width of the sofa, seraphine, and large French bedstead, was a nice fit for one end of the room. The lounge and handsome secretary, with a chair at each end of it, filled in between the bedstead and another one at the other end of the room. Centre-table stood a little in front of the secretary, with a vase of beautiful flowers, and jewelry case upon it. A large Boston rocker, with mahogany squab-seat chairs and cricket, made up the movable furniture. A family portrait gallery adorned the walls. There were pictures of beautiful little children, and pictures, also, of scriptural design, drawn from the times of the Saviour. This room was set apart for Mrs. S. and I, and, though one could hardly take two steps without moving a chair, we soon felt quite at home. There was a number of boarders in the house, and in the two families keeping the house only thirteen children. This house, at the time of the constitutional convention, accommodated seventy boarders.

The ladies of Topeka, with their wealth of social feeling, soon called to see us. The sewing-circle and temperance society also held their meeting while we were there. The ladies, coming from almost all states in the Union, seemed to be bound together in strong bonds of friendship, and the partiality they feel for Topeka above other settlements is not only felt but loudly expressed. It is doubtless true that the residents of other settlements are as strongly impressed with the advantages of their own. It is a singular fact, and one often remarked in this country, that, if we were to judge by the observations of others, or our own feelings when in different localities, each place is "the most beautiful of all." Almost every person seems to think their own claim the best, and it can only be accounted for by the acknowledgment of the fact that an exceeding loveliness is spread over the whole face of the country, and actual possession of such beauty doubles its value to the possessor.

Towards evening of one of the days we were at Topeka, the commissioners, Gov. Reeder, and several others, arrived from Tecumseh. The house was indeed full. Doctor went out to some of his acquaintances, to see if he could not find lodgings for us elsewhere, that he might, by giving up his bed in the general sleeping-room, make room for more; but every one's house was full. The necessity of the case then demanded that two sleeping apartments should be made of one room, and, by driving some nails in the beam overhead, and hanging Mr. S.'s large, red, double blanket in the centre, this was quickly done.

The same day one of Buford's men was at Tecumseh with a subpœna for Gov. Reeder to appear as a witness before the grand jury at Lecompton He declined answering the summons, on the ground of his business before the commissioners — that he was exempt from appearing as a witness. Open threats were being made at this time against Gov. Reeder's life. Major Clark, the murderer of Barber, was drilling a company of fifty men at Lecompton, daily, and the Buford men were gathering at Lecompton. We passed them in companies of eight or ten as we went to and from Topeka. They have no money, only the clothes they wear, and a rifle, for which they have given their notes to Major Buford. They looked, indeed, like the very offscouring of all creation.

When they landed at Kansas city they had no money to pay

for their night's lodging, and did not meet with that free, whole-hearted support which they expected from the many calls made upon them to come to the territory. One of the men was forcibly ejected from the pantry of the hotel there, that not being the landlord's usual place of entertaining his guests. The same evening, after reaching Kansas city, Major Buford called his men on to the high hill back of the hotel, and laid down the orders to them. He bound them upon an oath taken upon the Bible to remain in the territory to vote, and at all times to hold themselves in readiness to fight while they did remain. Some of the party, who, by false representations, had been induced to join the company, became disgusted with the new phase affairs were taking, and immediately left for home. Others would have done the same, but for want of passage-money.

A member of that company, now in the government employ, told me the offer of Major Buford was, to pay their expenses here, support them twelve months, and set them upon claims which were already selected for them, and he was then to have a share in the claim. Being poor, these inducements to get a living were a temptation, and the lure was successful. How different was the reality when they arrived here! This man also stated that the first time they heard that fighting was to be their business was when they arrived at Kansas city. Hence the disgust with which many returned to their homes. That they are, as a whole, a poor, degraded, ignorant set of beings, one glance will suffice to show. Complaining as one of them was to a free-state man, for years a resident of the territory, of his bitter fate, the latter said to him, "Why don't you get some work to do?"

"I can't work; I never worked a day in my life."

"Then you will have to buy a negro, and let him work for you."

"I have no money to buy anything."

What can such a community as this do in Kansas? Is there anything left for such creatures to do but kill, plunder and destroy? It has been the threat of some pro-slavery men, that when the free-state men should be driven out, they would take their houses and claims. Is this the selection of claims Major B.

had reference to, in promising claims to his men? While such men as these were making Lecompton their head-quarters, and Major Clark was drilling his fifty men, Judge Lecompte delivered his extraordinary charge to the grand jury. As a legal curiosity it deserves preservation, and will be regarded with interest by all who have fallen under the jurisdiction of a judge as much more infamous than Judge Jeffries as his consummate ignorance renders him more despicable. A portion of it reads thus:

"This territory was organized by an act of Congress, and so far its authority is from the United States. *It has a legislature elected in pursuance of that organic act. This legislature, being an instrument of Congress by which it governs the territory, has passed laws.* These laws, therefore, are of United States authority and making; and *all that resist these laws resist* the power and *authority of the United States, and are, therefore*, guilty of high treason.

"Now, gentlemen, if you find that any person has resisted these laws, then you must, under your oaths, find bills against them for high treason. If you find that *no such resistance has been* made, but that combinations have been formed for the purpose of resisting them, and individuals of influence and notoriety have been aiding and abetting in such combinations, then must you find bills for constructive treason." To make the matter so plain that even the dullest of his hearers may not fail to comprehend his meaning, he states that some who are "dubbed governor, lieutenant governor, etc., are such individuals of influence and notoriety."

Before this famous charge of Judge Lecompte, on the 8th of May, as Gov. Reeder had returned from Tecumseh, and was conducting the examination of a witness before the committee at Lawrence, Deputy Marshal Fain appeared in court, and served a writ of attachment upon Governor Reeder. He arose and informed the committee of the fact, and gave the three following reasons for his not obeying the subpœna of the day before; namely, informality in the writ, insecurity of person at Lecompton, and privilege as a member of Congress. The writ was not properly addressed to any officer; it did not specify the day in which it required him to appear; it was not properly attested. He stated further, that the House of Representatives had recognized him as a claimant for a seat in that body, as a delegate from Kansas; that he was, therefore, entitled to the same privileges as a member of Congress, conferred by the sixth section of article first of the federal constitution. It was also the opinion of the majority of the committee that Gov. Reeder would be privileged from arrest to the same extent that a member of the committee would be, and that his duty required him to attend the sittings of the committee instead of those of the territorial courts. Gov. Reeder was a contestant for a seat in Congress; his memorial had been received; the committee was sent to Kansas to take testimony in his case; and his attendance, in obedience to the summons of the committee, is essential to the prosecution of their labors. He must judge for himself upon his course of action. Gov. Reeder then informed the officer he should not be arrested, and, if he attempted it, it would be at his peril. Soon after the deputy left, however, he sent a letter to Judge Lecompte, saying he would appear before him as a witness, if he would promise him protection while in Lecompton, and grant him a safe return to Lawrence when he should have given in his testimony. The answer of the judge was, that "the matter had gone out of his hands."

The committee being about to leave for Leavenworth, Governor Reeder was warned not to go with them if he would escape assassination; but his reply was that he should go. It was not unknown to many that, on his first arrival in Kansas, in May, coming to Lawrence by way of Leavenworth, he had only left the last-named place when a band of men threatened to assassinate him if he could be found. These threats had not grown less bitter or more rare, and reports from Wyandot, Leavenworth, and Kansas city, showed that a new invasion was being planned against the territory. On the tenth, word came into Lawrence of these plans of the borderers. They were crossing into the territory and forming about Atchison, ready to march at any time. Their first plan was, by forced and stealthy marches, at night, to surprise Lawrence. But, seeing the impracticability of such a procedure, another plan more sure was adopted, and, on the eleventh of May,

United States Marshal Donaldson issued his proclamation of falsehoods.

"PROCLAMATION!

"TO THE PEOPLE OF KANSAS TERRITORY.

"Whereas certain judicial writs have been directed to me, by the First District Court of the United States, etc., to be executed within the County of Douglas; and whereas an attempt to execute them by the United States deputy marshal was violently resisted by a large number of the citizens of Lawrence, and as there is every reason to believe that an attempt to execute these writs will be resisted by a large body of armed men; now, therefore, the law-abiding citizens of the territory are commanded to be and appear at Lecompton, as soon as practicable, and in numbers sufficient for the proper execution of the law.

"Given under my hand, this 11th day of May, 1856.

"J. B. DONALDSON,
"*U. S. Marshal for Kansas Territory.*"

My husband, going upon business to the East, was also taken prisoner on the tenth of May, by a gang of Missourians at Lexington. They declared he was running away from an indictment, and by their whole conversation showed themselves better acquainted with the designs of Judge Lecompte and Gov. Shannon than the people of this territory. They sent word to this tool of theirs, who bears the title of governor of the territory, and he recognized them as his agents and accomplices.

Letters written by H. C. Pate, filled with utter falsehoods, calculated to arouse the passions of the border men, were published in the St. Louis *Republican.* In a letter dated Palermo, K. T., May 5, and published in the *Republican,* he made an untrue statement with regard to Jones, then stated that a man by the name of Harper had been shot in or near Lawrence, and went into doleful strains on the want of compassion of the people of Lawrence for the bereaved wife and children; all of which was a sheer fabrication — no man of the name of Harper having lived in Lawrence, or any man been molested; and another proof was given of the old adage, that "an idle man's brain is the devil's workshop." He closed his letter, however, by an appeal for present help, saying, "I think I shall be able, in a few days, to give you something of an interesting and conclusive character."

In this way was every means used to create a war in the territory. The St. Louis *Intelligencer* published the following letter, dated

"PARKVILLE, Mo., *May* 16, 1856.

"Prepare for an awful shock! Hold a steady helm, or the old ship will be wrecked! Armed men are rushing into the territory. The destruction of Lawrence is meditated. Civil war is just before us. Couriers just from Lawrence say they have from one thousand to fifteen hundred men, while there are from eight hundred to one thousand around the place, but increasing fast. It is thought the destruction of the committee and evidence is the cause of the outbreak, or at the bottom. We pray the Almighty God to avert these dreadful evils. The secret border league is at the head of this affair. It is expected to result in disunion. The ultras on both sides are dangerous men. Strike boldly for the union of this great country, and may God bless you. It is said the ladies of Lawrence are arming. The Platte city cannon and many men have gone over. None have yet gone from Parkville. It is not advised by the masses; most good citizens are against it."

While this shows the state of things in the Missouri border, outrage and pillage were already committed by the ruffians arrived in the territory. As a party of free-state men, on the fifteenth of May, were quietly at work in a field in Benicia, a little town about eight miles from Lawrence, unarmed, they were suddenly surrounded by twenty-five Missourians, wholly armed, who, without any warrant or authority, took them prisoners. They carried them into a neighboring cabin, and, with many threats of instant death, ordered them to leave Kansas. "G—d d——n you, if you are ever caught here again you shall be strung up! Go to Nebraska, d——n you! You have no right in Kansas!" was the language of these ruffians. "We are coming to Lawrence in a few days, to wipe out the d——d abolition city, and to kill or drive off every one of the inhabitants," was the *finale* of all their threats. All the prisoners except a Mr. S., of Worcester, Mass., were soon released. He had answered them like a man, and was reserved for further punishment. The following is the speech of Major Herbert, the leader of the ruffians:

"GENTLEMEN: The cause of our being together to-day is of a peculiar character. The condition of things at this time, and things that have been said and done, you are better acquainted with than I am. I have been here but a short time. What you know are facts; what I know is hearsay, but my information is such that it becomes facts.

"I now want to give you a piece of advice. You are in a state of *rebellion*. You have been aiding designing men in carrying out their *point*, which has brought this *Union* almost or quite into a state of dissolution. You have been offering resistance to the laws of the territorial Legislature, which was no doubt a legal one. The President has declared it legal; Congress has declared it legal; and resistance to those laws is TREASON!

"What did you come here for? Why did you not go to Minnesota, or Nebraska? It is not half settled, and is as good country as this. But, no; you must come here. You want to get the whole of the territory. That belongs to the South.

"We are going to drive you all out. We are going to Lawrence to take their arms. We are going to take every d——d thing they have got. The South asks nothing of the North. Now my advice to you is this: keep on at your work here, stay at home, have nothing to do with elections or voting. If you do you will be liable to be hanged on the first tree you come to.

"Every man has a right to his opinions, and a right to express them openly. Do you suppose I would go into a free-state camp and tell them that I was a free-state man? No, by G—d! I should hope I had more respect for myself or country. I told my people, before I left home, that I would see that this *was made a slave-state, or die*, and, by G—d, it shall be done, or every pro-slavery man in the territory will die in the attempt. It will be done peaceably if it can; if not, by G—d, it shall be by the point of the bowie-knife!

"This territory belongs to the South, and, by G—d, the South will have it! Is not this so, boys? [turning to his posse. 'It is,' was the response.] You have offered no resistance, and I hope that you will not. If you do you will be dealt with in a more summary manner. Gentlemen, you are released."

Cows and other animals had, for several days, been killed and carried off to the camp of the invaders at Lecompton. One free-state man was obliged by the ruffians to drive his own cow there, where they killed her before his eyes.

On the evening of the 13th of May, Mr. J. Weaver, assistant sergeant at arms of the congressional committee, was returning to Lawrence with one of the witnesses whom he had subpœned. Not finding his way to the ferry readily, a United States dragoon, whom he met, offered to show him the way, and as they came in sight of the ferry, they were just upon a camp of one hundred men, armed with revolvers, bowie-knives, United States muskets, and bayonets. They rode through the camp to the ferry-landing, and dismounted. As they did so, several men lying about on the ground exclaimed, "What in the h—ll does that mean?"

A crowd from the camp gathered around them, and one, coming in front of Mr. Weaver, asked where he was from, and where going; to which he replied he had been up north, and was going to Lawrence; when one of the ruffians remarked, "You won't get there very soon." He then asked "how he was on the goose?" to which he replied, "he was on the right side," but did not enter into any explanations of what, in his estimation, the right side might be. This answer raised the ire of the ruffian, and he said Mr. Weaver was "a fit subject to stay with them over night."

At this remark a number of the men gathered around with muskets in their hands. Another man, who had been talking with the dragoon, came up and said to the man, "It would be better not to interfere with Mr. Weaver, as he was in charge of the dragoon." Mr. Weaver then said "he was not in charge of the dragoon, but was himself a United States officer," and to the question of what kind of an officer, he replied, " he was an officer of the U. S. House of Representatives, and was called sergeant-at-arms."

His papers were then called for, and he handed his subpœna to a man they called colonel, who had the appearance of a man who might read.

After a thorough examination of the papers, and some consultation, he told Mr. W. "his case would be considered," asking him if " he did not know these were war times."

When Mr. W. expressed his ignorance of such a fact, the ruffian replied, "he would inform him these were war times, and folks must be on their guard; that it was a matter of importance that people be examined who do not show a plain front." He finished his dissertation by saying " that Mr. W. could not be released from custody, as the captain was not in camp."

Mr. W. told him "it was a matter of importance that he be not detained, as he must appear before the committee of investigation at Lawrence;" and, after a good deal of urging, another examination of his papers, and a new consultation among the ruffians, it was decided that Mr. W. and the witness should be sent under a guard of armed men to Lecompton, to be examined by Col. Wilkes, commanding at that time. So, after a detention of an hour or more, they were sent to Lecompton, and delivered to Col. Wilkes. After an examination of the papers, assisted by a Gen. Cramer, Col. W. told Mr. Weaver he thought "he was entitled to pass without molestation; but the forces in the territory being still unorganized, he would be liable to interruption and detention by the way."

He told him, also, "if he was hailed by any of the parties, to answer immediately, by all means, else he would certainly be shot."

At the request of Mr. W., to save detention by these parties, Col. Wilkes gave the following pass:

"LECOMPTON, KANSAS, *May* 13, 1856.

"TO ALL WHOM IT MAY CONCERN: This is to certify that I have examined the papers of Mr. J. A. Weaver, in company with

Gen. Cramer, and I am satisfied that he is acting under authority of the U. S. House of Representatives, and should pass unmolested.

"WARREN D. WILKES,
"*Of South Carolina.*"

This is a South Carolina pass; and the party who arrested Mr. W. claimed to be from South Carolina. Wilkes is one of Buford's men, a lieutenant in the band of ruffians. He is one of the self-constituted regulators in the territory in the affairs of actual settlers; was one of the destroyers of Lawrence, and was afterwards the leader of a gang of brutal men at Leavenworth, who arrested peaceable citizens without authority, and at the point of the bayonet.

On the 16th May, as Mr. Stowell was coming in from Kansas city to Lawrence, passing through Franklin, his wagon was stopped, and some boxes of guns broken open, and contents taken. Also a wagon-load of flour was taken possession of by the marshal's posse.

About the same time, Dr. Root and Mr. Mitchell, only a little time in the territory, having been down below Lawrence to look after some teams which they thought were delayed unnecessarily, on their return to Wabousa, left Lawrence on the afternoon of the 16th. On passing an encampment of Marshal Donaldson's, it being already dark, they were fired upon by a company of fifteen or twenty men, who rushed from a small cabin near the road, shouting and firing as they came. They were taken prisoners by them, while two gentlemen ahead of them, on fleet horses, escaped the whizzing balls. Hence the intelligence which went over the country that Dr. Root and Mr. Mitchell were killed.

About the same time, Judge Conway and P. C. Schuyler, returning to the territory from a tour in the states, were taken off the William Campbell by a mob. Their appeal to the officers of the boat availed them nothing. They only learned from them the simple fact that the affair was a "matter between them and the mob." The mob pretended "these gentlemen were endeavoring to leave the territory, and that writs were out against them."

Their coming into, instead of going out of, the territory was sufficient to show the falsity of such a pretence, and they expressed their willingness to answer to any charge before any court. The gentlemen preferring to trust their safety in the hands of friends, turned a deaf ear to the suggestions of one of the border ruffians, "that they were better off where they were than in the territory; for there was a heap of trouble there now, and, from what they believed, would be much safer in Parkville." Some of the more respectable people in Parkville interfered, and procured the release of Judge Conway and Mr. Schuyler from the ringleaders.

On the night of the 13th, Mr. Jenkins and G. W. Brown, of Lawrence, were taken prisoners by a band of ruffians, half-way between Westport and Kansas city, on their way to Lawrence.

Travelling was unsafe in the territory, bands of these ruffians being encamped at many points. About the 18th, armed men were camped on the "Big Stranger," waiting for the water to abate before they could cross with their two brass six-pound howitzers, and their ammunition and provision wagons. There was the camp of desperadoes at Lecompton, and bands of armed men infesting the usually travelled route from Lawrence to Kansas city. People passing on the highways were stopped, searched, and robbed of anything which pleased the invaders. These highwaymen and freebooters were called into the territory by the marshal's proclamation of the 11th, and their expenses were to be defrayed by the general government. Our people were annoyed beyond endurance. Their property was destroyed, their lives in jeopardy, and their rights trampled upon by these vile minions of a viler administration. United States muskets were put in the hands of these Carolinians and Alabamians, not one month in the territory, by Gov. Shannon, thus making himself a tool in the hands of the President, to consummate his infamy. The following pass is proof positive that Gov. Shannon is implicated in all these villanies:

"EXECUTIVE OFFICE,
LECOMPTON, K. T., *May* 17, 1856.

"The bearer of this is Jesse Newill, an acquaintance of mine from Ohio, who is now in this territory with the view of looking out for a situation to locate a saw-mill. He desires to examine the country and select a place well provided with timber. He is accompanied by his son, John Newill, Joseph Fitzsimmons, his brother-in-law, and a Dr. Gamble.

"They are no way identified with the present troubles in this territory.

"Now, therefore, I have to request all persons to permit the said Jesse Newill and his comrades to pass and repass throughout the territory without molestation.

"WILSON SHANNON,
"*Governor of Kansas.*"

The following pass also deserves preservation, as it emanated from the executive department of the territory. There are many more of the same kind afloat:

"let this man pas for i no him to bee a law and abiding man.
"Samuel Salters."

Gov. Shannon's pass was given under these circumstances: Mr. Jesse Newill, recently from Ohio, after having been arrested several times in going near Lecompton, at last entered the town, and, seeing the governor, rode up to him, saying, "What does all this mean?"

The governor, falling back on his dignity, of which he has no small share when he is enjoying a sense of security, both from friends and foes, said, "There is no use of complaining. The territory is under martial law, and a civil war is inevitable."

The governor seemed uneasy to get away from being questioned by an old friend. His conscience, although of the gutta percha kind, might have given an occasional twinge, when pressed by the close queries of a man of sense. On parting, he gave Mr. Newill the above characteristic pass.

Thus, while the people of Missouri arrest the leading men in the territory, Gov. Shannon accepts their services; while several are actually indicted upon a charge of high treason, — while the marshal has called in these Missourians to meet at Lecompton for siege upon Lawrence, — the Washington *Union* is out, with the bloodthirstiness of the border papers, for the extermination of the free-state men in Kansas. It expresses its hopes "that an example will be made of some of the ringleaders," and says, "It is high time that rebellion and treason should be brought to the bar of justice." What could better express the purposes of this administration, whose real head is Jefferson Davis and Caleb Cushing & Co.?

White servitude is the order in Kansas; but the more galling the bondage, the sooner will its reign be over, and the chains which bind us will drag down eternally, deeper than plummet hath ever sounded, our infamous oppressors. Let the *Union* talk of "treason and rebellion" to a tyrannical usurpation being brought to justice. There is no justice in Kansas. Let Douglas say, "I will subdue you," and let this subjugation be accomplished by President Pierce's "army and navy" at the point of the bayonet and the murderous rifle. Death, too, may come at his hands; but with it the soul wins immortality. The "traitor" may expiate his love of freedom on the scaffold of his building; but the world will see in it the pedestal of honor.

"For humanity sweeps onward; where to-day the martyr stands,
To-morrow crouches Judas, with his silver in his hands;
While the howling mob of yesterday in silent awe return,
To glean the scattered ashes into History's golden urn."

CHAPTER XVI.

THE ATTACK UPON LAWRENCE.

Surely the web has been woven around the little city of eighteen months' existence. Its prosperity has excited the envy of the spoiler, and gradually now the vile men under J. B. Donaldson, United States Marshal, are drawing nearer; the circle about the beleaguered town is continually growing less. They come with United States authority. The President seeks renown in the bombarding of a poor little town on the far-western prairies; and his hordes, suggesting to all beholders the idea of a resurrection from the infernal regions, or a sudden leap into Dante's Inferno, are gathered here. Gov. Shannon lends his servility to the scheme. But let the facts be stated; let the documents which passed between our people and their (?) governor be proof in the matter.

Rumors, well authenticated, were afloat in the community that large companies were gathering into the territory at different points; that they were drilling and preparing for an attack upon Lawrence. The last rumor was that a demand would be made upon the town for Reeder and Robinson and others, both of those named already being absent; that, if these were not given up, the town should be sacked. It was stated, further, that a large posse would enter the place, and, after making arrests, the posse would be disbanded to sack the town. The marshal's proclamation was issued on the 11th. This was not sent to Lawrence, nor any means used to acquaint the people with the designs of the officers. The people, however, acting upon the continual threats of invasion, called a meeting, and appointed a committee of three to wait upon Gov. Shannon, and apprize him of the real state of affairs, and ask his interference in their behalf. The following letter was sent from Lawrence by the committee to Gov. Shannon:

"LAWRENCE CITY, KANSAS, *May* 11, 1856.

"DEAR SIR: The undersigned are charged with the duty of communicating to your Excellency the following preamble and resolutions, adopted by the citizens of Lawrence at a public meeting holden at this place at seven o'clock this evening, viz.:

"'Whereas we have the most reliable information, from various points of the territory and the adjoining State of Missouri, of the organization of guerilla bands, who threaten the destruction of our town and its citizens, therefore,

"'*Resolved*, That Messrs. Topliff, Hutchinson, and Roberts, constitute a committee to inform his Excellency Gov. Shannon of these facts, and to call upon him, in the name of the people of Lawrence, for protection against such bands by the United States troops at his disposal.'

"All of which is most respectfully submitted, by order of the people of Lawrence.

"Very truly, etc.,

"C. W. TOPLIFF,
JOHN HUTCHINSON,
W. Y. ROBERTS."

After Gov. Shannon had held a consultation with several of the leaders at Lecompton, he returned the following missive, of doubtful import:

"EXECUTIVE OFFICE,
LECOMPTON, K. T., *May* 12, 1856.

"GENTLEMEN: Your note of the 11th instant is received; and, in reply, I have to state that there is no force around or approaching Lawrence, except the legally constituted posse of the United States Marshal, and Sheriff of Douglas County, each of whom, I am informed, has a number of writs for execution against persons now in Lawrence.

"I shall in no way interfere with either of these officers in the discharge of their official duties.

"If the citizens of Lawrence submit themselves to the territorial laws, and aid and assist the marshal and sheriff in the execution of processes in their hands, as all good citizens are bound to do, when called on, they or all such will entitle themselves to the protection of the law.

"But so long as they keep up a military or armed organization to resist the territorial laws, and the officers charged with their execution, I shall not interfere to save them from the legitimate consequences of their illegal acts.

"I have the honor to be

"Yours with great respect,

"WILSON SHANNON.

"Messrs. C. W. TOPLIFF,
JOHN HUTCHINSON,
W. Y. ROBERTS."

The citizens of Lawrence will be entitled to protection while they submit to the territorial laws. He is very careful, however, not to promise such protection; and the non-committal essay leaves room for the belief that, if the people did not yield like slaves to the insolence of an irresponsible mob, they would be regarded by him as outlaws, and be wholly given over to his reckless gang of desperadoes. "No military or armed organization to resist the territorial laws, and the officers charged with their execution," has ever been formed in Lawrence, which Gov. Shannon knew well. There have been military companies with stated drills, and these have constituted all the organizations entered into, save the one which he himself commissioned, gladly availing himself of its protection from the lawless mob he had precipitated upon us.

On Tuesday, the 13th of May, one of the marshal's proclamations was brought into town, and its charges were so entirely false and cruel in their intent, that the citizens immediately came together in public meeting, Judge W. presiding, and the following resolutions were adopted:

"Whereas, by a proclamation to the people of Kansas Territory, by J. B. Donaldson, United States Marshal for said territory, issued on the 11th day of May, 1856, it is alleged that certain 'judicial writs of arrest have been directed to him by the First District Court of the United States, etc.. to be executed within the County of Douglas, and that an attempt to execute them by the United States Deputy Marshal was violently resisted by a large number of the citizens of Lawrence, and that there is every reason to believe that any attempt to execute these writs will be resisted by a large body of armed men,' therefore,

"*Resolved*, by this public meeting of the citizens of Lawrence, held this 13th day of May, 1856, that the allegations and charges against us, contained in the aforesaid proclamation, are wholly untrue in fact, and the conclusion entirely false which is drawn therefrom; the aforesaid deputy marshal was resisted in no manner whatsoever, nor by any person whatever, in the execution of said writs, except by him whose arrest the said deputy marshal was seeking to make; and that we now, as we have done heretofore, declare our willingness and our determination, without resistance, to acquiesce in the service upon us of any judicial writs against us by the United States Marshal for Kansas Territory, and will furnish him a posse for that purpose, if so requested; but that we are ready to resist, if need be, unto death, the ravages and desolation of an invading mob.

"J. A. Wakefield, *President*.

"John Hutchinson, *Secretary*."

The same evening (Tuesday, the 13th) Mr. Cox, a pro-slavery man, of Lawrence, was requested by one of our leading citizens to ascertain from Marshal Donaldson if any peaceable arrangement could be entered into to prevent his monster posse from entering the town. Mr. Cox remained all night with Donaldson, and, on his return to Lawrence the next morning, reported the following conversation as having passed between himself and Marshal D.:

Mr. Cox asked, "Will you be able to control these men, if they enter the town?"

The marshal replied, "I don't know that I will."

Mr. Cox then asked, "Can anything be done, on the part of Lawrence, to prevent your coming in with so large a force?" He replied, "The three following demands must be complied with, before I shall consent not to enter Lawrence with all my force. First. That every man, against whom a warrant is issued, shall be surrendered. Second. All munitions of war, in Lawrence, shall be delivered up. Third. That the citizens of Lawrence shall pledge themselves implicitly to obey the present enactments of Kansas — test-oaths, taxes, and all."

Upon the receipt of this reply, on the morning of the 14th, the citizens immediately held a public meeting. That no means should be left untried for the protection of the citizens, — that the marshal should have no grounds for misapprehension in reference to the intentions of the people, — the following letter was prepared and sent to the marshal, by Mr. Cox:

"LAWRENCE, *May* 14, 1856.

"J. B. DONALDSON, U. S. MARSHAL FOR K. T. — Dear Sir: We have seen a proclamation issued by yourself, dated 11th May inst., and also have reliable information this morning, that large bodies of armed men, in pursuance of your proclamation, have assembled in the vicinity of Lawrence.

"That there may be no misunderstanding, we beg leave to ask respectfully, that we may be reliably informed what are the demands against us. We desire to state, most truthfully and earnestly, that no opposition whatever will now, or at any future time, be offered to the execution of any legal process by yourself, or any person acting for you. We also pledge ourselves to assist you, if called upon, in the execution of any legal process.

"We declare ourselves to be order-loving and law-abiding citizens, and only await an opportunity to test our fidelity to the laws of the country, the constitution, and the Union.

"We are informed, also, that those men collecting about Lawrence openly declare that their intention is to destroy the town, and drive off the citizens. Of course we do not believe you give any countenance to such threats; but, in view of the excited state of the public mind, we ask protection of the constituted authorities of the government, declaring ourselves in readiness to coöperate with them for the maintenance of the peace, order, and quiet of the community in which we live.

"Very respectfully,

"ROBERT MORROW,
LYMAN ALLEN,
JOHN HUTCHINSON."

On the morning of the fifteenth, Mr. John Hutchinson was bearer of a despatch to Col. Sumner, at Fort Leavenworth, requesting him, if he had no power to assist the citizens in defending the town, to station a body of troops in the vicinity, that their presence might act as a preventative to the sanguinary measures with which the mob threaten it. The majority of the investigating committee also asked for the interference of Col. Sumner, on the sixteenth. To them both the reply was similar: he wished he could do something, but he had no power to move without orders. Early Thursday forenoon, the fifteenth, Lieut. Gov. W. Y. Roberts, C. W. Babcock, and Josiah Miller, went to Lecompton to receive Marshal Donaldson's answer. The following is the document:

"OFFICE OF THE U. S. MARSHAL,
LECOMPTON, K. T., *May* 15, 1856.

"MESSRS. G. W. DIETZLER AND J. H. GREEN, LAWRENCE, K. T.: On yesterday I received a communication addressed to me, signed by one of you as president, and the other as secretary, purporting to have been adopted by a meeting of the citizens of Lawrence, held on yesterday morning. After speaking of a proclamation issued by myself, you state, 'That there may be no misunderstanding, we beg leave to ask respectfully, that we may be reliably informed, what are the demands against us. We desire most truthfully and earnestly to declare that no opposition whatever will now, or at any future time, be offered to the execution of any legal process by yourself, or any person acting for you. We also pledge ourselves to assist you, if called upon, in the execution of any legal process,' etc.

"From your professed ignorance of the demands against you, I must conclude that you are STRANGERS, and not CITIZENS, of Lawrence, or of recent date, or been absent for some time; more particularly when an attempt was made by my deputy to execute the process of the First District Court of the United States for Kansas Territory, against ex-Gov. Reeder, when he made a speech in the room and in the presence of the congressional committee, and denied the power and authority of said court, and threatened the life of said deputy, if he attempted to execute said process, which speech and defiant threats were loudly applauded by some one or two hundred of the citizens of Lawrence, who had assembled at the room on learning the business of the marshal, and made such hostile demonstrations that the deputy thought he and his small posse would endanger their lives in executing said process.

"Your declaration that you 'will truthfully and earnestly offer now, or at any future time, no opposition to the execution of any legal process,' etc., is indeed difficult to understand. May I ask, gentlemen, what has produced this wonderful change in the minds of the people of Lawrence? Have their eyes been suddenly opened, so that they are now able to see that there are laws in force in Kansas Territory, which should be obeyed? Or is it that, just now, those for whom I have writs have sought refuge elsewhere? Or it may possibly be that you now, as heretofore, expect to screen yourselves behind the word 'legal,' so significantly used by you. How am I to rely on your pledges, when I am well aware that the whole population of Lawrence is armed and drilled, and the town fortified — when, too, I recollect the meetings and resolutions adopted in Lawrence, and elsewhere in the territory, openly defying the laws and the officers thereof, and threatening to resist the same to a bloody issue, and recently verified in the attempted assassination of Sheriff Jones, while in the discharge of his official duties in Lawrence? Are you strangers to all these things? Surely you must be strangers at Lawrence. If no outrages have been committed by the citizens of Lawrence against the laws of the land, they need not fear any posse of mine. But I must take the liberty of executing all processes in my hands, as the U. S. Marshal, in my own time and manner, and shall only use such power as is authorized by law. You say you call upon the constituted authority of the government for protection. This indeed sounds strange, coming from a large body of men, armed with Sharpe's rifles and other implements of war, bound together by oaths and pledges to resist the laws of the government they call on for protection. All persons in Kansas Territory, without regard to location, who honestly submit to the constituted authorities, will ever find me ready to aid in protecting them; and all who seek to resist the laws of the land, and turn traitors to their country, will find me aiding in enforcing the laws, if not as an officer, as a citizen.

"Respectfully yours,

"J. B. Donaldson,

"*United States Marshal of Kansas Territory.*"

It is unnecessary to characterize it as most heartless and insulting. Let its spirit of revengeful exultation strike terror into the heart of any, who, by word or deed, would aid the purposes of the slave power, which, like the deadly upas-tree, casts blight and mildew over all within its shadow, while its already monstrous growth threatens to strike the blow at the foot of all republican liberty.

Gov. Shannon treated the messengers from Lawrence coldly, and would say nothing to them. While Messrs. Roberts and Parrott were there, Miller was accosted by Major Clark, to whom Miller extended his hand; but, without taking it, the murderer of Barber said, "D—n you, I won't shake hands with you! I believe you published an article in your paper about me. I will settle with you to-night."

As they were returning to Lawrence, a party came out upon them, and asked if Miller was among them, and if he was from South Carolina. Upon this, Mr. Miller replying that he was, one of the banditti said, "Come with us. I am from South Carolina, and we have an account to settle with you to-night." Mr. Miller showed the pass the marshal had given him; but the leader said 'he did n't care a d—n about the marshal."

They seized and dragged him away, in spite of the protestations of Messrs. Babcock and Roberts, and would not allow them to accompany their friend.

Mr. Miller was tried with a mock trial by these South Carolinians, Dr. Stringfellow presiding as judge. The charge w—

of treason against South Carolina, and Mr. Miller was released, minus his money, revolvers, and horse.

The communication of the marshal being received in Lawrence, all hope of safety from any action of his was at once abandoned. The evident design of the authorities was to force the people into resistance to the United States authorities, in acts of self-preservation, or to gain possession of the town by process of law, and then give it up to unrestrained outrage. The officers showed no disposition to restrain the lawless acts daily committed by their "legally authorized militia," and there is no reason to suppose they desired to do so.

At this time, beside the breaking open of goods, robbing and plundering, thirty men had been arrested without any legal process, and treated with every indignity, while some still remained at the mercy of the robbers. The people of Lawrence, still wishing peace, made one more effort with the marshal, and on Saturday, the 17th, sent him the following letter:

"J. B. Donaldson, U. S. Marshal of K. T. — Dear Sir: We desire to call your attention, as citizens of Kansas, to the fact that a large force of armed men have collected in the vicinity of Lawrence, and are engaged in committing depredations upon our citizens — stopping wagons, arresting, threatening, and robbing unoffending travellers upon the highway — breaking open boxes of merchandise, and appropriating their contents — have slaughtered cattle, and terrified many of the women and children.

"We have also learned from Gov. Shannon, that 'there are no armed forces in the vicinity of this place, but the regularly constituted militia of the territory.' This is to ask you if you recognize them as your posse, and feel responsible for their acts. If you do not, we hope and trust you will prevent a repetition of such acts, and give peace to the settlers.

"On behalf of the citizens,

"C. W. Babcock,
Lyman Allen,
J. A. Perry."

Col. Eldridge, with his brother, being desirous, if possible, to save the new hotel, of which he was the proprietor, went to Lecompton on the 18th, Sunday. Gov. Shannon talked with them of sending for the troops, to have them stationed at Lawrence, to protect the citizens from the marshal's mob, while they made the arrests; their arms to be given into the keeping of the troops, until the search was over, and the posse gone. This proposition was to be made to the people of Lawrence, and the Messrs. Eldridge were to return on the morrow to report their decision. This they did. The proposal had been acceded to by the citizens of Lawrence.

Gov. Shannon declared, on the 19th, that their arms must be delivered to the posse; that the hotel and printing-presses must be destroyed; else — let the reason of this wise execution of the law be taken note of— "the South Carolinians will not be satisfied." The Messrs. Eldridge immediately replied, that "This the people of Lawrence will never do; they will fight first." When this partisan governor, the weak tool of South Carolina and Missouri, leaving the room, said, "Then war it is, by G—d!"

On Monday also word came into Lawrence of the murder of a young man by the name of Jones, the support of his widowed mother. He had been to Lawrence for a bag of meal, and, returning, was ordered to halt, by a band of the marshal's posse, near Blanton's Bridge. He obeyed the order of the ruffianly assassins, and they disarmed him. Then they ordered him to proceed, and as he did so, two of the posse exclaimed, "Let 's shoot the d—d abolitionist!" Suiting the action to the word, the balls sped on their swift errand, and the recording angel wrote against the names of some high in power another murder.

Several young men immediately left Lawrence to go to the spot where young Jones fell a victim to the bloody tools of slavery · and about a mile from Lawrence they met two men from Westport. Another ball did the bidding of the slave interest, and another witness appeared against its supporters in the high court where perjury enters not, and packed juries are unknown.

The body of young Stewart, so lately come among us, was brought into town, and laid in the hotel. So sudden was his passage from this to the unseen life, that the placid countenance wore, not the aspect of death, but the beautiful repose of a dreamy sleep.

Illinois furnished the first victim. Will she hear the startled cry of young Jones, "O God, I am shot!" and the desolate plaint of the widowed one, now mourning like Israel's singer, "My son, my son, would God I had died for thee"? Will she do her uttermost to strike down the black piratical flag, borne aloft by her traitorous son, continually hissing, "I will subdue you"?

New York, in the murder of one of her young men, is reminded of the peril of all who bow not their knee to the Moloch of slavery.

The Messrs. E. returned to Lawrence. The people still loving the United States government, and having declared that they would never resist its authority, although the tyranny of the present administration is without its parallel in history, they refused all the proffered aid of the neighboring settlements, notwithstanding they well knew that with a small force they could have wiped out all these "territorial bands of militia" as easily as the melting away of the mist before the sun-rising.

It was necessary that the peace should be preserved under all these provocations, that the whole country might realize the sincerity of their declarations to obey the general government, notwithstanding the upholders of the administration have so loudly stigmatized them as "traitors" and "rebels." It was necessary that the whole country should be convinced of the real meaning of the words, "enforcing the laws," used so often by United States officials in the territory, as well as at Washington.

The proposition was made to have men armed, and at a proper distance from Lawrence to protect the inhabitants, should any outrages be attempted after the arrests were made. This seemed plausible; but would the apathetic, money-loving North believe this was the real object for which any means of defence had been prepared? Would not the border ruffian papers in the North, even the few which taint the moral atmosphere of fair New England, howl with another cry of rebellion in Kansas? So the people of Kansas feared; and the cool, calm heads of Lawrence decided, while the pale faces of two unburied victims attested to the malignancy of the slave power, and warned them of the imminency of their own peril, that, come outrage, pillage and death, at the bidding of United States officials, they would occupy a right position before the American people, and before wondering Europe, who sees freedom lie bleeding in a boasted republic.

Do any charge them with cowardice? Let them leave their quiet homes, where just laws hold wicked men in check, and the public safety is inviolate, and dwell where continued outrage and murder stalk abroad in the light of day,—where the United States government counsels violence, and is the real perpetrator of these wrongs,—and then, removed from the help of friends, with hordes of these vile men threatening their destruction, their extermination, lay by all means of self-defence, and with the calm spirit of endurance wait the issue. Is there not rather the sublimest courage in the act, and a beautiful, silent expression of their faith in the eternal law of right; that in reality "our wrongs will be our strength?" Thus the people thought, and, laying by their arms in safe places, they waited the action of the United States Marshal.

Tuesday, the 20th, was a still, calm day. O how calm it was! The hurrying bands of horsemen, brutal in their aspect, and uncouth, that had been for days flying over the prairies, making a blot on creation's fair face, were nowhere to be seen. No more the vile men, in companies of two, three, or more, came spying about the dwelling on Mt. Oread, to ask for water, and saying "The head of the house is not at home?" knowing well by what acts of villany he was taken prisoner at Lexington, and was yet a prisoner. So perfect was the semblance of quiet and peace, that a little party, who sat in the evening's twilight, in front of the same dwelling, wondered if indeed the threatened evil might not again pass by, as on so many previous occasions. A smaller guard than usual were actually on the watch. But, when the morning sun arose on the 21st of May, 1856, hordes of men, armed with United States muskets, were marshalled upon Mt. Oread. While wronged inno cence had slept quietly, they in the darkness had gained the height. The fair summit of Oread never before witnessed such an assemblage of creatures calling themselves men. Humanity stands aghast at the idea of brotherhood with such a ragged, filthy, besotted set. But it is only tools the slave power wants, and these could steal, plunder and kill. What more does the administration ask of its supporters in crushing Kansas? If peace had been desired, the United States troops would still have been called into service, for in no instance had resistance been offered them. Col. Sumner was not the officer whom Gov. Shannon dared ask to batter down a civilized town, and destroy presses; and his soldiers have the hearts of men in their bosoms, and, with too little alacrity to please government officials in Kansas, have they hunted down peaceable men. Hence the governor left them at Leavenworth, and relied upon his mongrel crew of Carolinians, Alabamians, and Missourians, as better instruments to do his bidding. This is why, on the last week of spring, the morning air freighted with perfume of flowers, and the carol of birds, on Mt. Oread, was mingled with oaths and ribald songs, as it ascended to heaven. Between the hours of eight and nine o'clock a part of this band moved down from Capitol Hill, above our house, nearer the town, upon the table land where the house stood. Runners were sent down to Massachusetts-street in the forenoon, and they reported, on their return to the hill, "All quiet in Lawrence; the few men there busy about their usual employments." The five hundred men on Mt. Oread had divided into two parties, one of which surrounded our house; the other planted their cannon on the brow of the hill. About eleven o'clock, W. P. Fain, United States Deputy Marshal, with eight men, went into the town. They went directly to the hotel, and were respectfully received. The marshal summoned four prominent citizens of Lawrence to assist him in arresting others of our citizens. Without resistance, Judge G. W. Smith and G. W. Dietzler were arrested. Col. Eldridge had but just removed his family to Lawrence, and this was the first public dinner given in the hotel. Marshal Fain, with his posse and prisoners, partook of the hospitality of the house. Col. Eldridge then took the prisoners and a part of the posse to our house, which had been taken possession of, by the "legally authorized militia," for their head-quarters. The United States Marshal then dismissed his monster posse of two hundred and fifty horsemen, and five hundred infantry, telling them "he had no further use for them, but Sheriff Jones has writs to execute, and they were at liberty to organize as his posse."

Sheriff Jones, who, through all the border papers, had been reported "dead," and "dying," rode forward, and was received with yells of applause. He spoke to the motley group of his attempted assassination, and informed them of certain writs in his hands, and asked their aid.

About one o'clock, at the head of a posse of twenty or twenty-five mounted men, armed with United States muskets and bayonets, this immortal sheriff rode into Lawrence, to the door of the hotel, and asked for Gen. Pomeroy. This gentleman soon answering the summons, Jones said, "I have been resisted several times in this place, and attempts have been made to assassinate me. Now I am determined to execute the law, if it costs me my life. I demand of you, as the most prominent man in the place, the surrender of all the cannon and Sharpe's rifles you have;" and, taking out his watch, he added, "I give you five minutes to decide whether you will give them up." He said, moreover, "I am authorized to make this demand by the First *District Court* of the *United States.*"

Gen. Pomeroy went to the committee room, and, returning in a few minutes, said, "The cannon will be delivered up, but the rifles are private property, and will be retained." The cannon was taken out of its safe retreat by Gen. Pomeroy. Cheerfully, until then, our people had looked on; but it was too humiliating to give up this brass six-pounder, which had been welcomed with shouts, during the fall invasion, strengthening their means of defence when the peril was imminent. The curses of the few free-state boys yet remaining in town (most having left when they found no defence was to be made) were muttered, but deep, and the dissatisfaction was general.

In the mean time, the forces, variously estimated from five hundred to eight hundred, had been marched down to the base of the hill and formed into a hollow square. Gen. D. R. Atchison made the following speech, which was received by the unceasing yells of the crowd:

"Boys, this day I am a Kickapoo Ranger, by G—d. This day we have entered Lawrence with Southern Rights inscribed upon our banner, and not one d—d abolitionist dared to fire a gun.

"Now, boys, this is the happiest day of my life. We have entered that d—d town, and taught the d—d abolitionists a Southern lesson that they will remember until the day they die. And now, boys, we will go in again, with our highly honorable Jones, and test the strength of that d—d Free-State Hotel, and teach the Emigrant Aid Company that Kansas shall be ours. Boys, ladies should, and I hope will, be respected by every gentleman. But, when a woman takes upon herself the garb of a soldier, by carrying a Sharpe's rifle, then she is no longer worthy of respect. Trample her under your feet as you would a snake!

"Come on, boys! Now do your duty to yourselves and your Southern friends.

"Your duty, I know you will do. If one man or woman dare stand before you, blow them to h—l with a chunk of cold lead."

As soon as he had concluded, the militia moved towards the town in solid column, until near the hotel, when the advance company halted. Jones told Col. Eldridge the hotel must be destroyed; he was acting under orders; he had writs issued by the First District Court of the United States to destroy the Free-State Hotel, and the offices of the *Herald of Freedom* and *Free State.* The grand jury at Lecompton had indicted them as nuisances, and the court had ordered them to be destroyed. The following is a copy of such indictment:

"The Grand Jury sitting for the adjourned term of the First District Court, in and for the County of Douglas, in the Territory of Kansas, beg leave to report to the Honorable Court that, from evidence laid before them showing that the newspaper known as *The Herald of Freedom*, published at the town of Lawrence, has from time to time issued publications of the most inflammatory and seditious character — denying the legality of the *territorial authorities;* addressing and commanding forcible resistance to the same; demoralizing the popular mind, and rendering life and property unsafe, even to the extent of advising assassination as a last resort.

"Also, that the paper known as *The Kansas Free State* has been similarly engaged, and has recently reported the resolutions of a public meeting in Johnson County, in this territory, in which resistance to the *territorial laws* even unto blood has been agreed upon. And that we respectfully recommend their abatement as a nuisance. Also, that we are satisfied that the building known as the 'Free-State Hotel,' in Lawrence, has been constructed with the view to military occupation and defence, regularly parapeted and portholed for the use of cannon and small arms, and could only have been designed as a stronghold of resistance to law, thereby endangering the public safety and encouraging rebellion and sedition in this country, and respectfully recommend that steps be taken whereby this nuisance may be removed.

"Owen C. Stewart, *Foreman.*"

Jones gave Col. Eldridge from that time — about half past three o'clock — until five o'clock to remove his family and furniture, which it had taken weeks to put in order. Seeing the impossibility of removing the furniture, Col. Eldridge said, "he had bought the furniture to furnish the hotel, not to stand in the streets." Longer time for the removal being denied, he said, "Give me time to remove my family (a sick daughter being of the number), that is all I ask." A part of the furniture was thrown out by the rabble, mirrors and marble-top tables being thrown from the windows. The house had been furnished at an expense of ten thousand dollars, and was by far the most elegant house west of St. Louis. The cellar was stored with provisions, advantage having been taken of the high water in the Kansas to bring up several months' supply.

The posse, growing weary of removing furniture, even in the expeditious manner of dropping it from the windows, began to ransack drawers, cupboards, and cellar, carrying with them boxes of cigars, wines, oysters, sardines, cans of fruit, etc.

This "legally organized militia" came into Lawrence with banners flying. We thank them heartily, that the United States flag was not desecrated by waving over their pollution. They had chosen their banners with singular appropriateness. One was a white flag with black stripes, and one had a white star on a red surface. This banner bore the inscription "Southern Rights," and on the opposite side was "South Carolina" in black paint. Another flag had, in blue letters on a white ground,

"Let Yankees tremble, abolitionists fall,
Our motto is give Southern Rights to all."

The precise bearing of these mottoes upon Marshal Donaldson's writs has not yet been explained.

The *Free State* office was first destroyed, the press being thrown into the river, while exchange papers and books were thrown into the street, and destroyed. The types of the *Herald of Freedom* office were also put into the Kansas, and the press broken. The red flag of the South Carolinians was first hoisted upon this office, and in about fifteen minutes was removed to the hotel. The building was fired several times, but put out by the bravery of some of the young men in Lawrence, who were not deterred by the threats of the mob. Sheriff Jones placed two companies to carry the types of the offices to the river, and break the presses.

After the red flag had been hoisted upon the hotel, four cannons were stationed about one hundred and five feet distant from it, and pointing towards it. The first command was given to fire, and the balls went far above the hotel, and over into the ravine beyond the town. When the cannonading commenced, it was thought prudent for women and children to leave the town, and many went across the ravine to some houses west of Lawrence. *Thirty-two* balls were fired, doing little damage to the hotel, the balls easily going through the concrete. Was the number significant of the admission of Kansas into the sisterhood of states? The walls of the hotel stood firmly, almost uninjured, and the patience of the posse, at so slow a progress, was getting weary. Their anticipations had been disappointed; for, on the first fire, the cry had been raised, "Now here she goes!"

Amid the continued roar of the eighteen, twelve, and six

pounder, the yells were terrific. By all who listened, it is averred they never before had heard such unearthly sounds. Some kegs of powder were carried into the cellar; for "law and order" was not blind, and the continued display of plunder gained by others of the mob excited their covetousness, and a more summary way of "removing the nuisance" was desired. The result was only a little smoke, and the shivering of a few windows. The order was then given to the military commander, Col. Titus, just arrived from Florida, to fire the building. By setting fires in each of the rooms, the large hotel was destroyed, nearly the entire wall falling in.

At the commencement of the cannonading, Jones had been asked, "Can you feel no pity for the sufferings you have caused?"

His reply was, "The laws must be executed." And, turning to two of his posse, he said, "Gentlemen, this is the happiest day of my life, I assure you. I determined to make the fanatics bow before me in the dust, and kiss the territorial laws."

Then, as another round was fired, with a bitter, scornful sneer he said, "I have done it, by G—d! I have done it!"

When the walls of the hotel had fallen in, he turned to his posse and said, coolly, "You are dismissed; the writs have been executed."

This was the signal for a general plunder of private houses, and as the drunken gang rushed from place to place, they took anything of value upon which their eyes fell. They rifled trunks, taking letters, money, drafts, apparel, both ladies and gentlemen's, and destroyed anything that would break, even to daguerreotypes and children's toys. Before the day was over, many of the citizens recognized, upon the before ragged persons of the militia, a hat, coat, vest, or pair of pantaloons, to which they had had previous title, with some of the heavy curtain-cords and tassels, taken from the hotel, worn around them in lieu of sashes; and, with expensive silk or satin dresses on their arms, they marched about, evidently elated with their transformation. In many houses, whatever they left was mutilated and defaced, and the people, on returning to their homes, found only a wreck of those things which had condr;ed to their comfort. Stores were broken open. Letters were pilfered from the post-office, and opened. From the same building, occupied as a store, Dr. Stringfellow carried off under each arm a box of cigars, having helped himself to them behind the counter, saying, as he did so, "Well, boys, I guess this is as good plunder as I want." He was particularly busy during the day in inciting the heroic band to such deeds of valor. Major Buford, of Alabama, was also conspicuous as a leader. Mr. Hutchinson's store was broken into by Col. Titus, saying, "I think there are Sharpe's rifles in there; stave her in, boys, if she is locked!" They obeyed him by breaking in the windows with the butts of their guns, and then crawled in through the aperture.

The cry of "There 's Reeder trying to escape!" at one time caused some excitement. One of the ruffians, attempting to shoot the man, who did not prove to be Gov. Reeder, while his horse was on a full gallop, fell from it and broke his leg. Another was killed instantly by the falling of a brick from the hotel. The South Carolina flag, waving on the roof, whipped it off one of the chimneys.

Some ladies, sitting upon College Hill west of the town, during the cannonading, were fired upon by a party of Buford's men, who came from town. When about a hundred yards distant, they levelled their guns at them deliberately, and, without one word being said, fired. The balls went whizzing through the air near the ladies. South Carolina's gallant sons then threw down their guns and shouted, while swinging their hats, "Hurrah for South Carolina! Down with the abolitionists! Slavery in Kansas, by G—d!"

Again they picked up their arms, and levelled them towards the ladies, who were standing still, looking at them, when one of the four said, "Don't fire; I would n't." Then, singing Katy Darling and Lily Dale, they went up the hill.

Our house was nearly vacated as night approached, and a neighbor passing, stepped in to see how matters looked. Furniture, which had been thrown out of the house, he set back, and finding only one of the Missourians in the lower rooms, and he busily engaged in looking for liquors, the way into the cellar, etc.

he went up stairs. In one room, a man with gloves on was rummaging bureau drawers. He had a large pile of letters in one hand, and a daguerreotype in the other. Trunks which had been locked were opened, their contents strewed everywhere, and a fire was blazing in the bed. After throwing the bed out of the window, this friend went into another chamber, and put out the fire which was kindled in a closet.

This man, so busily prying into bureau drawers and private correspondence, was one of the principal men in the "law-and-order party." O, southern honor! how her gloss has become dim, when her chief men, the self-constituted champions of southern institutions, attempt to gain their ends by stealing private correspondence, and pillaging a lady's drawers!

About seven o'clock, the semi-human creatures began to leave the town. The large covered wagons, which stood near our house to receive the spoils, moved off. Houses out of town, which had escaped molestation, were opened for the reception of the destitute and homeless.

About nine o'clock the flames burst forth from the home on Mt. Oread, and the "legally organized militia" had completed their work. Many thousand dollars' worth of property had been destroyed. People had been robbed of their all. Lawrence was destroyed; and the President bears the signal honor. Crown his brows with asphodel and wormwood, ye American people, for he has wrought for your fellow-countrymen bitterness and woe!

CHAPTER XVII.

THE "REIGN OF TERROR" IN KANSAS.

THE end is not yet. While these outrages were being committed, and fiend-like, with hideous yells, these officials rushed from spot to spot, to make the ruin complete, the people of Lawrence looked on in silence. They could hardly believe that men could be so transformed into demons of darkness, or that these acts were committed at the instigation of United States appointees. But cheerful, for the most part, was the silence. It is ever better that the foe one contends with should be clothed in his own panoply. If that panoply be sin, darkness, degradation, let them form the external covering. So, now, the slave power, blood-thirsty, and still crying more victims, had sent its own tools, — ragged, ignorant, debauched, semi-savages, the very offshoot and growth of its peculiar institution, — to destroy a quiet town, to steal, destroy, and outrage its inhabitants. The work has been accomplished. The first time in the history of the American people has an American town been besieged and its inhabitants robbed, by forces acting under the instructions of U. S. officers. Every outrage committed was in direct violation of that act in the constitution, which provides for the rights of the people in their persons, houses, papers and effects ; but it was done by the administration, acting as the servile tool of the slave power. Can any freeman decide what other provision of the constitution cannot as easily be set aside, when it stands in the way of the slave power's subduing intentions ? Was it ever heard in this country, or in England, before the times of Judge Lecompte, that a judge had legal authority to order the destruction of a press, which the grand jury, under his instructions, might find a nuisance ? Are one and all the presses in this country exposed to momentary irruptions upon them? We boast of the freedom of the American press. But let the bold assertion that freedom of speech, of action, and the press, is the birthright of an American citizen, no longer be heard.

Louis Napoleon gave three distinct and formal warnings, in the last French revolution, before dealing the fatal blow. But it was reserved for the administration, in the year 1856, in the year of our independence the eightieth, to summarily demolish a free press as a nuisance, and to bombard a little town on the western frontier. "O, shame! where is thy blush?"

If the American people desire the discontinuance of such unprecedented horrors, let them wake to the designs of the slave interest. Let them shake off the shackles which are continually growing more galling. The power which has struck this blow in Kansas meditates no less designs on any other part of the free North, when the opportune moment arrives.

Lieut. Warren D. Wilkes, of the South Carolina banditti, one of the self-constituted regulators in the territory, wrote the following to the *Charleston Mercury*:

"The importance of securing Kansas for the South may be briefly set forth in a positive and negative form:

"1. By consent of parties, the present contest in Kansas is made the turning point in the destinies of slavery and abolitionism. If the South triumphs, abolitionism will be defeated and shorn of its power for all time. If she is defeated, abolitionism will grow more insolent and aggressive, until the utter ruin of the South is consummated.

"2. If the South secures Kansas, *she will extend slavery into all territory south of the fortieth parallel of north latitude, to the Rio Grande, and this of course will secure for her pent-up institutions of slavery an ample outlet, and restore her power in Congress.* If the North secures Kansas, the power of the South in Congress will be gradually diminished; the states of Missouri, Kentucky, Tennessee, Arkansas and Texas, together with the adjacent territories, will gradually become abolitionized, and the slave population, confined to the states east of the Mississippi, will become valueless. All depends upon the action of the present moment."

On the 22d of May, the Platte County Rifle Company — one hundred armed horsemen, under the lead of Gen. D. R. Atchison — passed through Lawrence, over the ferry, on their way back to Missouri. They clenched their guns nervously, but no one offered them any molestation. In safety they passed through the town they had helped to devastate.

The threats of the men were bitter against the hotel at Kansas city. Murder and robbery were the order of the day. The horses and other property of free-state men were continually pillaged by the "chivalry," and travelling in the territory was unsafe. When the "militia" left Lawrence on the 21st of May, it was with the design of attacking Topeka. But a messenger having been despatched to Gov. Shannon, at Lecompton, with a report that "Topeka was on the march to destroy Tecumseh," Gov. Shannon sent to Col. Sumner for troops to be stationed at Topeka, to preserve order. An appeal had previously been sent to him from the citizens of Topeka, but they had no expectation of the granting of their request.

After Lawrence was destroyed, Gov. Shannon ordered troops there also to preserve the peace. A part of the "militia," after leaving the sack of Lawrence, proceeded to Fish's, the Shawnee Indian's. Having put him under guard, they robbed his house and store, took everything which could be eaten from his house, tore up the fences, and took his horses from the wagons. The reason was, his sympathies were with the free-state men.

A party of the southern youth encamped between Kansas city and Westport, and robbed all teams which passed, even stopping the mail, and examining the way-bill, on the 20th, 22d and 23d of May. Capt. H. C. Pate was the leader of the gang. He examined papers, trunks, valises and carpet-sacks. He obliged some of the passengers to take off their boots, that he might look into them. One passenger, upon whom he found a letter, he detained. When the driver grew impatient, and would have gone along, a man passed around in front of the horses, and presented a pistol at him. Coleman, the murderer, also threatened the mail-carrier so repeatedly that he spoke to Col. Boone, P. M. at

Westport, of the matter, and he advised him to leave the line, and get some one else to drive in his place, as "Coleman was a desperate man."

While such outrages were being committed between Kansas city and Lawrence, the reign of terror was complete at Leavenworth. On the morning of the 28th an exciting extra, issued at the office of the *Westport News*, headed "War! War!" was received at Leavenworth. The ruffians immediately held a secret session, and appointed themselves a vigilance committee. All persons, who could not answer "All right on the goose," according to their definition of right, were searched, kept under guard, and threatened with death by the rope or rifle. A company, under the lead of Warren D. Wilkes, of South Carolina, armed with United States muskets and bayonets, were paraded through the different streets of the town. They surrounded the house where a portion of the investigating committee boarded, while two or three entered and took prisoner Judge M. F. Conway, who was acting for the committee in the capacity of clerk. Forming a hollow square, and placing him in the centre, they marched through several streets. As they passed the office of Miles Moore, the Attorney General under the free-state constitution, they arrested him, also M. J. Parrott, a law partner of Moore. Mr. Sherman, one of the investigating committee, was conversing with them at the time, and Mr. Sherman inquired of Wilkes "if he had arrested one of the clerks of the committee upon any legal process." He replied, "he had not, but, at all hazards, he should arrest those whose names he had on his list."

Attacks were nightly threatened upon the houses of those free-state men who had stood firmly by their principles, and the committee were in hourly danger of violence. A threatening message was sent them with the significant signature of "Capt. Hemp." Violence had been contemplated both against the committee and my husband. It was rather too bold a step to attack the United States officials.

The exact state of things at this time may be better realized by statements of prisoners in the camp of the invaders. Dr. Root and Mr. Mitchell had been taken prisoners about the 15th May, being fired upon by a part of the marshal's posse. The balls whizzed about them fearfully, and finally they reined in their mules and asked the reason of such a murderous fire. Their answer was substantially that, in firing before ordering a halt, they had acted in obedience to the marshal's orders. The prisoners were taken by the ruffians one mile and a half to the encampment, and their pistols and valuable papers were taken from them by Capt. John Donaldson, the auditor. They were then put under guard. The reason of their detention was not given, but a promise was made that they should be told in the morning. Letters which Mr. Mitchell was carrying from the mail at Lawrence, to a friend, and supposed to contain several hundred dollars, were taken from him.

The next forenoon they were ordered to appear in the august presence of Dr. Stringfellow, who, however, gave no reason for the detention, but stated that he was acting wholly under the command of the United States Marshal. Sometimes they had two meals a day, and sometimes were deprived of food for twenty-four hours. The consolation, that "prisoners often fared worse, and they deserved to be hung," was freely given. On the fifth day of their imprisonment, having fasted twenty-four hours, the ruffians ordered Mr. Mitchell to cook something for himself and Dr. Root. On his declining to do so, never having been educated in the culinary department, he was commanded to appear immediately at Dr. Stringfellow's tent. There he was pressed upon by officers and men, crying "Kill the d—d rascal!" "Hang him, hang him!" At the same time a rope was thrown over his head, the men springing for the other end. Mr. Mitchell, being of agile motions, avoided this new test of the mercy of the ruffians. Seven prisoners were in camp at this time, whom Dr. Stringfellow insulted by asking the most disgusting questions, such as "Would you steal a nigger?" "Would you sleep with a nigger?" etc. The principal theme of conversation, in the camp was the proposed destruction of Lawrence.

The night before the bombarding, the prisoners were marched about six miles, and within two miles of Lawrence, being guarded on all sides by United States muskets in the hands of Southerners and Missourians. The ground was wet with heavy dew, and, as they reached the tent about nine o'clock, without any blanket under or over them, they were obliged to take what rest such accommodations and such surroundings might afford. After the marshal's posse had finished breakfast, they were drawn up into a hollow square, and into this Marshal Donaldson and Gen. D. R. Atchison were introduced. The red flag, with the lone white star, and "Southern Rights" and "South Carolina," floated over them. The marshal gave his orders for the day, and loud hurrahs rent the air. Then "Old Dave" was greeted with yells terrific. The green prairies almost trembled with the hideous sound. The tall form of him who had been vice-president of the United States was seated on his beautiful horse, now waving this hand, and now that, as he pointed first to their southern homes, and then to the doomed city. Surrounded by the restless mass of brutal men, he urged them on to deeds of violence, "not to leave it or the territory until they have quenched out every vestige of free-state principles."

A little time more elapsed, when the cavalry under the command of Col. Titus, Major Clarke, etc., came up from Lawrence, where they had been to learn of their defences. They reported there were no signs of defence, and there was exceeding joy manifested; this kind of fighting suited them. Before noon all the posse had left the camp, save about twenty-five in charge of the prisoners. At about three o'clock, United States Marshal Donaldson came and asked for the prisoners of the sergeant, who fired upon them at the time of the arrest, and others standing by. He asked the reason of their detention with all the dignity his office imposed upon him. No one was able to make any charge against them. His orders alone were the occasion of the detention. When arrested, the following receipt was given for articles taken: "Dr. J. P. Root, one mule, bridle, saddle, two Whitney's revolvers, brass spurs, blanket, lariettes."

The following general order was given: "Capt. Donaldson and other captains will release all the within named prisoners immediately after the reception of this order, and all their property to be restored to them without delay."

There was also this order:

"Let Dr. J. P. Root pass unmolested. He is entitled to receive his mule, saddle, bridle, spurs, blanket, lariettes, and two Whitney's revolvers.

"J. B. Donaldson,
"May 21, 1856. *U. S. Marshal.*"

Addressed to "*Captain J. Donelson, Present.*"

The release was effected as the firing upon the hotel commenced; and against the advice of the U. S. Marshal, who saw danger in the attempt to go to Lawrence, they made their way thither. When half way there they met the sergeant who arrested them at first. With an appearance of sincerity, he advised them not to enter into the besieged town, as "he knew the men better than they did, and it was not safe for them to go further." In the conversation with the U. S. Marshal, something in regard to the fare they had received was said by the guard, when a native of fair Erin, who was an officer of the day, stepped forward, and, in a low, rich brogue, with hand uplifted, and in a truly dramatic style, said, "This abuse these men have received is registered in heaven."

On the 22d, Dr. Root, accompanied by Mr. Mitchell, visited Marshal Donaldson at Lecompton, to recover their property. The marshal had acknowledged, by his orders, his responsibility in the arrest and robbery, but he refused to give up the goods. While there Dr. Root saw a bill of sundries charged to the U. S. Marshal's posse. The whole bill amounted to $370 85, which comprised whiskey at $1 00 per gallon, and French brandy at $8 00 per gallon. The bill was accepted, and no fault found except for a charge of five gallons of whiskey, which at first was claimed not to have been received. While they sat in the office of the marshal, Col. Titus and a man by the name of Elliot came in. Titus, with oaths, was talking about Capt. Walker, a brave free-state man, a native of Ohio. He said "he would have his head, on or off his shoulders, and for it he would give any man five hundred dollars." In this his faithful ally, Elliot, joined, and the marshal, as usual, ready to do the vile work of killing honorable men, said, "If you wish it I will send a posse immediately for him." It is such men as these who receive from the government daily wages in the glorious employment of hunting, robbing and killing innocent men, on this western soil.

The principal officers in the camp were D. R. Atchison, Col. Buford, Col. Abel (law partner of Gen. Stringfellow), Dr. Stringfellow, Col. Titus, and other men of similar stamp. Such are the men, residents of Missouri, and Georgians, and Floridians, just arrived in the territory, upon whom Marshal Donaldson called to assist him in "enforcing the laws."

Information being reliably received by Capt. Walker that his house was to be burned by the "law-and-order" party, a few neighbors gathered to protect it. About midnight a party of twelve men came down the Lecompton road, and halted in front of the house. As they were fastening their horses to the paling, the party in the house fired upon them, killing a horse in the gateway, and severely wounding one man. In the scattering of the "law-and-order" party which followed, two or three hats, several bowie-knives, and two Sharpe's rifles, taken at the sack of Lawrence, were left as relics. Also a part of a coat-skirt, with a bottle of whiskey in the pocket, was left hanging to the paling, which gave the impression of the owner's having made a desperate leap for life, Gov. Shannon's son was of the party.

The next day, Gov. Shannon made himself busy drinking whiskey, and outraging peaceable citizens in their own houses. He and his party, Col. Titus and confreres, were met upon the California road by several ladies, and Gov. Shannon was so drunk he reeled backward and forward on his horse, scarcely keeping his seat. Upon reaching home, he staggered around, holding upon the furniture to keep himself from falling. He was busy feeling mattresses, peeping into closets, emptying trunks, looking under beds, and used language which shocked those obliged to listen.

At the house of a Mr. Hazeltyne, which he visited in this drunken condition, he inquired of Mrs. Hazeltyne for her husband; upon her replying that she did not know where he was, the Governor of Kansas Territory replied, "I'll cut his d—d black heart out of him, and yours too, madam, if you don't take care." Gov. Shannon called the same day at the house of Capt. Thomes, and the following conversation passed between Gov. Shannon and the wife and little daughter of Capt. Thomes. As Gov. Shannon rode up to the house with his men, he asked for water, and then said:

"Who lives here?"

Daughter. — "Capt. Thomes."

Gov. S. — "What is he captain of, — Walker's company?"

"No, sir, he is a sea-captain."

"Where is he?"

"Gone to Lawrence."

"What has he gone to Lawrence for? To get up a company, eh?"

"No, sir, gone to get lumber to fence his claim with."

"Fence his claim with lumber? Eh? Well, my girl, I am Gov. Shannon."

At this time Mrs. Thomes came to the door from the garden, where she had been at work. Her daughter gave her an introduction to the governor, but she declined taking his extended hand, on the plea of her soiled hands.

Gov. Shannon replied, "Never mind, madam, give me your hand."

A similar conversation to the above passed, when the governor said, "I am around to see who is who, who to have killed, and who not."

Mrs. Thomes said, "Gov. Shannon, I hope you won't kill me nor mine."

"No, no, madam, you are peaceable citizens, an't ye, eh?"

"Yes, sir, we try to be."

The governor, wheeling his horse, called to Col. Titus to come forward. "Colonel, I want you to take particular notice of these premises, and not have this family harmed. Do you hear, eh?"

"Who did you say live here?"

"Capt. Thomes."

Col. Titus promised protection. Then Gov. Shannon addressed Mrs. Thomes again. "Madam, tell your husband to come to Lecompton and see me; he may rest assured that he will find a warm-hearted friend in me." He added further, "I am out to put a stop to these G —d d—d guerilla parties."

On the last day of May, an attack was made by some Georgians on the house of Mr. Storrs, who lived nine miles from Lawrence. Since the sacking of Lawrence, they had been encamped in that region. They came early in the morning, driving before them a man who lived with Mr. Storrs, and had been out to hunt the cattle, firing upon him three times. They demanded that a very valuable horse standing near should be given up. Mrs. Storrs asked, "By what authority?" The captain of the robbers replied, "By the authority of Gov. Shannon, and if she said a word, he would shoot her; he would kill every d—d abolitionist in the territory." They took the horse. The family for safety moved to Lawrence. Horses were continually being pressed into the governor's service, taken from teams on the highway, and in the furrow.

At one place, when the presence of some young ladies seemed to have some effect upon the chivalry, they declaring "they should return to Alabama in the fall, and would like to take some wives with them," the horses were left. They said, however, "they didn't know what the old man (meaning Gov. Shannon) would say, if he knew they did so."

Arrests are in no instance made of the men who commit such outrages; none of the Georgians attacking and destroying private dwellings, none of the Lecompton gentry who make midnight sallies upon quiet settlers, ever being arrested; but, per contra, warrants were issued for all who were known to be concerned in defending Capt. Walker's house.

Such is "law and order" in Kansas, whose governor, drunken and debauched, insults women in their own dwellings, with language too profane for insertion here, and heads gangs for searching settlers' homes.

CHAPTER XVIII.

ARREST OF G. JENKINS AND G. W. BROWN.

On the 14th of May, about two o'clock in the morning, as Mr. Jenkins and G. W. Brown were returning to their homes in Lawrence, they were arrested by armed men, between Kansas city and Westport, and taken to the house of Milton McGee, a most bitter pro-slavery man. The same forenoon they were taken to the Harris house, in Westport, and placed under strong guard in rooms in the third story. Mrs. Jenkins, having received word from her husband, left Lawrence on Friday, P. M., the 16th, in a driving rain, and reached Westport, Saturday, P. M., about four or five o'clock. Mr. Jenkins' brother accompanied her. She found her husband quite ill from fatigue and excitement, his strength having been impaired before leaving home by the watching and anxiety attending the severe illness of one of his children, as well as by the ill-treatment he had since received. Mrs. Jenkins laid aside bonnet and shawl. Crowder, a man who pretended to be one of the deputy marshals, had just been in the room to say that the papers they were expecting from Kansas city, in reference to Mr. Jenkins' release, had not come, and they would stay at Westport another night. Scarcely had he gone out, when Mr. Jenkins, seeing his horse in the street, a valuable one, which they had taken from him the night he was taken prisoner, went down with his guard to see if he could not have it restored to him. Mrs. Jenkins seated herself in one of the deep window-seats, and looked out upon the motley group in the street. A hack drove around to the door, and the loud, harshly-spoken words, "Come along," attracted her attention. The moment she looked her husband was literally pushed into the carriage by several men. Sick as he was, no time was given to get his overcoat, for which he asked. Almost flying down the two stairways, Mrs. Jenkins arrived at the door only in time to see the carriage driving away. She ran to Mrs. Brown's room, who had arrived in Westport one day before her, and Mr. Brown too was gone. He had been called down stairs on some trivial pretence, and was also forced into the hack. Mrs. Jenkins inquired of Mr. Harris and others where they were going, and why they were taken away in such a hurried manner. To all of which questions they gave indefinite answers, or plead ignorance. Before this, however, another hack had driven to the door, with fine, large horses, and the gentleman promised Mrs. Brown he would take her to her husband. He said, "he would drive on until he overtook the other hack." Upon Mrs. Jenkins asking, "if he would take her too," he replied in the affirmative; when a loud dispute arose among the besotted crowd, and threats of "We will shoot you, if you attempt to carry these ladies, and we'll shoot you, if you get into that carriage," resounded on every side, with brutal imprecations mingled. The man, however, took his seat in the carriage, and asked Mrs. Brown to get in also; but, as he said at this time he would only take her, she declined going.

Mrs. Jenkins then found her brother. He harnessed the horses quickly, which had scarcely been put in the stable, and they started in pursuit of the party. By asking of persons whom they met, "if they had seen a hack," they found they were on the track, and, about two miles from Westport, they overtook the carriage, stopped by the way, and its escort of twenty men preparing supper. As they drove up by the side of the carriage, and the astonished posse saw who they were, loud and bitter were the curses. They were told they should not stay with their husbands; but Mrs. Jenkins, excited by fears for her husband's safety, by the strange movements of the mob, as well as by his haggard looks, induced by constant illness for the last few days, as soon as her carriage ceased moving, was in the other with her husband. She did not wait for the convenience of open doors, but made her entrance through the window. Mrs. Brown also soon entered it, while the posse continually declared the ladies "should not remain in the hack." They said "if the ladies would return to Westport, where they could have comfortable quarters for the night, they could reach them in the morning before they should leave." Or, if they would go on to "Donaldson's (a stopping-place for travellers), they would call for them in the morning."

But the reply of the ladies was the same: "We will remain by our husbands, and share their accommodations." The distress of the ladies, occasioned by the strange conduct of the men, at last softened somewhat their hearts. They brought them supper, and said "they would use their influence with Capt. Pate, when he should come from Westport, that they should not be separated from their husbands." The hack-driver declared, with feeling, "they should have the carriage to themselves."

The difficulty which had been suggested by the men, of there being a want of room for all the posse, should the ladies remain in the hack, was at once remedied by Mr. J.'s offer of their carriage and his brother to drive it. The matter was at last adjusted, and the *cortege*, forgetful of their declaration, made again and again, that this was to be their camping-ground for the night, moved on. Horsemen in front, at the sides, and in the rear, guarded the prisoners in the hack. Instead of passing Donaldson's, where they had desired the ladies to sleep, promising to call for them in the morning, they took the Santa Fe road. Not long after they started, two horsemen, who always rode some distance in front of the rest, as a kind of scout, turned suddenly, and upon full gallop returned to the party. They reported a large body of men advancing towards them, and they apprehended an attack. "Halt!" was the word of command, given by the gallant Capt. Pate; "form into line!" followed with other orders in quick succession. For the advantage of all other brave men in similar circumstances, let the facts be stated. The men were drawn up in readiness for battle *behind* the carriage in which were seated the prisoners. Thus, breastworks were formed against the approaching enemy. The courageous band waited. They lingered. No foe came. The two horsemen again went out a short distance. They wheeled and galloped in furiously. They reported no enemy in sight. Some fence stakes, in the distance, had probably looked to their excited imaginations like so many legions. They reached an

Indian house about two o'clock, A. M., and, with oaths and curses which made the listener shudder, the posse attempted to sleep on the wet ground, while the occupants of the hack got some rest, although anxieties and suspense made sleep broken, and of little worth. Breakfast of fat bacon and corn bread could hardly be eaten. There was no way to wash their faces but in a brook near by, using handkerchiefs for towels. In the afternoon of that day they stopped a little time at a trading post on the Santa Fe road, and a pleasant house. Mrs. J. procured some medicine for her husband, and he felt somewhat recruited after an half hour's sleep on the lounge. They reached Blue Jacket's, at the crossing on the Wakarusa, towards night on Sunday the 18th, having been part of the night and nearly all the day reaching a point which might have easily been gained on the usually travelled road in five hours. They had supper there. From this place word was sent to the camp at Franklin of the arrival of the posse at Blue Jacket's, and thirty men came down to meet them. The heavy rain of the Friday preceding had completely flooded the low grounds of the Wakarusa, and it is impossible to describe the ludicrous appearance of the newly-arrived escort, as they ploughed their way along, first knee-deep in water, then as deeply sinking in the heavy, deceitful mud. The party arrived at Franklin, and, as they halted before the log cabin, christened hotel, the gathered crowd, which the camp near by had emptied forth, was large and full of curiosity. Repeatedly the prisoners, still seated in the hack, heard their curiosity syllabled forth in "Which is Jenkins?" and "Is that Brown?" Their prying looks exceeded far the bounds of etiquette. The proposal was again made and urged that the ladies should sleep in the house; but their decisive reply, "Accommodations which are good enough for our husbands are good enough for us," settled the matter, and the hack, with its curtains lowered, again answered for a sleeping apartment.

The prisoners with their wives went to the house when breakfast was ready, with a strong guard of "guns" on all sides of them, themselves being the centre of a hollow square. A disturbance arose here among the guard, as to who should sit at the first table. The landlady's ire was a little aroused, but the difficulty was settled without an appeal to arms.

Monday morning, the 19th, the cavalcade, with a large additional guard, making in all about one hundred men, started for the main camp, some twelve miles distant. This group of men was made up of all kinds. There were a few young men of education, accustomed to the refinements of life, and others brutal and ignorant. Their dirty dress gave to them an elfish look, and many lookers-on declared they had not supposed God's beautiful earth contained such desperate, brutal-looking men. They were obliged to pass along the prairie only a mile south of Lawrence, and, as they approached the long, steep hill on the California road, a quarter of a mile beyond Mt. Oread, they sent scouts all over the hills. They commenced whipping their horses at the base, and, as one of the prisoners expressed it, " they went kiting up the hill, and for nearly a mile after the summit had been gained."

Many of this posse had never been in the territory before, and, as they looked at Lawrence and its surroundings, of river flowing beneath the dim forests, the beautiful uplands and emerald slopes, and the distant highlands surging against the azure sky, like the deep blue ocean-wave, they broke forth in exclamations of rapture and delight. But Lawrence, with her large stone buildings, and little homes, made rich in experience of the past and hope for the future, was doomed — yes, doomed to destruction! for the strong arm of the government so willed it, and the wail of its desolation has gone up to Heaven against its officials, who, by their base proclamations, had brought this infamous horde upon us.

About two miles from Lawrence, a Mr. W., passing near his home, hunting for his cattle, was made to dismount by the posse and give up his horse to them. They reached Judge Wakefield's at two o'clock, P. M., and Capt. Donaldson, who seemed to have the command at this time, went into the house, then returned to the hack with a lady who was stopping there. She invited the ladies to remain with them over night; but, firm in their determination to stay by their husbands until forced from them, they declined the invitation, and went with the posse to the camp, one and a half miles distant. As the cavalcade approached the tents, hundreds of men, unwashed and unshorn, cursing and reeling in their inebriation, came around the carriage. Dr. Stringfellow was the officer of the day of this "law-and-order" crowd. He ordered the prisoners to alight, and immediately closed the doors upon their wives. Their tears fell like rain, and, distinctly above the cursing, that "all should be served alike," "men and women should be strung up together," were heard their sobs, which came from hearts near bursting. The suspense, the untold weight of bitterness crowded into these moments of separation from their husbands, having fearful reason to suppose it was the last earthly parting, cannot be measured in words. But Stringfellow was inexorable. He said "the northern press would say he had taken women prisoners, and it should not be said." When the hearts of some of the invaders had softened at their distress, and they promised to do all they could for the protection of the prisoners, Dr. Stringfellow said, "Mark my words; if any resistance is offered at Lawrence, or any attempt made to rescue the prisoners, the orders are to shoot them first of all."

Mrs. J. asked him, "could she be safe in driving a team to Lawrence and back again, to bring some bedding and clean clothes for Mr. J.?" Stringfellow said yes, but she soon learned that the span of large bay horses and the carriage she had already there, were "pressed" into the service, and could not be taken from camp. Mr. J.'s brother had been driven away at the point of the bayonet. She, with Mrs. B., then returned to Judge Wakefield's in the Westport hack, whose driver offered them seats. Taking his horses from the plough, Judge W. sent a son to carry the ladies to Lawrence. They returned as quickly as possible, and, before sundown, through the wet grass, with clean clothing on their arms, they went to the camp. The carriage-bed was carried into the tent to keep them from the wet ground, and, with some comfortables, a bed was made. The ladies then returned to Judge W.'s. About two o'clock A. M., Mr. Jenkins also arrived there, having been released. His horses had broken from the camp, and, during the night, Judge W.'s horses had been stolen. Mr. J. went to Lawrence on foot, and returned with another pair of horses for his wife. He recovered, on his second trip down, the bay horses. The fine horse first stolen he has never been able to recover, notwithstanding an order given him by those in authority, at the time it was taken.

This was Tuesday, the 20th. Mrs. Brown went over to the camp early; and her husband was already on horseback, surrounded by a guard of mounted men, to be taken to Lecompton.

On the afternoon of the 21st, after Judge Smith and G. W. Deitzler had been taken to the "head-quarters," the house on Mount Oread, Mr. Jenkins was again taken prisoner. He was taken from his bed, being wholly exhausted with his illness and fatigue, and with the rest carried to Lecompton. On the morning of the 22d of May they appeared before Judge Lecompte to answer to the charge of treason. The cases were continued until the second Monday in September. A request to be discharged on bail was made and denied. The crime was alleged to have been committed on the 1st, 17th, and 21st of May. G. W. Brown and Mr. Jenkins proved that nearly the whole time they were in the hands of the mob, who held them without warrant or law, and a part of the time in Missouri. G. W. Brown had been for weeks absent from the territory, and was returning to his home when arrested. Judge G. W. Smith had been only four days in the territory since the last of January. He had always recommended resistance to the laws through the legal tribunals. G. W. Deitzler also showed his position to be similar. Should bail have been allowed, the design for which they were taken prisoners would have been frustrated, viz., that of leaving the people without some of their leading and active men, that more easily the whole free-state movement might be crushed.

Mrs. J. and B. went to Lecompton on the 22d. They, with the four prisoners, had one small room in a frame house, the guard occupying the other room. Mrs. J. and Mrs. B. were allowed to take their meals at the public house, while those of the prisoners were sent to them. Thus, in a little room, in the intense heat, six persons were obliged to stay, night and day. The threats of mobbing them were also so great that Marshal Donaldson slept one night in the house, and another sat up on the outside. Mrs. J.

went to Lawrence on the 23d, returning the next day with some articles to add to the comfort of the prisoners, such as bedding, luncheon, water-pails, wash-basins, soap, towels, etc. The few days they had been in Lecompton, notwithstanding their frequent request of the marshal, they had only a two-quart pail for water; and, in making their toilet, they had had to pour water into their hands, and use handkerchiefs for towels. Mrs. J. says, "You never saw a more pleased set of fellows than they were when they saw the pails, soap, and towels." On the 26th the marshal proposed to Mrs. J. and Mrs. B. to board the prisoners, as the house they were in must be given up. They concluded to do it, thinking to make them more comfortable; and the next day, towards night, Mrs. J. returned from Lawrence with her span of white mules, which have been in her service ever since, going to Lawrence for provisions once or twice a week. She brought everything needed to commence housekeeping in a tent. The tent was already up; the stove soon was set; and, by all lending a helping hand, the supper was soon prepared. To shade the table, poles were set, and quilts and blankets thrown over them. To sit down once more at a table, and eat of food cooked in a home-like way, brought a ray of sunshine to the prisoners' hearts.

The military officer in command was of strong southern proclivities, and, one would judge from his words and manner, of unpleasant nature. The prisoners were not allowed to see their friends. When Mrs. B. returned, after an absence of a few days, he made loud complaints, saying "he wished they would either stay out or stay in."

Mrs. J. suggested the marshal's request, and that "if they boarded them, they must have provisions."

He replied, in a surly, insulting way, "We can find some one to get provisions, and you can stay away altogether."

A lady from Lawrence carried up the mail. While she was allowed to see the prisoners only at a distance, the officer carefully took from the papers the New York *Tribune*, allowing the rest to go in. Upon whose soul rests the sin of these indignities offered to peaceable, honorable men, and of the sufferings caused to innocent women?

ARREST OF GOV. ROBINSON.

My husband and myself left Lawrence, on his way to Washington, in the public hack for Kansas city. We reached that point about six o'clock. The Star of the West, Capt. Dix commanding, soon after came down the river; and the doctor immediately went on to the boat, entered his name on the clerk's book, and procured a state-room. We remained at the hotel over night, and took passage on the boat the next morning about six and a half o'clock. There were very few passengers; everything was quiet; and we were making a quick trip. In the afternoon we procured some books, and went into our state-room. From reading we soon fell asleep. At Lexington I was awakened by a noise as of many coming on to the boat. It having subsided somewhat, I was drowsing again, when the captain came to our state-room door, opening upon the guard, with a red-faced, excitable-looking person, of short stature, whom he introduced to my husband as Gen. Shields. Whether this title of General was acquired by Mr. Shields' visit to the territory at the time of the "Shannon War," last December, or whether it arose from the necessity which western men seem to feel, that of bearing some title, I have been quite unable to learn. That he was prominent in inciting that invasion, as well as others in the territory, is true. Another person, of larger figure, and more quiet, dignified air, came soon, and was introduced as Mr. Bernard, of Westport. After stating "they had come upon an unpleasant errand," they proceeded to state its purport — that of detaining my husband in Lexington, as he was fleeing from an indictment. He assured them such was not the case; that he had at all times been in Lawrence, or at places where he could have been arrested, had the authorities desired his arrest; but they had made no effort to serve any process upon him, and, so far as he knew, there was no indictment out against him.

The two gentlemen were reïnforced, as the moments passed, by eight or ten of the "first citizens in Lexington." "They had heard there was disturbance at the wharf, and had come down to see the cause of it." Gen. Shields stated that "they had been talking to the mob fifteen minutes, endeavoring to persuade them to leave the boat; but none would be satisfied unless the governor was retained in Lexington," while others said, "Drag him out." His own manner was sufficient to show that, had the mob acted upon the advice as reported, there would have been at least one of "the first citizens" wofully disappointed. He said, moreover, "Had it not been reported that your lady was on board, violence would at once have been offered; and no restraint could have been held over the crowd." The Yankee spirit of the lady rose at this, and a mental review was made upon such chivalry, such gallantry, of men who hesitate not to steal and invade the rights of others on the public thoroughfares. Such gallantry is the index, in all nations where it prevails, of the real want of morality and principle — a false glitter, where the whole under-current of the body politic is corrupt. The various propositions of sending a committee to St. Louis, that my husband might there transact as much of his business, which was urgent, as he could, and then return, if they should find, by their proposed express to Gov. Shannon, there was an indictment, did not meet with favor from this gallant band. His request to talk to the crowd, whom Gen. Shields declared to be in numbers "a cabin full," and "infuriated by the liquors on the boat, of which they were drinking freely," was also refused, with a look of utter disdain. My husband told them "he would never think to escape from an indictment for a political offence, and, had he been doing so, of all places he would have avoided the Missouri river and Lexington." By way of suggestion, he added, "that even in such a case he saw no reason for another state to interfere," at which the excitable elements in Gen. Shields' character became yet more aroused, and he said, "he did not wish to get into an argument, but," he continued, "I warn you, not as a friend, for I am not your friend,"— (to which my husband laughingly said, "I do not wish any one to claim to be my friend who is not,") —"but I warn you that this delay in consenting to leave the boat is only making the matter worse."

They said the carriage was ready to take us to the town; that in two or three days, or perhaps by the next boat, they would learn if there was an indictment, and, as soon as the messenger to Gov. Shannon should return, if they did not learn sooner there was none, they would leave him to pursue his journey. My husband, desiring to do that which was right in the matter, although his feelings prompted him to a forcible maintenance of his rights, let the consequences be what they might, asked me "what he should do." My counsels were to decline going with them. This was an unexpected phase of the matter; but the clerk of the boat stepped into our state-room at this juncture of affairs, and advised me, for the sake of my husband's safety, to consent to his going with them. The gentlemen gathered about the door pledged themselves to protect him from all violence. The exact value of such pledges I was unable to estimate, not knowing why men who would invade all the rights of American citizens on the public thoroughfares, would not as easily, without compunction of conscience, break their plighted word, if policy whispered a different course. My only hope at that moment was in this matter of policy, and I at last consented to go off the boat at Lexington.

Having accepted the hospitalities of Mr. Sawyer, by far the most gentlemanly man present, and whose face betokened kindliness of heart, we made preparations to leave the boat, which Gen. S. observed must be done without the knowledge of the "cabin full" of "drunken men." We passed out on the guard of the boat. The ruffianly horde were standing all around the gangways, and on the levee. One captain, so drunk he could not talk plain, was ordering his men. Another boat soon came, and the crowd rushed on it to search for Gov. Reeder, who was still in Lawrence. At night four men stood guard near Mr. Sawyer's. The next morning, having decided to continue my own journey, Mr. S. kindly took me to the boat. The following day my husband went with Mr. S. to his office, and was there introduced to several of the principal citizens, with whom he had familiar conversation. During the day, two men, known for their boasting and cowardice, came into Lexington from the country, and tried to excite the people to some violence against him. At last, some one, who knew them well, proposed to let them meet him, equally well armed as themselves. This proposal at once produced quiet. The week passed away without any word being brought back from Gov.

Shannon. Whether it required all this time to make out the necessary papers, after finding the indictment, we have no means of knowing. It was rumored that Gov. Shannon had sent a requisition upon the Governor of Missouri for the return of my husband to the territory. A few evenings after his detention at Lexington, a Dr. McDonald, of California, who tended upon him when he was shot in Sacramento, and who was temporarily in Lexington, called to see him. The people imagined he was some person from Lawrence, and that a rescue was in contemplation. In a very short time several hundred men had gathered around Mr. Sawyer's house. Mr. S. disliked such a state of things, and my husband preferred to go to the hotel; so, with a large guard, he went down to the hotel between eight and nine o'clock in the evening. The steps were full of men, and he passed in through them. After sitting a while in the parlor, conversing with the landlady and other ladies, he was attended to his room by a guard of three men. After a day or two, he took his meals in the public dining-hall. Many of the citizens called to see him, and were acquainted with all the plans of the new invasion. They said, "there would be a fight."

He told them "he did not think so; there would be no occasion for a fight. No one intended to resist the arrests of the United States Marshal."

They said, "it would make no difference whether they resisted the marshal or not,— they were determined to have a fight. They would attack and destroy Lawrence, then the other towns generally, and drive the free-state men from the territory." A few of them said, "they did not care for Kansas particularly, or the laws, but were determined to get up a fight; then the North would be aroused, a general war ensue, and the dissolution of the Union would be the result." Others said, "it was to be a war of extermination; if the free-state men could sustain themselves against the pro-slavery men, they would acquiesce and give it up."

Col. Preston returned from his interview with Gov. Price on Sunday, the 18th He had orders from the governor, to the sheriff of that county, to deliver my husband into Col. Preston's hands. A boat being at the wharf, it was decided to go on board;

but just as he was retiring for the night to his state-room, Col. Preston altered his mind, and they returned to the town. Col. Preston and Wm. Donaldson, with the prisoner in a carriage, left Lexington on the 19th, and reached Independence the same night. The next day they went to Westport, and remained there until the 22d, they declaring, without any hesitancy, that "Lawrence would be attacked, and they wanted him to remain in Westport until after it was done." On the night of the 22d, having had the additional guard of Capt. Long's party of Wyandot Indians, they arrived at Franklin. They told him repeatedly that in case his friends attempted to rescue him, they should kill him the first thing. About midnight, all having retired for the night, at Franklin, word came from Gov. Shannon, to Col. Preston, to return to Leavenworth by way of Kansas city, as there was danger of a rescue; that "he should hold him responsible for Gov. Robinson's safety, and if any harm befell him it would bring on civil war." (At Leavenworth he was informed that Gov. Shannon feared a rescue from his own men.)

So, the long way to Westport and Kansas city, through the swollen creeks and deep ravines, and in the darkness of the night, was to be retraced. They reached Kansas city the next evening, having taken a longer route to avoid the Westport and Kansas city road. Whether this was done through fear of attacks from the bands of South Carolina foot-pads infesting the usually travelled way, was not stated. After a little rest, a boat-whistle sounded on the night air. The officers, with their prisoner, were again astir, and the morning of the 24th found them at Leavenworth. The prisoner was delivered into the hands of the deputy sheriff of Leavenworth, who appointed Capt. Martin, of the Kickapoo Rangers, and three others, his guard. On the 28th, when the general reign of terror commenced at Leavenworth, those who had constituted themselves a committee of vigilance were determined to drive from the country every free-state man, and they made many threats of taking my husband from the hands of his keepers, and hanging him. Capt. Martin, learning of this intention, and determined no ill should come to him while in his charge, sent for more of his men. The marshal and Judge Lecompte came into Lawrence in the afternoon, and the threats of the mob became less loud. But the most bitter feeling was prevalent among the pro-slavery men.

Mr. S., of the investigating committee, called upon Gov. R. soon after his arrival in Lawrence, and, while talking with him, a pro-slavery man present interrupted him with, "You had better not talk so much."

Mr. S. looked at him in astonishment, and the man continued. "G—d d—n you, I 'd as soon put a bullet through your abolition head as not!" The fierceness of the man's character was prevented from further development by the interposition of the marshal. Judge Lecompte also made a formal call upon the prisoner, when he took the opportunity to ask of him the nature of his indictment, and if there was more than one against him.

The "Little Territorial Court," the red-faced, chubby man, making an effort towards dignity, replied, "There are two; one for usurping office, and one for high treason."

"Does the bill for usurping office include all my connection with the free-state movement, or is the indictment for treason founded upon this also?"

Judge Lecompte replied, substantially, "The indictment for usurping office relates to the state movement, and the office you have assumed under it. You are indicted for treason because you have organized and counselled forces to act against authorities recognized and appointed under the Kansas-Nebraska bill. You have assisted in arming men, thus resisting the movements of a legal body, and thus waging war against the United States."

"Does that relate to the occurrences in Lawrence in last November and December?"

"Well, such things, of course, cannot be plainly stated; but that is its chief basis, I suppose."

Let it be sounded in the ears of the American people, that high treason against the United States consists in arming one's self and friends, in defence of homes and property, in face of a mob, who threaten innocent men with death, and timid women with a fate in comparison with which death were infinitely preferable.

On the first of June, my husband, under the charge of his guard, arrived at Lecompton, and was placed in a tent with the other prisoners; thus making seven persons crowded into one tent.

CHAPTER XIX.

EXCITEMENT IN MISSOURI — OUTRAGES IN THE TERRITORY.

I ARRIVED at Kansas city on the night of June 3d, at twelve o'clock, after my eastern flying trip, and in hopes soon to join my husband. I had reached Chicago, on the homeward journey, when the first uncertain news of the sacking of Lawrence came. A few hours' delay, in order to gain more certain intelligence, followed, and the unexpected arrival of a friend from the ill-fated city gave to the wearing suspense of uncertainties the vividness and sadness of realities. He was doubtful as to the fate of any prisoners in their hands, yet for them he feared the worst. Still hoping all things good, however, with the habitual buoyancy of my character unsubdued, I pursued my journey, receiving from strangers in Illinois many tangible proofs of their sympathy for Kansas, and for those battling in the cause. The last day or two of the trip on the Missouri river rumors of war became more frequent. Inflammatory extras were thrown upon the boats at different landings. People at Lexington, and other points along the river, were much excited, and preparing for a new invasion. The extras stated the murder of eight pro-slavery men, by the abolitionists, and the cruel mutilation of their bodies; the death of the United States Marshal, of H. C. Pate, and J. McGee. Deeds of blood and violence, of which they were hourly guilty, were charged upon the free-state men. The following is a sample of the incendiary extras which flew through the border counties: "Murder is the watchword and midnight deed of a scattered and scouting band of abolitionists, who had courage only to fly from the face of a wronged and insulted people, when met at their own solicitation. Men, peaceable and quiet, cannot travel on the public roads of Kansas, without being caught, searched, imprisoned, and their lives, perhaps, taken. No Southerner dare venture alone and unarmed on her roads!" Such were the false statements made to arouse the passions of the border men.

A short colloquy on the boat between one of the surveyors in the employ of Gen. Calhoun, and others, will show the bitterness of their feelings. As the boat left Lexington he came into the ladies' cabin, and said to his wife, the daughter of a Wyandot, that "Donaldson was killed."

I said to him, "Will you tell me what Donaldson it is?"

"John Donaldson," was his curt reply.

Not knowing their Christian names, I asked, "Is it the United States Marshal?"

He then said, showing a very evident desire to make no explanations, "He was auditor;" and his wife, showing more animation than from her listless manner one would have supposed possible, added, "He was a very fine man."

To my question, "Were there others injured?" the surveyor said, "Yes, the abolitionists have killed several other persons."

This seemed to me a doubtful story, and I so stated my belief, adding, that "such stories were put in circulation for the purpose of exciting another invasion." Reliable persons had informed me that the sacking of Lawrence without resistance to the "regularly organized militia," was regarded by them as signal a defeat as the Dec. invasion; the invaders having made preparations for a siege, and the want of defence on the part of Lawrence had again foiled their plans. These reports of outrages committed by the free-state party seemed but another scheme to bring about civil war.

The Wyandot lady, with great bitterness, replied, "These stories come from the right side to be true!"

As I was revolving in my mind with what simplicity she had revealed her proclivities, a gentleman sitting by said to the surveyor, "Are these Buford men enlisted in the territorial militia?"

With some hesitancy, yet a half leer of satisfaction spreading itself over his broad, bloated face, he replied, "They are residents of the territory." I suggested their residence was of short duration, when the lady, who was "R. G. Q.," said, "These men and the Missourians went into the territory to make homes, while the eastern people went there to vote, and then returned."

Such astounding developments, coupled with the statement that had fallen from her lips the same morning, "that her husband was the handsomest man on the boat, and because of his beauty she married him," seemed to me all I had better try to believe at once. So I retired to my old seat to ruminate upon wars in Kansas, and the blessings resulting to mankind in general from a large diversity of tastes and dispositions.

There were several pro-slavery families on board, very pleasant people. There was a lovely girl going to her home, in Missouri, from a boarding-school in Illinois. There was a young lady from Kentucky, of intelligence and refinement, pro-slavery, yet with her I had many pleasant talks. A Missourian returning to Missouri with a Texan bride, delicate and pale as the light gossamer robes in which she floated, was very affable and intelligent. The young Shawnee girl, with her white husband, on her bridal tour, was educated, and pleasant, and from all, with the exception named, I received the common courtesies of life. This Wyandot lady also stated, with great satisfaction of manner, that "Gov. Robinson would be hung;" and was not a little displeased that her listeners doubted the statement.

On arriving at Kansas city we found the stage would go to Westport early in the morning. There were four of us to go, and we would attempt the passage together, notwithstanding bands of armed men were infesting the highways. Arrangements were made, and I slept a few hours. As I sat with bonnet and shawl on, the next morning, watching the stage, I saw it leave the door without passengers, and the clerk of the house following after. He asked the driver, "Why he left his passengers? Would he return? Would he wait for them to come where the coach then was?" To all his questions he received sullen, indefinite replies. The gentleman, knowing our anxiety to get into the territory, coaxed and threatened. But it all proved useless. He would not carry us to Westport, where we could meet the stage for Lawrence, and no carriage could go from the hotel, because horses were continually taken from wagons, carriages, or riders, and pressed into the service of "law and order." So, until the day after the next, as the stage went out only three days in the week, returning on the alternate days, we would be obliged to remain. This would have been unendurable had not the hotel still been in the possession of Massachusetts gentlemen. Five Massachusetts families were still in the house, also Mr. C., of Philadelphia, who had sometimes made a home with us, had just returned with his wife from the Quaker city.

The threats of destroying this hotel were still frequent, and nightly the danger of attack was imminent. The mayor of the city had kept out a guard one or two nights. But he had declined doing this longer, and, a meeting of the citizens being called, it was decided to ask the "Eldridges" to sell the hotel, to save it from the fury of South Carolinians and border men; they expressed to them at the same time their regret that such was the excitement against it.

Again and again the mob had assembled, and with groans, whose hideousness no one can appreciate who was not forced to listen, and with yells, declared the house should come down. The "Eldridges" proposed their terms, which were accepted, and, on the morning of the tenth, the hotel passed into the keeping of two pro-slavery men. Little curly, woolly heads, sitting in the doorways, proclaimed also the house was under a new rule. One, with skin slightly colored, and fiery red hair, looked oddly, and bore a marked resemblance to the little boy of his own size, whose attendant he seemed to be.

On the second of June a battle was fought near Prairie city. For several days, a portion of the posse, Buford men and Carolinians, together with Missourians, had been committing depredations upon the settlers, taking several of them prisoners. Capt. Brown, on hearing of the outrages, called his company together, and started on the eve of Sunday, travelling all night. At daylight, Capt. Brown made the attack upon Pate and his company, who were arranged behind their wagons. Pate also placed the unarmed prisoners, whom he had taken, in front of them, as a shield. The forces were not far from equal, Pate's party numbering a few more than the other. After a two hours' fire, Pate sent forward one of his men, with a prisoner, and a white flag, and surrendered unconditionally. A few of Pate's company fled to Missouri. Among them was Coleman, the murderer; twenty-six men were taken prisoners by Capt. Brown. A quantity of goods, stolen from Lawrence, was found in their wagons. A day or two after this, bands of South Carolinians were threading their way towards Bull Creek, and men from Independence, Lexington, Westford, and Clay county, generally, were fast going up the Santa Fe road to join the same bands. One hundred and eighty men, who had been camped near Bull Creek, went nearer Palmyra, and camped back of the town, in a ravine. About one hundred free-state men were in camp about two miles beyond. From near Hickory Point and Lawrence one hundred men were marching to reïnforce those last named. Whitfield left his seat before the investigating committee, June 2d, at the head of a large body of armed men, to conquer, I suppose, his constituents in the territory, his stated object to relieve H. C. Pate. While Gov. Shannon, in every instance, has stationed troops in a town after it has been sacked, he now saw the free-state men rallying to protect themselves, and feared the slave power would lose the ground gained through his servility. He heard, too, of aid coming from out of Kansas, and issued a proclamation on the fourth, "commanding all persons belonging to military companies unauthorized by law to disperse, otherwise they would be dispersed by the United States troops." It required all civil officers of the government to be watchful in enforcing the laws, and protecting the property and persons of all law-abiding citizens. All aggressive parties outside the territory will be repulsed. The President's proclamation of February 11th was appended, and Gov. Shannon stated that it would be strictly enforced. A requisition was also made upon Col. Sumner for a force sufficient to compel obedience to the proclamation.

On the fifth, Col. Sumner broke in upon the free-state camp, and released Capt. Pate and fellow-prisoners. Col. Sumner ordered the free-state men to return quietly to their homes, and then, turning to Pate, said, "What business have you here?"

"I am here by orders of Gov. Shannon."

"I saw Gov. Shannon yesterday, and your case was specially considered, and he asserted you were not here by his orders." He then added, "You are Missourians, all of you, and when you crossed your state line, you trampled on state sovereignty. Now, go, sir, in the direction from whence you came;" and, as he closed his remarks, Col. Sumner waved his hand for Pate and his party to leave. So the brave H. C. Pate returned to Westport and Kansas city. He acknowledged the bravery of Capt. Brown, for he said Capt. Brown rode about them sword in hand, and commanded a surrender, and they were obliged to make it. He spoke well of them in their treatment of him while a prisoner, but with Col. Sumner's treating him with so little deference he felt quite outraged, and talked of a challenge.

The pro-slavery camp was also visited by Col. Sumner, and ordered to leave the territory. A part did so; but another part of Whitfield's force went towards Osawattomie. On the sixth, at four o'clock in the afternoon, one hundred and fifty of them, fully armed and much intoxicated, entered Osawattamie, and commenced their work of house-breaking, burning and pillage. They sacked the town, taking everything of value, money, provisions, clothing and jewelry. Sixteen horses were taken, while the owners looked on. Among them were two from the United States mail coach, running between Fort Scott and Westport.

On the eighth, Capt. Brown's company, having been disbanded at Palmyra, was disarmed. Hearing of the sack of Lawrence, they had again organized, and were deliberating how best to protect themselves, and neighbors, when the troops, who should have protected Osawattomie, came upon them, and took their arms. Word had been sent, previous to the attack, to some of the free-state camps, and messengers were immediately sent to the nearest camp of the dragoons, asking for protection for Osawattomie. The messengers stated that the free-state men had been disbanded with the promise of protection. Now, Osawattomie was calling to them for aid, and unless they would march to their relief, the free-state men would rally, and at once go to their assistance.

Lieut. McIntosh said he had heard rumors of an attack, similar to those brought by the messengers, and that he had sent an express in the morning, to the camps near Osawattomie, informing them of the contemplated attack. The messengers stated that unless they could carry back word that something definite would be done, for the protection of Osawattomie, they would immediately march to that place. The lieutenant then stated that everything that could be done, would be; that he would himself start for the camp below. While he was preparing to leave, he accused the free-state people of being unwilling to obey the Draconian laws of the territory. He was on his way toward Osawattomie.

The free-state men, thinking their friends would be protected, returned to their homes, leaving the field to the dragoons. The next night brought the intelligence of the sack of Osawattomie. The troops *could* not save Lawrence, because Col. Sumner had no orders to act. They *did* not save Osawattomie. Neither did they protect Leavenworth, only three miles from the fort, during its reign of terror. While the free-state men showed a disposition to protect themselves, they were not allowed to do it; yet robberies and murders were repeated every day, in the early part of June. Every evening's intelligence was of some fresh outrage.

On the evening of the fourth, Mr. C., counsel for the prisoners, with his wife, returned from Lecompton. Judge C. was also with them, having gone as a witness in the case. At Lecompton both of them were ordered from the town by a bully from Leavenworth, by the name of Kelly. He ordered Judge C. to leave, and when he applied to Gov. Shannon for protection, the reply of the governor of the territory was, "Your people are shooting down our people, and I can give you no protection." The meaning of this is, the free-state people are shooting down the pro-slavery, which was false in reality, and which still further proved the partisan character of the government. After ordering Judge C. to leave, he met Mr. C., as he was returning from the clerk's office (where he was having some papers necessary in my husband's case made out) to Shannon's office.

The following dialogue took place:

Ruffian, in a rough manner, — "You are ordered to leave Lecompton."

Mr. C., in a very composed manner, asked, "Do you order me to leave upon your own responsibility, or at the suggestion of others?"

"I tell you you are ordered to leave Lecompton."

"Yes, but such proceedings are not usully executed so summarily, and it would gratify me to know who takes the responsibility of ordering me from Lecompton."

"I take the responsibility; so do others. I tell you to leave."

"Well, what may your name be?"

The ruffian demurred at giving his name; but, as Mr. C. assured him that, in all civilized countries, the accused were allowed to know the names of their accusers, he said, "You know me. You saw me at Leavenworth at the first election."

"I do not recollect having had the honor of your acquaintance; but of course you are an honorable man, and are not ashamed of your name."

"Well, my name is Kelly; and you are ordered to leave Lecompton."

Mr. C. retained his seat, while Mr. Kelly, like a witness on the stand, was standing before him, and the highly honorable governor was sitting by.

"In all courts of justice it is customary for the accused to make a defence before judgment is pronounced, and it would please me to know of what I am accused."

After refusing, for a time, to make any charges, Mr. Kelly said, "You have written articles for the *Herald of Freedom.*"

"That is a misstatement. What other charges have you?"

"You have been connected with the free-state movement."

"You are so honorable a man, you will, of course, allow me to bring witnesses to prove this charge untrue."

"Well, you are known to be the intimate friend of Gov. Reeder and Gov. Robinson."

Mr. C., rising, said, "That is sufficient;" and, turning to Gov. Shannon, asked, as counsel for Gov. Robinson, — having come there expecting an examination in his case, — if he had no protection to offer him. The governor signified he had none. Then Mr. C., gathering up his papers in a dignified manner, bade him "good-afternoon," and walked out of the house. The governor seemed to have a sudden thought. He stepped out after him, and spoke to some of the ruffians a moment, when one of them told Mr. C. "he could stay in Lecompton as long as he wanted to."

Judge C., with the wife of the counsel, rode out of town a short distance to wait for her husband. They were stopped by three men, armed with U. S. muskets, as they approached Westport, on their way back to Kansas city. The question whether they were armed was asked by one of the foot-pads; to which Mrs. C. replied, "No, sir." They were then allowed to pass. Westport was full of armed men, and a large company were drilling in front of Milton McGee's, two miles from Kansas city; but, for some reason, they were allowed to pass unmolested.

The next morning, June 4th, Judge C. was sitting in the parlor, relating to three or four of us ladies his adventures of the three last weeks, his detention at Parkville by a mob, his arrest at Leavenworth by a gang of self-constituted authorities, and his being driven from Lecompton by an Irish bully, the governor acquiescing. We were all laughing merrily at the pictures he drew of his forlorn condition, being marched about at the point of the bayonet, and assuring us, in his own peculiar way, that it "did confuse a fellow's ideas somewhat when he expected a punch from the bayonets every moment." But, at this instant, a rough, burly fellow, red-faced, and with hair of yet more fiery color, came through the reading-room into the parlor. He came a little way towards Judge C., and called him to him. He then asked, "Is your name C.?"

"It is, sir."

"You are my prisoner."

"By what authority?" said Judge C.

The only reply was a rough grasp of the shoulder and wrist of Judge C., with the words, "Come along," as he rudely drew him into the reading-room. Mrs. C., the Philadelphia lady, and a brave Massachusetts woman in the house, were close to Judge C.'s side. The rude law-and-order man stated that Jones had just been shot, and was dead, and that Judge C. was the murderer.

Mrs. C. said, "Judge C. is a friend of ours, and he is an innocent man."

Some men of Kansas city, at work on the levee, in front of the hotel, had gathered near. The official appealed to them for help; but not a hand was raised to aid him, while he declared "he would not give a 'fip' for such a town as that." Seeing how matters stood, that he was to get no help, he said "he was mistaken in the man," and spoke of two other free-state men as implicated in the pretended assassination of the day before, who had been in the states since January, and were not yet in the territory.

He then said, "Were you not driven out of Leavenworth?"

"I was told to go, sir."

To Judge C.'s explanation that he was now on his way to Baltimore, his home, the burly fellow said "it was also his home."

"What may your name be? perhaps I may know you," said the judge.

"My name is Hughes." Then Mr. Hughes made his parting address; "Well, C., you go to your home, and do as man ought to do to man."

"I will, sir."

"Don't tell any of your infernal lies when you get to Baltimore."

"I shall tell no lies, sir."

The truth in his case, he doubtless thought, as we did, would be all-sufficient to rouse the feelings of American citizens against the outrages committed here at slavery's bidding. A gentleman from Lawrence, whom Brewerton had pointed out as having shot at a Mr. Cox, in the meleé passed directly through the crowd from the office, to a safer place. Another, from St. Louis, was introduced to the same Hughes, by a bystander, as a "shipper of Sharpe's rifles." The law-and-order man dilated his eyes, and asked the gentleman if that was his business. He replied, "he was a commission merchant, and whatever boxes came, shipped to his care, he sent forward." "Did he not know he had no right to send rifles to Kansas?" "I have lived several years in St. Louis, and have never broken any law of the state." To such indignities and questionings have gentlemen been obliged to submit at the hands of men who have been convicts for years in the penitentiary. It was amusing to see the indignation of the last gentleman, at such an examination, not having been through so thorough a process of breaking-in as Judge C. Every day only added to the enormities of the pro-slavery party.

A Mr. Cantrell, recently from Missouri, but a free-state man, was taken prisoner on the evening of the 5th of June, by one of Gen. Whitfield's scouting parties. On the next day he was carried down the Sante Fe road. At Cedar Creek he was taken out into a ravine by two men. Then there was a shot; — then the cry, "O, God, I am shot! — I am murdered!" Then another shot, and a long, piercing scream; — another shot, and all was still!

A Mr. Bailey narrowly escaped a violent death, and through many sufferings at last reached his friends. He had started from his home to get a load of provisions for himself and his neighbors. When near Bull Creek, Coleman, who had twenty men encamped close by, came and ordered him to stop there over night. Among these twenty men were Buckley and Hargous, his accomplices in the murder of Dow. In the morning his horses were missing their halters having been cut. The men expressed sympathy for his loss, and told him the horses could be found in the camp at Cedar Creek, and they proposed to go with him to find them. Before reaching Cedar Creek they met a company of two hundred men. A consultation was held with them, and Coleman said, "There may be treachery used."

Soon after the company had passed on, three men took Mr. Bailey into the prairie about one hundred yards from the road, and demanded his money; without hesitation, or one word of objection, he gave them forty-five dollars, all he had. One of the men then raised his gun as though he would fire. Mr. Bailey said, "If you mean to kill me, you will kill a better man than yourself;" to which the ruffian, lowering his gun, replied, "I wish you to take off those pantaloons; perhaps they will get bloody." But Mr. Bailey said, "They are mine as long as I live."

This tool of the administration, armed with a U. S. musket, again raised his gun, and fired. The ball struck Mr. Bailey in the side, glancing along the ribs, and lodged in the back. Mr. Bailey fell, and was struck at again and again with the musket. Then two of the men disappeared, and left this more than demon to finish the work of killing a peaceable man. He jumped on the body of the prostrate man, stamping on his face and head. But as Mr. Bailey caught hold of the musket, and was able to hold on upon it, the murderer ran after the others, calling upon them to return. They, however, were too far away. After lying in the grass three hours, Mr. Bailey attempted to find his way home. In doing so, he passed near their camp the next morning at daybreak, and for a while lay hid in the grass, to learn their movements. While there, he heard a cry, "Are you going to hang me?" and no reply, save the ringing of a bell. In about five minutes, he heard a shot, then a whistle, and six other shots at intervals of five minutes. He lay in the woods all that day, and at night crawled along about two miles; was hid near the Wakarusa all the next day; saw a wagon stopped by five men; heard angry words, and a shot fired. In the night, worn down by his sufferings from the wound and bruises, having had nothing to eat for three days, and nothing to drink but stagnant water, he reached the house of Dr. Still, at Blue Mound.

A young man, by the name of Hill, was going to Missouri, also for provisions, and as night came, he asked two men on the road where he could find water for his horses. They said they would show him, if he would go with them. When he had gone with them to the ravine, where they said he would find water, they searched him, took whatever he had of money, and threatened to kill him. He told them he had a mother, and young brothers and sisters, dependent on him; that day after day, as she looked out for his coming, and night only brought a renewal of the sad suspense as to his fate, in sorrow she would go the grave; but there was no pity in their hearts, no mercy. They tied the young man's arms behind him, and, bending his feet backwards, tied them also to his arms, then put a stick an inch and a half wide in his mouth, prying it open, and tied the string back of his head. Then, more barbarous than the New Zealanders, they cut places in his hat, and tied that also over his face, and laid his face downwards on the stones. They went away leaving him to die.

After a time they came back; and, as one placed his pistol directly over his eye, he feeling its pressure through the hat, the other said, "Don't shoot him; he will not go any further on his journey to-night." They left again to report at the camp, probably, another victim to the vile tools of slavery propagandism.

When this young man found himself again alone, and thought they would not return, he commenced making an effort to extricate himself from his painful position. By working his boot upon the sharp stones, he found the rope loose enough for him to draw his foot out. His feet were thus left at liberty, while one boot was swinging on his back. By working his hat between his knees, he was able to pull it off his face. Then with the strip of board still lacerating his mouth, and hands fastened with strong cords behind him, he set out to find some house in the darkness of the night.

He had come from Iowa in the spring, and was but little acquainted with the country. After travelling eleven miles, he knew, by the barking of the dogs, he was near a house, but was unable to get over the fence. The strange cries he made at last attracted the attention of the family, but, supposing him to be a drunken Indian, they did not at first come to his aid. He was, however, cared for by them. Elliot, who with Titus pledged five hundred dollars for the head of Capt. Walker, when the U. S. Marshal, with his usual servility, offered to send a posse for him, was one of the actors in this savage transaction. Other men were continually shot and robbed.

A man, who had a pass from U. S. Marshal Donaldson, with a load of freight, was returning to his home in the territory. The same evening of the day he left, he returned, robbed of his money, wagon and oxen, and saved his life only by a promise to leave the territory. The men who attacked him were encamped about two miles from Westport, armed, as all their men are, with U. S. rifles and side arms.

The questions asked of him were, "Where do you live? Where are you from? What are your politics? How much money did that d—d Emigrant Aid Society give you to come out here? What the h—l did you come out here for? Did you come to make Kansas a free state? Why did n't you go to Nebraska? That 's a good country, and you d—d Yankees may have it; but Kansas you 'll have to fight for, and we 'll whip h—l out of you, but we 'll get it, Union or no Union! That 's a game that must win, I am thinking." The question was finally asked, "If we will let you go, will you take a gun and march with the pro-slavery party?"

"*Never!*" was the invariable reply. In an instant, the cry resounded through the camp, "The ropes, boys, the ropes!"

It was thrown over his head, and he was dragged to the nearest tree, exclaiming, "You do not intend to kill me in this manner, do you?"

The reply was, "Yes, G—d d—n your abolition heart, and all like you!"

He asked, if he was thus to be sacrificed, for time to collect his thoughts, and arrange his worldly affairs. The fiends told him he could have ten minutes to make any disposal of his property, and his peace with God. He then gave a list of his effects to one of the captains, asking him to send it east to his friends; and, at the expiration of the ten minutes, the rope was thrown over a limb, and they jerked him from the ground. After being let down, he was asked, "Will you leave the territory, if we 'll spare your life?"

The prisoner objected, stating he had broken no law, and infringed upon no man's rights. The leader, who had ordered him let down when hanging, again interposed, saying he must make this promise, or lose his life. He told the men that this gentleman had a "right to be a free-state man, though no right to hold such views in Kansas; that he was guilty of no crime." With a guard he was sent back to Kansas city.

Others, going out with loaded teams, soon returned, having

gone through the same operation of questioning and hanging. In one instance, as one was released, and left the camp, he heard the screams of another man in the camp across the road. Mr. Upton, the sergeant-at-arms of the investigating committee, was also threatened with hanging, but he was very firm in his expressed opinions that they would n't do it. When at last he told them who he was, they looked frightened, and were glad to be rid of him.

A young man and his wife, formerly from Iowa, came to Kansas city. They were fearful, and dared not stay longer in the territory. Nine yoke of cattle, which he was going to take into Iowa to sell, were taken from him by a ruffianly band just as he approached Kansas city. Some gentlemen stopping at Kansas, who had lost teams on their way down, were anxious to get back into the territory. They started one day, but returned ere its close. They thought, by going on foot, and keeping off of the travelled roads, they should be able to get through without molestation; but, when about twelve miles out, they fell into the enemy's hands. They were released after a time, and advised to return to Kansas city, "as they would meet other bands, where they might fare worse."

A clergyman, from Vermont, whom I met on my tour East, and who spoke to me then of visiting the territory, to look after an insane brother, reached Kansas city on his return, having been in perils many and oft. At Westport, he stated himself a clergyman, his object in visiting the territory, and tried to hire a horse of Mr. Harris, of the Harris House. There seemed to be objections, but the matter was at last arranged. A man proposed to go with him, who also had a sick brother. Coleman stood near them as the arrangements were made. As Rev. Mr. Webster and the other man were travelling along, he noticed another man keeping always the same distance in the rear. A few miles out of Westport, the man proposed watering the horses; and, as Mr. W. dismounted, he was informed by the other man, "that he was taken out here for the purpose of an examination, to see whether the stories he told were true." The papers he found on the minister corroborated his statements, and satisfied the man. The one following had also arrived there, and entered into the examination. Mr. W. was then informed that if he went on to Prairie city, he must do so on foot, as he had orders to take the horse back to Westport. Mr. W. was unable to walk so far, and concluded to go back and make another trial. On retracing his steps, he was taken into a camp of the highwaymen, and marched about at the option of the vile men. He was surprised to find there, also in bonds, two Virginians who had made the passage of the Missouri at the same time with himself. They had promised to travel with him, to be a mutual protection, but by some means they had lost sight of each other. And they, not willing to go all lengths of robbing and shooting, in their defence of slavery, had fallen under the surveillance of these brutes in form of men.

Reports of five men hanging on the trees between Westport and Palmyra came in at Kansas city. One of the pro-slavery proprietors of the house had his information so direct that he said "he had no doubt it was true."

Some free-state families were leaving, but they were mostly those who had but recently come into the territory, and had not established themselves, and become a part of the great question of slavery and freedom. Timid men turned back when their feet had hardly pressed the rich soil of Kansas; but the old settlers, undaunted by past disasters and present confusion, stood firmly upon their rights. Having put their "hands to the plough, they would not look back." In some regions, where husbands and brothers were in arms to protect some other settlement, or to drive out marauders, delicately reared and intelligent New England women were busy in the fields. Their horses and oxen stolen they were at work earnestly to get in the crops. Two beautifu and accomplished girls, thus at work, said to a friend of mine, "Those who would think less of us for working in the field, may say what they please; we do not value their opinions."

Forbearance has been the motto of our people. No means have been left untried to arouse them against national authority, but, with the trusting, peace-loving spirit, which has no parallel in history, they have cherished a *faith,* in the final righting of their wrongs, which indeed "hopeth all things and endureth all things."

None but the intelligent, strong-hearted class of people, who have passed into Kansas, could have reached such an acme of endurance. Now another desperate effort is put forth to possess the land. Attempts are made unceasingly to drive off the timid, to harass the settlers generally, by placing the love of life in the scales with a love of freedom; by keeping in prison the leading men, and by preventing the incoming of new free-state settlers by every possible means.

CHAPTER XX.

TWO WEEKS IN JUNE ON THE MISSOURI BORDER.

Every succeeding day's fresh enormities clearly show the base intention of the pro-slavery men. Major Richardson, Buford, Donaldson, and others, who are foremost in this cruel war upon the free-state men, often dined at the hotel in Kansas city. The threats of Buford's men against him were neither few nor mild. Many of them, without hesitation, said "they would shoot him the first chance they could get," and he at last went down the river. His men came in, every day, worn out and sick. A free-state man, pitying the utter wretchedness of one of them, took care of him a few days, and sent him down the river. I saw him frequently carrying some little nourishment from the hotel to the store where the sick man was. A gentleman in from Chicago reported help near. He brought letters from well-known friends of Kansas. The rumor spread abroad. Its soothing effect upon the overwrought passions of the border men could not escape notice. Their anxiety in the matter was intense. One of them, a native of Burlington, Vt., of fine family, but who has been connected with a rabid pro-slavery paper here, though now apparently leaning to the other side of the question, had his seat next me at the table. This gentleman said to me, "It is said two thousand men are coming from Chicago; but I think the trouble is confined here; it reaches but a little distance." The reply made was, "You cannot have been East lately, for there is intense feeling throughout the North, and they will not be backward in sending many times that number, if emergencies require it." A report of five hundred men coming from Wisconsin also had a wonderfully subduing effect upon the Leavenworth law-and-order men, and soon after Col. Sumner disbanded their Vigilance

Committee. For many days the ferry-boat had been plying busily backwards and forth across the river, bringing over the Clay County boys. As they landed but a few rods below the house, and I saw their besotted, rough, unintelligent faces, I wondered less at the barbarities we heard daily. The intellectual was blotted out, the animal, the sensual part of human nature alone remaining, rendering them fit instruments, in the hands of a corrupt administration, in aiding and abetting the interests of the slave power. They came back in two days, and went on the boat quietly, no yells resounding through the grand old woods on the further shore, as when they came over. Col. Sumner had at last driven them out. There were Wyandots returning drunk, who yelled in front of the hotel, and brandished their pistols, daring one another to fight. One of my husband's guard at Westport was at the hotel, and desired to see me. He seemed to be a man of kind heart, and evidently thought he was conferring a favor by telling me how much "the guard thought of Gov. Robinson; that he was a gentleman, and they treated him as such; that Capt. Martin was very much attached to him, and declared no injury should come to the governor in which he did not share." As we were talking familiarly, I asked him "how it happened that Gov. Shannon was so long in sending for my husband." He said, "I suppose they had to wait for papers to be made out." "Then they found there was no indictment when we left Lawrence?" And he was forced to say there was none at that time. He was very anxious to get to Lecompton, but pretended to think the people of Lawrence would attack him if he attempted to pass there, and, if I would go with him, he would protect me by their camps, while my presence would be a safeguard for him at Lawrence. The mutual advantages of the arrangement did not strike me so forcibly as him, and I preferred to stay longer here to getting into a worse place. Gov. Shannon came to Kansas city on the 9th. It was known that he met a large party of Georgians at Westport, just arrived; and the streets were full of the noisy, drunken crowd. He stated his intention to go down the river. Poor man! he feared for his own safety. He was despised by both parties, and a curse to himself. As a man who had lost his cattle was speaking to the governor, trying to get some redress, it was amusing to watch the expression of his face. There was a look of utter weariness, of inability to do anything, of incapacity to know what to do. Instead of going down the river, he took the first boat to Fort Leavenworth, and the next day sent a sealed despatch to the President. Gov. Shannon was frightened, and, as he repeated some things about the invasion to Col. Sumner, the colonel grew angry, and talked plainly to the governor, telling him "he would have driven out the ruffians long ago, had he had the power, and now he had, he would drive them over the state line, or to h—ll." The colonel, with Shannon under his wing, started off with another company of dragoons, three brass six-pound field-pieces, and a quantity of stores. Col. Sumner was very indignant at the Osawattomie affair.

The investigating committee had also arrived on the 9th, having finished their laborious work in the territory, and their last sittings at Leavenworth and Westport being in the midst of war, arrests of their clerks, their witnesses, and in general confusion. Every day at Westport armed bands of infuriated, drunken men, were marshalled in the streets. Their threats were open and violent against the committee. Whitfield had left his position before the committee to carry fire and sword into the territory. The last afternoon there was an effort made to create a disturbance, but the firmness of the majority of the committee effectually quelled it.

The people of Westport soon began to grow weary of the troublesome men whom they had invited into their midst. Not content with robbing free-state people, the Westport people said, "No man was sure, when he fastened his horse and went into a store, that he would find it on his return." Such an experience was a little troublesome, so they called a meeting to express their disapprobation of this invasion into the territory, to state that they had no sympathy with it. But the insincerity of the movement was expressed by the total failure of the meeting, only six persons remaining until its close. They probably forgot that at the same time a call was in all the papers, signed by one of the most influential citizens of Westport, for "provisions and horses to carry on the war." A few days after, another meeting was called, and a resolution was passed to the effect that they had taken no part in this invasion upon the territory, in the outrages, such as murder, hanging, etc. A man, who shot Mr. Cantrell, voted for this resolution. Another man, more honest at least, arose and said he was of a party which had gone through a mock hanging; but the resolution passed.

Business was dead at Kansas city. For the few last days I was there nothing was stirring where before, for the press of teams, a person could pass with the greatest difficulty; scarcely any one could be seen. The warehouse men had received word from Lawrence that all freights in their houses, consigned to merchants there, must be shipped to Leavenworth. This made them anxious, for through their pockets their feelings had been reached. The business men invited conversation with some eastern men. They said they would call meetings expressive also of their disapprobation; but they were assured the move was too late; that it would not be regarded as sincere; that eastern capital was timid, cautious; that it would not be convinced; that money, which would have come in here, would go where life and property are safe; that eastern travel would leave the Missouri river for a northern route.

One man, who brought the governor's proclamation down to Westport and Kansas city, was on the way, through the border town, to raise more men for the war. Wm. Donaldson, several days after, was at Independence, endeavoring to induce men to go up and attack Topeka. The following letter from Independence states the fact:

"INDEPENDENCE, Mo., *Thursday, June* 12, 1856.

"POSTMASTER, LAWRENCE, K. T.: There were some men here yesterday trying to get men to go with them to the territory, for the purpose of going to Topeka to burn it up. Now, for God's sake, send an express immediately to that place, and get the people there to send for the United States troops to protect them. One of the men that were here was named William Donaldson (brother of Postscript D.), and he said that Shannon had left the territory and gone home, leaving Secretary Woodson as acting governor, and that *he* would let the pro-slavery party do as they pleased, and that *now was the time* to burn out, kill and drive every free-state man from the territory.

"I am a pro-slavery man myself, but I want things done honorably, and give you the warning now. Do not delay, for they will be in Topeka in a very few days. Respectfully,

"James Brown.

"P. S. — This is not my proper name, but what is said is true."

Several women, whose lives had been passed amid the influences of slavery, were a novel study. One who boarded in the hotel, a lady in manner, seemed anxious to know all that was transpiring in and around the house, and to gain such knowledge did not hesitate to listen at the doors of other people's rooms. One evening, three several times was she found standing in the dark passage-way near a room, where several of the free-state people were chatting socially.

Another, a young girlish thing, full of quick wit and ready repartee, though as uncultivated as the unhewn rock, occasioned us many a laugh. She was a native of this far west, and it seemed to be as natural for her to swear as to breathe. Almost every sentence, besides the oath, either began or finished with the assertion "I am a real border ruffian." She talked a good deal of a proposed visit to her husband's parents in Vermont, and wondered "what they would say when they saw a live border ruffian."

There was another person, whose languid airs and affected manner of speech would entitle her, in the great world of fashion, to the name of lady. The subject of temperance lectures being one day incidentally introduced, she said, "It was not because her husband was a seller of liquors that she never attended such lectures, but where she had lived it had not been considered respectable for ladies to attend them." She concluded by saying "that in these days of isms she supposed some would attend them."

There was another woman, native-born, who came to the house, occasionally, at the time it was passing into new hands. She owned one of the colored "boys," who was hired in the hotel. She came to make some arrangement with the new proprietor. She was a maiden lady, considerably on the down-hill side of life, large, portly, with most expressionless face, but she had "raised" the "boy," and she "wanted him treated kindly." She said, "she had thought she would let him have what wages he made through the summer." When the proprietor, quite harshly, said, "it did not do to treat negroes well," she said "she had never struck the boy a blow in her life, and she would have him well treated; he could stay a month, and if he did not like he could leave."

In a conversation with a little daughter of the former proprietor, she said, "Where are you from?"

"Massachusetts."

"What county is that in?"

"Massachusetts is a state," timidly replied the sensitive girl, not liking to show any superiority of knowledge.

"Yes, I know that; but what county is it in?"

There seemed to be a confusion of ideas. She knew she lived in Jackson County, and to her, probably, that comprised all Missouri. As far as native intelligence went, the colored boy was her superior, and she evidently regarded him with the same affection she would a white boy whom she had reared.

A most forcible display of the evil passions aroused and strengthened by the system of slavery, and the effect which absolute power over one's fellow-creature has upon the character, was made one day at dinner. A stranger unfortunately had taken the seat which this boarder usually occupied. He came late to his meal, and saw the seat was occupied, and, as he stood in the doorway, looking up and down the table, turning his head this way and that in most furious manner, there was in his face scarcely one expression of the "human face divine." He was an intemperate man, and now, when his passions were aroused, his appearance suggested wild animals, a whole menagerie. Seeing his strange actions and looks, we supposed he was looking for some one at the table, against whom such wrath had concentrated, but he finally turned and told the proprietor, "he should leave the house before the sun-setting, and he would have it torn down; not another night should it stand." Thus he raved all that afternoon, in the house and out of the house, endeavoring to gather a crowd; but toward evening another dram gave him a quietus for the night and the next day, and the matter ended.

It was at last decided by Col. Sumner, that, for the present, he would keep the prisoners at Lecompton, as so many of his forces must be drawn away from the fort. It was impossible to get to Lawrence by way of Westport, and all travellers thither must go up the river to Leavenworth, and across the Delaware Reserve. The boats were getting scarce. One came up heavily loaded with Mormons; every place on the upper deck was crowded with large emigrant-wagons, and the living freight packed in at every corner. Dirt and filth were visible, and the looks of these women, "sealed" to the Mormon faith and their tyrannical husbands, was one of utter misery. About the same time, one of the down boats carried, as passengers, two of the Mormon elders on their way to Washington, on business relating to the admission of Utah as a state. Several ladies on board were able to distinguish them, among the crowd, from their coarse, brutal looks.

At last the Keystone came, and, on the evening of the 13th, in company with a gentleman and lady from Massachusetts, whose intelligence and pleasing ways had contributed much to the comfort of my detention in Kansas city, I left for Leavenworth, and they for a summer stay at Council Bluffs.

On the boat we overheard a conversation between a Kentucky lady and a lady from Missouri. The former said,

"They are having exciting times in Kansas!"

"Yes; a great many have gone over from the border counties."

"Well, Kansas will be a free state in the end. The Yankees have determined upon it, and when they have determined upon a thing, they have so much more energy than the Southerners, they will accomplish it."

The idea did not seem to please the Missouri lady, but she replied, "If I lived in Kansas, I would want it a free state; but to live in Missouri, I want it a slave state."

"We had slaves in Kentucky, but we preferred to come to Kansas, because we know property is more valuable in a free state, and its institutions are more desirable. Many people in Kentucky are of the same mind."

The rudder of the boat was slightly damaged by running into the bank in the fog of the morning, and, becoming more dense every moment, it was impossible to keep the boat under way. Hence, when we reached Leavenworth, the stage had gone to Lawrence. The next day was Sunday, and it rained heavily, and all the morning of Monday, but an acquaintance was over from Lawrence, and "if I would risk getting a drenching," he said, "we would start." I was enough of a water-fowl not to mind rain, and, to the surprise of the pleasant Kentucky family with whom I stopped, I appeared all ready for a drive when the little blue bit of sky was continually varying from the size of one's hand to that of a yard square, and the sun was playing "hide-and-seek" with the dark clouds. Save the driving out of our way at one time, and the slippery state of the roads, we had a pleasant ride through the beautiful Delaware country. It needs only some pleasant houses, grouped among the clumps of trees, to give it the look of a long-settled country.

Leavenworth, situated on the Missouri, has the finest landing for many miles. The site of the town is broken with small hills, and some fine swells in the distance invite residences. Tasteful hands prepared the town-site, and left many trees and shrubs standing. The advantage Leavenworth has over the other settlements, in procuring pine lumber directly from St. Louis, shows itself in the good-sized dwellings built with porticos and piazzas, and yards neatly fenced. There are, at present, no large public buildings. Thirty stores stand near the levee, and have done a large business. The present state of things in the territory has produced a general depression in trade, and none feel it more than people at Leavenworth. The majority of the settlers are free-state people, mostly from Pennsylvania. Owing to its nearness to Missouri, and ease of access to the border men, they have come over in crowds, and, uniting with the few "fire-eaters" in and around Leavenworth, have controlled everything, making mob-law the rule. Leavenworth must, unavoidably, be a large commercial point in the West, and now holds the first rank in size in the territory.

As the evening was fast coming, we emerged from the heavy timber on the north bank of the Kansas, and waited for the ferry-boat on the other side of the river.

Desolation sat in the despoiled city; the one broken wall of the hotel was yet standing; there was no home on Mt. Oread; plunder and fire had wrought the ruin there, and the destructiveness of the mob had only been satiated by the girdling of every tree transplanted there.

Still there was a home-feeling in getting back to Lawrence, notwithstanding my husband was in prison and myself homeless. And most heartily were the glad assurances of welcome and interest, from many friends clustered around, reciprocated.

There was a new excitement in Lawrence. A man, by the name of Hopkins, had been shot the evening before. He was found dead in the house of a new comer, named Haney. The circumstances seemed to prove that, in attempting to rid the world of a monster who had boasted of having killed three men and four Indians, he was himself shot. The immediate cause of the feeling against Haney was, his having acted as deputy sheriff of Douglas County in the arrest of David Evans, familiarly known as "Buckskin." This Evans was the man who effectually cowed the pro-slavery men, and especially the Hungarian doctor, in the case of the free black man, the summer before. Evans, being a Missourian, and a free-state man, was exposed, as all other free-state men coming from slave states are, to the intense bitterness of the border ruffians. The dragoon government was set in motion. Haney, with fourteen dragoons, stopped and inquired for "Dave." He being the one accosted, and suspecting some foul play, told them he was "round there." As they went to look for him, "Dave" was fast nearing the ravine; but they espied him, and, with a loud halloo, hastened after him, while Haney shouted, "Shoot him! shoot him! shoot the d——d rascal!" The officer in command cried, "Don't shoot," but at the cry, "shoot him," Dave had stopped. Haney demanded his arms, but Evans, disdaining to notice him, said to the officer of the dragoons, stepping near him, "I can't give my pistol to that d——d rascal, but if you want it, captain, here it is." Lecompton was the destination of the prisoner, and he rode by the side of the officer, declaring, "he would not keep company with the d——d sneaking scoundrel." Haney showed no writ, and the threat, "I 'll subdue you," was carried out by the U. S. dragoons. Evans was taken to Lecompton, and put in chains, like a felon.

CHAPTER XXI.

THE U. S. CAMP — DISPERSION OF THE LEGISLATURE.

Early on the morning of the 17th, with a brother of my husband, and a friend, I left for Lecompton, or for Uncle Sam's Bastile on the Kansas prairies, which had been moved a mile and a half, or two miles, from that tribunal of justice. It was only a day or two since persons had been allowed to go in, and some doubt existed whether I could have the privilege. We came in sight of the tents. There were three in one row, with poles set along in front, and cloth spread over them, and upon the tents, making a long shady place, which E. told me was called the "pavilion." The tents being a few feet apart, the cloth stretching over them, made a fine place to sit, for the table and all culinary arrangements. Another row of tents was pitched in front of these, with only a driveway between, while the captain's tent was on a rise of ground a little distant.

The carriage was driven to the officers' tent, and A. went to inquire if we could go in. He looked vexed as he returned, and said, "You can go in." I said, "Can't you go too?" "Not without going to Jones, for a pass, and unless C. wants to see me very much, I'll not go to him."

I ran down, and met my husband just outside the tent; the sentinel was pacing back and forth, close to the pavilion, musket in hand. He stopped a half moment at the sight of a new face, then resumed the everlasting tread. I went back to tell A. that C. wished to see him, and he started for Lecompton. The prisoners looked well, with the exception of Judge S., who was suffering with chills, and were contented, and hopeful that their imprisonment would accomplish more good than their liberty could. The prison-

UNITED STATES CAMP NEAR LECOMPTON.
From the Daguerreotype taken for Mrs Robinson.

ers now had their papers, and letters, and two or three friends had been in. Some books also had been sent up. For exercise, they walked in front of the tents, brought wood from the timber close by, and water from the spring a little distant. They notified the guard of their desire to take these short trips, by saying, "I want a gun;" and a man with a musket would be provided. The screeching of the trumpets, calling the soldiers to their various duties, added not a little to a headache, induced by weariness and anxiety. If ever I realized that there was more truth than poetry in the words of Mrs. Swisshelm, when she said, "I never see a man in regimentals but I think somebody has lost his monkey," it was when I saw daily the want of power to act out one's manliness, while remaining in the army. One's feelings were continually outraged by arrests made, the troops acting as "posse comitatus." To join the army is to become an automaton, in action at least.

On the 19th, Haney again appeared in the streets of Lawrence, at the head of about forty dragoons. Mr. Legate was in the street. Haney commanded him to assist in arresting a Mr. Colburn; he refused to do it.

"Haney became excited, and ordered the troops to arrest Mr. Legate, and take him to the camp. They then commanded the prisoner to walk before them, which he refused doing under any circumstances whatever. One of the dragoons then dismounted, and Legate took his seat in the saddle, and a company of horse conducted him to the camp.

"Haney then rode up and down Massachusetts-street with the troops, looking for some one to make prisoner; at the same time swearing vengeance against the people of Lawrence, and declaring that 'he would keep the troops here until the snow fell, if necessary, to arrest the free-state men or abolitionists;' 'the d—d town must be subdued,' etc.

"At this time he saw Major Hoyt walking across the street. He immediately drove up to where Hoyt was, followed by the dragoons, and said:

"'Mr. Hoyt, you are my prisoner.'

"'By what authority do you arrest me?' asked Hoyt.

"'By the authority of the territorial laws,' replied Haney.

"Hoyt then demanded to see the writs for his arrest. The deputy said he had none. Hoyt then refused to be molested by him, and proceeded to walk across the street. Haney did not know what to do at this crisis. He was relieved from his dilemma by the lieutenant of the company, riding up to Hoyt, and commanding him to halt, and saying,

"'I arrest you; you are my prisoner, and must go with me.'

"The dragoons surrounded their victim, and he was forced to go to the camp. The soldiers soon returned, and went to a grocery, where they were all treated to a drink. The whiskey was passed around among them in large wooden buckets, and they were allowed to drink as they could. They then returned to camp and took the prisoners to Lecompton.

"When they reached there, Gov. Shannon refused to recognize Haney as having any authority to arrest prisoners, and informed the worthy that he had no right to bring prisoners there.

"Sheriff Jones was on hand, and prepared papers for the reärrest of the prisoners instanter.

"Gov. Shannon, seeing that Jones had the advantage of possessing 'legal' papers for the arrest, said no more, and the prisoners were then taken to a cabin. Mr. Legate was put in irons by order of the sheriff, and they were both locked up for the night."

The same night, the soldiers, in a state of intoxication, were prowling about Lawrence, breaking into houses, and making a noise generally. At this time the people of Lawrence came in carriage-loads to see the "traitors." Capt. Walker, the officer in command, had power, for a few days, to allow any persons to come in. The opportunity was improved. They came bringing books, strawberries, gooseberries, figs, lemons, prunes, ice-creams, and early vegetables. There was a general thoughtfulness for the "prisoners," and none came empty-handed. Little Marshal Cramer, whose inferior, even distressed looking face, has gained him the soubriquet of "monkey-faced," called one day with Col. Preston, who had been one of my husband's guard on his removal from Lexington. He did not say anything, but he evidently thought the prisoners were bearing the changes of life too lightly. He gave the captain orders not to let any one in, or even letters. Then there was a day or two, when persons coming were not allowed to see the prisoners, but Mrs. J. and I could go out to the captain's tent, and see them. I was much amused one day, when a gentleman from Lawrence with his wife came. He had also with him the wife of a gentleman, against whom the pro-slavery party had some bitterness, and she was introduced to the captain and lieutenant by her maiden name. She was very young and girlish looking, and as she was talking pleasantly with the lieutenant, though earnestly, upon the outrageous course of President Pierce, he, in a laughing way, said, "You are a little fanatic, but you 'll marry some Southerner one of these days." She laughed, and went on talking. The lieutenant is of southern birth, but is far from intolerant, and no one could have treated the prisoners more gentlemanly. Capt. Walker too seemed to feel hurt at this "shutting down" upon the prisoners, and told me "he would do anything he could for them, but he must obey orders." Marshal Donaldson came in a day or two, and denied having sent any new orders to Cramer, and again any one could come in.

Evans was released toward the last of June. Efforts had been made to bail him out, but the bogus Probate Judge, Dr. J. N. O. P. Wood, of former notoriety at Lawrence, fixed the bail at five thousand dollars. The love of freedom is a crime in Kansas. The probable reason of the release was a disinclination on the part of the pro-slavery men to bear the extra expense of prisoners. Not being "traitors," the United States government could not be charged with their support.

On the 26th, two young men arrived in Lawrence, from New York, by means of a pass from Atchison. Sixty men coming to settle in the territory, with ploughs, harrows, and all farming implements, were turned back, after being disarmed, first at Lexington, then at Leavenworth, by Atchison and Stringfellow.

The Missourians not only have become plunderers and highwaymen, but pirates, in the service of the present administration. A few days after, Dr. Cutter's party, from Massachusetts, were also robbed, and sent back. At Liberty, the cannon on the shore was fired, and directions were given to the gunner "not to fire too high, as people were on the opposite bank." At Weston, Buford, and twenty others, came on board, and kept them under strict surveillance until the boat reached St. Louis.

While such deeds of blood and violence were being committed on the river, the Indian agent, Gay, was killed, near Westport, by some of Buford's men. Upon his replying in the affirmative to the question, "Are you in favor of making Kansas a free state?" he was immediately shot.

Bands of the marauders infested the woods on the Westport route. They plundered wagons of provisions, for subsistence, and struck down the unwary. In camp we were awakened one morning by loud words near by. One of the "chivalry" was talking to Col. Sumner in no gentlemanly way.

When the news of the nomination of Buchanan and Breckenridge was received in Lecompton, a meeting was called. The celebrated "Sheriff Jones" was the president of the meeting, while kindred spirits filled the other offices. The following resolutions were unanimously adopted:

"*Resolved*, That we have entire confidence in James Buchanan and John C. Breckenridge, as sound and true national democrats, and believe them to be the best men who could have been selected as the exponents of the principles of the platform adopted by the Cincinnati convention, and noble standard-bearers, who will rally to themselves and their platform all Union-loving men and true democrats.

"*Resolved*, That we do most heartily approve and endorse the leading measures of the administration of Franklin Pierce, and have the utmost confidence in the integrity and patriotism of S. A. Douglas; and while some of us may have preferred the nomination of one or two other of these able statesmen, yet we do heartily endorse the nomination of James Buchanan, and look upon his election as necessary to the stability and safety of the Union."

On the 23d the prisoners received an accession to their numbers in the persons of Capt. John Brown, Jr., and H. H. Williams, likewise dignified with the name of "traitors." The former was still insane from the ill-treatment received while in charge of the troops. These gentlemen, upon hearing of the intended attack upon Lawrence in May, had, in company with one hundred others from the region of Osawattomie, left their homes for her defence. Having heard, when a few miles distant, that the people of Lawrence would make no resistance to the force brought against them, they returned to their homes. Fifteen of them were at first taken prisoners by a part of Whitfield's gang of ruffians. Seven were rescued, and eight taken for trial to Tecumseh, after being kept in irons two weeks, under the guard of United States troops, Capt. Wood, of company C., commanding.

Capt. Brown had a rope tied around his arms so tightly, and drawn behind him, that he will for years bear the marks of the ropes, where they wore into his flesh. He was then obliged to hold one end of a rope, the other end being carried by one of the dragoons; and for eight miles, in a burning sun, he was driven before them, compelled to go fast enough to keep from being trampled on by the horses. On being taken to Tecumseh, they were chained two and two, with a common trace-chain, and padlock at each end. It was so fixed as to clasp tightly around the ankle. One day they were driven thirty miles, with no food from early morning until night. The journey in a hot June day was most torturing to them. Their chains wore upon their ankles until one of them, unable to go further, was placed upon a horse.

The testimony at Tecumseh was general against them, all alike; but five were released, while the three, who are members of the Topeka Legislature, were retained.

The people of Lecompton, hearing of the new arrival of the free-state men in the territory, were in continued fears of attacks. Their days were filled with rumors of intended attacks, and their nights with vigils. For several days before the 3d of July, Col. Titus, and other choice spirits, had called upon Capt. Walker more frequently than usual, and the 31st of June was spent by them in consultation. July 1st, about eleven and a half o'clock, Mr. P., of the *N. Y. Tribune*, and E., the young lady who had been part of my household, came from Lawrence. Our plan had been for E. to remain with me a few days, while Mrs. J. could go down to look after her family at home. They were informed by the captain that they "could not come into the tents." Afterwards an unwilling consent was given that "E. could come in, and Mrs. J. go to Lawrence; but Mrs. J could not come back until after the sixth, and not then if there was any trouble at Topeka."

Mr. P. asked "what authority he had for such restrictions;" and the officer's reply was, "I have authority." Mr. Deitzler also asked him "if he had orders from the marshal;" and his reply, given with a good deal of hesitancy, and an evident effort at dignity, "I do not act without orders," was certainly equivocal.

After the carriage conveying our disappointed visitors back to Lawrence was fairly out of sight, Capt. W. returned to our tents, saying, "I forgot to mention that I shall move camp in about an hour. I will have a wagon here to convey you there." So, with finishing getting dinner, etc., the hour passed away, and Col. Titus' big wagon, greasy from having transported bacon, was obliged to wait a half hour, while I washed, and Mr. Deitzler dried the dishes, Judge Smith and my husband packing them in boxes and baskets. Mrs. J. was busy in other matters preparatory to a move, while the rest were striking the tents, and taking down our pavilion. At last we were packed in with bags, baskets, and anything we preferred carrying in our own care, and jolted along the mile and a half in a scorching sun. A mule team was in advance. Some of the blue coats rode each side of us, and the main body of this portion of the President's army of subjugation brought up the rear. Out in the prairie, less than a mile from Lecompton, we came to a double log cabin, and as we alighted, and our chairs were taken from the wagon, the captain, pointing to the right hand cabin, said, "You can go in there, and stay." We went in. There was no window, and no air in the cabin; but a woman, dressed in bright-red calico, with blue undersleeves, black mits, and shingle sun-bonnet, sat there sewing on a muslin of gay colors, in stripes of exceeding width. My husband said something to her; but she seemed anything but social, and we took our chairs and walked out again. The space between the buildings was shady; so we sat there and read our newspapers, and looked at the men as they pitched the tents in the rear of the cabin.

The other room was occupied by the owner of the place, a Pennsylvanian and a free-state man; and for a week only had this cabin been rented to a pro-slavery family. Neither of these families had been consulted in this arrangement of the camp; but a brother of the pro-slavery man, living in Lecompton, had expressed his approval. When the pro-slavery man came home at night, he made loud threats of "driving off the free-state man, and holding his claim."

Towards evening a padlock was tried upon the door, and at dark we were ordered to sleep in the log cabin, the family being driven from their home. It was the intention of Capt. W. to lock the door; but Messrs. J. and D. talked to him so rousingly, telling him, "if they were to be hung, he had better begin then, as it would be better than suffocation," that he failed to carry his plans into execution. So seven men and two women had to stay in one little room without a window. The mattresses lay so close upon the floor that ours was slid partly under the bedstead, upon which Mrs. J. sat up to fan herself until near morning, when she retreated to the tents for a short nap. Had the want of air, and the oppression been less, sleep would have been prevented by the continual noise during the night. Fifteen "law-and-order" men, from Lecompton, came in at different times in the night to offer their services in case of a rescue; and that Capt. W. took them to his tent and "treated" them, has never been denied. All night "Halt!" "Who goes there?" "A friend." "Sergeant of the guard!" Advance!" resounded.

July 3d.—Yesterday and to-day the heat has been oppressive. Some of the prisoners suggest that it is greater on account of our proximity to Lecompton. They say "they can smell the brimstone and see the smoke." A part of our things were not brought from the other camp, as promised, and, without any shade, we have to cook and eat, suffering much from the heat. If we did not laugh and make merry, the wrinkles in our faces would become indelibly fixed. While we, as all dwellers in Kansas, feel a terrible hatred to tyranny, which those living in quiet homes can never appreciate, we are still quick to catch the stray sunbeams on our pathway, and to our courage add cheerfulness. Judge S., with his dry sayings, would make the longest and most sedate countenance shorten in a smile; and no company of the same number could have been found with a more pervading love of fun, and a greater fund of good-humor. So, however "dark the cloud, we find the silver lining."

There is an ever-present indignation at the course of the administration and its underlings; but with it there is the realization, strong as the "everlasting hills," that its villany will work its own ruin.

Woodson, Fain, and other "law-and-order" men from Lecompton, were in camp yesterday. Several of these men have sat in their wagon watching us a long time to-day. They tried quite perseveringly to learn who were the tenants of the various tents, and "which was which" of the prisoners. One of them came into our tents without asking permission of the captain, and was ordered away several times by the guard before leaving. They appeared to feel themselves particularly privileged above other men, and it was amusing to see them march along with great nonchalance in spite of the sentinel's cry of "Halt!" but it was more so when a sudden period was put to their locomotion, as the guard levelled his gun at them, and they, with an assumed air of innocent ignorance, cried, "Halt! halt! is it us you are hallooing at?"

Capt. Brown has been ill several days; and, for a day or two, delirious. To get the air, he lay out upon the ground in the shadow of the tents. Physicians from Lawrence were sent for; also provisions.

Towards evening great preparations for defence were made. Large government wagon-bodies were taken from the wheels, and placed against the open space between the cabins. They were filled with corn, barrels, and sacks. Capt. W. flitted around, as though he had the affairs of a continent resting upon his shoulders, until the barricades were completed. He also compelled the free-state family to vacate their room. He knocked the chinking out of the walls and took possession.

The family went half a mile to their nearest neighbor's to sleep, and every night and morning we had a general move between the house and tents. When the "tattoo" sounded, it was our signal for retreat to the poor little prison.

Drs. P. and T. did not arrive at camp until after nine o'clock, and Capt. Brown was obliged to go to the officers' tent to see them. Provisions and clothing, brought in by another team, were taken there, as well as the mail, and not an article escaped strict search.

4th. — There were three men in from Lecompton last night. The captain took them into his cabin to show them the port-holes. There was also a ruse last night. A pistol-shot was fired; then the word came that the picket-guard had been fired upon. Capt. W. was in motion; but some little time elapsed before he sent any one down to the guard. The matter was probably understood among the men.

There has been no battle yet! The wagon-bodies are all whole, and the corn-bags yet undisturbed! Capt. W.'s head is yet safe, and the world moves on! At daybreak there were three more ruffians at the captain's tent. About eight o'clock Crowder, one of the pretended officials, came also to his tent, and had a long conference. The horses of the privates are continually lent to these men, of which they complain bitterly. We did not receive our papers from the officers' tent until the middle of the forenoon. (A letter was never given to one of the prisoners.)

Was there ever such a glorious country as this, with petty tyrants made weak-headed by a little power? Austrian despotism is liberty in comparison.

We heard this morning, from Lecompton, that the cause of our removal here was to protect that town; an agreement of mutual protection having been entered into by the people there and Capt. W. We are also acquainted with the movements of our friends, notwithstanding the watchful vigilance of our heroic keeper.

5th. — Last night brought the intelligence of the dispersion of the Legislature at the point of the bayonet. Col. Sumner arrived here this morning, and three companies of troops passed by. Capt. W. came down to our tents with Col. Sumner. Col. S. said "he was sorry the Legislature did not disperse at the reading of the proclamation; that the free-state men had injured their own cause."

My husband replied, "that he was sorry they dispersed until he fired upon them, and, if he had been there, he would have obliged him to do so."

"You could not have obliged me to do it, for I should not have fired." When Col. S. was asked what he would have done, he said, "I might have tied your arms behind you."

My husband told him the constitution gave them a right to meet and memorialize Congress. The treatment we had received the last week was also plainly stated to Col. S., and he at once ordered our letters given us, and our friends to be allowed to come in. Judge S. was very ill again, and in his delirium the week's course of discipline seemed to be on his mind.

Another page has been written, in the history of the American people, in unparalleled infamy. Another scene in this dark and tragic drama of crushing out a free people has been enacted. Instead of the brilliant panorama and festive scenes which for years past, on this anniversary, have spoken the heart-gladness for liberties gained through years of struggle, the people of this mighty nation wear sackcloth and mourning. The star-spangled banner no longer waves over a free people, but is draggled through the blood of those slain, at the bidding of a merciless administration, on Kansas plains. Mr. P., an eye-witness, eloquently tells the thrilling story:

"The national flag floated proudly over Topeka on the Fourth of July; and over the hall of legislation, or state buildings, was displayed a flag, American in every respect, save that among the stars was a larger additional star on the corner — the orphan star of Kansas.

"Around the large new hotel the convention had assembled, and proceeded to transact its business. Some half a dozen military companies, in handsome uniform, paraded about. Ladies promenaded, with little banners flying from their parasols. The scene was highly interesting.

"In spite of the apparent indifference, many hearts throbbed anxiously for the denouement of the day's proceedings. It was well known that nearly all the military force in Kansas was concentrated within a few hundred yards in Topeka, and that in the camp of Col. Sumner was Secretary Woodson, the infamous Jeffreys Lecompte, Donaldson, who led on the plundering hordes to the sack of Lawrence, Judges Cato and Elmore, and other influential pro-slavery men; and it was also known that those men, who have shown the most inveterate hostility to the settlers of Kansas, were plotting mischief against them. All this was known, and, although it might make the pulsation of some hearts beat quicker, it neither disturbed nor affected their action.

"About ten o'clock, United States Marshal Donaldson, accompanied by Judge Elmore, entered the town, and gave it to be understood that he had a proclamation to read. The convention paused in its business, and invited these gentlemen to the stand. Donaldson being, like Moses, not particularly well qualified for public speaking, called on his Aaron, in the shape of Judge Elmore, who read the proclamation of the President, dated in February — a law-and-order document, the signification of which was comprehended at the time, and which was now made to do its work in the drama, 'We will subdue you.' Next was read the second proclamation of Gov. Shannon, issued a month ago; and then followed the proclamation of Secretary Woodson, which, acting under presidential authority, commanded the Legislature to disperse, and threatened it with violence from the troops in case they did not submit to this order. The proclamation being read, these gentlemen made their exodus as they had made their advent, neither being accompanied by any external or visible symptoms of a moral earthquake; and the convention proceeded with its business, which had been interrupted. This evidently chagrined Donaldson, who turned round and interrupted the debate upon a resolution, by asking if we had any reply to carry down to Col. Sumner. The president informed Mr. D. that this assemblage was not the Legislature, to which the proclamation had been specially addressed, but asked him if it was desired that we should send any reply. Donaldson said No, but, if we had anything to send, he would convey it. The president, on behalf of the convention, informed him that we had no communication to send.

"These gentlemen left, and matters went on as before. It was nearly twelve o'clock, the sun was blazing down, and the thermometer stood at 100°, when we learned that Col. Sumner, with five companies of cavalry and two pieces of brass cannon, were leaving their camp and approaching Topeka in full military array. Although they were only two hundred yards off, the report did not disturb the convention or other matters. If resistance had been intended, Col. Sumner never would have entered Topeka, and would have been met before he could get possession. It had been determined that no resistance should be offered the United States troops, but that we should proceed with our business, and let them do their worst.

"But Col. Sumner fulfilled his duty in as gentlemanly a manner as such wretched orders could be obeyed. At the moment of his approach, the two Topeka companies, F. and G., were drawn up before the legislative hall building. They had just marched up the street, preceded by martial music, and had formed in front of the State House to receive a banner the ladies had made for company G. The street was filled with a crowd, among whom were many ladies and children, when Col. Sumner appeared with his forces, rapidly debouching into Kansas Avenue. With great rapidity and considerable military skill he threw his men forward, and by rapid orders, shouted in a stern, shrill voice, formed his companies into the strongest form they could occupy for their service. Perhaps many hearts beat faster when they thought that a scene of carnage might in the next few minutes blot out the startling and brilliant panorama. On the one hand, the armed and uniformed dragoons, with flashing sabres; on the other, only two Topeka companies, with their two banners, one of them just received, bearing the inscription, 'Our lives for our rights.' Nobly they stood. While the dragoons approached, the band was playing, but the drummers continued to drum until the drumsticks nearly touched the noses of the advancing horses of the dragoons, and only stopped when Sumner requested them. One little boy was beating the kettle-drum, and rattled it manfully, never turning to look at the dragoons. In the rapid movements of the dragoons in forming into position, they pressed on the Topeka companies, but those men kept their position, and only stepped out of their ranks when the horses were ridden up to them, and only then far enough not to be trampled on. The sharp, shrill voice of Sumner rung through Kansas Avenue and all around the State House, as he gave orders, and the dragoons wheeled into form. The two pieces of artillery were planted about a hundred yards up the street. They were said to be loaded with grape. The slow-match was lighted.

"After the dragoons were placed so as to suit Col. Sumner's taste, he dismounted, and walked towards the Assembly rooms. Both Senate and House stood adjourned to meet at twelve o'clock; a fact of which Col. Sumner appeared to be aware. The lower house was just assembling, when Col. Sumner inquired in the hall where the Legislature met. Mr. S. J. Tappan, Clerk (the Speaker, Mr. Minard, being absent), called the Legislature to order by rapping with the gavel on the Speaker's desk. He then called the roll, and, there not being a quorum, sent the Sergeant-at-Arms after the absentees. When Sumner had first entered, and had been invited forward, he was offered a chair at the desk; he jocularly asked if they wanted to make him Speaker. This was received by a hearty shout and laughter. The rooms were crowded by the citizens to witness the spectacle, and some ladies got into the room. The roll was again called by Mr. C. S. Pratt, Recording Clerk, and the absentees marked, when Col. Sumner rose and said:

"'Gentlemen, I am called upon this day to perform the most painful duty of my whole life. Under the authority of the President's proclamation, I am here to disperse this Legislature, and therefore inform you that you cannot meet. I therefore order you to disperse. God knows that I have no party feeling in this matter, and will hold none so long as I occupy my present position in Kansas. I have just returned from the borders, where I have been sending home companies of Missourians, and now I am ordered here to disperse you. Such are my orders, and you *must disperse.* I now command you to disperse. I repeat that this is the most painful duty of my whole life.'

"Judge Schuyler asked, 'Col. Sumner, are we to understand that the Legislature are driven out at the point of the bayonet?'

"Colonel Sumner: 'I shall use all the forces in my command to carry out my orders.'

"The Legislature dispersed. Some of the members in town did not appear at the hall; but the immortal number who responded to their names occupy a proud position. Some pleasant interchange of civilities occurred between Col. Sumner and persons in the hall — members and others. He left the hall, and mounted his horse, when he was reminded that he had not dispersed the Senate. He dismounted, and returned to the Senate Chamber, Donaldson going with him; Donaldson having also been present at the dispersion of the Legislature. The Senate had not yet been convened, as it was but very little past the appointed hour; but Col. Sumner, addressing them in their collective capacity, proceeded to disperse them in terms something similar to those used in the hall below. When he concluded there was a pause, the senators standing in a circle silently but respectfully. No one was in the hall but the senators, the Senate officers, Col. Sumner, Donaldson, and your correspondent. Col. Sumner broke the pause by asking if they intended to disperse. With calmness and dignity, Mr. Thornton, President of the Senate, replied that the Senate had not yet convened, and could not make any reply. He asked Col. Sumner if he could convene the Senate, so that they could make a reply to him. Col. Sumner replied that his orders were to prevent them from meeting, and that they could not convene, but must disperse.

"Here Donaldson stepped forward, and made the outrageous demand that the senators should promise not to assemble again, or he would arrest every member. Monstrous usurping villany for a federal officer! If he had writs from a court to serve on either of these officers, it was his duty to serve them independent of any contingency; if he had none, he had no right to arrest or molest a man, and as little thus to insult popular representatives thus assembled. Several senators told Col. Sumner that, when thus dispersed by him, they would of course disperse. Mr. Pillsbury said that they were there in no condition to resist the United States troops, and must of course disperse. Thus was the Senate dispersed.

" When Col. Sumner first entered the town, a committee from the mass convention immediately waited on him to ask if he intended to disperse the convention, or disband the military companies on parade. He replied that he did not; he merely intended to disperse the Legislature. While the dragoons were thus drawn up, and while Col. Sumner made this reply, three cheers were given for Col. Sumner. Mr. Redpath cried, 'Three cheers for Gov. Robinson!' which were given very heartily, and then three cheers for liberty. After Col. Sumner had dispersed both branches of the Assembly, and just as he proceeded to march off with his forces, in order to show that they respected him for his gentlemanly conduct, and did not hold him responsible for the grievous outrage, three cheers were given for Col. Sumner again, three cheers for the national flag, three cheers for the State Legislature, three cheers for John C. Fremont, which were given as the dragoons were moving off, and three groans for Pierce."

CHAPTER XXII.

"LAW-AND-ORDER" MEN—FREE-STATE MEN AROUSED.

July 7th. — We experienced a heavy rain yesterday. It poured through the tents, wetting everything. This tent-life in the burning sun and pouring rains will be a good recipe for ague or cholera. So, besides the discomfort of the present, we have these in anticipation. Capt. W. left on Saturday, and Capt. Sackett, a noble-looking man, has the prisoners now in charge.

To-day a gentleman has been in camp from Illinois. He with a party of seventeen were robbed at Leavenworth of their arms and farming utensils. Several of them were hunted for their lives. (Aid was afterwards asked of Gen. Smith in recovering these goods, a letter being sent to him from Woodson counselling such interference; but he declined giving it.) Also, eight families from Illinois, when near Platte city, were turned back by one hundred and fifty men, armed with United States muskets and bayonets. The stereotyped questions of "Where are you from?" and "Where going?" were put to the emigrants. The leader of the ruffians said, "I suppose you 've hearn that we don't allow any movers to go through into the territory." When the ruffians proclaimed their intention of searching the wagons, an Iowa man objected, but a revolver was quickly drawn upon him. After searching their wagons twice, and taking all the arms, they took them back under guard to Liberty, Missouri, telling them "they could go where they pleased, so they did not go into the territory."

What new scheme of villany, for the subjugation of Kansas, shall we hear? Step by step the work has gone on. Missourians have invaded the territory, and, by force, taken possession of the polls. They have trampled upon the right of the people to make their own laws. They have framed a code of laws which would have disgraced the dark ages. They have denied the citizens of the territory the right of free speech. They have, for weeks, besieged a town under the leadership of the governor. They have burned and sacked towns under the United States Marshal, the aforesaid governor offering no word of disapproval; they have murdered, with all the cruelties of the Fejee islands, peaceable settlers. Without restraint they have robbed and pillaged. They have blockaded the Missouri river. No more bloody or meaner pirates, sailing under black flags, ever infested the high seas, years ago. Now the debauched and desperate robbers search and send back peaceable emigrants, their wagons laden with the emblems of their occupation, ploughs, and farming implements.

We have moved camp again to-day, two miles further from Lecompton. It was my first experience in the inside of these huge covered wagons. I protested that I would rather walk than attempt to mount into such a vehicle; but they all said ride. By extra effort E. and I got in, attempting to find a place to sit among the mattresses. At first move, one of the mules, by rapidly throwing up his feet, was soon out of harness. The jolting of the wagon was intolerable when the mules travelled faster than a walk.

29th.—July days are passing with little variety. We have a great deal of company; many days four or five carriage loads. They are people from Lawrence, and other settlements, while many strangers travelling in the territory call to "look in upon the traitors." A number of ladies living on claims some miles from Lawrence, whom we had never met, have visited us in camp. They are very intelligent and refined.

Gen. Smith has arrived in Leavenworth. As he was passing Delaware, a little settlement among the hills, the boat was hailed, and obliged to stop. A band of ruffians, gathered from the "four corners of Satan's dominions," demanded, "Are there any abolitionists on board?" Gov. Shannon and his wife also came up the river in the same boat. They came through in the stage from

Kansas city to Lecompton. When passing places of more than usual loveliness, she would say, "she should like a plantation there, with about two dozen negroes." To the question how she liked "border ruffians," she said, "she liked them infinitely better than Massachusetts paupers." Every time any attempt was made by others in the stage to vindicate the free-state cause, she remarked, "she did not wish to hear anything about it." She remained scarcely a week in Kansas, and, in reply to the question, "Will you return to Kansas?" she said, "I should like to live in Kansas if it is a slave state, I suffer so much where I am in associating with abolitionists." It would be kind in the governor to have regard for her sufferings, and go into some obscurity, where she could be relieved from the enlightened intelligence of Ohio.

Col. Titus, a few days ago, told a man who came to him for money to buy a claim, with oaths, "Wait, and we will get it any how. Now is the time to drive out the d—d Yankees."

Acting upon this impression, probably, two days since, he attacked a young man, living on a claim two miles from Lecompton. After beating him severely, and jumping upon him, he ordered an accomplice, standing by, to fire his house. A free-state man immediately talked plainly to Gov. S. in relation to it, and concluded by telling him, "if he did not prevent such outrages, the people would."

Gov. S. immediately sent for troops to protect Titus. Free-state men are driven from their claims, beaten and killed. Then the governor employs the troops to protect the assassins. Such is dragoon government in Kansas. It leaves the free-state people exposed to all outrages; and, when they would assert their rights, and take care of themselves by driving out the ruffians, the dragoons protect them by orders of the governor. Gov. Shannon has said, repeatedly, that the state "prisoners, if charged, would be tried; if tried, convicted; and, if convicted, hung." Judge Lecompte has made similar statements. Woodson has said, "they did not expect there would be a trial, but they meant to keep them imprisoned."

W. P. Fain, who acted as deputy marshal in arresting Judge

Smith and G. W. Deitzler, was in camp the other day. While talking of the Toombs bill, the prisoners stated "that they had no confidence in the President appointing men who would take the census fairly." He replied, "I would do it."

When they asked him, "if he was to be one of the commissioners," he replied in the affirmative, thus showing the whole matter to have been arranged before Stringfellow went to Washington. There was a heavy shower a few nights since. Our tent being the poorest shelter from rain of all, Capt. Sackett urged us to sleep in one of his; but we preferred staying in our own. When the storm came, the wind was terrible. The rain came through in streams, and little lakes were standing in every hollow on the bed. At this unpleasant juncture, the captain sent down an India-rubber blanket, and, by removing the wet ones, no one suffered very severely. Towards morning, a heavy wind tore up a part of the stakes, and a drenching rain came full upon us. There was not a dry spot in the bed, and no more sleep for us. We had, however, a hearty laugh with Capt. Sackett, for the tent he had kindly assigned us was prostrate; the only one which had been so essentially affected by the storm.

31st. — A man, by the name of Le Hays, active in the plundering of Lawrence, has boasted much of the spoils which fell to his share — silver ware, ladies' apparel, besides guns. On the night of the 18th his house was entered by a party of men, and the guns were taken. Gov. Shannon is much excited about it. He says they were men from Lawrence and vicinity, and reports the house generally plundered. A strong guard was forthwith set around Lecompton. On the 20th, Cramer, the deputy marshal, came to camp, and ordered Capt. Sackett not to allow any person to converse with the prisoners privately. "His responsibility, since the sacking of Lawrence, in regard to the prisoners, had weighed upon him much." But Capt. Sackett at once informed him, "he need give himself no further trouble on the subject, as the responsibility of their safe-keeping rested upon him." The little fellow appeared pleased; but his wrath was only pent up. He met a man, soon after leaving camp, and poured it forth in execrations upon the captain, declaring that "Robinson was more the governor of the territory than Shannon;" that "the prisoners should be taken from Capt. Sackett's charge, and that their lives would not be safe an hour." On the 21st the little deputy came again, with a letter from Gov. Shannon, in which he advised that "persons and letters be not allowed to go into camp; that the territory had never been in so bad a condition; that he believed the prisoners were implicated in these disturbances, and in great measure the occasion of them." Cramer, at the captain's tent, also said, "The governor don't know what to do." He talked so loudly, it was quite impossible not to hear what was said. It will be remembered that only two days had passed since the governor had been informed, that, if such outrages as that of Titus continued, the people would try to suppress them. Word was returned to the governor from Capt. Sackett that "he had his orders from Col. Sumner to give up the prisoners to the civil authorities, if unnecessary restrictions were placed upon them." Gov. Shannon immediately sent to Capt. Sackett, that "he did not know he had orders from Col. Sumner, but, if he had, of course he must obey them." He swore, however, "he would see if he could not make Capt. Sackett obey orders," and sent an express to Gen. Smith at the fort. Gen. Smith proposed not to interfere in matters in the territory, and, no change being made in the treatment of the prisoners, the governor was disappointed, and unable to carry out his threats. On the 19th he was heard to say, as at many other times, that "Gov. Robinson would be hung."

A wagon of provisions for Palmyra was robbed at Westport a few days since, and, on the 22d, Mr. P., a daguerrian of Lawrence, was nearly killed about a mile from town, by three men from Franklin. He was fired upon, and so badly wounded by their jumping upon his body, that he was very ill, and it is feared will never recover. Several bowie-knives were found in the grass next day. Major Sedgwick protected Titus only one night, and removed his camp about a fourth of a mile from Capt. Sackett's camp. Then Titus gathered about him a gang of desperadoes like himself. Major Richardson is reported to have gone up north to intercept emigrants coming into the territory. Three men from Lecompton have been to see Capt. Walker, of the free-state forces. They desire all matters amicably adjusted. There is talk of vigilance committees of equal numbers, free-state men and pro-slavery, to try offenders. Gov. Shannon has expressed himself in favor of letting the territorial laws go, as the House has admitted free Kansas. Woodson is very strongly opposed.

A few days since, a free-state man, in Lecompton, was ordered out of town by Wm. Donaldson. The people there, effectually frightened at the turn affairs are taking, returned the compliment, ordering Donaldson to leave town. They immediately had a circular printed, inviting people into their town, and promising them safety.

Mr. Wilson and daughter, from South Carolina, were in camp a little time on the 21st. They were strangers in the territory. When Mr. Wilson returned to Lawrence, he refused to pay the four dollars for the team, which he promised on taking it. Chapman, one of the Shawnee council, declared he would have the one dollar still retained by Mr. Wilson, and the next morning, as Mr. W. was going to Westport in the stage, Chapman asked him again for the money. Upon his refusing, Chapman struck him on the head with a heavy stick. After the wound was dressed, against the advice of others, he continued his journey to Westport, and died soon after reaching there. Chapman was examined before a justice at Lecompton, and released on bail, $3,500. Sam Salters and Haney were his bondsmen, both notorious for their villany, and pecuniarily irresponsible. The bail asked in the case of Evans, free-state, by an impartial *in*justice, at Lecompton, was $5,000, and in case of young Doy, also free-state, taken on charge of horse-stealing, no bail could be admitted. Chapman has also been notorious for his threats against the lives of several of the citizens of Lawrence.

All kinds of vegetables have been bountifully supplied to the prisoners for many weeks by their friends. In some cases they have brought of the first fruits of their fields. Wild grapes and apples are growing plenty now. To-day some gentlemen, concert-singers, brought their melodeon and sang to us. It made quite a variety in camp life.

August.—The first Sunday in August we had preaching in

camp. Mr. N., and a large number of people, came from Lawrence. As many as possible sat under the pavilion, while others occupied the carriages. The officers and soldiers attended, and all together we made a goodly number. A melodeon was also brought up from town. Major Hoyt brought a large number of beautiful pond lilies, which, at his suggestion, were placed on the table, before the preacher.

On the first day of August, Fain was in Lawrence attempting to assess taxes. He was waited upon by a committee, and recommended to leave. A very intelligent lady, recently from Delaware, visited us in camp. The camp of the invading horde in May was close by her house, and from their brutal conduct she suffered much. One of the captains of the gang has since apologized to her, saying, "that if his mother in Virginia knew in what company he had been, or what he had been doing, she would grieve herself to death." She has recently buried a little daughter, who, in the first of her illness, was constantly saying, "Mama, don't let the Kickapoos shoot me." She thinks fear was the occasion of the child's death. These men were cursing and swearing about their house nights, and firing their guns in the day-time, so that the balls whizzed past her. When asked by her "if they had commands to disturb peaceable houses on the Sabbath day," they replied, "they had orders to go where they chose, and when they chose; they were here by President Pierce's authority, and acting under the directions of Gov. Shannon." It is said in Lecompton to be the plan of the ruffians to kill the prisoners on the day of the trials. Pro-slavery men from the same place stated, that, on the 5th, Jones, Clark and Titus, were urging the governor to call out the "militia," for further outrages. Word had been received from Col. Boone, of Westport, that "now was the time to drive out the free-state men." Shannon had sworn he would not call out the "militia" again, and the above named "law-and-order" men threatened to put him in the river, and were holding a secret session as to the course to be pursued. On the 6th news came of Gov. Shannon's removal.

Robberies on the Westport road are becoming more frequent. Preparatory to the expected passage of the Toombs bill, many

Missourians and Southerners have been coming into the territory. They have not taken claims and built houses upon them, but have built forts and stocked them with provisions and munitions of war. It all looked like a war of extermination, and preparations for a general siege, although many Missourians had said they were coming in to vote. The principal head-quarters for the invaders were the fort near Osawattomie, one on Washington Creek, at Franklin, and the house of Col. Titus. From the latter, morning and evening, we heard the report of fire-arms, as his gang were firing at a mark. Depredations being committed by the men at all these places, it was decided to drive them out. About the eighth, a party of free-state men reached the fort on Sugar Creek, but Dame Rumor had flown in advance of it, and the fort was vacated. The invaders had gone back to their homes in Missouri, leaving a load of flour, sugar, hams, etc. The flour and sugar were taken, while the bacon was burned with the fort.

Several of the free-state scouts to the upper country have returned. They report the emigrants making roads, and bridging streams. Some of the scouts went through to Iowa. The reports of the emigrants being intercepted by Missourians were false. There are over four hundred emigrants on the way. The train is more than a mile and a quarter long. Such a body of men looked formidable to the spies of the enemy, and they returned to report larger numbers.

The people at Lecompton are exceedingly alarmed for the safety of their town. For a week or two they have been so worn out, keeping a nightly guard, that they have hired a guard, paying each man two dollars a night. At several different times they have been awakened in the night by a courier going in with the false report of the free-state men close at hand. Early on the morning of the 12th, Titus sent in word that he had seen one hundred and seventy-five free-state horsemen approaching the town, which at once created a panic. On the night of the 13th, we heard firing in the direction of Lawrence, and before sunrise the next morning, an express was sent to Maj. Sedgwick. As he rode in by our tents, the sentinel hailed him with, "What news?" His reply was, "War! war!"

The free-state men made an attack upon a building in Franklin. It was the same building that was stormed in the little battle of the 4th of June, but, as a block-house, had been considerably strengthened since then. It was the first station of the Georgians beyond Westport, and contained, besides a quantity of small arms, a six-pounder brass cannon, which had been brought into the territory in May. They called upon those in the block-house to surrender, before firing at all. After three hours' brisk firing, the free-state men, having one man killed and several wounded, drew a wagon load of burning hay against the building, when the cry for "quarter" was heard. The hay was soon drawn away, and the occupants of the fort threw down their arms and fled. The guns and cannon were taken by the free-state men.

The immediate occasion of the attack at Franklin at that time, was the sad news of the murder of Maj. D. S. Hoyt, which had been received that day.

For some time the settlers along the Wakarusa, and near Washington Creek, had been much harassed by Georgians at that fort. Their threats of extermination of the free-state settlers were repeatedly heard, and robberies by them were of frequent occurrence. The settlers had sent messengers to Lawrence, and other points, at different times, asking help. Several appeals had been made to the troops, but Maj. Sedgwick declined doing anything, as he had no authority to act.

On the eleventh and twelfth, messengers were again sent to him, asking him to do something quickly for the protection of the settlers in that region. He had been informed by Capt. Anderson, of the troops, whose company during the summer had recruited some of Buford's men, that the camp was a peaceable one, and he so stated to the gentlemen from Lawrence. At the request of the people of Lawrence, Major Hoyt went out to the camp. He was most brutally murdered by the Georgians, his body being riddled with bullets. Major Hoyt was an efficient aid to the free-state cause, and was universally esteemed.

This outrage aroused the free-state men yet more to the necessity of breaking up the stronghold of these barbarians; and on the afternoon of the 15th, the fort on Washington Creek was burned.

The fort was strongly garrisoned and provisioned, and contained many articles taken at the siege of Lawrence. Without striking a blow the Georgians fled. In the night, Titus' band was out, as usual, stealing horses. They had taken three, when they came upon the advance guard of the free-state men. Titus, seeing the numbers upon which he had fallen, fled, they following but a little way, and taking one or two prisoners.

About sunrise the next morning, the 16th, firing was heard near our tents, and one of the cannon balls whizzed past us. Two or three horsemen were standing upon a high hill, a half a mile distant, apparently watching the troops in camp. A heavy shower came up; the rain poured in torrents. Our breafast had been set upon the table, but the frail cloth overhead was like a sieve, and each of us caught some of the dishes, and ran into the nearest tent. A messenger from Gov. Shannon had come to Major S.'s camp. The bugle-call had sounded, and the troops were soon on their way to Lecompton. At the moment the troops started, the horsemen on the hill disappeared. As we sat in a little tent, *à la Turque*, eating our breakfast, with our plates in our laps, one of the persons looking out, said, "Titus' house is on fire. The black smoke is rising over the hill."

A little time passed, and a wagon, with a lady and several children, of various shades of color, came to Capt. Sackett for protection. It was Mrs. Woodson and her household, who, fearful, had fled from their house, one half mile distant from Titus'. When Lieut. Carr reached Lecompton, in accordance with Major Sedgwick's orders, Gov. Shannon was nowhere to be found. It was only after repeated inquiries, he received the reply, "You may find him by the river." Going there, he found the executive getting into the scow to go across the river. How one's imagination brings up the picture of Cæsar crossing the Rubicon! As he returned with Lieut. C., and met Major S. at the point designated, he was asked "what were his orders."

He replied, "I don't think I will have anything done with them; but we will go and see if they have disturbed Major Clarke" (the murderer). The four hundred free-state men, going over the prairie on their way back to Lawrence, looked too formidable to the pusillanimous governor. Major C.'s residence was found deserted, the doors wide open, furniture left as just used, and everything betraying that some great fear had driven them from their homes. The fright and confusion at Lecompton were terrible. Any way to get over the river seemed to be the desideratum; many even, in their haste, jumped in to swim over. Col. Titus and eighteen men were taken prisoners. Among them was Wm. Donaldson, who had been my husband's guard on his way from Lexington. Titus had several prisoners in his house, — men just arrived in the territory. The order of the previous evening had been to shoot one of them that morning.

Some of the type of the *Herald of Freedom* office had been taken from the Kaw, and melted into slugs. These were used to load the cannon in the attack upon Titus' stronghold. At the first fire, the cannoneer cried, "This is the second edition of the Herald of Freedom."

The prisoners were taken to Lawrence. The next day, Sunday the 17th, Maj. Sedgwick, Gov. Shannon and Dr. Rodrigue, of Lecompton, went to Lawrence to make a treaty. The two latter were ready to make terms anyhow. They trembled like aspen leaves for fear. Gov. Shannon's second treaty with the people of Lawrence was concluded. The five free-state men arrested after the attack at Franklin, under the bogus laws, and the howitzer taken from Lawrence in May, were to be exchanged for Titus and his band. There were also to be no more arrests under the territorial laws.

Gov. Shannon made a speech, in which he stated "he wished to set himself right, before the people of Lawrence; that he desired peace and harmony for the few days of his continuance in office;" and concluded by saying, "and the few days that I remain in office shall be devoted, so help me Heaven, in carrying out faithfully my part of the agreement, and in preserving order."

Capt. Shombre, of the free-state party, was mortally wounded, but his expressed sentiment was, "Willingly I yield my life for freedom." When they told him of the treaty, like Wolfe, he said, "I die happy." He died, much regretted by our people, on the evening of the 17th. The treaty was carried into effect the next day. Titus and Donaldson begged most piteously for their lives. It was humiliating to see men, who had no mercy for any who fell into their power, yet beg so humbly for their own lives. They said "they would go to their old homes, and would never strike another blow for slavery in Kansas."

But Titus, safely in Lecompton again, has sworn vengeance. He was badly wounded in the shoulder and hand, and one of his men was killed. Dr. Rodrigue and family passed down to Westport on the 18th, on their way to Virginia. Judge Elmore, with his family and slaves, left the territory the same day. Gov. Shannon asked for a military escort out of the territory, but was told the people would call him a coward in truth. The difference in men fighting for their homes and lives, and their oppressors, has been clearly marked in this contest. Fear has been the daily and nightly portion of the people of Lecompton since their attack upon Lawrence. Now, when their gangs of desperadoes have been routed in three or four positions, the panic has become general, and the leading men of the pro-slavery party remove their families from the territory. Women leave their homes to ask protection of military commanders, and pro-slavery towns beg a dragoon guard.

Gov. Shannon, immediately after the treaty at Lawrence, sent for all the troops in the fort. When asked by one of the military officers what was the message he sent, he said "he did not know, as he had sent his papers, among which was the copy of his letter to Gen. Smith, by his son, to Westport." Wholly different from this was the course of the men and women of Lawrence. Calmly they looked upon the devastation, and awaited the hour when God would avenge them. People upon claims, close by the ruffians' camp, remained at their homes. Faith in the final upholding of justice was their shield.

CHAPTER XXIII.

NEW INVASION — RELEASE OF STATE PRISONERS.

On the 19th of August another most brutal murder was committed near Leavenworth. A gentleman named Hops, from Griggsville, Ill., only six days in the territory, was shot and scalped by a man named Fugert, who belonged to Atchison's ruffian band encamped near Leavenworth. He had made a bet of six dollars against a pair of boots, that in less than two hours he would have an abolitionist's scalp. He returned to Lawrence, received the boots, and exhibited the scalp as a token of his prowess.

Mr. Hops had hired a house in Leavenworth, intending to locate there. He then brought his wife to Lawrence, to remain a few days with her sister, Mrs. Nute, wife of the Unitarian clergyman. Upon his return, within two miles of Leavenworth, the horrid deed was committed. It will be remembered that Fort Leavenworth, where United States troops are stationed, is only three miles distant. A German, who spoke freely of the atrocity of the deed, was shot upon the spot.

A day or two after, a young free-state lady, of Bloomington, was carried from her home a mile and a half, by four ruffians, her tongue drawn out of her mouth as far as possible, and cords tied tightly around it. Her arms were pinioned, and she was otherwise so wantonly abused, that for days her life was despaired of.

On the twenty-first, Woodson, declaring the territory in a state of insurrection, called out the militia. For several days Woodson, Jones, and others, at Lecompton, had been trying to induce Gov. Shannon to resign his office, as he would not call out the militia, that Woodson might do it. The ruffians were very loud in their praises of him, saying, "he was just the governor they wanted."

The plan was to have a general war of extermination before Gov. Geary could arrive. Gov. Shannon, most urgently solicited, at length resigned the morning of the day his papers of dismissal came from Washington. He again asked for an escort from the territory; but the military officer declined, upon the plea that the free-state men had asked for an escort upon the same road, stating it was unsafe for them to travel, being infested by pro-slavery camps. The ex-governor's angry retort was, "Then, by G—d, I 'll fight my way through!"

On the twenty-second, a party of Georgians made a descent upon the Quaker Mission in the Shawnee Reserve, plundering it of horses and other property, while they treated the people with barbarity.

On the twenty-third it was ascertained that Atchison's force, numbering four hundred and fifty men, were mustering at Little Sante Fe, on the border of Missouri, and about thirty-five miles from Lawrence, preparatory to another invasion of the territory. At Lawrence there were about two thousand people, men, women, and children. There was great scarcity of provisions, and not twenty sacks of flour in the whole town. People from the Big Stranger Creek, about half way between Lawrence and Leavenworth, had been driven from their claims, and in some instances both men and women had been most barbarously treated. It was considered unsafe to send teams for provisions past the camps of the ruffians. The route to Kansas city was also blockaded. Three times an escort had been asked of the highest officer in command, out of the fort, and *three times been refused.*

On the 24th of August, five of the citizens of Lawrence called upon Woodson. They found him in the tent of the officers in command of the troops. The committee stated that the people of Lawrence were out of provisions, that their roads were blockaded by armed mobs. They asked whether he intended to allow this overwhelming force to murder, burn, and pillage? He replied, "if the people of Lawrence would obey the laws, this thing (meaning the invasion) could be settled in five hours." C. W. Babcock then said, "Governor, are we to understand that your position is this: that if we obey the bogus laws, you will protect us with the whole force under your command (meaning the troops), and, if not, you will allow us to be murdered? Is that your position?" Woodson replied, "The laws must be obeyed, and writs executed." The committee concluded that they must depend wholly upon the strength of the free-state men, if Lawrence was attacked. Volunteers were continually arriving, and Lawrence again looked warlike. The forts built last winter were repaired, and new ones were built. Wheat and hay were carried in so near town that they could not be destroyed by the marauders. The wheat was ground as a substitute for fine flour, and many cattle were driven in near town. A strong guard was again placed around the town, while the scouting guard were on duty miles away. It was estimated that in twelve hours' time from fifteen hundred to two thousand men could be rallied to defend Lawrence.

On the twenty-fifth, Col. Cook, commandant at Fort Riley, arrived at the spot where Capt. Sackett was in charge of the state prisoners. He came with a large additional force, which numbered, with the companies called in from different parts of the territory, about five hundred troops. They had five pieces of artillery, and, as they came in over the hills to our quiet little camp, they looked quite formidable. The care of the prisoners at once devolved upon Col. Cook. He manifested the responsibility he felt by putting on an extra guard, with another to stand by to listen to conversation when any company was in the tents. Capt. Sackett, with thirty-five men, had found, for seven weeks, one guard all-sufficient for the *protection* of the prisoners. Col. Cook, with five hundred, must have felt strangely insecure.

On the twenty-seventh, Mr. Nute, with his widowed sister-in-law, and John Wilder, a merchant of Lawrence, with a number of teams for provisions, started for Leavenworth. They had been advised by the military commanders to attempt this journey. When near Leavenworth the whole party were captured by a band of ruffians under Capt. Emory. The body of Mr. Hops had been buried, by the troops, in Pilot Knob cemetery, and his widow was denied the consolation of looking upon his grave. After continued refusals by the ruffians, she at last succeeded in getting on board a boat bound down the Missouri. The others were retained as prisoners of war, and untold anxiety was felt for their safety.

When this intelligence reached Lawrence, G. W. Hutchinson, one of the merchants whose wagons had been taken, and Mr. Sutherland, the mail-carrier between Lawrence and Leavenworth, whose hack and driver were of the same number, were despatched to Woodson, also to Col. Cook, to inform them of the facts. Col. Cook could not move with his troops to Leavenworth without orders from Woodson. He advised these gentlemen to see Woodson. They went to Lecompton, and while in his office were taken prisoners by his brutal "militia," he offering no word of protest. When Col. Cook heard of this unprecedented outrage, he sent again and again to Woodson, demanding their release. His invariable reply was, "They were taken as spies, and we hold them as prisoners of war."

The same day eighty of the troops went to Lawrence under command of Deputy Marshal Newsem, who had rendered himself conspicuous by breaking open and searching the trunks of five free-state men on the road a few days before. He had a writ of replevin for a horse, and a writ of habeas corpus for a man who had been detained at Lawrence over night as a spy, but who had been released the same morning. He read his writ, signed by John P. Wood, Judge of Probate for Douglas County. It was directed to "James H. Lane," "the Safety Committee," and the people of "Lawrence generally." There was too large a share of the ridiculous in this parade of troops on so trivial a matter to occasion any show of dignity among the people at Lawrence. So the free-state boys laughed with the soldiers, and made sport of the simpleton who held the writ. When they left, the boys gave three cheers for the troops, and a groan for the official.

On the thirtieth, Saturday morning, about six o'clock, Frederic Brown, son of Capt. John Brown, walking on the road near his house, not far from Osawattomie, was shot by two scouts of the invaders. Two hours later, a force of three hundred men under Gen. Reed attacked Osawattomie. Seeing the vast superiority of numbers, Capt. Brown retreated with the small free-state party under his command, between thirty and forty men, to the timber on the river. The battle lasted several hours, until the ammunition of the little party gave out. They were then ordered to retreat to the river. The Missourians charged upon them with horses, and, being wholly undisciplined, came up in crowds, so that the sure aim of the little band in the woods thinned their ranks. The free-state party lost two men killed in the battle; one man murdered afterwards. As nearly as could be estimated, the enemy lost thirty-one killed, and thirty-two wounded. Three wagon loads of dead and wounded were taken from Osawattomie. After the battle the ruffians burned the town, between twenty and thirty houses and stores, and pilfered letters from the post-office, etc. They burned, also, the house of "Ottawa Jones," who had a fine residence half way between Lawrence and Osawattomie. This news being received at Lawrence, Gen. Lane with a strong force went out to meet Reid's army. He came near them at Bull Creek, and camped for a battle at sunrise on the morrow. In the night Reid's army retreated, and Gen. Lane drove them to Missouri.

This portion of the invaders had intended to march nearer Lawrence, and attack it upon one side, expecting to be reïnforced by other parties gathered at Lecompton.

On the thirty-first, Sunday, P. M., a woman, residing a mile distant from the camp, came and reported to Col. Cook that some ruffians from Lecompton had gathered at her house, with threats to destroy it. He sent four soldiers back with her to guard it. After their arrival the party left. Mrs. H. gathered together some of her goods, and three small wagon loads were brought to her mother's near the camp. Some of the soldiers returned with the wagons. Soon after they started with the last load, about one hundred and fifty of these Missourians, under the lead of Dr. Stringfellow, appeared, and set the house on fire. They at first took the gun from the one soldier then there, but soon returned it. A few of them surrounded the wagon, and "ordered a surrender." But the woman with her escort came on to the camp. Soon the dense smoke arose over the hill, and the Missourians came up in sight of the camp, and formed in line of battle upon a very high point only a quarter of a mile distant. It looked like a defiance to the troops. Col. Cook with his officers stood by his tent, with a spy-glass, watching them. He was evidently surprised at the boldness of the movement.

Soon the bugle sounded for "boots and saddles," and the soldiers, with loud shouts, and on a full run, started for the horses. They thought they were to have the opportunity of driving off the Missourians. The colonel, being a Southerner, was annoyed by the shouting, and commanded them to be quiet. The Missourians soon left the hill, and the soldiers had their regular Sunday drill.

In a little time two more houses, a short distance away, were fired. Before sundown Deputy Marshal Cramer rode up to the officers' tent to say, that "the houses were set on fire by free-state men." Col. Cook quite indignantly replied, "I saw the smoke of the fire, as your men rode from it on to the hill."

The evening of the next day, five other houses of the settlers were burned, and another, around which the mob gathered, was saved by the lady of the house showing a paper which Marshal Donaldson had given them as a means of protection during the spring invasion. Most of the fires were seen at the camp. Some of the houses had been vacated, the families having gone to Lawrence for safety. The occupants of others were driven from their homes at midnight, only escaping with their lives. One woman, with a number of young children, whose husband could not remain with his family in safety, saved a few things by carrying them into the woods. The next day the house near the camp was full of these homeless ones. There were families without their natural protectors, because they had been previously driven from their homes. There were men, whose families had been removed to Lawrence a few days before, while they had remained at their houses attempting to get their goods ready to move, when they were obliged to fly. No free-state men could now travel between Lawrence and Lecompton. The man who carried meat to the camp daily was taken prisoner by Stringfellow and his scouting party, and retained in camp over night, notwithstanding he showed his contract with the quarter-master.

2d. — "Gen. Strickler of the territorial militia, with Cramer, called on Col. Cook. Cramer introduced the general. Col. Cook seemed to think it militated against his own dignity somewhat to be "ranked" by such a stripling, and he replied, "General?" Cramer said, "Yes," and the usual courtesies passed between them. Then Cramer said, "We want you to hold yourself in readiness to act when called upon; for there may a contingency arise when we shall need you." He also added that "Lane was *cavorting* around the territory."

Mrs. Jenkins, with a military escort, went to Lawrence on the second, for provisions for the prisoners. Upon her return, the next day, she passed through the most of the "territorial militia," about six miles from Lawrence. They were very free with their threats of the destruction of Lawrence; and swore it would be accomplished that night. Mrs. Jenkins met several free-state men, flying as fast as their horses would carry them, to notify Lawrence of the approach of the invaders. One of their scouts was sitting quietly in a ravine, eating a watermelon, before he noticed this force almost upon him. Quickly mounting his horse, he sped towards Lawrence, while four of the invaders pursued him, continually firing. Three of the pursuers soon relinquished the chase, and he was able to outstrip the speed of the fourth.

Dr. Stringfellow was in bad repute with the other officers, as well as with the men. Many of them left when they found that house-burning was to be the principal work. One or two of the captains, on learning the true state of things, immediately left Lecompton, returning over the river.

On the fourth, Marshal Donaldson, and his deputies, Cramer and Newsem, took one hundred and sixty of the troops to Lawrence to arrest Lane, Walker, Grover, and others. They came back wholly unsuccessful. It seemed to be the impression at Lawrence that Lane was not a resident there, and the particular location of the house or boarding-place of others inquired for was not very clearly defined in the minds of those questioned.

The same day three men from Leavenworth, who had never taken any part in the free-state cause, attempted to go from Leavenworth to Lawrence. They were shot by the ruffians. Two were killed, and the other was supposed to be dead by the cruel men. With his head awfully mangled, by the aid of a Delaware Indian, he reached Lawrence. Sicoxie, chief of the Delawares, on the 4th, sent to the camp for troops to protect them from the continual robberies and depredations of the marauders. Captain Sackett, with his company, was sent out. The bodies of the two murdered men were buried by them.

On the same day one hundred and fifty men were ordered to cross the Kansas river, and march upon the north side as far as Lecompton. They arrived at this point about dark. Colonel Harvey so arranged his men that it would have been impossible for a much larger force than his to retreat past them. They lay all night upon their arms, in one of the most violent storms of the season, hungry and supperless. The confusion, the next morning, in Lecompton, was unprecedented even there. Many of the Missourians, who had come to quell "outrages and disturbances by the abolitionists" upon the pro-slavery settlers, finding these acts perpetrated by the "law-and-order" party, were disgusted and sick of "the wars." Wishing to go home to Missouri, they found their retreat cut off. About four o'clock, P. M., Gen. Lane had taken possession of the hill overlooking Lecompton, and the foundation of the capitol, which was used by the enemy as a fortress. He had planted two pieces of artillery, before any intimation had been given in Lecompton of the approach of "Lane's army."

Three messengers from Lecompton, to Col. Cook, followed each other in quick succession. They reported one thousand men about to attack Lecompton. There was soon an unusual stir in the camp. The different bugles sounded, and, in just thirty-five minutes after, the troops began to move towards Lecompton; not in a body, but at the earliest moment each company was ready. The artillery went out, mingling its deafening sound of heavy metal with that of iron hoofs, and the clanking of the sabres of their riders.

Mr. Branscomb and Capt. Cline had been deputed by Gen. Lane to go into Lecompton and make a demand of all prisoners there. They rode in, bearing a flag of truce, and halted before the fort. The following conversation was held:

Mr. Branscomb: "Who has command of the forces here assembled?"

Several voices: "General Richardson."

"Can I see General Richardson?"

Here General Richardson stepped forward and bowed.

"General Richardson, are you in command of the forces here assembled?"

"Well, I don't know as I am."

An individual here stepped forward, and inquired as follows:

"General Richardson, do you still retain the command?"

"No, I suppose not; I resigned this morning," was the reply.

This individual then turned to Messrs. Branscomb and Cline, and said, "I am in command of the forces here assembled, and am ready to receive any proposition."

Mr. Branscomb: "Who are you, sir?"

Individual: "I am General Marshall."

"I am directed by General Lane, commander of the free-state forces of Kansas, to demand of you the *unconditional and immediate release* of all the free-state prisoners now in Lecompton."

General Marshall: "We wish to make no compromises with General Lane, only that he shall treat our prisoners as kindly and courteously as we treat his."

"Do I understand you to refuse to surrender the prisoners demanded?"

"Such is the understanding."

Messrs. Branscomb and Cline were about to return to General Lane's lines, when General Marshall requested them to wait a few minutes. They did so. After a private consultation with some others, the general returned, and gave Mr. Branscomb the strange intelligence that all the prisoners demanded had been released that morning, and that provision had been made to obtain an escort of United States dragoons to attend them to Lawrence the next day. He then told him that he made a demand on General Lane for all the pro-slavery prisoners which had been taken, and asked Mr. Branscomb to state the demand. This ended the interview.

Colonel Cook reached Lane's lines about the time the messengers to Lecompton got back. Colonel Cook said to General Lane and his staff, "Gentlemen, you have made a great mistake in coming here to-day. The territorial militia was dismissed this morning; some of them have left, some are leaving now, and the rest will leave and go to their homes as soon as they can." Mr. Parrott, of Leavenworth city, who was twice sent down the river by the ruffians, replied to him as follows: "Colonel Cook, when we send a man, or two men, or a dozen men, to speak with the territorial authorities, they are arrested and held like felons. How, then, are we to know what is going on in Lecompton? Why, we have to come here with an army to find out what is going on. How else could we know?" To this, Col. Cook made no reply.

The prisoners came over to the camp at evening, and, under military escort, went to Lawrence the next day. Gen. Richardson, of the "Kansas militia," made a visit in Lawrence. He was received kindly by General Lane, who escorted him on his way to Franklin. He stated "he was on his way to disperse the Missourians who were coming into the territory."

A lady from Leavenworth, about this time, having a brother at Lawrence, succeeded in getting through to the latter place. She walked the entire distance, thirty-five miles, and, by prudence, eluded the watchfulness of the enemy.

For some weeks mob-law had raged at Leavenworth. Hordes of the vilest of the Missourians were continually crossing the river into the city. On the first of September a municipal election was to be held. Capt. Emory, the mail agent, at the head of one hundred ruffians, drove from the city all free-state men, declaring that "all who did not leave should be killed."

They attacked the house of William Phillips, a lawyer of Leavenworth. Knowing that it was their intention to murder him, he told them "he should defend his home;" and, as they rushed upon him, he drew his revolver and killed two of them, when he was pierced with a dozen bullets, and died instantly. The brother of Mr. Phillips had his arm badly shattered. Some buildings owned by Mr. P. were burned; also some others. On the Saturday before, and during the night, also, the excitement was intense. The groceries were continually frequented, and the firing of guns was incessant. All of Sunday night companies of thirty or forty men went over the whole city, crying, at the top of their voices, for "all who would not take up arms to enforce the territorial laws, to leave the territory immediately, or suffer the consequences."

On the first of September, about fifty of the inhabitants were obliged, by Capt. Emory and his band, to take passage on the Polar Star for St. Louis. The next day eight hundred men, commanded by Capt. Emory, paraded on the levee in front of the Emma. Capt. E. ordered the captain of the boat not to leave the landing until he gave directions. Then, at the point of the bayonet, were men, women, and children, more than one hundred in number, driven, like cattle, from their homes, to satisfy yet further this guilty administration. Men of property were obliged thus to leave it to the mercy of the mob; and, in some instances, had not means with them to pay their passage to St. Louis. The goods of some of the merchants, together with ten thousand dollars' worth in the warehouses, for traders in Lawrence, were confiscated by the ruffians. In many instances they laid aside their shabby and soiled garments, and were loud in their praise of the excellent fits they found among the clothing designed for merchants in Lawrence. No free-state man dared venture in the streets of Leavenworth. Many fled into the bushes and escaped to the fort. Thirty or more families found safety there.

When the fourteen prisoners at Lecompton were released, Rev. Mr. Nute, and Mr. Wilder, about whom great anxiety had been felt, were discovered not to be among them. Col. Cook provided Mr. Whitman, Mr. Sutherland, and Mr. Wilder, father of young Wilder, an escort, in Sergeant Cary, to go to Leavenworth to attempt their release, if they were there. Within a short distance of the town, after passing several picket guards, they were taken prisoners by Capt. Emory's band. After a little consultation, the leaders concluded it was advisable to release Sergeant Cary. Riding post-haste, he reached the fort and stated the facts. Soon there was a bustle among the soldiers, and two hundred of them marched to Leavenworth. Two hours later, they returned, bringing in Capt. Emory's band of thirty horsemen, with the three gentlemen last taken prisoners in the rear.

Mr. Nute and Mr. Wilder had been released that morning. They had been, for a part of the time, imprisoned in a seven-by-nine stone building with grated windows. There was not an article of furniture in the room.

In such a place, without ventilation, with thirteen others, they were kept one day, without anything to eat from early morning until five o'clock, P. M. Then, some dry bread and coffee were brought in. The prisoners said they could not eat without going into the fresh air; and, on being taken out doors, were scarcely able to stand from faintness.

Gov. Geary arrived at the fort on the morning of the ninth. He was there when Sergeant Cary reported his seizure by the ruffians. He declared that peace should be restored; that every one who was not an actual settler should be driven out; and that the rights of all men should be protected. To some officials under government, with whom he conversed on his way to the territory, he stated, as the urgent necessity for this peace, "the impossibility of carrying Pennsylvania for Buchanan without it."

Rev. Mr. Nute and friends reached Lawrence on the evening of the 10th. On the 6th September, Col. Cook's camp moved within a half mile of Lecompton. On the eighth, a number of the citizens of Lawrence came up to attend the trial of the state prisoners. No officer of the court could be found; neither judge, jury, clerk or marshal. The next day they appeared in Lecompton, and an attempt was made by the counsel for the government, C. H. Grover, to postpone the trials until April, alleging that the County of Douglas was in a state of insurrection, caused by the introduction of large bodies of armed men, whose purpose was to resist the laws of the territory; that jurors and witnesses were prevented from attending court thereby.

Mr. Branscomb and Mr. Parrott, counsel for the prisoners, opposed the motion. Mr. B. stated, the prisoners had been ready for trial the last term. They were ready now, and, as a right, they demanded an immediate trial. Although no summonses had been issued to jurors or witnesses, there were jurors present who would answer to their names, and there was no evidence before the court of such insurrection as the counsel for the government had stated, etc.

Mr. Grover, in reply, said, "he could bring any amount of proof of such insurrection. There was the *London Times*. The *London Times* said that not only Kansas, but the whole country, was in a state of insurrection."

Judge Lecompte overruled the motion, stating that there was not sufficient evidence before the court of such a state of insurrection as to deter witnesses and jurors from appearing.

The docket was then taken up. The first case called was, "The Territory of Kansas against Charles Robinson, for usurpation of office." The same reasons for continuance of this case were brought up by Mr. Grover. Also their witness, P. Hutchinson, who, they said, had been summoned, was not present. He is a man unknown to the prisoners, their counsel or friends never before having heard of him.

Judge Lecompte then gave his decision. He would continue the case on the ground of there being so great an excitement in the country as to prevent a fair trial. The prisoner was admitted to bail in the sum of five hundred dollars.

The other cases were then called, — "The United States against Charles Robinson and others," — and continued. The prisoners were released on bail of five thousand dollars each.

Judge Lecompte accepted the bail offered, and seemed anxious to get the cases off his hands.

John Brown, Jr., and H. H. Williams, who had never been indicted, were also released on one thousand dollars bail.

On the afternoon of the 10th September, just four months from the day my husband was taken prisoner, and nearly four months since the arrest of the others, the tents on "Traitor Avenue" were struck. Three wagons were filled with the furniture and valuables of the prisoners.

While all were getting ready, a party of us rode into Lecompton. It is a little town down in the ravines. The air was hot and stifling, and we wondered any one should locate a town there, when the breezes on the high grounds are so fresh and invigorating. There were two or three tents still standing, the remnant of the invaders' camp. Everything was quiet, and perfectly dull. With two carriages of gentlemen, which came from Lawrence in the morning to attend the court, the ambulance, and two others under military escort, we left for Lawrence. Within a mile of the town, the "Stubs" were waiting to welcome us. Soon after, we were met by Gen. Lane and his staff, who led the way into Massachusetts-street, where crowds of people had gathered to greet their long-absent townsmen.

My husband made them a short speech. In the evening the people had a jubilee of rejoicing, and short speeches from several of the prisoners. The arrival of Mr. Nute and fellow-prisoners, the same evening, added not a little to the enthusiasm of the hour.

On the fourteenth of September a new invasion was made against Lawrence. Gov. Geary was notified of the fact, and he commanded their dispersion. They burned several houses, and the saw-mill in Franklin, and drove off two hundred head of horses and cattle.

A part of the same force passed up to Lecompton on the sixteenth, and killed David Buffum, a reliable free-state man, the same who brought the little howitzer into Lawrence, during the fall invasion, by singular skill and bravery.

Rumors having come into Lawrence of the invaders committing depredations on the northern part of the territory, by the advice of Gov. Geary's friend, a few men were sent to drive them out. On their way back to Lawrence, they were taken prisoners and carried to Lecompton, where they have since been retained. The horses of free-state men are being taken by the other party, under forms of law, and the system of robbery and outrage has received no check.

Two gentlemen, new-comers in the territory, on the twenty-second were taken from the stage, as they were passing from Lawrence to Kansas city, and one is still missing.

The promised peace has not yet come to Kansas. Hopefully the settlers have waited for it; but their hope in the present administration has turned to despair. With many fears, and many sufferings before them in the cold months coming, they still look forward to a day of deliverance when the genial breath of spring shall have melted winter's icy bands, and the new reign of peace and righteous laws takes the place of oppression and tyranny.

CHAPTER XXIV.

AN APPEAL TO THE AMERICAN PEOPLE.

Two years have passed since the territory of Kansas was thrown open to settlement. Under the Squatter Sovereignty bill, expecting to be protected, settlers came from the far East and North, as well as from the more Southern and Western States. They had a right to look for such protection to the President of these United States in the very provisions of that bill. How have they been protected? Let his infamous appointees in the territory — the vile tools of tyranny — answer to an enlightened public sentiment. Let freemen, imprisoned for months on the prairie, under the burning sun, and amid drenching rains, for no crime but the innate love of freedom, tell the tale. Let the booming cannon battering down hotels, and printing-presses thrown into the Kansas river, tell afar the bloody despotism that rules our land. Let the bristling bayonets of the United States army tell how the free settlers have been outraged and plundered, while ruffian bands have been protected by it, under Gov. Shannon's orders. Let the loud moan of lone men, murdered by these hordes of the administration, and the bitter wail of desolate homes, borne on every gale, tell to the world the blackness of the demon Slavery, and the unmitigated villany of those who have aided, abetted, and connived at all these atrocities — those who have brought disgrace upon our country's name, and clothed their own in darkness so dense, that no after acts of a lifetime can erase the stains of blood and guilt. While the ghost-like forms of their murdered victims flit around their nightly pillows, and the cry, " O, God! I am murdered!" comes to them on every morning breeze, and the low plaint of the insane widow, as she starts and listens at every footstep, saying,

"Is it my husband?" as he comes never more, "O, my soul, come not thou into their secrets!"

The appointees of the President in this territory, both judicial and executive, have, with two or three exceptions, in every possible way aided these invasions of the territory, the mobs, the murders, the downfall of freedom by fire and sword. When Gov. Reeder acted out his manliness, and refused to be a tool to carry out the nefarious plans of the administration, he was dismissed on a charge so false that even the vile minions of slavery denounced the President.

This dismissal did not come, however, until the President had urged Gov. Reeder to resign, promising him an appointment upon a foreign mission. Then a new governor was appointed. He declined the appointment. Then another was found mean enough to accept the appointment, after a dismissal of the former governor under such circumstances, and the refusal to accept of the second appointee. And well has he fulfilled the promise of meanness, heartlessness, and perfect servility to the great Moloch of Slavery, an acceptance, at such a time, warranted us to expect. He made a league with our enemies before he set foot in the territory. He brought them against Lawrence, in December, 1855, by a tissue of lies. He made a treaty with his own people, when he found his fiat was not sufficient to annihilate them. When he feared his own life was in danger, he gave the people of Lawrence a right to protect themselves, and him. In May a new horde of blood was brought against Lawrence. The protection of this instrument of the slave power was implored again and again; but the last conference was closed by his demand of the guns being given up, because one hundred South Carolinians, just arrived in the territory, would not be satisfied without, and the hotel must be destroyed for the same laudable reason. Magnanimous governor! What laurels will crown his brow, as his name goes down to posterity; and how the closing remark of that conference will add lustre to them!

This brave champion for slavery has dared to tell lone women on the Kansas prairies he would "cut their d—d hearts out!" He has given passes to a few men travelling in the territory, showing his connection with the murders and outrages daily committed. He has at all times, when outrages have been committed by his accomplices, and he feared the just wrath of the people, protected them by United States troops. He has, when fearing an attack upon Lecompton, been seen entering the scow to cross the river to save himself, and, under the protection of Major Sedgwick, has made his second visit to the people of Lawrence, and made another treaty with them. He has asked for an escort to get him out of the country. But the President, at last, seeing the Democratic party in danger, has numbered the days of the governor. Let " de mortaibus nisi bonum " be our motto. Judge Lecompte was particularly qualified to be the chief justice in Kansas, by his want of legal knowledge, and lack of intellectual ability. His particular forte in packing juries, and instructing grand jurors to indict freedom-loving citizens for high treason, as well as hotels and printing-presses as nuisances, has probably fulfilled the President's expectations in regard to him, as well as made him a worthy fellow-worker with the decapitated governor. Another of the judges declared that he would leave the bench to assist in arresting persons who said they would pay no regard to the territorial laws. Such has been the partisan character of all these appointees.

When Congress was memorialized as to these grievances of the people, and a plain statement was laid before the President of the invasion of March thirtieth, he signified his alliance with the ruffians by removing Gov. Reeder. During the siege of Lawrence, in which Gov. Shannon had for his counsellors men from Westport and Independence, when Clark, the Indian agent, in a most wanton manner, murdered an unarmed man, Judges Lecompte, Elmore, Johnson, Cato, and Burrill, being of the same party, as they left Lecompton, on their way to head-quarters on the Wakarusa, the President was silent. He offered no protection to the people of Lawrence. He has done nothing since towards the removal of the murderer. When, however, a new invasion being in preparation, word was sent to him, he suddenly found that some things in Kansas required his interposition. His special message was crowded upon the House, and his proclamation soon followed. Did he speak of the murder by his official ? Not one word. Did he reprove the governor — the very man after his own heart in guilty weakness — for his unparalleled course of oppression? O, no! He told the peaceable settlers in Kansas, who had asked his protection, that he would "enforce the laws" of the Legislature, elected by Missourians, "with the army and navy of the United States." He, moreover, intimated very strongly that treason had been or would be committed.

Again and again irruptions were made into the territory. The ballot-boxes were taken by force; and on the seventeenth of January another murder, so terrible in all its barbarities that the mind shudders at the thought, was committed in the territory. The people, oppressed by cold unprecedented, and many of them suffering for the actual wants of life, were harassed hourly by fears of the assassin. Yet the President was dumb. Spring came, and earth and sky rejoiced with mutual gladness in the balmy airs and up-springing verdure. Business revived, and the people hoped in some measure to retrieve their losses of the last fall's invasion; but the demon Slavery was yet insatiate. Armed bands from Missouri, South Carolina, and Alabama, poured into the territory. They openly proclaimed they came to "fight and to vote, and would return to their homes." These things were known to the country. Was the President one of those who, "having eyes, see not, and ears, hear not"? They came, and were enrolled as the militia of the territory — men so degraded, so debauched, that one of their officers in camp said "they never had had so good a home as that before." They were the proper instruments to do the work desired by the administration — sacking towns, robbing and murdering innocent people; and this they did under the orders of the United States Marshal. The way, they thought, was open for a general extermination of free-state people, because, by the orders of Judge Lecompte, a few of the leaders had been thrown into prison, and others driven off.

Lawrence was destroyed. Osawattomie was sacked. Guerilla bands blockaded the highways, and murdered peaceable citizens. Did the President do anything? When by a word he could have given Kansas the long-sought-for peace, he said it not.

The White House rose between him and the suffering dwellers in Kansas. He had been struck with official blindness, and saw not how, when he had been their willing agent, their pliant tool, the southern party would cast him off as a worthless thing. He had gone too low; he had crouched too humbly; he could not be trusted. So they gave him a complimentary vote when he came before that Cincinnati Convention, in the words of a Massachusetts senator, "with the lurid light of the sacked and burning dwellings of Kansas flashing on his brazen brow, and with the blood of the people of Kansas dripping from his hands." When our people attempted to right their wrongs by assembling to memorialize Congress, an armed body of United States troops rushed in upon them, and commanded their dispersion. This act, on the Fourth of July, 1856, makes the third act of this kind chronicled in history. While such things are being sanctioned in Kansas, the Missouri river is infested by pirates, and closed to peaceable citizens. The President still looks on unmoved, and permits outrages which long ago would have been made the pretext for a bloody war, had one tenth part of the wrongs been committed by a foreign power.

We have fallen upon the evil times, in our country's history, when it is treason to think, to speak a word against the evil of slavery, or in favor of free labor. In Kansas, prisons or instant death by barbarians are the reward; and in the Senate, wielders of bludgeons are honored by the state which has sent ruffians to desolate Kansas. But in this reign of misrule the President and his advisers have failed to note the true effect of such oppression. The fires of liberty have been rekindled in the hearts of our people, and burn in yet brighter flame under midnight skies illumined by their own burning dwellings. The sight of lawless, ruthless invaders, acting under the United States government, has filled them with that "deep, dark, sullen, teeth-clenched silence, bespeaking their hatred of tyranny, which armed a William Tell and Charlotte Corday." The best, the boldest utterance of man's spirit for freedom will not be withheld. The administration, with the most insane malignity, has prepared the way for a civil war, and the extermination of freemen in Kansas. With untiring malice, it has endeavored to effect this by the aid of a corrupt judiciary, packed juries, and reckless officials. In violation of the Constitution of the United States, no regard was paid to the sacred rights of freemen in their persons and property. Against the known sentiment and conviction of half the nation these deeds of infamy have been plotted, and have been diligently carried on. That a people are down-trodden is not evidence that they are subdued. The crushed energies are gathering strength; and, like a strong man resting from the heats and toils of the day, the people of Kansas will arise to do battle for liberty; and, when their mighty shouts for freedom shall ascend over her hills and prairies, slavery will shrink back abashed. Life, without liberty, is valueless, and there are times which demand the noble sacrifice of life. The people of Kansas are in the midst of such times; and amid discomfiture and defeat men will be found who for the right will stand with sterner purpose and bolder front. Kansas will never be surrendered to the slave power. God has willed it! Lawrence, the city where the plunderer feasted at the hospitable table, and, Judas-like, went out to betray it, will come forth from its early burial clothed with yet more exceeding beauty. Out of its charred and blood-stained ruins, where the flag of rapine floated, will spring the high walls and strong parapets of freedom. The sad tragedies in Kansas will be avenged, when freedom of speech, of the press, and of the person, are made sure by the downfall of those now in power, and when the song of the reaper is heard again over our prairies, and, instead of the clashing of arms, we see the gleam of the ploughshare in her peaceful valleys. Men of the North, shall the brave hearts in Kansas struggle alone?

APPENDIX.

MESSAGE OF GOVERNOR ROBINSON, OF KANSAS, TO THE NEW LEGISLATURE.

Fellow-Citizens of the Senate and House of Representatives:

HAVING been chosen by the people to occupy the executive chair of the new State of Kansas, it becomes my duty, under the constitution, to communicate to the General Assembly the condition of the affairs of the state, and recommend such measures as I shall deem expedient for their action. While gratitude to the people for the confidence their suffrages evinced, and for the honor bestowed, will induce me to enlist all my energies in their service, inexperience in public life, and a lack of ability and information, will cause me to speak with diffidence upon the various subjects to which your attention will be invited.

The organization of a new government is always attended with more or less difficulty, and should, under the most favorable circumstances, enlist the learning, judgment and prudence, of the wisest men in all its departments; the most skilful workmanship is requisite, that each part of the complicated machinery may be adapted to its fellow, and that a harmonious whole, without jar or blemish, may be the result. In Kansas, especially, is this a most delicate and difficult task. Our citizens are from every state in the Union, and from nearly every country on the globe, and their institutions, religion, education, habits and tastes, are as various as their origin. Also in our midst are several independent nations, and on our borders, both west and east, are outside invaders.

In our mutual endeavors to set in motion a state government, we have a common chart for our guide, the Constitution. The duties of the General Assembly, as designated by this instrument, are:

To provide for the Encouragement of Education and Religion;
The Registration of Electors;
To provide for the Returns of Elections;

For the Election of Officers;
For the Filling of Vacancies;
For the Number of Senators and Representatives;
For Apportionment;
Against Special Legislation;
For Publication of Laws;
For Taking the Census;
For Salaries of Officers;
For Surveyor General, State Geologist, and Superintendent of Common Schools;
For Judicial Districts and Jurisdiction of Courts;
For Publication of Decisions of Supreme Court;
For Duties of Clerk and Reporter of Supreme Court;
For School Fund, University, Normal Schools, etc.;
For State Asylums for Blind, Deaf, Dumb, Insane, Idiots, and the Poor;
For Houses of Refuge for Juvenile Offenders;
For State General Hospital;
For Seat of Government and State House;
For Militia;
For Finance and Taxation;
For Counties, County, City and Town Officers;
For Commissioners to arrange Rules of Practice in the Courts of Record;
For Bureau of Statistics and Encouragement of Agriculture;
To secure the separate Property and Custody of Children to Wife;
For Election of two United States Senators;
For Banks and Banking;
For Redemption of Certificates of Indebtedness; and for Enforcement of the Sixth Section of the Bill of Rights.

Also, the people, by a separate and direct vote, have instructed the Assembly to provide for the exclusion of free negroes.

Education of the people, common school education, is the palladium of our liberties. Without this, free institutions cannot exist; with it, tyranny and oppression must disappear. A thorough and efficient system of education is a better and cheaper corrective and preventive of poverty, degradation and crime, than the poor-house, house of refuge, or penitentiary. This subject will not fail to receive its full share of your attention. That the common school may be put on a permanent basis, the proceeds of the school lands, or other educational income, should be carefully husbanded, till a fund shall accumulate amply sufficient to give to every child in the state a liberal common school education.

Second only to the common school in importance are the University and Normal Schools. For these, also, the constitution suggests that you provide at an early day.

Of the public charitable institutions named in the constitution, a General State Hospital calls most urgently for consideration. In a new country, many must necessarily suffer from sickness and poverty, and, in the present unsettled condition of the people, it is eminently proper that the state should provide for their relief.

The subject of finances and taxation is one of primary importance in every state, and particularly in a new one. Onerous taxes and large indebtedness should be guarded against as far as possible, and economy without niggardly parsimony should be the rule of action. For the present state of the finances you are referred to the report of the executive committee.

Exposed as our citizens are to the scalping-knife of the savage on the west, and to the revolver and hatchet of the assassin on the east, a thorough and early organization of the militia is urgently called for. By the constitution, this duty devolves upon the General Assembly. Measures should at once be taken to encourage the organization of volunteer companies, and to procure the arms to which the state is entitled.

The disposition of the public lands is a matter for serious consideration. Under existing laws, they belong to the general government, and are used as a source of revenue. The policy of such a use is at least questionable. The amount received into the treasury from the sale of public lands is inconsiderable, amounting in the aggregate to about two millions of dollars annually.

This sum, distributed among the states where the lands are situated, would aid essentially the cause of education, or the establishment of charitable institutions, but it is entirely unnecessary in the already overflowing treasury of the general government. Even as a matter of revenue, the treasury gains nothing by selling the public domain to the people, for the principal revenue is derived from the products of the soil, and these will be increased as the number of land-holders increases, and in proportion to the capital invested in its cultivation. The one dollar and twenty-five cents per acre, laid out on the land, will produce far more revenue to the government in a few years, than if deposited in the treasury. The true policy for any government is to give, to every citizen who will cultivate it, a farm without price, and secure it to him for a permanent homestead. Especially should the citizen who deprives himself of the blessings of home and civilization for a time, to reclaim the wilderness that it may be added to the commonwealth, be allowed his land gratis.

But if the land must be sold, and the proceeds applied to defray expenses of government, the state should be the recipient, and not the general government. Every new state must incur extraordinary expenses in setting its government in motion. It has its public edifices, State-house, Asylums, Penitentiary, Universities, School-houses, Railroads, etc., to construct, and limited means at command. Should Congress, in its wisdom, donate, as we have reason to believe it will, all the public lands of Kansas to the state, it will then be the duty of the assembly to dispose of them. In such an event, by donating one hundred and sixty acres as a homestead to each resident of five years, and allowing no one person to purchase of the state more than one hundred and sixty acres additional, the state would become rapidly settled, and at the same time secure a fund for educational and other purposes equal to its necessities.

The indiscriminate sale of intoxicating drinks in a state like Kansas, where are numerous Indian tribes, is productive of much mischief. Some tribes within our borders are still uncivilized, and indulge their appetites without restraint, while many of the other tribes are equally unfortunate. It is a duty we owe to the Indian, that we not only cultivate the most friendly intercourse, but that we protect him from injury ; and this subject should not be overlooked by the General Assembly.

The use of intoxicating drinks, as a beverage, impairs the health, morals, good order and prosperity, of any community, and the traffic in them is an unmitigated evil, and it is for the Legislature in its wisdom to adopt such measures as shall best secure the public welfare.

It will be remembered that a skeleton of a government still exists in our midst, under the territorial form, and although this was but the foreshadowing of a new and better covenant, collision with it should be carefully guarded against. A territorial government is transient in its nature, only waiting the action of the people to form a government of their own. This action has been taken by the people of Kansas, and it only remains for the General Government to suspend its territorial appropriations, recall its officers, and admit Kansas into the Union as a sovereign state.

The reasons why the territorial government should be suspended and Kansas admitted into the Union as a state, are various. In the first place, it is not a government of the people. The executive and judicial officers are imposed upon the people by a distant power, and the officers thus imposed are foreign to our soil, and are accountable, not to the people, but to an executive two thousand miles distant. American citizens have for a long time been accustomed to govern themselves, and to have a voice in the choice of their officers ; but, in the territorial government, they not only have no voice in choosing some of their officers, but are deprived of a vote for the officer who appoints them.

Again : governments are instituted for the good and protection of the governed ; but the territorial government of Kansas has been, and still is, an instrument of oppression and tyranny unequalled in the history of our republic. The only officers that attempted to administer the laws impartially have been removed, and persons substituted who have aided in our subjugation. Such has been the conduct of the officers and the people of a neighboring state, either intentionally or otherwise, that Kansas, to-day, is without a single law enacted by the people of the territory. Not a man in the country will attempt to deny that every election had under the territorial government was carried by armed invaders from an adjoining state, and for the purpose of enacting laws in opposition to the known wishes of the people.

The territorial government should be withdrawn, because it is inoperative. The officers of the law permit all manner of outrages and crime to be perpetrated by the invaders and their friends with impunity, while the citizens proper are naturally law-abiding and order loving, disposed rather to suffer than do wrong. Several of the most aggravated murders on record have been committed, but as long as the murders are on the side of the oppressors, no notice is taken of them. Not one of the whole number has been brought to justice, and not one will be, by the territorial officers. While the marauders are thus in open violation of all law, nine tenths of the people scorn to recognize as law the enactments of a foreign body of men, and would sooner lose their right arms than bring an action in one of their misnamed courts. Americans can suffer death, but not dishonor ; and sooner than the people will consent to recognize the edicts of lawless invaders as laws, their blood will mingle with the waters of the Kansas, and this Union be rolled together in civil strife.

Not only is this territorial government the instrument of oppression and subjugation of the people, but under it there is no hope of relief. The organic act permits the Legislature to prescribe the qualification of voters, and the so-called Legislature has provided that no man shall vote in any election who will not bow the knee to the dark image of slavery, and appointed officers for the term of four years to see that this provision is carried out. Thus nine tenths of the citizens are disfranchised and debarred from acting under the territorial government if they would.

Even if allowed to vote, the chief executive of the country says he has no power to protect the ballot-box from invaders, and if the people organize to protect themselves, his appointees intimate that they must be disarmed and put down ; hence, whether allowed to vote or not, there is no opportunity for the people of the territory to rule under the present territorial government. Indeed, the laws are so made and construed that the citizens of a neighboring state are legal voters in Kansas, and of course no United States force can be brought against them. They are by law entitled to invade us and control our elections.

According to the organic act the people have a right to elect a Legislature, and that Legislature has a right to make laws, establish courts, and do everything but choose their executive and supreme judicial officers. If they have the right to do the one, they undoubtedly should have the right to do the other. The principle of squatter sovereignty, upon which this act is said to be based, knows no distinction between the power to legislate and the power to adjudicate or execute. If the right of one department of government is inherent in the people, so is the other. On this subject there is high authority. Gen Cass, in the Senate, said : " The government of the United

States is one of limited authority, vested with no powers not expressly granted or not necessary to the proper execution of such as are."

"There is no provision in the constitution granting any powers of legislation over the 'territory or other property of the United States,' except such as relates to its regulation and disposition. Political jurisdiction is entirely withheld, nor is there any just implication which can supply this defect of original authority."

Again he says, "I shall vote for the entire interdiction of all federal action over this general question, under any circumstances that may occur." But the executive and judiciary of Kansas are the creatures of the federal government, and under its control, and the governor has a negative legislative power equal to two thirds of both branches of the Legislature, leaving to the people of the territory only one third of one of the three departments of government, and to the general government all of two departments, and two thirds of the other.

Also, he says, "Leave the people who will be affected by this question (slavery), to adjust it upon their own responsibility and in their own manner, and we shall render another tribute to the original principles of our government, and furnish another guaranty for its permanency and prosperity." But how can this or any other question be adjusted by the people, while ruled by a foreign executive and judiciary?

Mr. Douglas says, "I have always held that the people have a right to settle these questions as they choose, not only when they come into the Union as a state, but that they should be permitted to do so while a territory." If the people have this right, then the federal government has no right to interfere with it, and the people of Kansas have a right to demand that the present territorial government of Kansas be withdrawn, and that they be allowed to choose *all* their officers.

Mr. Henn, of Iowa, in Congress, said, "I would that Congress would recognize the doctrine of 'squatter sovereignty' in its length and breadth; that the citizen, wherever he may settle, if on American soil, shall have all the rights and privileges of citizenship, and be consulted by executives as well as by representatives. This would be right. This would be simple justice. It is a doctrine that was broadly asserted, and with firmness maintained, by the fathers of our republic."

In the organic act of the territory, section 14, is the following: "It being the true intent and meaning of this act not to legislate slavery into any territory or state, nor to exclude it therefrom, *but to leave the people thereof perfectly free to form and regulate their domestic institutions in their own way*, subject only to the constitution of the United States."

But how can this "intent" be carried out with an executive and judiciary, and two thirds of the legislative power, in opposition to the will of the people, and with an overwhelming invasion at every election by permission of these officers?

In the President's annual message to Congress, for the current year, he says, "In the counsels of Congress there was manifested extreme antagonism of opinion and action between some representatives who sought, by the abusive and unconstitutional employment of the legislative powers of the government, to interfere in the condition of inchoate states, and to impose their own social theories upon the latter ; and other representatives, who repelled the interposition of the general government in this respect, and maintained the self-constituted rights of the states. In truth, the thing attempted was in form alone the action of the general government, while in reality it was the endeavor, by abuse of legislative power, to force the ideas of internal policy, entertained by particular states, upon allied independent states. Once more the constitution and the Union triumphed signally. The new territories were organized without restrictions on the disputed point, and were thus left to judge in that particular for themselves."

If it would have been an "abuse of legislative power" for Congress to "force the ideas of internal policy entertained by particular states" upon Kansas, by what reasoning does he justify the executive in the exercise of that power? That the officials of his appointment are to-day endeavoring to do this very thing, against the sentiment of a large majority of the people, cannot admit of a doubt.

Again he says, "The measure of its repeal (Missouri Compromise) was the final consummation and complete recognition of the principle, that no portion of the United States shall undertake, through assumption of the powers of the general government, to dictate the social institutions of any other portion."

The people of Kansas have reason to feel that the "complete recognition" of the principle, unless carried into practice, is of no avail to them, and that the recognition of this principle by Congress, while the opposite is acted upon by the executive, would be simple mockery.

Once more; "If the friends of the constitution are to have another struggle, its enemies could not present a more acceptable issue than that of a state, whose constitution clearly embraces a republican form of government, being excluded from the Union because its domestic institutions may not in all respects comport with the ideas of what is wise and expedient entertained in some other state." "If a new state, formed from the territory of the United States, be absolutely excluded from admission therein, that fact, of itself, constitutes the disruption of union between it and the other states. But the process of dissolution could not stop there. Would not a sectional decision, producing such a result by a majority of votes, either northern or southern, of necessity drive out the oppressed and aggrieved minority, and place in presence of each other two irreconcilably hostile confederations?"

Thus it will be seen, by the highest democratic authority in the country, that the people of Kansas have a right to demand the removal of the present oppressive territorial government, and also that they be admitted into the Union as an equal and independent state.

Knowing that one great party in Congress, with the President at its head, was in principle committed to our defence, and believing that many from the other parties would, if not from principle, as an act of justice, be induced to look upon us with favor, we had a right to anticipate a speedy termination of our present thraldom. However, owing to an apparent misunderstanding of the constitutional movements in Kansas, the President intimates in a special message that Congress must interfere and make the people undo what, with great care and expense, they have so well done. This message, as it refers exclusively to Kansas, should receive some attention from the General Assembly. Kansas men, "squatter sovereignty" men, cannot fail to be somewhat surprised at its purport. It is somewhat belligerent in its tone, threatening to bring against the people of Kansas the army and navy of the United States; and, should this force be inadequate to the task, the militia of the several states are to be brought into requisition to compel the people to submit to what they do not recognize as laws, and to laws, according to his own showing, the people of Missouri, with the aid of the executive which he appointed, have enacted.

But it is to be hoped that, by the time his forces are raised and marched into the territory, he will find, like His Excellency Governor Shannon, that the people are not so deserving of annihilation as he had supposed.

The President gives the details of the invasion of Kansas and the Governor's connection therewith, and does not deny that the so-called territorial Legislature was elected by the people of Missouri; but because the Governor, his appointee, chose to grant certificates of election to a majority of persons elected by the people of a neighboring state, therefore their laws are binding upon the people. To strengthen his argument, he might have accused the Governor of still further complicity with the invaders, and have said that although this territory is hundreds of miles in extent, and the people were politically unorganized, yet he gave them but four days in which to contest the election, and would not extend the time one hour; for it is said that a protest arrived at one o'clock on the morning of the fifth day, which, had it been regarded, would have changed five seats in the Legislature; but it was too late by one hour, and could not be received.

The argument of the President may be good against any objection to the acts of the Legislature on his part, as, in the first place, he refused to protect the ballot-box from fraud, and, in the second place, so far as lay in his power, his appointee legalized it; but is it good against the people?

The organic act provides for a Legislature to be elected from, and by, the voters; and a voter is to be "an actual resident of said territory;" and if any other set of men, either with or without the sanction of the executive, claim to be the Legislature, are the people bound to regard them as such?

Also, this act says, "It is the true intent and meaning of this act to leave the people of the territory perfectly free to form and regulate their domestic institutions in their own way, subject only to the constitution of the United States," *not* subject to the people of Missouri, or the executive, or both of them together. How can the true intent of this law be carried out by a Legislature elected as was that on the thirtieth of March last? Yet that Legislature, elected from and by the people of a neighboring state, have assumed to pass laws for the people of Kansas, and also to "legislate slavery into the territory," which Congress itself professed not to have the right to do; and these are the so-called laws that the President says must be enforced, even though it require all the army and navy of the United States and the militia of the several states. Undoubtedly one half of this force will be all-sufficient to enable him to enforce any process, or to chop, shoot and hang all the inhabitants. But all the armies and navies in the world could not make the people believe he had a right to do it, or that the enactments of that border Legislature were binding upon the people of Kansas. If squatter sovereignty means simply that Congress has no right to interfere with the affairs of a territory, but that the executive and the people of another state have, then most certainly that doctrine will be very unpopular in Kansas.

Other reasons might be given to show that no legal Legislature have ever passed laws in Kansas besides the above, as the removal of the sittings from Pawnee to the Shawnee Mission, which is on the Shawnee Reserve, as it is understood, and can, consequently, "constitute no part of the territory of Kansas." The organic act provides that "the persons having the highest number of *legal* votes in each district for members of the Council (or House of Representatives) shall be declared by the Governor to be duly elected." From this decision there is no appeal, according to the act; yet nine persons, declared to be duly elected by the Governor, were ejected by the Legislature, and others admitted. But one person, it is believed, was duly elected by the legal voters of the territory, and he resigned his seat, regarding the whole body illegal. His seat was filled without an election, and by the Legislature; hence, probably, not one of the members of the body could have received the suffrages of the legal voters in the districts they pretended to represent.

It is the enactments of such a body of men that the army, navy and militia of the country are to enforce upon the people, who were told they should "be free to form and regulate their domestic institutions in their own way;" a body of men elected by a neighboring state; who did not sit at the seat of government as required; who *did* sit at the Shawnee Mission, understood to form no part of the territory of Kansas; who turned out nine of its legally elected members and received in their stead nine persons not legally elected; who filled a vacancy by appointment, and not by election of the voters of the district, etc., to say nothing of the Draconian character of the enactments.

The President says, "The constitutional means of relieving the people of unjust administrations and laws, by a change of public agents, and by repeal, are ample." This is usually the case, and ought always to be so; but the case of Kansas is an exception. The administration of Kansas has its head at Washington, and we have not so much as a vote in favor of its continuance or removal; while the repeal of any laws, under present arrangements, by the people, is out of the question, as the Legislature has disfranchised a large majority of them. No man, in favor of a change or repeal of certain laws, can vote under our new order of things; and, consequently, no peaceable way of establishing a government of the people is left but to form a state constitution, and ask for admission into the Union. This has been done; but the President objects to our constitution, and calls the movement for a state government revolutionary, and intimates that the forces of the Union must, if necessary, be brought against it, although he admits that it was not revolutionary for other territories to do precisely what we have done — as California, Michigan, and others. His reason is, that the constitution of Kansas was formed by a party, and not by the whole people. What are the facts? A bill, calling for a convention for the formation of a state constitution, is said to have passed through one house of the Mission Legislature, and was defeated in the other only because they feared the result would be a free state. In July and August a paper was circulated for the signatures of all such persons as were desirous of forming a state government, and between one and two thousand persons signed it. August 15th, a general mass meeting of citizens, irrespective of party, was held at Lawrence, pursuant to a public call, signed "Many Citizens," "to take into consideration the propriety of calling a Territorial Delegate Convention, preliminary to the formation of a state government, and other subjects of public interest." At this meeting all parties participated, and the following preamble and resolution were adopted, with but one dissenting voice, and that was an acknowledged disunion abolitionist, the only one of that party at the meeting.

"Whereas the people of Kansas Territory have been, since its settlement, and now are, without any law-making power; therefore, be it

"*Resolved*, That we, the people of Kansas, in mass meeting assembled, irrespective of party distinctions, influenced by a common necessity, and greatly desirous of promoting the common good, do hereby call upon and request all bona fide citizens of Kansas Territory, of whatever political views or predilections, to counsel together in their respective election districts, and in mass convention, or otherwise, elect three delegates for each representative to which such district is entitled, in the House of Representatives or the Legislative Assembly, by proclamation of Gov. Reeder, of date 10th March, 1855; said delegates to assemble in convention at the town of

Topeka, on the 19th day of September, 1855, then and there to consider and determine upon all subjects of public interest, and *particularly* upon that having reference to the speedy formation of a state constitution, with an intention of an immediate application to be admitted as a state into the Union of the 'United States of America.'"

This was the first public action taken by the people in their sovereign capacity upon this subject, and all parties and sects participated.

The next action was at a party convention held at Big Springs on the 5th and 6th of September. A committee on state organization was appointed, and made the following report:

"Your committee, after considering the propriety of taking preliminary steps to framing a constitution, and applying for admission as a state into the Union, beg leave to report that, under the present circumstances, they deem the movement untimely and inexpedient."

The following was offered as a substitute for the report:

"*Resolved*, That this convention, in view of its recent repudiation of the acts of the so-called Kansas Legislative Assembly, respond most heartily to the call made by the people's convention of the 15th ult., for a Delegate Convention of the people of Kansas Territory, to be held at Topeka on the 19th inst., to consider the propriety of the formation of a state constitution, and such other matters as may legitimately come before it." This substitute was agreed to.

Thus it appears that this party convention simply approved of the action of the citizens' convention at Lawrence, and let the matter rest.

A Delegate Convention, irrespective of party, was held at Topeka, Sept. 19th and 20th, agreeable to the call of the mass convention of the 15th of August, and the following preamble and resolution were unanimously adopted:

"Whereas the Constitution of the United States guarantees to the people of this republic the right of assembling together in a peaceable manner for their common good, to establish justice, insure domestic tranquillity, provide for the common defence, promote the general welfare, and secure the blessings of liberty to themselves and their posterity; and whereas the citizens of Kansas Territory were prevented from electing members of a Legislative Assembly, in pursuance of a proclamation of Gov. Reeder, on the thirtieth of March last, by invading forces from foreign states coming into the territory, and forcing upon the people a Legislature of non-residents, and others, inimical to the interests of the people of Kansas Territory, defeating the object of the organic act, in consequence of which the territorial government became a perfect failure, and the people were left without any legal government, until their patience has become exhausted, and endurance ceases to be a virtue; and they are compelled to resort to the only remedy left — that of forming a government for themselves; therefore,

"*Resolved*, By the people of Kansas Territory, in Delegate Convention assembled, That an election shall be held in the several election precincts of this territory, on the second Tuesday of October next, under the regulations and restrictions hereinafter imposed, for members of a convention to form a constitution, adopt a bill of rights for the people of Kansas, and take all needful measures for organizing a state government, preparatory to the admission of Kansas into the Union as a state."

At this convention a Territorial Executive Committee was appointed, and the committee, in accordance with the instructions of the convention, issued a proclamation, commencing as follows:

"TO THE LEGAL VOTERS OF KANSAS.

"Whereas the territorial government, as now constituted for Kansas, has proved a failure — squatter sovereignty under its workings a miserable delusion — in proof of which it is only necessary to refer to our past history, and our present deplorable condition; — our ballot-boxes have been taken possession of by bands of armed men from foreign states, and our people forcibly driven therefrom; persons attempted to be foistered upon us as menbers of a so-called Legislature, unacquainted with our wants, and hostile to our best interests, some of them never residents of our territory; misnamed *laws* passed, and now attempted to be enforced by the aid of citizens of foreign states, of the most oppressive, tyrannical, and insulting character; the right of suffrage taken from us; debarred from the privilege of a voice in the election of even the most insignificant officers; the right of free speech stifled; the muzzling of the press attempted; — and whereas longer forbearance with such oppression has ceased to be a virtue; and whereas the people of this country have heretofore exercised the right of changing their form of government when it became oppressive, and have, at all times, conceded this right to the people in this and all other governments; and whereas a territorial form of government is unknown to the constitution, and is the mere creature of necessity, awaiting the action of the people; and whereas the debasing character of the slavery, which now involves us, impels us to action, and leaves us the only legal and peaceful alternative — the immediate establishment of a state government; and whereas the organic act fails in pointing out the course to be adopted in an emergency like ours; therefore, you are requested to meet at your several precincts in said territory hereinafter mentioned, on the second Tuesday of October next, it being the ninth day of said month, and then and there cast your ballots for members of a convention, to meet at Topeka on the fourth Tuesday of October next, to form a constitution, adopt a bill of rights for the people of Kansas, and take all needful measures for organizing a state government preparatory to the admission of Kansas into the Union as a State."

On the fourth Tuesday of October, the Constitutional Convention assembled at Topeka, and drafted a constitution, which was submitted to the people on the fifteenth of December, and by them approved, by a very large majority — men of all parties voting.

Such, in brief, is the history of the constitutional movement in Kansas; and, if this is a party movement, it is difficult to see in what way a constitution can be framed and adopted not open to this charge. If the people or any other portion of them failed to participate, it was their own fault, and not the fault of those who were active. Democrats, Hards and Softs, Whigs, Hunkers and Liberals, Republicans, Pro-Slavery and Anti-Slavery men of all shades participated in the formation of the state government, and if it be a party movement at all, it certainly cannot be a movement of one party alone. In a republican government, the majority has no power to compel the minority to vote on any question ; neither has the minority a right to object to the action of the majority, because they did not choose to act with them.

The President says: "No principle of public law, no practice or precedent under the constitution of the United States, no rule of reason, right or common sense, confers any such power as that now claimed by a mere party in the territory. In fact, what has been done is of a revolutionary character. It will become treasonable insurrection if it reach the length of organized resistance by force to the fundamental or any other federal law, and to the authority of the general government."

"No principle of public law"? What is the principle of squatter sovereignty, then? "No precedent"? What did Michigan, California, and other new states do? "No rule of reason, right, or common sense"? Is popular sovereignty unreasonable, unjust and nonsensical? Suppose the *party* comprise an overwhelming majority of the people, what then?

James Christian, Esq., a very honorable and high-minded pro-slavery gentleman, writes to a friend in Kentucky as follows: "I believe I informed you before that I have been appointed clerk of this (Douglas) county, under the territorial Legislature; but we are in such a horrible state of confusion in regard to the laws that it don't pay anything. The free-soilers are in a large majority in the territory, and they are determined to pay no regard to the laws ; consequently they will not sue nor have any recording done, so my office is only in name. It is the same all over the territory."

According to the President, this "large majority" can have no rights, because they happen to think alike on a certain subject, or belong to the same "party." It was formerly a principle of democracy that the majority — especially "large majorities" — should rule ; but times must have changed.

If this "large majority" persist in setting in motion a state government, it will be "treasonable." It was not so, however, in Michigan, California, and other states. But the people of Kansas do not propose to reach the point of "organized resistance by force to the fundamental or any other federal law, and to the authority of the general goverment," unless our state, "whose constitution clearly embraces a republican form of govern ment, is excluded from the Union because its domestic institutions may not in all respects, comport with the ideas of what is wise and expedient, entertained in another state."

If our *state* "be absolutely excluded from admission therein, that fact of itself (*may*) constitute the disruption of union between it and the other states. But the process of dissolution could not stop there," and we should have the chief executive on our side in such an event. But no such result is to be anticipated. When the President fully understands our case, he can do no less than withdraw his recommendation for an enabling act to form another constitution, and Congress will admit us without delay.

Also we have confidence that no attempt will be made by the federal authorities to enforce the enactments of a foreign Legislature upon the people of Kansas. Mr. Christian, the pro-slavery clerk of Douglas County, says, the people of Missouri came into the territory on the thirtieth of March last, "bearing with them their peculiar institutions — bowie-knives, pistols and whiskey — to the amount of five or six thousand, carried the election by storm, and elected every pro-slavery candidate that was in the field, by overwhelming majorities, thus securing every member of Council and House of Representatives, in some instances driving from their seats the judges appointed by the governor, and placing judges from their own number in their stead, who paid no regard to the instructions of the executive," etc.

It cannot be that the President, after permitting the people of another state to take from the legal voters their constitutional and organic rights, will add to the outrage by compelling the people of Kansas to submit to their authority and obey their enactments. It is bad enough to be deprived of the right to make laws for ourselves, but it is worse to be compelled to submit to the laws of those who deprived us of that right. Although there has been and there will be no organized resistance to the self-styled territorial Legislature, yet nine men out of every ten spurn it with contempt as a gross outrage upon American citizens, and it is highly proper for the General Assembly to memorialize Congress upon this subject, as with reference to the admission of the state into the Union.

The President apologizes for the frequent invasions of Kansas, on the ground that some northern people talked about the repeal of the Missouri Compromise, and subjects connected with the extension of negro bondage, and because an emigrant aid association had been formed.

The people of this country have been in the habit of talking about the affairs of government ever since the Mayflower discharged her cargo on Plymouth Rock, but this is the first time that it has been considered an apology for the invasion of a distant state or territory. If the people of Kansas were accountable for the loquacity of the North or the silence of the South, the case might be different.

Emigrant aid associations are nothing new in the United States. When

California was first opened to settlement the same kind of associations were formed, with only this difference : in one case, each party had an agent of its own for the purpose of procuring tickets, arranging details, &c. ; while, in the other, all the parties have a common agent. There is, however, connected with the aid society for Kansas emigrants, a stock company, for the purpose of erecting mills, hotels, etc., in the new country ; but the agent of this society will purchase tickets for a slave-holder as soon as for a free-state man, and the investments are for the benefit of all settlers alike. No questions are asked, and no distinctions are made.

Had the President visited Western Missouri before any aid society had been formed at the East, he might have found a secret, oath-bound association, pledged to make Kansas a slave state, peaceably if they could, forcibly if they must. This society has been in active operation since its inception, and now threatens to deluge Kansas with the blood of American citizens, for the *crime* of preferring a free to a slave state.

Also, it is only necessary to read a few southern journals to see accounts in different parts of the South, not of emigrant aid societies, but of Emigrant buying or hiring societies, which do not simply procure tickets for the emigrants, at cost, irrespective of party or condition, but which pay the fare and expenses of the *right kind* of emigrants, and support them in Kansas one year, more or less. However it may be, the "king can do no wrong," although it may be wrong for the common people to do as the king does.

The people of Kansas will not object to aid societies, whether North or South, so long as they treat all parties alike. Emigrants from all parts of the country are received with a hearty welcome, and the investment of capital, whether eastern or western, northern or southern, is greatly needed.

The settlers of Kansas have suffered severe losses and injury from repeated invasions from a neighboring state, and it is highly proper that Congress be memorialized upon this subject. Especially should the general government repair the injury it has inflicted. All the invasions have been permitted by the officers of the government, without any opposition, while at least one was invited by them. It is the duty of the federal government to protect infant territories in their rights ; but Kansas has not only not been protected, but it has been actually oppressed by those whose duty it was to defend it.

It is unjust to any community to send among them officers, with government patronage, whose political sentiments are opposed to the sentiments of the people, particularly when those officers mount the stump and shoulder the rifle for the purpose of crushing out all who differ from them. Some of the federal officers of Kansas are charged with undignified conduct, and one of them, at least, with high crimes ; and it is the duty of the Legislature to memorialize the President, that our citizens may be protected in their lives and inalienable rights, and from unwarrantable interference of officials in the management of their internal affairs. It is manifestly improper for the federal officers to *dictate* into, or out of Kansas, an institution over which Congress professes to have no authority.

It is understood that the deputy marshal has private instructions to arrest the members of the Legislature, and the state officers, for treason, as soon as this address is received by you. In such an event, of course, no resistance will be offered to the officer. Men who are ready to defend their own and their country's honor with their lives, can never object to a legal investigation into their actions, nor to suffer any punishment their conduct may merit. We should be unworthy the constituency we represent, did we shrink even from martyrdom on the scaffold, or at the stake, should duty require it. Should the blood of Collins and Dow, of Barber and Brown, be insufficient to quench the thirst of the President and his accomplices, in the hollow mockery of "squatter sovereignty" they are practising upon the people of Kansas, then more victims must be furnished. Let what will come, not a finger should be raised against the federal authority, until there shall be no hope of relief but in revolution.

The task imposed upon us is a difficult one ; but with mutual coöperation, and a firm reliance on His wisdom who makes "the wrath of man praise him," we may hope to inaugurate a government that shall not be unworthy of the country and the age in which we live.

C. ROBINSON.

TOPEKA, March 4th, 1856.

CHARGE OF THE BORDER-RUFFIAN BRIGADE.

From the New York Evening Post.

"OUR forces amounted to *eight hundred* strong. * * * When we first reached Lawrence not a human being could be seen. In about an hour there gathered, in the streets, in front of the hotel, some hundred and fifty men. * * * *When they agreed to surrender*, our men were marched down in front of the town, and one cannon planted on their own battlements. Cannon were brought in front of the house, and directed their destructive blows upon the walls; the building caught on fire, and soon its walls came with a crash to the ground. Thus fell the abolition fortress!"—*Lecompton* (border ruffian) *Union*, the editor of which was one of the gallant eight hundred.

I.

Half a league, half a league,
    Half a league onward,
All to the fated town,
    Rode the Eight Hundred.
"Charge!" was the captain's cry;
No foeman's bayonet nigh,
No gun to make reply—
"Charge!" was the gallant cry,
And into the fated town
    Rode the Eight Hundred!

II.

No cannon to right of them,
No cannon to left of them,
No cannon in front of them,
    Volleyed and thundered!
Stormed at by shot nor shell,
Boldly they rode and well,
Cowed by no fear of death,
Cowed by no fear of hell,
    Rode the Eight Hundred!

III.

Flashed all their sabres bare,
Flashed all their guns in air,
The gallant Southrons there,
Charging like fury, while
    All the world wondered!
Seeing no battery smoke,
Their southern courage woke,

Then rapid was their stroke,
And through the lines they broke,
And Lawrence plundered ;
Then the ruffians scampered back,
All the Eight Hundred !

IV.

No cannon to right of them,
No cannon to left of them,
No cannon behind them
Volleyed and thundered !
Stormed at by shot nor shell,
They, that had robbed so well
Ran, their exploits to tell,
Back to their dens again,
Back to their border-hell,
The whole black horde of them,
All the Eight Hundred !

V.

Honor the brave and bold !
Long shall the tale be told,
Yea, when our babes are old,
How bravely they plundered !

PENNYSON.

A LIST OF BOOKS

RECENTLY PUBLISHED BY

CROSBY, NICHOLS, & CO.,

111 WASHINGTON STREET, BOSTON.

A MEMOIR OF WILLIAM ELLERY CHANNING, with Extracts from his Correspondence and Manuscripts. Edited by his nephew, WM. HENRY CHANNING. Comprised in three volumes, of from 450 to 500 pages each, uniform with the best edition of the Works. Two very superior portraits of Dr. Channing appear in the volumes; one from a painting by Allston, the other by Gambadella. Price $ 1.50.

CONTENTS. — *Part First*, — Parentage and Birth; Boyhood; College Life; Richmond; Studies and Settlement. *Part Second*, — Early Ministry; Spiritual Growth; The Unitarian Controversy; Middle-age Ministry; European Journey. *Part Third*, — The Ministry and Literature; Religion and Philosophy; Social Reforms; The Antislavery Movement; Politics; Friends; Home Life; Notes.

NOTICES OF THE PRESS.

"A more interesting and instructive biographical work we have never read. High as was our opinion of Channing, — of his intellectual and moral worth, — the perusal of this work has convinced us that we never duly estimated him. . . . . . His letters reveal his character more fully than his sermons and essays. In his letters he lays his heart entirely open; and no man, no matter what his opinions or prejudices, can read them without saying, — 'Channing was, indeed, a great and good man, — one who lived for the world!' " — *Christian Messenger.*

"Only one who was similar in purpose and temper, — who felt like aspirations, hopes, and faith, — could at all do justice to the distinguished subject. The present book must, therefore, we are sure, give us Channing's character in its completeness, and true harmony and proportions of parts." — *Salem Observer.*

"These memoirs of a great and good man will, we apprehend, obtain an uncommonly extensive circulation, not only among the denomination of Christians in which he ranked himself, but with all who reverence purity of character, an enlarged philanthropy, and eminent talents, guided by virtue and piety." — *Salem Register.*

"If we mistake not, now is the very time in God's providence when the biography of William Ellery Channing could best make its appearance. We have heard that a distinguished divine, of different speculative religious views from Dr. Channing, has recently said, — 'Channing is greatly needed among us at this present moment.' Behold him here! We doubt not that the biography thus prepared is to make a great impression on the age that is passing, and that is yet to come" — *Christian Register*

MEMOIR OF MARY L. WARE, Wife of Henry Ware, Jr. By Rev. EDWARD B. HALL. With a fine engraving on steel. Seventh Edition. 12mo. Price, $1.25.

"A book like this is a great gift to the world. It is a light in the pathway of every-day life. . . . . . It is a judicious, affectionate record of a strong, earnest, consistent Christian life. . . . . . It is delightful to see a character so thoroughly religious as was Mrs. Ware's." — *Buffalo Com. Advertiser.*

"Among the biographies of Christian women, eminent for their piety, their meek devotion to their religious profession, and their holy conduct in all the walks of life, this Memoir of Mrs. Ware deserves to take a high rank." — *Philadelphia Bulletin.*

"No one could desire, for sister, daughter, or friend, a more instructive, pleasing, or touching lesson of the quiet, unobtrusive, simple virtues of domestic life, than this unpretending volume, prepared by one at once so appreciative of the virtues of his subject, and so well qualified to do them justice." — *Boston Atlas.*

"The book is a treasure, and belongs to the permanent riches of our devotional literature." — *Christian Inquirer.*

THE SICKNESS AND HEALTH OF THE PEOPLE OF BLEABURN. 1 vol. 16mo. Price, 50 cents.

"The story is one that no person will think of laying down, when once they begin to read it, until the last word of the last page has been reached." — *Traveller.*

THE PROPHETS AND KINGS OF THE OLD TESTAMENT. A Series of Sermons preached in the Chapel of Lincoln's Inn. By Rev. FREDERIC DENISON MAURICE, Chaplain of Lincoln's Inn, and Professor of Divinity in King's College, London. Second Edition. 12mo. Price, $1.25.

"Rich in learning and thought and practical views of life." — *Christian Observer.*

"We can assure our readers that the volume will be found full of instruction and eminently suggestive. . . . . . We have followed his instructive pages with delight." — *Christian Examiner.*

THE CHILD'S MATINS AND VESPERS. By a Mother. Comprising Meditations and Prayers for Morning and Evening, &c. Second Edition. 32mo. Price, 37½ cents.

"A capital little book to lay on your child's table beside the Bible, that good and holy thoughts may be the first and last every day." — *Ohio Inquirer.*

"The parent who wishes to keep the heart of the child pure, to form habits of prayer, to inspire the young mind with profitable reflections, and lead the early years into proper spiritual habits, will be greatly assisted by this little volume." — *Christian Era.*

LECTURES TO YOUNG MEN. By Rev. WILLIAM G. ELIOT, Jr. 1 vol. 16mo. Price, 62½ cents.

CONTENTS. — An Appeal. Self-Education. Leisure Time. Transgression. The Ways of Wisdom. Religion.

"The practical wisdom, the habits of close observation, and the sincere piety of Mr. Eliot, united with what we must consider an essential element in his success, — his sympathy with the young, — have fitted him to discharge his task successfully." — *Christian Examiner.*

LECTURES TO YOUNG WOMEN. By Rev. WILLIAM G. ELIOT, Jr. 1 vol. 16mo. Price, 62½ cents.

CONTENTS.—An Appeal. Home. Duties. Education. Follies. Woman's Mission.

"We know of no book which we can recommend so unhesitatingly as this of Mr. Eliot." — *Christian Examiner.*

REMINISCENCES OF THOUGHT AND FEELING. By the Author of "Visiting my Relations." 16mo. Price, 75 cts.

"A very interesting, piquant book, and every body is reading it. . . . . . It will do a great deal of good by clearing up people's morbid moods of mind, and showing that an entire trust and reliance on God are the best medicine of the heart. This work shows how valuable a book can be written out of the history of a private life." — *Cincinnati paper.*

GOD WITH MEN; or, Footprints of Providential Leaders. By Rev. SAMUEL OSGOOD. 1 vol. 12mo.

SERMONS. By Rev. A. A. LIVERMORE. 1 vol. 12mo.

HOW I BECAME A UNITARIAN, explained in a Series of Letters to a Friend. By a Clergyman of the Protestant Episcopal Church. 12mo. Price, 75 cents.

*SERMONS IN THE ORDER OF A TWELVEMONTH By Rev. N. L. FROTHINGHAM, D. D. 12mo. Price, $ 1.00.

"As a writer, Mr. Frothingham ranks among the best of New England divines. . . . . . His sermons are prepared with great care, and possess, on account of their moral tone, their fervent spirit, their earnest pleadings for duty, a high value." — *New Covenant.*

THE MISCELLANIES OF JAMES MARTINEAU. Edited by Rev. THOMAS STARR KING. 12mo. Price, $ 1.25.

"Mr. Martineau's productions are distinguished by a loftiness of tone, a catholic candor, a severity of logic and intellectual fidelity, a clearness of moral discrimination, and an affluence of imagery, and vigorous precision of expression."

THE CHRISTIAN DOCTRINE OF THE FORGIVENESS OF SIN. By JAMES FREEMAN CLARKE. 16mo. Price, 50 cts.

"This is the work of a thoughtful, serious man; on a topic of great practical importance. . . . . . It contains much that richly deserves the serious consideration of all readers." — *Traveller.*

ST. PAUL'S EPISTLE TO THE CORINTHIANS; an Attempt to convey their Spirit and Significance. By Rev. JOHN HAMILTON THOM. 12mo. Price, 75 cents.

"Its deeply religious and tolerant spirit, and its clear expositions, will render an instructive and agreeable book to the Biblical scholar and devout Christian of every faith."

RELIGIOUS THOUGHTS AND OPINIONS. By WILLIAM VON HUMBOLDT. 16mo. Price, 62½ cents.

"It cannot be read without imparting strength and comfort, especially to those who are called to endure the misfortunes of life." — *Christian Witness.*

"To read them seems like being admitted to a personal and privileged interview with one of the greatest men of the age."

COMMUNION THOUGHTS. By Rev. STEPHEN G. BULFINCH. Author of "Lays of the Gospel," &c., &c. 16mo Price, 62½ cents.

"We especially commend it to all those who are desirous of becoming religious professors, but hesitating about their fitness. . . . . . No one can read it without becoming better." — *Taunton Whig.*

THE CHRISTIAN PARENT. By Rev. A. B. MUZZEY, Author of "The Young Maiden," &c., &c. 16mo. Price, 75 cts

"We regard the book as one of the best of its kind which has appeared for several years, ... and we would, after a careful perusal of this volume, own our obligations to the author for very many valuable hints and suggestions set forth with clearness and force." — *Cambridge Chronicle.*

THE STARS AND THE EARTH; OR THOUGHTS UPON SPACE, TIME, AND ETERNITY. Third American from the Third London Edition. 18mo. Price, 25 cents.

It contains a vast amount of thought, clothed in a religious garb, and throughout which flows an exalted view of argument, inducing lofty aspirations and clearer views of the wisdom of our Creator, as the reader proceeds step by step from the opening page to the close." — *Taunton Whig.*

ECHOES OF INFANT VOICES. 16mo. Price, 50 cents.

"The selections are made with good taste and judgment, from the best English and American poetry of Caroline Bowles, Mrs. Hemans. Longfellow. Lowell, Bryant, W. B. O. Peabody, and others. The little work seems admirably calculated to accomplish its mission of sympathy and kindness." — *Cambridge Chronicle.*

SUNDAY SCHOOL AND OTHER ADDRESSES. By FREDERIC T. GRAY, Pastor of the Bulfinch Street Church. Price, 62½ cents.

"Mr. Gray speaks from personal knowledge, and the Addresses before us contain facts of great interest, which, but for some such record, would soon be lost." — *Christian Examiner.*

FAMILIAR SKETCHES OF SCULPTURE AND SCULPTORS. By Mrs. H. F. LEE, Author of "The Old Painters," "Luther and his Times," "Cranmer and his Times," &c., &c 2 vols. 16mo.

DISCOURSES ON THE CHRISTIAN SPIRIT AND LIFE. By C. A. BARTOL, Junior Minister of the West Church, Boston. Second Edition, revised, with an Introduction. 12mo Price, $1.00.

DISCOURSES ON THE CHRISTIAN BODY AND FORM By C. A. BARTOL. 12mo. Price, $1.00.

"The highest praise that we can give these Discourses is, to say that they have all the marks and features of Christian sermons. . . . . . Their eloquence is that of deep religious conviction, and of fervor as calm as it is earnest, as earnest as it is calm." — *Christian Examiner.*

LECTURES ON THE JEWISH SCRIPTURES AND ANTIQUITIES. By JOHN G. PALFREY, D.D., LL.D. Volumes Three and Four. 8vo., cloth. Price, $5.00.

SERMONS ON CHRISTIAN COMMUNION. Designed to promote the Culture of the Religious Affections. Edited by Rev. T. R. Sullivan. 12mo. pp. 403. Price, 75 cents.

This work is not confined to the subject of the Lord's Supper, but "forms a series of practical discourses of the persuasive kind, relating to repentance, or the duty of commencing the Christian course, — to edification, or the encouragements to progressive Christian improvement, — and to the eucharistic service, as affording exercise for all the grateful and devout affections of the heart in every stage of its subjection to Christian discipline." — *Preface.*

The following is a list of the writers: —

Rev. H. A. Miles, Lowell.
" F. Parkman, D. D., Boston.
" S. Judd, Augusta.
" F. D. Huntington, Boston.
" C. T. Brooks, Newport.
" N. Hall, Dorchester.
" J. I. T. Coolidge, Boston.
" G. W. Briggs, Plymouth.
" A. A. Livermore, Keene.
" J. Whitman, Lexington.
" J. W. Thompson, Salem.
" H. W. Bellows, New York.
" E. S. Gannett, D. D., Boston.
" A. P. Peabody, Portsmouth.
" J. Walker, D D., Cambridge.
" C. Robbins, Boston.
Rev. G. E. Ellis, Charlestown.
" G. Putnam, D. D., Roxbury.
" J. H. Morison, Milton.
" A. Young, D. D., Boston.
" E. B. Hall, D. D., Providence.
" S. G. Bulfinch, Nashua.
" O. Dewey, D. D., New York.
" S. Osgood, Providence.
" A. Hill, Worcester.
" W. H. Furness, D.D., Philadelphia.
" N. L. Frothingham, D.D., Boston
" E. Peabody, Boston.
" S. K. Lothrop, "
" C. A. Bartol, "
" A. B. Muzzey, Cambridge.

"The design of the work is admirable, and we doubt not it is admirably executed, and will promote the best interests of our churches. We chanced to open at Sermon XVIII., on Christian Education, and were pleased to see the idea of Dr. Bushnell's celebrated book on 'Christian Nurture' illustrated and urged in a sermon by Dr. Putnam, preached two years before Dr. Bushnell's book made its appearance." — *Christian Register.*

"The tone of these sermons, their living interest, their unpremeditated variety in unity, fit them well for this purpose,— close personal influence on minds of widely differing views, united in the one great aim of a Christian life. We shall probably take an early opportunity of making some selections." — *Christian Inquirer.*

"We think the volume is upon the whole one of the best volumes of discourses ever issued from the American press." — *Boston Daily Atlas.*

THE GOSPEL NARRATIVES, their Origin, Peculiarities, and Transmission. By Rev. Henry A. Miles. 16mo pp. 174. Price, 50 cents.

This work is designed for families and Sunday Schools, and contains a comparison of each Gospel with the education, life, and character of its author, and with the purpose which he had in view in its composition; as also an account of the transmission of the Gospels down to our time, and the evidence of their uncorrupted preservation.

"This volume by Mr. Miles has substantial value. It is by the circulation and use of such books that Christian knowledge is to be extended, and Christian faith confirmed. By a thorough study even of this small work in child hood, many persons might have the satisfaction of carrying through life a clear and connected idea of the biographies of Jesus, and of the nature of the external evidence in their favor, instead of remaining in vague uncertainty on the whole subject. Bringing into a simple and popular form, and small compass, information not hitherto accessible, except to a limited number of persons, the 'Gospel Narratives' will be interesting to the general reader, whether youthful or adult. It must, without doubt, be introduced in all our Sunday Schools, and will rank among the most important manuals."

NAOMI; or Boston Two Hundred Years Ago. A Tale of the Quaker Persecution in New England. By ELIZA BUCKMINSTER LEE, Author of "The Life of Jean Paul." Second Edition. 12mo. pp. 324. Price, 75 cents.

The first edition of this popular book was exhausted within a month after its publication.

"Mrs. Lee has given the public a most agreeable book. Her style is elevated and earnest. Her sentiments, of the pure and the true. The characters are well conceived, and are presented each in strong individuality, and with such apparent truthfulness as almost to leave us in doubt whether they are 'beings of the mind,' or were real men and women who bore the parts she assigns them in those dark tragedies that stained this 'fair heritage of freedom' in the early days of Massachusetts." — *Worcester Palladium.*

"We have been exceedingly interested in this book, and recommend it as a beautiful picture of female piety and quiet heroism, set in a frame of history and tradition, that cannot fail to please every one connected, however remotely, with the land of the Puritans. The accomplished author of 'The Life of Jean Paul' has produced an American novel which we should like to see followed by others illustrative of the facts and manners of the olden time." — *Christian Inquirer.*

THE MARRIAGE OFFERING. Designed as a Gift to the Newly-married. Edited by REV. A. A. LIVERMORE. 16mo. pp. 215. Price, 62 cents.

"It was a happy thought that suggested such a volume. We were not aware before that there was so much and so various Christian literature on the subject." — *Christian Register.*

MARTYRIA; a Legend, wherein are contained Homilies, Conversations, and Incidents of the Reign of Edward the Sixth. Written by WILLIAM MOUNTFORD, Clerk. With an Introduction to the American Edition, by REV. F. D. HUNTINGTON. 16mo. pp. 348. Price, 75 cents.

"The charm of the book lies in the elevated tone of thought and moral sentiment which pervades it. You feel, on closing the volume, as if leaving some ancient cathedral, where your soul had been mingling with ascending anthems and prayers. There is scarcely a page which does not contain some fine strain of thought or sentiment, over which you shut the book that you may pause and meditate.

"We recommend the volume to our readers, with the assurance that they will find few works in the current literature of the day so well worth perusal." — *Christian Register.*

"This is really an original book. We have seen nothing for a long time more fresh or true. The writer has succeeded wonderfully, in taking himself and his readers into the heart of the age he describes. What is more, he has uttered words and thoughts which stir up the deep places of the soul. Let those read who wish to commune with the true and unpretending martyr-spirit, the spread of faith and endurance, courage, self-denial, forgiveness, prayer.

"Of all the treatises we have ever read on marriage, we have seen none so good as one here called a 'Marriage Sermon'; not that we would ask any couple to hear it all on their marriage day, but we commend it to all who are married, or intend to be. The whole book is precious." — *Providence Journal.*

"There are few religious books which breathe a finer spirit than this singular volume. The author's mind seems to have meditated deeply on the awful realities of life. In the thoughtful flow of his periods, and the grave, earnest eloquence of particular passages, we are sometimes reminded of the Old English prose writers. The work is a 'curiosity' of literature, well worth an attentive perusal" — *Graham's Magazine.*

www.ingramcontent.com/pod-product-compliance
Lightning Source LLC
LaVergne TN
LVHW020123110826
845151LV00001B/254

* 9 7 8 1 4 2 5 5 4 1 8 6 6 *